Knights Across the Atlantic

The Knights of Labor
in Britain and Ireland

STUDIES IN LABOUR HISTORY 7

Studies in Labour History

'...a series which will undoubtedly become an important force in re-invigorating the study of Labour History.' *English Historical Review*

Studies in Labour History provides reassessments of broad themes along with more detailed studies arising from the latest research in the field of labour and working-class history, both in Britain and throughout the world. Most books are single-authored but there are also volumes of essays focussed on key themes and issues, usually emerging from major conferences organized by the British Society for the Study of Labour History. The series includes studies of labour organizations, including international ones, where there is a need for new research or modern reassessment. It is also its objective to extend the breadth of labour history's gaze beyond conventionally organized workers, sometimes to workplace experiences in general, sometimes to industrial relations, but also to working-class lives beyond the immediate realm of work in households and communities.

Knights Across the Atlantic

The Knights of Labor in Britain and Ireland

Steven Parfitt

LIVERPOOL UNIVERSITY PRESS

First published 2016 by
Liverpool University Press
4 Cambridge Street
Liverpool
L69 7ZU

Copyright © 2016 Steven Parfitt

The right of Steven Parfitt to be identified as the author of this book
has been asserted by him in accordance with the Copyright, Designs and
Patents Act 1988.

All rights reserved. No part of this book may be reproduced, stored in a
retrieval system, or transmitted, in any form or by any means, electronic,
mechanical, photocopying, recording, or otherwise, without the prior written
permission of the publisher.

British Library Cataloguing-in-Publication data
A British Library CIP record is available

ISBN 978-1-78138-318-6 cased

Typeset by Carnegie Book Production, Lancaster
Printed and bound in Poland by BooksFactory.co.uk

Contents

Acknowledgements	vii
Introduction: The World of the Knights of Labor	1
1 Origins	20
2 The Rise of a Transnational Movement	50
3 Organisation, Culture and Gender	79
4 The Knights in Industry	109
5 The Knights and Politics	135
6 The Knights and the Unions	164
7 The Fall of a Transnational Movement	196
Conclusion: The Knights of Labor in Britain and Ireland	223
Appendix: List of Known Assemblies of the Knights of Labor in England, Scotland, Wales and Ireland	233
Bibliography	239
Index	256

Acknowledgements

This book would not have happened without the help of many people in many different ways. The first of them are my PhD supervisors, Professor Chris Wrigley and Dr Nick Baron. Your willingness to very often meet and talk about my research, read whatever I sent you, and provide useful guidance and advice throughout all three years of the PhD, made those three years as rewarding, productive and stress-free as any PhD can possibly be. I must also thank Paul Taillon, my supervisor at Honours and Masters level at the University of Auckland, who read drafts on occasion and remained incredibly supportive even though I was no longer your student and not even in the same country, and my external examiner, Neville Kirk, whose comments on this book helped it to assume its final shape. In all cases I have been given the best possible understanding of what it means to be a historian and I hope that any future students I might supervise will learn as much from me as I have from you.

Without my parents, Julia and Graham, this book would also not have been possible. You provided me with an early love of reading and learning, and instilled in me an interest in current and past events. Without all of those I would not have written this book. Your financial support during my PhD studies made this research possible, and you deserve thanks as well as my love. My friends in New Zealand, and friends I made in Nottingham – Anas, Dominik, Mike, Laura, Maria and Christeena, amongst many others – also kept me sane during the three years and made it such an enjoyable experience. Thanks especially to Michael, Josh, Jeremy and Jou-an, Paula and Philip, and Richard, Julie, Kirk, Claire and Dan, for putting me up on my many trips to London and sharing the odd drink or two. There are too many other people to name here but I thank you all. And finally, to Elizabeth, who demonstrated amazing patience with me during the last several months and kept me going. I love you.

I would also like to thank the Economic History Society, the Society for the Study of Labour History and the Royal Historical Society for providing me with the necessary funds to conduct research in the United States, and the University of Nottingham for providing me with an International Research Excellence Scholarship that allowed me to study in the UK. Thank you as well to the archivists at the Modern Records Centre at Warwick, the Catholic University of America, the British Library, National Library of Scotland, the Library of Congress, and the Local History Centres at Liverpool, Birmingham, Sandwell, Dudley, Wolverhampton, Walsall, and Rotherham, for making the task of research that much easier. Thanks to Valida and Chris Walker for making my stay in Washington DC so enjoyable and productive. Finally, I would like to thank the editors at Liverpool University Press and Alison Welsby in particular for your friendly and efficient help in the preparation of this book. Though this book bears my name, it was only possible because of a wide cast of people. I thank you all once again.

Introduction
The World of the Knights of Labor

On 9 December 1869, the members of the Garment Cutters' Association of Philadelphia met to dissolve their organisation and divide its funds amongst themselves. After that meeting ended, some of them convened elsewhere to create a new, secret association. Nine men, joined by five more two days later, founded the first assembly or branch of the Noble and Holy Order of the Knights of Labor, although they only adopted that name on 28 December.[1] The leading spirit behind that new order, Uriah Stephens, a man trained for the Baptist ministry before economic circumstances forced him to seek work in the garment trades, designed the Knights of Labor along the lines of a fraternal order with an elaborate ritual based on Freemasonry. The Knights kept their name and existence hidden from the public, even from the workers they sounded out as members. They announced their meetings in a cryptic code scrawled on the walls of public buildings. From these unlikely beginnings the Knights of Labor became one of the great social movements of nineteenth-century American history.

The Knights grew slowly during the 1870s. That decade was marked by the Panic of 1873, a global financial crisis that left economic depression in its wake, and by the Great Uprising of 1877, when the first nationwide railroad strike in American history took place and in some cities and acquired the feel of an armed struggle between workers, employers, local police and state militias. The Knights were only marginally involved in these battles and in 1878, at their first General Assembly, or national convention, they mustered around 10,000 members. As the trade unions succumbed to depressed economic conditions or to the counter-attacks of employers after the Great Uprising, the Knights moved slowly, at first, into the spaces they left behind.

---

[1] N. Ware, *The Labor Movement in the United States, 1860–1895: A Study in Democracy*, 2nd ed. (New York: Vintage Books, 1964), p. 23.

They exploded onto the American social and political scene in the 1880s. From 50,000 members in 1883, 70,000 in 1884 and 100,000 in 1885, the Knights of Labor approached the staggering figure of 1 million members in the early months of 1886.[2] In that year, known to historians as the Great Upheaval, American workers struck in unprecedented numbers, formed numerous labour parties that contested and often won elections, and flocked to labour organisations, whether the Knights or the trade unions, in their hundreds of thousands. The economic and political rulers of the United States found themselves facing a mass mobilisation from below that threatened to redraw the American social landscape on cooperative rather than competitive lines. The Knights of Labor became the symbol of and the banner for that mass mobilisation. Yet only ten years later the Knights were effectively dead. Employers and their allies in government launched a fierce attack against the Order and rooted it out of workplaces across America. Rival trade unions fought the Knights out of their industries and took many of their members. Knights fought amongst themselves for control of the Order's leadership and over its tactics, strategy and political orientation. The Knights of Labor disappeared from American life almost as quickly as they had entered it, and in 1917 their last General Master Workman, the top executive position in the Order, deposited its records in a shed behind an office in Washington DC, and formally brought the Order to an end.

The rise and fall of the Knights of Labor remains one of the most dramatic episodes in American and Canadian labour history. But the Order became more than just a North American movement. Over the course of their history the Knights established assemblies in Belgium, England, Wales, Scotland, Ireland, France, Italy, South Africa, Australia and New Zealand. There are suggestions that the Knights also extended into Germany, Mexico, Scandinavia and even India. This book tells a part of this international story. It explores the history of the Knights of Labor in Britain and Ireland, which began in 1883 with an assembly in Wales and ended in 1894 with the collapse of the last surviving English assemblies.

The British and Irish Knights never became anything like as powerful as the Knights in the United States. Their assemblies never organised more than ten or fifteen thousand workers, only a fraction of the million that belonged to American assemblies in the summer of 1886. Yet British and Irish Knights won the allegiance, at various times, of influential figures in British and Irish political life. The Knights of Labor became part of the great changes that took place in the British labour movement in the late 1880s and early 1890s, from the extension of the trade unions beyond their traditional home in the skilled trades to the early development of working-class politics

---

[2] Ware, *Labor Movement*, p. 66.

independent of the Liberals and Conservatives – a process that, within little more than a decade, culminated in the birth of the British Labour Party. The Knights were more than a footnote in British and Irish labour history: they were an important, if brief and under-recognised, part of it.

The history of their order has undergone sweeping changes and revisions over the course of the nineteenth, twentieth and twenty-first centuries. American labour historians began to write the history of the Knights of Labor even as Terence Powderly remained the General Master Workman between 1879 and 1893. Powderly, George MacNeill, another Knight, the German-American socialist Friedrich Sorge and economist and Christian Socialist Professor Richard T. Ely all placed the Knights of Labor at the heart of American labour history.[3] As labour history became an academic discipline during the early twentieth century, however, its early practitioners saw the Knights as a failed alternative to the American Federation of Labor (AFL), which fought with and defeated the Order in the 1880s and 1890s. John Commons, Selig Perlman, Robert Hoxie and, slightly later, Gerald Grob – the so-called Commons or Wisconsin School of labour history – all argued that the Knights represented a failed, utopian strain in American labour that the AFL, with its exclusive focus on economic objectives, especially wages and working hours, was bound to overcome.[4] Norman Ware, by contrast, described its history as a 'study in democracy' and claimed that the Order's demise was not inevitable at all, but he remained in a distinct minority during the first half of the twentieth century.[5]

From the 1960s onwards, however, labour historians rediscovered Ware's arguments and began to dismantle the binaries constructed by the Commons School. They increasingly saw the Knights not as a backward-looking reaction against the emergence of monopoly capitalism in the United States – as Commons, Perlman and Grob had – but as a valid, serious and forward-looking response to it. They emphasised the Order's pioneering role in

---

[3] G.E. MacNeill, *The Labor Movement: The Problem of Today* (New York, 1887); R.T. Ely, *The Labor Movement in America* (New York: M.W. Hazen Co., 1886); F. Sorge, *Labor Movement in the United States: A History of the American Working Class from Colonial Times to 1890* (Westport: Greenwood, 1977); Terence V. Powderly, *Thirty Years of Labor, 1859–1889* (Philadelphia: Excelsior, 1890). Powderly also wrote an autobiography in the 1910s that presented his view of the Order's history: Powderly, *The Path I Trod: The Autobiography of Terence Powderly* (New York: Columbia University Press, 1940).

[4] J. Commons, *History of Labor in the United States: Volume 2, 1860–1896* (New York: Macmillan, 1936); S. Perlman, *A Theory of the Labor Movement* (New York: Macmillan, 1928); R.F. Hoxie, *Trade Unionism in the United States* (New York: D. Appleton and Co., 1917); G. Grob, *Workers and Utopia: A Study of Ideological Change in the American Labor Movement, 1865–1900* (Chicago: Quadrangle, 1969).

[5] Ware, *Labor Movement*.

the organisation of female and non-white workers. They rejected even the idea that the AFL was bound to thrive and the Order bound to fail. Leon Fink's work on the many significant political ventures that the Knights pursued in the 1880s, Susan Levine's pioneering study of the Order and gender questions, Robert Weir's re-examination of its cultural practices and productions as well as its internal conflicts, are only a small selection of the scholarship that has enlarged and revised our understanding of the Knights of Labor in the past several decades.[6]

This book falls within that revision of American labour history and its emphasis on the importance, and the pioneering role, of the Knights of Labor. It also falls within the wider revision of labour history, as with other historical subjects, along transnational lines. Labour history has always dealt with international issues, at least since Marx issued his famous injunction for the workers of the world to unite, and earlier generations of historians by no means neglected the development of the labour movement, of socialist and anarchist currents, on an international scale. The great international movements of nineteenth-century labour, from the International Workingmen's Association or First International of Marx and Bakunin to the Second International that united the powerful socialist parties of Europe before the First World War, have long been the subject of scholarly interest.[7]

---

[6] Scholarship after Grob concerning American Knights includes, but is not limited to, L. Fink, *Workingmen's Democracy: The Knights of Labor and American Politics* (Urbana: University of Illinois Press 1983); R.J. Oestreicher, *Solidarity and Fragmentation: Working People and Class Consciousness in Detroit, 1875–1900* (Urbana: University of Illinois Press, 1986); B. Laurie, *Artisans into Workers: Labor in Nineteenth-Century America* (New York: Noonday, 1989); D. Brundage, *The Making of Western Labor Radicalism: Denver's Organized Workers, 1878–1905* (Urbana: University of Illinois Press, 1994); S. Levine, *Labor's True Woman: Carpet Weavers, Industrialization and Labor Reform in the Gilded Age* (Philadelphia: Temple University Press, 1984); C. Phelan, *Grand Master Workman: Terence Powderly and the Knights of Labor* (Westport: Greenwood, 2000); R. Weir, *Beyond Labor's Veil: The Culture of the Knights of Labor* (University Park: Pennsylvania State University Press, 1996); Weir, *Knights Unhorsed: Internal Conflict in a Gilded Age Social Movement* (Detroit: Wayne State University Press, 2000); M.A. McLaurin, *The Knights of Labor in the South* (Westport: Greenwood, 1978); M. Hild, *Greenbackers, Knights of Labor, and Populists: Farmer-Labor Insurgency in the Late-Nineteenth-Century South* (Athens: University of Georgia Press, 2007); K. Voss, *The Making of American Exceptionalism: The Knights of Labor and Class Formation in the Nineteenth Century* (Ithaca: Cornell University Press, 1993); J. Gerteis, *Class and the Color Line: Interracial Class Coalition in the Knights of Labor and the Populist Movement* (Durham: Duke University Press, 2007).

[7] See, for instance, G.D.H. Cole, *The Second International, 1889–1914* (London: Macmillan, 1956); J. Braunthal, *The History of the International, 1864–1914* (London: Macmillan, 1966); M. Drachkovitch (ed.), *The Revolutionary Internationals, 1864–1943* (London: Stanford University Press, 1966); J.B. Jeffreys, *The Story of the Engineers* (London: Lawrence and Wishart, 1945); J. Joll, *The Second International, 1889–1914* (London: Wiedenfeld and

Most labour historians, however, have concentrated on the story of their respective labour movements at a national level. This made sense. Trade unions, political parties and other working-class movements developed towards the end of the nineteenth century as national movements and engaged with national governments and, increasingly, national corporations. But as historians have argued more consistently in recent decades, viewing labour history through a national lens has obscured or downplayed some of the great processes, trends and movements that arose from and shaped nineteenth-century capitalism on a global scale. Much recent labour scholarship has stressed the importance of transnational processes like migration, the globalisation of capital, the extension of strikes and working-class solidarity across national borders, and myriad other trends that were not self-contained in any one country. Labour historians have also re-examined the famous movements of international labour, the relationships that developed between national movements, and have explored formal and informal associations between the workers of different countries that never or only barely appeared in earlier scholarship.[8] Their research has already begun to reshape our understanding of American labour history.[9]

But the transnational turn has barely touched the Knights of Labor. Aside from Canada, whose labour history is so closely bound up with that of the United States, and where Bryan Palmer and Gregory Kealey have provided such an excellent account of the Order's history, and New Zealand, where Robert Weir has unearthed the crucial role that Knights played in that country's early social and political history, the Order's history outside the United States remains largely unwritten. Maurice Dommanget explored

---

Nicholson, 1968); S. Bernstein, *The First International in America* (New York: Augustus M. Kelley, 1965).

[8] See, for instance, N. Kirk, *Comrades and Cousins: Globalization, Workers, and Labour Movements in Britain, the USA, and Australia from the 1880s to 1914* (London: Merlin, 2003); M. van der Linden, *Transnational Labour History: Explorations* (Aldershot: Ashgate, 2003); J.H.M. Laslett, *Colliers across the Sea: A Comparative Study of Class Formation in Scotland and the American Midwest, 1830–1924* (Urbana: University of Illinois Press, 2000); P. Katz, *From Appomattox to Montmartre: Americans and the Paris Commune* (Cambridge, MA: Harvard University Press, 1998); S. Milner, *The Dilemmas of Internationalism: French Syndicalism and the International Labour Movement, 1900–1914* (New York: Berg, 1990); L. Fink (ed.), *Workers Across the Americas: The Transnational Turn in Labor History* (Oxford: Oxford University Press, 2011). A useful overview is offered by N. Kirk, D.M. MacRaild, and M. Nolan. 'Introduction: Transnational Ideas, Activities, and Organizations in Labour History 1860s to 1920s,' *Labour History Review*, 74:3 (2009), pp. 221–32.

[9] See, for instance, L. Fink, *The Long Gilded Age: American Capitalism and the Lessons of a New World Order* (Philadelphia: University of Philadelphia Press, 2015); R. White, *Railroaded: The Transcontinentals and the Making of Modern America* (London: W.W. Norton, 2011).

the activities of Knights in France at book length some time ago. Leon Watillon's pamphlet from the 1920s remains our only source concerning the Belgian assemblies. Several research articles deal in passing with Knights in Australia. Paragraphs in several works provide a brief introduction to the Order in South Africa. Knights in Italy and the other continental European countries appear largely in footnotes or stray sentences without much in the way of explanation. Assembling a comprehensive international history of the Knights of Labor out of these fragments is a task that historians have not yet attempted.[10] This book is a part of that unfinished project.

The history of the British and Irish Knights also remains to be written. Henry Pelling provided the only short account of that history in 1956, and Ronald Bean and James D. Young fleshed out the Order's history in Liverpool and Scotland, respectively, two decades later.[11] Most subsequent historical writing that mentions the British and Irish Knights leans heavily on their work.[12] Taken together, these scholars provide the foundations

[10] A short and not exhaustive list of scholarship which touches on the Knights outside North America includes, for Australia and New Zealand: L.G. Churchward, 'The American Influence on the Australian Labour Movement,' *Historical Studies: Australia and New Zealand*, 5 (1953), pp. 258–77; B. James, 'The Knights of Labor and Their Context,' found at: http://www.takver.com/history/secsoc02.htm; B. Scates, '"Wobblers": Single Taxers in the Labour Movement, Melbourne 1889–1899,' *Historical Studies*, 21:83 (1984), pp. 174–96; B. Scates, '"Millennium or Pandemonium?": Radicalism in the Labour Movement, Sydney, 1889–1899,' *Labour History*, 50 (1986), pp. 72–94; H. Roth, 'American Influences on the New Zealand Labour Movement,' *Australian Historical Studies*, 9 (1961), pp. 413–20; H. Roth, 'The Distribution of New Zealand Radicalism: 1890–1957,' *New Zealand Geographer*, 15:1 (1959), pp. 76–83; R. Weir, *Knights Down Under: The Knights of Labour in New Zealand* (Newcastle: Cambridge Scholars Press, 2009). For Belgium: L. Watillon, *The Knights of Labour in Belgium* (Los Angeles: University of California Press, 1959). For South Africa: R.V. Turrell, *Capital and Labour on the Kimberley Diamond Fields* (Cambridge: Cambridge University Press, 1987). For France: M. Dommanget, *La Chevalerie du Travail Française, 1893–1911* (Lausanne: Recontre, 1967). Brief details on the Order's overseas branches can also be found in Cole, *Second International*.

[11] H. Pelling, 'The Knights of Labor in Britain, 1880–1901,' *The Economic History Review*, 9 (1956), pp. 313–31; R. Bean, 'A Note on the Knights of Labour in Liverpool,' *Labor History*, 13:1 (1972), pp. 68–78; J.D. Young, 'Changing Images of American Democracy and the Scottish Labour Movement,' *International Review of Social History*, 18:1 (1973), pp. 69–89.

[12] Works on British and Irish labour history that mention the Knights include: E. Taplin, *The Dockers Union: A Study of the National Union of Dock Labourers, 1889–1922* (Leicester: Leicester University Press, 1986); K. Coates and T. Topham, *The Making of the Labour Movement: The Formation of the Transport and General Workers Union, 1870–1922* (Oxford: Blackwell, 1994); A.B. Campbell, *The Scottish Miners, 1874–1939, Vol. 2: Trade Unions and Politics* (Aldershot: Ashgate 2000); H. Pelling, *America and the British Left, from Bright to Bevan* (London: Adam and Charles Black, 1956); H. Pelling, *The Origins of the Labour Party* (London: Macmillan, 1954); W.H. Marwick, *A Short History of Labour in Scotland* (Edinburgh: W. and R. Chambers, 1967); J.W. Boyle, *The Irish Labour Movement in the Nineteenth Century* (Washington, DC: Catholic University of America Press, 1992); S. McAteer, 'The New

for an in-depth study of the Order's British and Irish assemblies – but foundations are not a building, and this work provides the first comprehensive study of the Knights of Labor in Britain and Ireland. It draws on the insights of recent scholarship concerning the Knights in the United States, and concerning the transnational aspects of labour history. It is indebted to Robert Weir's pioneering work on the Knights in New Zealand, and to the impressive, if sometimes incomplete, database of the Order's thousands of assemblies that Jonathan Garlock compiled in the 1980s.[13]

The British and Irish Knights did their historians few favours. 'The story of the Knights of Labor outside North America,' as Robert Weir writes, 'is one constructed from slender threads framing suggestive holes.'[14] In Britain and Ireland these threads are quite slender indeed. Any internal documents they made have not survived, and the secrecy that they practised has further obscured their history. This book attempts to close as many of these suggestive holes as possible through extensive archival research across the United States and the United Kingdom. It relies especially on local newspapers around Britain, documentation from the Order's rivals in the British labour movement, the records of American Knights, the personal papers of Terence Powderly and John Hayes, the Order's Secretary-Treasurer and then General Master Workman after Powderly, the proceedings of the Order's annual General Assemblies and its official organ, the *Journal of United Labor*, renamed *Journal of the Knights of Labor* in 1890. Together these sources are sufficiently dense and numerous to construct a detailed narrative of the Knights of Labor in Britain and Ireland. First, however, we must place that narrative within its international context and within the global history of the Knights themselves.

The World of the Knights of Labor

The Knights of Labor made the transition from an American order to an international movement in an unprecedentedly globalised and interconnected world. Innovations from the steamship to the telegraph brought much of the earth closer together. Capital and trade extended throughout the world, aided by the growth of worldwide empires centred in Europe, North America and, increasingly, Japan, that subjugated or dominated great swathes of Africa, South America, Asia and the Pacific. The nineteenth

---

Unionism in Derry, 1889–1892: A Demonstration of its Inclusive Nature,' *Saothar*, 16 (1991), pp. 11–22.

[13] J. Garlock, *Guide to the Local Assemblies of the Knights of Labor* (Westport: Greenwood, 1982).

[14] Weir, *Knights Down Under*, p. 220.

century was an age of nationalism but, paradoxically, it was an age of internationalism as well. The great international exhibitions brought together the world's wares and attracted visitors from all over the planet. Lawyers and diplomats negotiated international treaties to govern the railroads, shipping and telegraph lines that did not remain conveniently within national frontiers. Scientists and middle-class professionals created international associations to exchange findings and methods in their respective fields. Social causes became international movements as well. Progressive reformers, as Daniel Rodgers explains, developed international networks to promote everything from the state regulation of public hygiene to cleaning up corrupt municipal governments.[15] The years from 1870 to 1890, Karen Offen writes, were an era of 'internationalizing feminism,' when bodies such as the International Council of Women and the Women's Christian Temperance Union brought women's rights activists together from across the globe.[16]

To the American economist, Richard T. Ely, the second half of the nineteenth century was an age of "economic internationalism" as well, and Ely was impressed most of all with the rise of labour as an international movement.[17] The birth of the Knights of Labor in 1869 coincided with the heyday of the First International, formed in 1864. The International fell apart after the repression that followed the defeat of the Paris Commune in 1871, after factional splits between the socialists and anarchists, and after the departure of many trade unionists. But working-class internationalism survived the fall of the International. Numerous international congresses of socialists, anarchists and trade unionists took place in the 1870s and 1880s even if they ended to little result.[18] Great international fraternal orders, of which the Oddfellows and Order of Foresters were only among the largest, provided social insurance and a social life for their mainly working-class members.[19] Advocates of cooperative enterprises from across the world met

---

[15] D.T. Rodgers, *Atlantic Crossings: Social Politics in a Progressive Age* (Cambridge, MA: Harvard University Press, 1998).

[16] K. Offen, *European Feminisms, 1700–1950: A Political History* (Stanford: Stanford University Press, 2000), ch. 5; M. McFadden, *Golden Cables of Sympathy: The Transatlantic Source of Nineteenth-Century Feminism* (Lexington: University Press of Kentucky, 1999); L.J. Rupp, *Worlds of Women: The Making of an International Women's Movement* (Princeton: Princeton University Press, 1997); I. Tyrrell, *Woman's World – Woman's Empire: The Woman's Christian Temperance Union in International Perspective, 1880–1930* (Chapel Hill: University of North Carolina Press, 1991); R.J. Evans, *Comrades and Sisters: Feminism, Socialism and Pacifism in Europe, 1870–1945* (Brighton: Wheatsheaf, 1987).

[17] R.T. Ely, 'Economic Internationalism,' *The Chautauquan* (February 1890).

[18] Braunthal, *History of the International*, p. 194.

[19] J. Baernreither, *English Associations of Working Men* (London: S. Sonnenschein, 1893);

at the annual British Co-operative Congresses to share their plans and experiences.[20]

Trade unionists across Europe and North America continued to support strikes, prevent the movement of strike-breakers and maintain correspondence with their colleagues in other countries. Individual unions such as the British Amalgamated Society of Engineers established branches across and even beyond the British Empire.[21] After a congress at Paris in 1889, a new, Second International finally emerged to fill the gaping hole left by the decline of the First. Between then and the outbreak of the First World War, this new International symbolised the arrival of labour as a powerful social and political force in national and world affairs.[22] International associations of trade unions developed alongside the Second International, some bringing together individual unions of the same trade, others bringing together the national federations of trade unions that emerged across Europe and North America from the 1860s onwards.[23] The Knights of Labor, in other words, were but one of many movements that united workers of different countries in the nineteenth century.

For a time that order became the largest labour organisation in the world, simply on account of its million American members. During the 1880s and 1890s the Knights became one of the most extensive international working-class movements in the world as well – matched, as Weir writes, only by internationalism and the followers of Henry George's single tax.[24] Their international history began in the period between the two nineteenth-century Internationals and overlapped with the early history of the Second, and I have elsewhere described the Knights as a "First and a half International," bridging the period between those two famous bodies and, as we will see in the following chapters, sharing some features with both of them.[25] The

---

H. Gosden, *Self-Help: Voluntary Associations in the Nineteenth Century* (London: Batsford, 1973).

[20] P. Gurney, *Co-operative Culture and the Politics of Consumption in England, 1870–1930* (Manchester: Manchester University Press, 1996), pp. 88–95.

[21] The *Dundee Courier*, *The Trades' Union Congress: Meetings in Dundee* (Dundee, 1889), pp. 12–13; Jeffreys, *Story of the Engineers*, pp. 61–62.

[22] Joll, *Second International*; Cole, *Second International*.

[23] See L.L. Lorwin, 'The Structures of International Labor Activities,' *Annals of the American Academy of Political and Social Science*, 310:1 (1957), pp. 1–11; Gary Busch, *The Political Role of International Trade Unions* (New York: St Martin's Press, 1983), pp. 7–18; G. van Goethem, *The Amsterdam International: The World of the International Federation of Trade Unions (IFTU), 1913–1945* (Aldershot: Ashgate, 2006).

[24] Weir, *Knights Down Under*, p. 206.

[25] Steven Parfitt, 'The First-and-a-half International: The Knights of Labor and the History of International Labour Organizations in the Nineteenth Century,' *Labour History Review*, 80:2 (2015), pp. 135–67.

following account of the Order's global history builds on Weir's final chapter, closes some of the gaps that remain in it and places the British and Irish Knights within the context of the great international movement of which they became a part.

The first recorded assembly of the Knights of Labor outside of North America began in 1883, when travelling organiser John Hughes established Local Assembly (LA) 2886 in Cardiff. In the following year, as we will see at length in Chapter 1, the American glass workers of LA300 went abroad to organise their fellow craftsmen in Europe, and created a Universal Federation of Window-Glass Workers, which united glass workers from across Europe and North America. Their first success in organising assemblies of Knights came in Belgium. There, the Order's representatives recruited the entirety of the Union Verrière, an association of glass workers in Charleroi that had already made contact with LA300 several years earlier.[26] Albert Delwarte, the leader of that union and a veteran of Belgian branches of the First International, also led the Belgian assemblies. With help from Isaac Cline, Andrew Burtt and A.G. Denny, organisers working on behalf of both LA300 and the Order's General Executive Board, the Belgian Knights quickly spread amongst other workers in Charleroi, including 3,000 coal miners by 1885 and many iron and steel workers.[27] Organisers also reached Brussels, where the Knights established assemblies of workers making gloves, leather, lace, carpentry, confectionary, fur and tin.[28] In 1887 the Belgian Knights brought their various assemblies under one central body, the State Assembly of Belgium. Albert Delwarte headed this body and represented it at the General Assembly in 1888, where Terence Powderly personally gave him gifts on behalf of the Order and where the assembled delegates paid him lengthy tribute.[29]

Robert Weir writes that 'the Belgian KOL was probably defunct by the time New Zealand Knights began to enjoy success' in 1890. That was certainly not the case. The Belgian State Assembly formally disaffiliated itself from the American Order at the end of the 1880s, not because it faced terminal decline itself but because its leaders wanted to distance the State Assembly from the severe problems then fracturing the American assemblies. Belgian Knights retained the allegiance of glass workers, miners, metalworkers and

---

[26] Watillon, *Knights in Belgium*, pp. 7–8; K. Fones-Wolf, 'Immigrants, Labor and Capital in a Transnational Context: Belgian Glass Workers in America, 1880–1925,' *Journal of American Ethnic History*, 21:2 (2002), p. 62.

[27] Watillon, *Knights in Belgium*, pp. 21–29.

[28] Watillon, *Knights in Belgium*, p. 34.

[29] *Proceedings of the General Assembly of the Knights of Labor* (Philadelphia, 1888), pp. 75–81. (Hereafter *Proceedings of the GA*.)

glove makers around Brussels and Charleroi into the 1890s, and one report claimed in 1891 that the Order organised 23,000 out of 30,000 coal miners in the latter city.[30] Their leader, Jean Callewaert, had lectured delegates to the first International Congress of Miners on the Order's principles the previous year.[31] Belgian Knights left a lasting imprint on their labour movement. Leon Watillon credits them with introducing mutual insurance schemes for sick and death pay into Belgian trade union practice, and from 1892 payment into such a fund was finally made compulsory for all Belgian Knights.[32] Robert Weir claims that the Knights 'helped nascent unions articulate goals, taught them how to mobilize, and educated them on a set of principles that aided in craft solidarity.'[33] The coal miners left the Order in 1895, but Belgian glass workers continued to use the Knights' name and practices into the 1930s, well after the American body had faded into complete insignificance and unimportance.[34]

The Order briefly found a foothold in Italy. Glass workers there certainly attended meetings of the Universal Federation. Some reports claimed that as many as 1,000 Italian glass workers became Knights in the mid-1880s.[35] Further reports in 1886 mention 'an organization of Italian operatives resembling the American "Knights of Labour,"' arrested *en masse* by local authorities, but provided no further details.[36] The only tangible evidence for Italian assemblies comes from Jules Corcodal, who had spent several years in the United States and decided on his return to Turin to open assemblies of the Knights of Labor there. Corcodal corresponded with the *Journal of United Labor* in 1888, and revealed that in the middle of that year he organised three local assemblies, one with 125 members, with the other two boasting more than 150 members each. A lack of money prevented further growth, and Corcodal and his colleagues seem to have given up soon afterwards.[37] But his calls for Knights to attend and present an exhibition at the Paris Exposition of 1889 left a more lasting impression on the Order's global history.[38] A number of local and district assemblies did indeed send over their flags, banners and other insignia. These were displayed alongside

---

[30] *1893–4 Royal Commission on Labour: Foreign Reports, Volume IV, Belgium*, pp. 13–14. Found at: *House of Commons Parliamentary Papers Online (HCPP)*.

[31] *Revue Socialiste*, 66 (June 1890).

[32] Watillon, *Knights in Belgium*, p. 32.

[33] Weir, *Knights Down Under*, p. 217.

[34] Cole, *Second International*, p. 620; Weir, *Knights Down Under*, p. 216.

[35] *Maysville Daily Evening Bulletin*, 16 July 1886.

[36] *The Times*, 29 June 1886.

[37] Jules Corcodal to Powderly, 17 June 1892, Box 72, *Terence Powderly Papers*, Catholic University of America History Research Center and University Archives (TVP).

[38] *Journal of United Labor (JUL)*, 1 and 22 November 1888.

bound copies of the *Journal of United Labor* and the proceedings of the general assemblies, as well as pictures of Powderly, Uriah Stephens and other of the Order's leading figures.[39]

The Knights also found lodgement in neighbouring France. Glass workers there affiliated with the Universal Federation but remained aloof from the Order itself. Several leading Knights and their sympathisers claimed assemblies in France as early as 1887 and 1888.[40] No further proof exists for them at that time; one solitary bookbinder from Ammonay, however, was so enthused by the Order that he applied to join the Knights as a member in 1886 and, with Powderly's help, was initiated by Knights in Belgium.[41] Between 1888 and 1890, two equally enthusiastic French labour activists, F. Veyssier and Abel Davaud, bombarded Powderly and the *Journal of United Labor* with news from France and with their desire to form assemblies in Paris and the provinces. They gathered together enough interested Parisian workers to form several assemblies and waited, as they told American Knights, for the repeal of legislation dating from the aftermath of the Paris Commune and from fears over the power of the First International, which prohibited French workers from joining international bodies with foreign headquarters.[42] At this point, French glass workers, according to Albert Delwarte, were also waiting for that repeal to become fully fledged Knights themselves.[43]

Like Corcordal in Turin, Veyssier and Davaud implored the American Knights to make a big impression at the Paris Exposition. Both eventually arranged the shipment of banners, flags, portraits and other paraphernalia from the United States to France and set up the Order's exhibition in the hall assigned to it. Though the *Journal of United Labor* predicted thousands of new recruits before the Exposition ended, a breakdown in communication meant that Powderly did not visit the Exposition, as the 1888 General Assembly had decreed and as he had told Veyssier and Davaud. Poor communication also ensured that the Knights actually forgot to recompense them for their work in arranging the Order's exhibition, which they had done out of their own pocket, and meant that Knights who did visit Paris failed to meet their French supporters. In the end, Veyssier and Davaud decided to form their own organisation, based to an extent on the Order's model but not affiliated with it, and the *Journal*'s high hopes were

[39] *JUL*, 28 February and 14 March 1889.
[40] *Birmingham Daily Post*, 21 October 1887; *Wichita Daily Eagle*, 15 February 1888; *Los Angeles Times*, 31 May 1888.
[41] B. Maurice to Powderly, 30 October 1888, Box 48, TVP.
[42] *JUL*, 25 October 1888.
[43] *JUL*, 6 September 1888.

smashed.⁴⁴ It was not until 1893, when Belgian Knights began to organise French assemblies on their own initiative, that the Order finally established itself in France. By then the American Knights were too absorbed with the problems of their declining order to help them in any practical way; but like the Belgian assemblies, those in France survived into the twentieth century.⁴⁵

The Knights made it into the southern hemisphere as well. Australian trade unionists wrote to the Order's headquarters in Philadelphia as early as 1886, requesting more information about the Knights and suggesting some kind of trans-Pacific alliance.⁴⁶ Carpenters in Brisbane also led a movement in 1887 for a 'Labour League, founded on the basis of the American Knights of Labour,' and their secretary established contact with the American Knights and declared his intention to form a '"Queensland Knights of Labour."'⁴⁷ Nothing came of that movement, although newspaper reports suggest that an assembly began at Adelaide in South Australia.⁴⁸ The history of the Australian Knights really began with the arrival of a Canadian organiser, W.W. Lyght, in 1888. He opened local assemblies in Melbourne and Sydney, while local labour activists like Larry Petrie and Samuel Rosa added to the number of assemblies and others, like Arthur Rae, who himself won political office as a Knight, extended the Order into Wagga Wagga.⁴⁹ Indeed, the Australian assemblies attracted a large number of other well-known Australian labour activists as well, including poets like John Farrell and Henry Lawson, writers like William Lane and J.R. Davies, and political figures like Dr William Maloney.⁵⁰

Despite these prominent supporters, however, the Australian assemblies struggled to attract a mass membership. They faced fierce opposition from local trade unionists: Knights in Melbourne, for instance, twice tried to secure affiliation with the city's Trades Council and were twice rejected.⁵¹ Trade unionists who initially saw the Knights as a shortcut to independent labour politics, Lloyd Churchward argues, found their solution in the Australian Labor Party instead.⁵² As a secret society, the Knights were

---

⁴⁴ C. Deville to Hayes, 28 July 1889, Box 55, TVP; F. Veyssier to Powderly, 20 September 1889, Box 56, TVP; F. Veyssier to Powderly, 28 February 1890, Box 59, TVP; *JUL*, 9 May 1889.
⁴⁵ *Proceedings of the GA* (1894), p. 167; Dommanget, *La Chevalerie du Travail Française*.
⁴⁶ W. Lane to Powderly, 12 May 1886, Box 21, TVP.
⁴⁷ *Brisbane Courier*, 28 May and 5 September 1887.
⁴⁸ *Brisbane Courier*, 12 October 1889; *Burra Record*, 15 February 1887.
⁴⁹ Weir, *Knights Down Under*, p. 228; *JUL*, 19 February 1891.
⁵⁰ Weir, *Knights Down Under*, pp. 227–28.
⁵¹ *Melbourne Argus*, 11 July 1891 and 15 April 1893.
⁵² Churchward, 'American Influence,' pp. 265–66.

refused admission to the inaugural congress of that party.⁵³ Cut off from the mainstream of the Australian labour movement for most of the 1890s, the Knights struggled on into the twentieth century with some minor successes among the miners of Western Australia.⁵⁴ They finally rejoined the mainstream in 1899 when their representatives attended the first Australian Trade Union Congress. Yet their numbers and influence remained modest. Only in the elaborateness of their ritual, conducted in locally designed regalia, did Australian Knights equal their American counterparts or those in many other countries.⁵⁵

They certainly failed to equal the achievements of their brethren across the Tasman Sea, in New Zealand. Between 1887 and 1889, local trade unionists in Christchurch and Auckland created their own assemblies, based on scraps of information gleaned from newspapers arriving on ships from the United States, although these disintegrated by the end of the decade.⁵⁶ As in Australia, the history of the Knights in New Zealand really began with the arrival of W.W. Lyght. He arrived in Auckland in February 1890, and lectured his way down the North and South Islands, explaining the Order's principles and in some cases creating local assemblies along the way. When he arrived in Christchurch the remnants of the New Zealand Knights of Labor, who had in the meantime experimented with alternative forms of organisation, returned to the Order's fold. And in the same year that Lyght helped place the Order in New Zealand on a solid footing, a series of strikes, particularly by seamen and dockers, inspired by related struggles in Australia and as far away as South Africa and Britain, fell to defeat. The Order's trade union rivals were decimated, and the membership of its assemblies swelled accordingly.⁵⁷

As New Zealand's Knights advanced through the first half of the 1890s they achieved political and industrial power, in proportional terms at least, in advance of Knights in any other country. That included, Robert Weir argues, the United States as well.⁵⁸ A significant fraction of the colony's legislators were Knights. It is likely that one Premier, John Ballance, was as well. In alliance with the Liberal Party, the Order became a national political force with few peers elsewhere in the labour world; one scholar has even described the Knights as New Zealand's first true political party.⁵⁹

---

[53] Weir, *Knights Down Under*, p. 228.
[54] *Proceedings of the GA* (1898), pp. 4, 49.
[55] Weir, *Knights Down Under*, p. 229–30; Bob James, 'Knights of Labor and Their Context.'
[56] Weir, *Knights Down Under*, pp. 1–2, 7–10.
[57] Weir, *Knights Down Under*, p. 18.
[58] Weir, *Knights Down Under*, p. 206.
[59] Herbert Roth, 'Knights of Labour,' in *An Encyclopaedia of New Zealand*, 1966, found at: http://www.teara.govt.nz/en/1966/political-parties/page-7.

Much of the social legislation that made turn-of-the-century New Zealand the envy of many reformers and trade unionists from all over the globe, from female suffrage to old age pensions and the compulsory state-run arbitration of industrial disputes, was due in large part to the lobbying and votes of Knights in and outside Parliament. Yet their numbers and influence soon waned. Their trade union rivals soon recovered from the defeats of 1890. Employers began to attack the Order's assemblies at the workplace. Ballance's successor as Premier of the Colony, Richard Seddon, saw the Knights more as an annoyance than an ally. Weir even claims that Knights lost momentum in the latter part of the 1890s precisely because so much of their programme had found its way into legislation. Few working-class organisations can attribute their demise to their own success, and when the New Zealand Knights disintegrated in the early twentieth century they had already reshaped the social and political landscape of the country.

Finally, the Order extended into Africa as well. Robert Weir surmised that 'oblique references' to South African Knights found in the *Journal of the Knights of Labor* probably referred to transient dockers and sailors in and around Cape Town.[60] These references actually referred instead to diamond miners in the town of Kimberley, the unquestioned centre of world diamond extraction, which had by then become concentrated in the hands of De Beers Consolidated Mines.[61] De Beers, one of the great international monopolies of the nineteenth (and twentieth) century, boasted among its directors the arch-imperialist Cecil Rhodes, who served, from 1890 to 1896, as Prime Minister of the Cape Colony. As De Beers restricted the supply of diamonds to raise their price on the international market, causing mass unemployment in Kimberley, miners attempted to work unused mines themselves. Since De Beers enjoyed complete power over local political machinery as well as the supply of diamonds, these attempts failed.[62] In February 1890, a small number of white miners founded the Knights of Labour of South Africa at the Burns Hotel.

Their new order freely borrowed from the practices of other fraternal orders. Adopting the motto 'Charity, Unity, and Fidelity,' South African Knights organised into 'temples' under a Grand Master and a Grand Council of 13, and created the ranks of first and second degree along Masonic lines. They practised absolute secrecy on the understandable grounds that De Beers, which maintained an extensive system of surveillance in the town, would quickly destroy an organisation based on open lines. While it is virtually impossible to ascertain their numbers, they published a manifesto which

---

[60] Weir, *Knights Down Under*, pp. 220–21.
[61] Turrell, *Kimberley Diamond Fields*, p. 4.
[62] Turrell, *Kimberley Diamond Fields*, pp. 122, 226–27.

claimed that 'our Society has been no unimportant factor in the politics and social events of Kimberley and the Colony at large.'[63] Nor was this merely the hopeful words of a few isolated militants. One intrepid reporter from a Cape Town magazine infiltrated the Knights and was amazed to find many of Kimberley's most prominent citizens as well as many local workers at their meetings.[64] South African Knights made contact with the Order's Philadelphia headquarters in 1891 and 1892. There are references to South African assemblies as late as 1895, but they seem to have faded away soon afterwards.[65] It remains difficult to provide a more detailed narrative of their history due to their absolute secrecy. Even a Royal Commission in 1892 found the task of finding any precise information about the Knights impossible 'except that the members were bound by oath to carry out any orders which they might receive.'[66] It seems likely that the South African Knights eventually fell before the combined might of De Beers and the Cape Colony government.

But their struggles led to some unusual consequences. Strict racial stratification of labour had long existed at Kimberley's mines. Colonial authorities kept black workers, recruited from neighbouring tribes, in 'compounds,' a euphemistic term for concentration camps that enforced brutal labour discipline and prevented them from leaving the mines while still under contract.[67] The South African Knights, many of whom used black workers as contractors, feared that De Beers was planning to either replace all white labour with black workers or reduce the wages and conditions of white workers to the level of black labour. Where American Knights sought to organise black workers, South African Knights hoped to protect the jobs and living standards of white workers through the maintenance of a strict colour line. All skilled labour would be reserved for whites. And as Ray and Jack Simons write, this idea 'of a war on two fronts, against Monopoly Capital and Cheap Coloured Labour, guided the thinking of organized white labour for many decades to come.'[68]

There are suggestions that the Knights established assemblies in other places as well. Several sources point to German assemblies and, given comments that A.G. Denny made in 1886 these assemblies, if they existed,

---

[63] *Manifesto of the Knights of Labour of South Africa* (London, 1891), p. 7.

[64] *Manifesto*, p. 10; 'Knights of Labour of South Africa,' *The Lantern*, 5 December 1891.

[65] *JUL*, 19 November 1891; Letter from John Law to Powderly, 16 May 1892, Box 72, TVP; *New York Times*, 22 October 1895.

[66] *1892 Royal Commission on Labour, Volume II, Foreign Reports, India and the Colonies*, p. 85. Found at *HCPP*.

[67] Turrell, *Kimberley Diamond Fields*, p. 11.

[68] J. and R. Simons, *Class and Colour in South Africa, 1850–1950* (London: Harmondsworth, 1969), p. 45.

were probably composed of glass workers.[69] At least one scholar refers to an assembly of glass workers in Portugal.[70] One solitary source refers to assemblies in Sweden, Norway and Denmark.[71] Interested parties from these countries certainly wrote to Powderly and other leading Knights, but no corroborating evidence exists for assemblies in any of them. Fragments also refer to assemblies in Mexico: G.D.H. Cole mentions only that some unions there 'became loosely attached' to the Knights while 'others imitated its methods.'[72] The most intriguing reference of all concerns India. The Indian philosopher and nationalist Amrita Lal Roy was so enthused by the Knights during his travels throughout the United States in 1886 that he promised to *John Swinton's Paper*, one of the largest American labour newspapers, that on his return to India he would preach the 'gospel of the Knights of Labor ... and their talisman of organization will yet revivify that land.'[73] No trace survives, however, of any Indian assemblies.

This was the world the Knights built. In some places their assemblies made little headway. Knights in Italy lacked the money to organise more than several hundred workers, those in Australia failed to overcome determined opposition from local trade unions, French Knights suffered from the prevarications and bureaucratic failings of the Order's American leaders and the South African assemblies crumbled before the corporate-political axis of De Beers and the Cape Colony. But the Knights of Labor also made significant and lasting contributions to the labour movements of many countries. They hastened the growth of trade unionism in Belgium, found enthusiastic supporters in France and Italy, attracted leading figures in the Australian labour movement, united South African diamond miners against one of the great corporations of the age and left deep marks upon the labour movement and political system of New Zealand. The British and Irish Knights never matched the numbers of the Belgian Knights or the political achievements of the Knights in New Zealand, but, as we will see, they made significant contributions of their own to British and Irish history.

The Knights of Labor in Britain and Ireland

This book tells their history through seven chapters, each organised on thematic lines but with due attention paid to the evolution of the British and Irish assemblies over the course of their existence. The first chapter

---

[69] *Sacramento Daily Record Union*, 3 July 1886.
[70] Fones-Wolf, 'Immigrants, Labor and Capital,' p. 66.
[71] *Wichita Daily Eagle*, 15 February 1888.
[72] Cole, *Second International*, p. 826.
[73] *John Swinton's Paper*, 30 May 1886.

addresses the origins of those assemblies and locates them in the unique conditions of the 1880s, where the American labour movement seemed on the verge of overtaking its British counterpart, and in the Knights' fears about uncontrolled immigration on the one hand and their commitment to universal brotherhood, a form of international solidarity, on the other. Chapters 2 and 7 address the rise and fall, respectively, of the British and Irish Knights and place their history in wider transnational context. They both look particularly closely at the role played by the growth and decline of the American Order in the shifting fortunes of their British and Irish branches. Chapter 2 also examines the significance of racial, imperial and, to an extent, religious questions in our story. Knights encountered these questions largely through the prism of the Irish question, and through the many links that connected Irish or Irish-descended workers in Britain, the United States and Ireland itself.

Chapters 3 and 4 explore the ways in which the Knights adapted their American Order to British and Irish conditions. The third concerns the ways in which British and Irish Knights interpreted the cultural practices and organisational forms of their order, and why they failed to follow their American cousins in one crucial respect: their complete lack of female members. The fourth deals with industrial relations, particularly how British and Irish Knights interpreted their order's positions on strikes, boycotts, arbitration and cooperation. Both chapters point to one major conclusion: regardless of any cultural differences between British, Irish and American workers, Knights in Britain and Ireland followed the advice and the guidelines that the Order's American leaders gave them more closely than many, probably even most, Knights in the United States.

Chapters 5 and 6 position the Knights within the context of the British labour movement. The fifth takes up the political ventures of the assemblies and places the Knights of Labor within the early movement for independent working-class politics. The sixth chapter deals with the Knights and the trade union movement, both in terms of the role played by conflict with rival unions in the Order's British and Irish history, and the Order's own influence over the development of the British and Irish labour movement. Both chapters demonstrate the significant role the Knights played in the great changes that swept through the British labour movement during the 1880s and 1890s. These changes, in time, led to the birth of the British Labour Party and the rise of the British trade unions as a movement truly representative of the British working class.

An appendix provides details of all the British and Irish assemblies, including, where known, their name, number, years of operation and the occupations they organised. British and Irish Knights, as Chapter 3 makes clear, followed the same hierarchical progression as the American Knights from the basic unit, the local assembly, to district assemblies, which brought together five or more local assemblies in the same geographical area, and finally to the General Assembly, which met once a year and proposed, debated and adopted resolutions that would be enacted by the general officers. Those officers were headed by the General Master Workman, a post that Terence Powderly occupied for all except the final months of the British and Irish assemblies, and included a General Secretary, General Treasurer (these last two posts were combined in 1888), and General Worthy Foreman, this last charged with overseeing the Order's ritual. Throughout this book I spell the Order's name in the American style and only refer to the "Knights of Labour" when that spelling is used in quotation. With those basic points in order, we now turn to the local, national and transnational forces that led the Knights of Labor to first establish their assemblies in Britain and Ireland.

1
Origins

At the end of 1881 the potters of Staffordshire went on strike; in 1882, they returned to work defeated. The potters had called that action to force their employers to participate in the formal arbitration and conciliation machinery that had governed the pottery industry until the end of the 1870. Their local unions emerged from the defeat in poor shape, and the potters' leaders decided that if they wanted to restore arbitration to their industry they needed a single, strong union that could negotiate on their behalf from a position of strength. When they met at Hanley to establish that union, the National Order of Potters, in September 1882, the potters emphasised their desire to break with the ineffective unions of the past by basing their new organisation on a model sourced from abroad. The newspapers all agreed that 'this new Trades Union shall be based upon principles in many respects similar to those of the new American Trade Organisation, known as the Knights of Labour.'[1]

The press could be forgiven for thinking that the Knights, already 13 years old, were in fact a new movement. Their leaders had only recently made the name and existence of their order public, and the Knights of Labor only became widely known in the United States, let alone elsewhere, two or three years later. In this context the decision of the Staffordshire potters to imitate an obscure American fraternal order becomes only more significant. The American pottery industry, writes Frank Thistlewaite, was 'the result of a direct colonization from the Five Towns of Staffordshire.'[2] Potters routinely

---

[1] H. Owen, *The Staffordshire Potter* (Bath: Kingsmead, 1970), pp. 216–17; F. Burchill and R. Ross, *A History of the Potters' Union* (Hanley: Ceramic and Allied Trades Union, 1977), p. 128; W.H. Warburton, *The History of Trade Union Organisation in the North Staffordshire Potteries* (London: George Allen and Unwin, 1931), p. 176; *The Standard*, 28 September 1882.

[2] F. Thistlewaite, 'The Atlantic Migration of the Pottery Industry,' *The Economic History Review*, 11:2 (1958), p. 265.

migrated back and forth across the Atlantic. Ties of kinship and friendship spanned the ocean too. When potters in Pennsylvania, New Jersey and Ohio became early recruits of the Knights of Labor, their colleagues in Staffordshire soon heard of it. After their local unions were smashed in the strike of 1881–82, the Staffordshire potters naturally turned to the Order of their American cousins as the model for their own new union.

The Staffordshire potters kept unusually well abreast of developments within the American labour movement, and were not representative of British and Irish workers as a whole. But the reasons behind their decision to base the National Order of Potters on the Knights of Labor illustrates the local, national and transnational processes, trends and considerations that led the Knights to establish their assemblies in Britain and Ireland. One of these was migration. The international movement of potters and other workers enabled the spread of new ideas and institutions across oceans and continents, but also raised fears among trade unionists that mass immigration might endanger the labour movement and drive down wages. American Knights held those fears particularly strongly. Their desire to regulate immigration, if not prevent it altogether, drove them to seek legislation from Congress but also, at the same time, to organise workers overseas before they immigrated to the United States. Another major factor behind the origins of the Knights in Britain and Ireland was the unusual relationship between the British and American labour movements in the 1880s. For most of the nineteenth century the American labour movement appeared to be a pale imitation of its British counterpart, organising proportionally less workers than in Britain and basing American trade unions on earlier British models. In the 1880s, however, that picture was turned almost upside down. During that decade the British labour movement faced severe challenges while the Knights of Labor led an unprecedented upswing of union membership and working-class struggles in the United States. Like the Staffordshire potters, some British workers and radicals now looked to America for solutions to the problems they faced at home.

The story of how the Knights of Labor established assemblies in Britain and Ireland also raises serious questions regarding a central theme in American labour history: American exceptionalism. For labour historians, that term refers to the fact that American workers never built a durable and influential labour or socialist party as their counterparts did elsewhere in the developed world, that American trade unions almost invariably organised a smaller proportion of the labour force than trade unions in other industrial countries, and that American workers supposedly never displayed the class consciousness so prevalent among workers in Europe.

The first systematic attempt to explain these differences came in 1906 with the German economist Werner Sombart's short work, *Why Is there*

No Socialism in the United States? Sombart put them down to the higher standards of living that American workers enjoyed, and their overwhelming interest in gaining immediate material benefits rather than in far-reaching social change.[3] John Commons, Selig Perlman and Gerald Grob, the leading representatives of the 'Commons' or 'Wisconsin' School, advanced Sombart's arguments still further. They described what Sombart saw as the overriding materialism of American workers as 'job-consciousness' in contrast to the socialist implications behind the term 'class-consciousness'. Perlman and Grob in particular saw the rise of the American Federation of Labor in the late nineteenth and twentieth century as the victory of that principle over a utopian strain, which Grob termed 'reform unionism,' present in the early American labour movement, and which culminated in the rise of the Knights of Labor.[4] Other historians, in the 1950s especially, added that any conflicts that arose in American society centred on status anxieties and not class conflict. Historians began to challenge these assumptions in earnest from the 1960s onwards. Many argued that the class consciousness of American workers fractured along racial, ethnic, religious, nationality or gender lines. Many also claimed that the severe repression that American employers and government directed against organised labour and radical politics accounted for the smaller size of the trade union movement and the lack of a labour or socialist party. Yet the idea of American exceptionalism, Sean Wilentz argued in an influential article in 1984, remained at the heart of their wider narrative.[5]

Wilentz disagreed with the tendency of American labour historians to make comparisons in which, as Michael Hanagan has more recently put it, 'American workers are denied class-consciousness while European workers brim over with it.'[6] Historians are often wont to generalise about the failings of their scholarly predecessors, and in the process they often fail to recognise the innovations, complexities and insights of those predecessors. American labour historians *ante*-Wilentz unearthed rich layers of militancy, class consciousness and radical politics. In recent decades, however, the arguments behind American exceptionalism have come under closer scrutiny and faced more serious challenges. Some historians, like Wilentz and Hanagan, reject exceptionalism altogether and see it as the consequence of an outmoded

---

[3] W. Sombart, *Why is there No Socialism in the United States?* (London: Macmillan, 1976).

[4] See especially Commons, *Labor in the United States*; S. Perlman, *Theory of the Labor Movement*; Grob, *Workers and Utopia*; Hoxie, *Trade Unionism in the United States*.

[5] S. Wilentz, 'Against Exceptionalism: Class Consciousness and the American Labor Movement, 1790–1920,' *International Labor and Working-Class History*, 26 (1984), pp. 1–24.

[6] M.P. Hanagan, 'An Agenda for Transnational Labor History,' *International Review of Social History*, 49:3 (2004), p. 457.

Marxist interpretation that compares all labour movements to an ahistorical, class-conscious and socialist gold standard.[7] Others, like Kim Voss, argue that the picture of an exceptional American labour movement remains valid in a twentieth-century context, but that this picture came about as the result of contingent historical events and processes, not because of essential characteristics inherent in American society or the American worker. American exceptionalism, Voss argues, was not inevitable: it was made.[8]

The Knights of Labor naturally figure prominently in these arguments, whether in terms of their international activities or their history in the United States. Voss argues that the main features of American exceptionalism developed after the Order's defeat in the United States. She adds that the lessons that American trade unionists took from that defeat, to avoid political entanglements and to view with caution any attempt to extend trade unionism beyond the skilled trades, ensured that the Americans fell behind their European counterparts. Robert Weir makes his rejection of American exceptionalism one of the major themes of his recent study of Knights in New Zealand.[9] It is also a major theme of this work. In chapters 5 and 6, which deal respectively with politics and the trade unions, we engage with the idea of American exceptionalism in more specific terms. The present chapter sketches the broad outlines of that debate and finds that the American labour movement was exceptional in the 1880s for its high numbers and strength, not for its weakness.

Lenin once wrote that in a revolutionary situation, 'it is usually insufficient for "the lower classes not to want" to live in the old way; it is also necessary that "the upper classes should be unable" to live in the old way.' To these 'objective' parameters he added 'subjective' ones: for a revolution to actually occur, the revolutionary classes needed the determination and will to topple the existing regime at a stroke.[10] Transnational organising has its own version of the same principle. Objectively, some latent desire must exist in the foreign country which the transnational body can satisfy; subjectively, that transnational body must have the motive, will and resources to expand outside its home country in the first place. This chapter follows that logic, and deals firstly with the objective side of the equation. We find that in the 1880s the unusual strength of the American labour movement, and the stagnation that afflicted its British counterpart for much of the decade, provided the

---

[7] For a recent treatment of the 'Sombart question,' see R. Archer, *Why Is there No Labor Party in the United States?* (Princeton: Princeton University Press, 2007).

[8] Voss, *Making of American Exceptionalism*.

[9] Weir, *Knights Down Under*.

[10] V.I. Lenin, *The Collapse of the Second International*, found at: http://www.marxists.org/archive/lenin/works/1915/csi/ii.htm

space for an American movement to take root on British soil. This chapter then explores the subjective side of the equation. We find that American Knights expanded overseas due to a combination of high-minded feelings of international solidarity, their desire to stem the tide of mass immigration and the initiative of an unusually powerful assembly of glassworkers, Local Assembly 300, whose deep pockets subsidised the Order's first organising missions in Europe. This chapter began with the potters of Staffordshire. We will end with the window glassworkers of England and America, and the Order's first significant British branch, Local Assembly 3504.

The Unique Decade:
British and American Labour in the 1880s

Comparisons between the British and American labour movements have generally followed a recognisable pattern. Most observers would have agreed with the American economist M.B. Hammond, who wrote in 1911 that:

> in nearly all its important aspects, the history of the labor movement in the United States repeats that of Great Britain ... English artisans brought the institutions of unionism to this country, and men trained in the English trade unions have not infrequently been the leaders in the class struggle in America.[11]

When Henry Pelling compared the two movements 43 years later he reached much the same conclusions: 'The American labour movement, in so far as it followed the British pattern at all, was about half a century behind it.' The Knights of Labor properly arrived on the American scene in the 1880s, about 50 years after Robert Owen's Grand National Consolidated Trades Union. Both organisations were general unions that aimed to replace private industry with a series of cooperative enterprises. The craft unions of the American Federation of Labor rose to pre-eminence in the 1890s, 40 or 50 years after the British new model unions, like the Amalgamated Society of Engineers, 'which they undoubtedly set out to imitate.' The Federation itself, Pelling adds, 'came into being as the expression of the interests of the skilled craftsmen; and it too represented for many years only a small "aristocracy" of the workers.'[12]

Yet a very different view prevailed in the 1880s, as two contemporary American economists writing about the British labour movement in 1889

---

[11] M.B. Hammond, 'Six Decades of Trade Unionism in America,' *The Dial* (1 November 1911).

[12] H. Pelling, 'The American Labour Movement: A British View,' *Political Studies*, 2:3 (1954), pp. 227–28.

made clear. 'There is nothing of the compactness and uniformity which were aimed at in a great centralized organization like the Knights of Labor in the United States,' wrote Edward Cummings. The English unions, he added, resembled 'some of the older unions in the United States.'[13] Professor Albert S. Bolles of the Pennsylvania Bureau of Labor Statistics observed, after returning from an investigation of labour conditions in Europe, that American trade unionists 'would do well to pattern after the English.' By that he meant that they should adopt conservative policies and strike less often.[14]

These views are difficult to square with a picture of American trade unions as unceasingly weak and backward compared with their British equivalents. They hint at the first part of our explanation of the origins of the Knights of Labor in Britain and Ireland. Even Pelling, who saw the Americans as 50 years behind trends in Britain, also claimed that the Knights became a mass movement at one of the few points in history when the American labour movement matched or even exceeded the numbers of its British counterpart, and when that British counterpart faced serious challenges from within and without.[15] To many British observers in the 1880s, the Knights represented the future of trade unionism, and the unions of the Trades Union Congress (TUC) represented its past. That unprecedented situation was largely the work of the Knights themselves, of course, and it provided unusually favourable conditions for an American working-class organisation to establish its branches in the home of the trade union movement.

The shifting fortunes of the British and American labour movements were in part the result of wider social and economic changes over the course of the nineteenth century. Pelling argued that the backwardness of the American trade unions was most powerfully shaped by the relatively late industrial development of the United States compared with Britain. He broadly shared that view with Friedrich Engels, who wrote in 1886 that Britain's foreign competitors 'have arrived at about the same phase of development as English manufacture in 1844. With regard to America,' he added:

> the parallel is indeed most striking ... we find in America the same struggles for a shorter working-day, for a legal limitation of the working time, especially of women and children in factories; we find the truck system in full blossom, and the cottage-system, in rural districts, made use of by the 'bosses' as a means of domination over the workers.[16]

---

[13] E. Cummings, 'The English Trades-Unions,' *The Quarterly Journal of Economics*, 3:4 (1889), p. 405.

[14] *Pittsburgh Dispatch*, 15 September 1889.

[15] Pelling, *British Left*, p. 62.

[16] F. Engels, '1886 Preface to the American Edition' in *The Condition of the Working*

A similar level of industrial development, in other words, ensured similar industrial conditions and, above all, a similar level of trade unionism, even when the two examples were separated by 40 years.

That equation, however, fails to capture some of the nuances of American labour history. As does Pelling's idea of a 50-year lag between the American and British labour movements. The Knights of Labor, for instance, began in 1869, less than 40 years after Owen's Grand National. The Order's American predecessor, the Brotherhood of the Union, created by the reformer and novelist George Lippard, had emerged nearly 20 years earlier, in 1849. The Brotherhood shared many characteristics with the Knights and the Grand National, including secrecy, fraternal ritual and regalia, and sweeping aims: to free workers, in Lippard's words, from 'the death-grip of the monopolist and the Tyrant' and to make 'the American Continent ... the Homestead of redeemed Labor.'[17] Pelling's narrative omitted the National Labor Union, which operated from 1866 to 1874 and at one point boasted a total membership of more than 100,000. The craft unions that eventually created the American Federation of Labor in 1886 were also closer in time to the new model unions on which they were based. Trade unionists such as Adolphe Strasser and Samuel Gompers developed organisations, like their own Cigarmakers' International Union, that combined the benefit plans and high dues of the new model unions in the 1870s, and even became known under the heading of the 'new unionism.'[18] The supposed 50-year lag is thus reduced to 15 or 20 years. This is not surprising given that British immigrants to the United States brought with them the latest ideas and methods, even if the American industrial scene did not permit them to flourish immediately.[19]

The difference between British and American industrial output, and industrial development as a whole, also narrowed over the course of the nineteenth century. For a long time, American industry followed the British lead, whether in the textile mills of Massachusetts, the coal mines of Pennsylvania, the iron and steel factories of the industrial North – and in the example that began this chapter, the pottery industry. Even after the great stimulus to industrial output provided by the Civil War, British industry continued to lead the way, a fact reflected in all the major indexes

---

Class in England, New York, 1887. Found at: https://www.marxists.org/archive/marx/works/1886/02/25.htm

[17] G. Lippard, 'Platform of the Brotherhood of the Union,' in D.S. Reynolds (ed.), *George Lippard, Prophet of Protest: Writings of an American Radical, 1822–1854* (New York: P. Lang, 1986), pp. 209–10; D.S. Reynolds, *George Lippard* (Boston: Twayne, 1982).

[18] P.S. Foner, *History of the Labor Movement in the United States, Vol. I* (New York: International Publishers, 1972), pp. 512–14.

[19] C.K. Yearley, *Britons in American Labor: A History of the Influence of the United Kingdom Immigrants on American Labor, 1820–1914* (Baltimore: Johns Hopkins Press, 1957).

of industrial development, from annual steel production to coal extraction.[20] This lead soon narrowed. Between 1870 and 1913, the British share of world industrial production fell from 30 to 15 percent.[21] By the end of the nineteenth century, both Germany and the United States produced more than the erstwhile workshop of the world. British industrialists learned the harsh lesson that industrial development, like other forms of historical development, is at once uneven and combined. Their rivals drew on British innovations and then, as the century came to a close, built on them with their own innovations. The laggards became the leaders and the old leaders, as British employers discovered, soon lagged behind.

A similar process of combined and uneven development conditioned the progress of the British and American labour movements too. Historians have often drawn analogies between the Knights and the Grand National Consolidated Trades Union, which shared more than an attachment to fraternal ritual and regalia. Michael Hanagan writes that these 'mass industrial unions' each spearheaded the development of the labour movement in their respective countries and, after they failed, were each succeeded by 'narrow craft unions led by conservative leaders who scorned the mass of unskilled workers and maintained an authoritarian control over their own membership.'[22] According to Pelling and Engels, at least, the similar evolution of these two movements can be explained by the similar level of industrial development in which each movement arose.

Yet the Knights of Labor arose in a very different context to the Grand National. Improvements in industrial technique at the end of the nineteenth century threatened to make the skilled worker completely obsolete, a process that had only begun in Robert Owen's day. The Knights concluded that craft unions, based on the skilled trades, also faced obsolescence and insisted that only the unity of what they called the 'producing classes,' under the Order's banner, could deliver workers from the evils of the wage system. The concentration of capital in the era of the Knights of Labor also reached levels undreamt of in the heyday of the Grand National. Knights, again, held that craft unions were no match for the great corporations, trusts and monopolies of the day, and that only a single organisation of all producers could wield the necessary industrial and, perhaps, political power to challenge the owners of concentrated wealth and prevent them

---

[20] N. Kirk, *Labour and Society in Britain and the USA, Volume 2: Challenge and Accommodation, 1850–1939* (Aldershot: Ashgate, 1994), pp. 11–13.

[21] J. Hinton, 'The Rise of a Mass Labour Movement: Growth and Limits,' in C.J. Wrigley (ed.), *A History of British Industrial Relations, 1875–1914* (Amherst: Harvester, 1982), pp. 21–22.

[22] M.P. Hanagan, *The Logic of Solidarity: Artisans and Industrial Workers in Three French Towns, 1871–1914* (Urbana: University of Illinois Press, 1980), p. 22.

from corrupting the democratic institutions of the Republic.[23] Both trends proceeded at a faster rate in the United States than in Britain: by the late 1880s, as Eric Hobsbawm recognised, American industry was on the whole more mechanised than its British counterpart.[24]

The Knights of Labor might have adopted the form and some of the content of the Grand National. The Order, however, was no throwback to the early nineteenth century, as Gerald Grob once claimed.[25] It emerged as a response to an American industrial scene fast becoming more mechanised, and more productive, than its British contemporary. By the end of the nineteenth century the Americans took the lead in industrial output and the British never regained it. For a time, the same trend started to develop among the respective labour movements of the two countries. When the Knights of Labor reached a million members in the summer of 1886, in addition to the several hundred thousand Americans enrolled in trade unions, for the first time the American labour movement organised more workers than the British TUC. At the same time that the United States began to emerge as the world's leading industrial power, it gave rise to an order that briefly became the largest labour organisation in the world.

The 1880s proved a crucial decade in the history of the British labour movement too. In 1880, membership of British trade unions stood at just over half a million and represented about 4 percent of the working population.[26] In 1888 that membership stood at 817,000 workers and then rose to 1,470,000 in 1890.[27] When the 1880s began, the TUC brought together a collection of unions that almost entirely represented male workers in skilled trades. The numbers organised into the unions of the TUC remained stagnant until the end of the decade, when the rise of the 'new unionism,' a subject we explore at length in Chapter 6, led to the extension of trade unions into less skilled occupations. The new unionism petered out in the 1890s, and it would take until the 1910s for the British labour movement to consolidate itself as representative of workers of all levels of skill, reaching 25 percent of the working population in 1914; but the 1880s saw the first major steps towards that level of representation.[28]

In that decade the British trade union movement faced serious challenges and underwent far-reaching changes. British trade unionists faced the

[23] Ware, *Labor Movement*, pp. 200–04.
[24] E.J. Hobsbawm, 'General Labour Unions in Britain, 1889–1914,' *Economic History Review*, 1:2 (1949), p. 139.
[25] See especially G. Grob, 'The Knights of Labor and the Trade Unions, 1878–1886,' *The Journal of Economic History*, 18:2 (1958), pp. 176–92.
[26] Hinton, 'Mass Labour Movement,' p. 20.
[27] J. Cronin, 'Strikes, 1870–1914,' in Wrigley, *Industrial Relations*, p. 89.
[28] Hinton, 'Mass Labour Movement,' p. 20.

prospect of mechanisation, skill dilution and the rise of a new layer of semi-skilled operatives who worked a growing number of machines, even if the markets of the Empire sheltered British industry from foreign competition and ensured that automation proceeded at a slower pace than in America. They faced a growing number of women entering the labour market.[29] They also faced new challenges to the Liberal orthodoxy that dominated working-class politics after the collapse of the Chartists. The Lib-Lab pact, as it was known, ensured that a number of trade unionists were returned to the House of Commons on a Liberal ticket, and in 1885 an unprecedented 12 working-class Liberals entered Parliament. Some historians even consider them the first Labour MPs.[30]

Working-class Liberalism had never entirely subsumed other radical working-class traditions, however. Movements for national rights and land reform in Ireland and Scotland became causes all over Britain and Ireland in the 1880s. Charles Parnell and Michael Davitt headed the Irish Land League, an organisation that aimed to free Irish farmers from the exploitation of landlords and argued for Home Rule. In 1881, the League inaugurated a campaign of ostracism against Irish landlords, named after Captain Boycott, who became its first victim. Home Rule became a central political issue in Britain and Ireland and led to a split in the Liberal Party between Gladstonians, who supported it, and Liberal Unionists, who opposed it. These questions also energised radical forces outside the Liberal Party. In Scotland the crofters, small tenant farmers in hock to (mainly) absentee landlords, resisted attempts by those landlords to drive them off the land. Their struggles gained them wide sympathy in Scotland and in the rest of Britain and Ireland. Representatives of the crofters even formed a political movement around the issue and elected several MPs in 1885.[31]

These movements did not seriously threaten the Lib-Lab pact. Yet the emergence of a new British socialist movement eventually did. The Social Democratic Federation (SDF), founded in 1881, the Fabian Society, created in 1884, and the Socialist League, formed in 1885 after a split from the SDF, all provided new critiques of British society and, as we will see in more detail in later chapters, also contributed to the rise of independent working-class politics and the new unionism. These groups all remained numerically

[29] G. Anderson, Some Aspects of the Labour Market in Britain c.1870–1914, in Wrigley, *Industrial Relations*, pp. 1–20.

[30] J. Shepherd, 'Labour and Parliament: The Lib-Labs as the First Working-Class MPs, 1885–1906,' in E. Biagini and A. Reid (ed.), *Currents of Radicalism: Popular radicalism, Organized labour, and Party Politics in Britain, 1850–1914* (Cambridge: Cambridge University Press, 1991), pp. 187–213.

[31] See, for instance, A.G. Newby, *Ireland, Radicalism and the Scottish Highlands, c.1870 to 1912* (Edinburgh: Edinburgh University Press, 2007).

small throughout the 1880s. Some historians have questioned whether they represented a significant or influential movement at all.[32] They did, however, recruit a number of trade unionists who would soon become major figures in the labour movement, including Tom Mann, John Burns and Ben Tillett, and gained notoriety when they led demonstrations of unemployed workers through the streets of London and held meetings on Trafalgar Square. Older strains of British radicalism, dating back to the Chartist agitation, also survived into the 1880s. London's Radical Clubs helped bring about the SDF. *Reynolds's Newspaper*, edited by an ex-Chartist, printed 'anti-monarchist and radical-patriotic sentiments' for hundreds of thousands of readers every day, as it had done since the 1860s. Like many other radicals, those who wrote for *Reynolds's* moved towards socialist positions and began to advocate 'collectivist social reform' in the 1880s.[33]

British radicals viewed the British trade unions of the early to mid-1880s as conservative and aloof or, at the very least, overly cautious. Tom Mann, both a socialist and a member of the Amalgamated Society of Engineers, summed up the view of this small but growing tendency when he insisted in an oft-quoted 1886 pamphlet that 'none of the important societies have policies other than endeavouring to keep wages from falling. The true union policy of aggression seems entirely lost sight of.'[34] Mann's manifesto did not herald an immediate transformation in the tactics or the considerations of the trade union movement. Even in the years of the new unionism his hopes were only partially realised. But others like him sought new ways to revitalise the unions and looked for alternatives to them. In chapters 5 and 6, especially, we will see how many of them found such an alternative in the Knights of Labor.

Similar criticisms extended to the record of the TUC leadership on the international stage. British trade unionists pioneered international working-class cooperation during the Chartist period. They built the First International in the 1860s. Their record in the 1880s, by contrast, was poor. They held two International Trades Union Congresses, one at Paris in 1886 and the other at London in 1888. At these Congresses the representatives of the TUC seemed more concerned with fighting socialism than promoting international labour cooperation. When a German socialist at the 1886 Congress described Henry Broadhurst, the secretary of the TUC's Parliamentary Committee

---

[32] For a summary of these arguments see D. Matthews, '1889 and All That: New Views on the New Unionism,' *International Review of Social History*, 36:1 (1991), pp. 37–39.

[33] N. Kirk, *Change, Continuity and Class: Labour in British Society, 1850–1920* (Manchester: Manchester University Press, 1998), p. 191.

[34] T. Mann, *What a Compulsory Eight Hours Working Day Means to the Workers* (London, 1886).

and a Lib-Lab MP, as a traitor to the cause of labour for accepting a post in the Liberal government, John Burnett of the Amalgamated Society of Engineers responded that 'the attack against English Trades Unions came very inappropriately from the representative of a nation which more than any other country helped to keep down the rate of wages.'[35] At the 1888 Congress, the Parliamentary Committee adopted the standing orders of the TUC and excluded representatives from political parties. As trade unions were illegal in Germany and some other European countries, this effectively meant, as the German Social-Democrat Eduard Bernstein noted, 'a simple exclusion of all German delegates.'[36] To its British critics, the TUC seemed both isolated on the international stage and incapable of representing more than a narrow aristocracy of British workers.

With the trade union movement showing its limitations, and with the emergence of new radical causes and the rejuvenation of old ones, it was only natural that many critics of the British labour movement looked to the United States for inspiration. British radicals had long looked to emulate American republican and democratic institutions.[37] Scottish and Irish radicals, thanks to the particularly strong flows of migration that connected them to the United States, held the American republic in especially high regard.[38] The case of *Reynolds's Newspaper* is especially relevant here as it became an early propagandist for the extension of the Knights of Labor into Britain and Ireland. In the 1860s, wrote Henry Pelling, 'its leading columns ... reveal a partisan enthusiasm for American institutions that can only be paralleled in modern times [the late 1950s] by the enthusiasm of the Communist *Daily Worker* for the Soviet way of life.'[39] In one celebrated article the paper even hoped that the United States would annex Canada.[40] That enthusiasm faded by the turn of the century; but in the 1880s *Reynolds's* remained the leading advocate of American democratic institutions across Britain and Ireland.

Aside from the Knights of Labor, three individuals demonstrated the unusually strong influence of American radicalism in Britain during the 1880s. The first was the economist Henry George, whose book *Progress*

---

[35] A. Smith, *Report of the International Trades Union Congress, held at Paris from August 23rd to 28th, 1886* (London, 1886), pp. 8–11.

[36] E. Bernstein, *The International Working Men's Congress of 1889: A Reply to Justice* (London, 1889), p. 6.

[37] Pelling, *British Left*, esp. chs 1–4.

[38] See, for instance, B. Aspinwall, *Portable Utopia: Glasgow and the United States, 1820–1920* (Aberdeen: Aberdeen University Press, 1984); T.N. Brown, *Irish American Nationalism, 1870–1890* (Philadelphia: Lippincott, 1966).

[39] Pelling, *British Left*, pp. 23–24.

[40] Pelling, *British Left*, p. 53.

and Poverty, first published in 1879, sold hundreds of thousands of copies throughout the English-speaking world. George had an enduring influence in Britain and Ireland.[41] According to David Guetze, he spearheaded 'the cross-fertilization of Progressivism in Britain and the United States.'[42] His single tax, a land reform which he presented as a panacea for all social ills, inspired such varied figures as Joseph Chamberlain, Tom Mann and Michael Davitt. When 51 Labour MPs were polled in 1906 for a list of the most influential authors in their lives, Henry George came in at the top.[43] George also became a hero to Irish nationalists when British authorities in Ireland imprisoned him during a speaking tour there.

Scottish crofters and their supporters used George's proposals for land reform as the basis for movements like the Scottish Land Restoration League, which arose out of the enthusiasm generated by George's speaking tour in Scotland in 1884.[44] At that point Glasgow, as Bernard Aspinwall writes, 'was a hotbed of Henry George's Single Tax enthusiasts, supported by two papers.'[45] The importance of land reform as a live political issue across Britain owed much to George's writings and his speeches around Britain and Ireland.[46] Although George was not a socialist, his work inspired the political careers of a whole generation of British socialists.[47] Tom Mann, for instance, traced his interest in political matters to the time when he first read *Progress and Poverty*.[48] Ironically, the attention that George paid to widening social inequalities in the United States actually helped to end British radicals'

[41] For an early survey of the historiography surrounding George and Britain see J. Saville, 'Henry George and the British Labour Movement,' *Science and Society*, 24:4 (1960), pp. 321–33.

[42] D. Gutzke, 'Britain and Transnational Progressivism,' in Gutzke (ed.), *Britain and Transnational Progressivism* (New York: Palgrave Macmillan, 2008), p. 25.

[43] E.P. Laurence, *Henry George in the British Isles* (East Lansing: Michigan State University Press, 1957); J.H.M. Laslett, 'Haymarket, Henry George, and the Labor Upsurge in Britain and America During the Late 1880s,' *International Labor and Working-Class History*, 29 (1986), pp. 66–82; P.T. Phillips, *A Kingdom on Earth: Anglo-American Social Christianity, 1880–1940* (University Park: Pennsylvania State University Press, 1996), p. 204.

[44] I. Wood, 'Irish Immigrants and Scottish Radicalism,' 1880–1906,' in I. McDougall and J. Donald (eds), *Essays in Scottish Labour History* (Edinburgh: Edinburgh University Press, 1976), p. 76; D.W. Crowley, 'The Crofters' Party, 1885–92,' *Scottish Historical Review*, 35 (1956), pp. 110–26; R. Douglas, *Land, People and Politics: A History of the Land Question in the United Kingdom, 1878–1952* (London: Allison and Busby, 1976), pp. 43–49; E.E. Barry, *Nationalisation in British Politics: The Historical Background* (London: J. Cape, 1965), pp. 59–62.

[45] B. Aspinwall, 'The Civic Ideal: Glasgow and the United States, 1880–1920,' in Gutzke, *Transnational Progressivism*, p. 75.

[46] J. Belchem, *Popular Radicalism in Nineteenth Century Britain* (New York: St. Martin's Press, 1996), pp. 150–51.

[47] M. Crick, *The History of the Social-Democratic Federation* (Keele: Ryburn Press, 1994), p. 19.

[48] T. Mann, *Tom Mann's Memoirs* (London: MacGibbon and Kee, 1967), p. 17.

enchantment with American democracy, as these inequalities suggested that democratic institutions alone were not enough to cure the social problems of industrial life.[49] This disenchantment, as James D. Young writes, was especially strong in Scotland.[50]

The second American was Edward Bellamy. His utopian – or dystopian, depending on one's point of view – novel, *Looking Backward*, followed a young American man who is transported forward in time to the year 2000, to a society where the social problems of Gilded Age society have been solved through the nationalisation of production and distribution.[51] It became an instant international bestseller on publication in 1887 and sold millions of copies worldwide.[52] In Australia *Looking Backward* became even more influential than *Progress and Poverty*.[53] The novel immediately spawned nationalist clubs, so named by Bellamy in an attempt to distance his utopia from the odious word socialism, and British enthusiasts set up the Nationalization of Labour Society with its own journal, the *Nationalization News*.[54] The orderly, planned and bureaucratic vision of the future outlined in *Looking Backward* also influenced the early development of the Fabian Society, and the English socialist William Morris conceived his own utopian novel, *News From Nowhere*, as a riposte to that vision.[55]

The third American was Laurence Gronlund, for some years a leader of the American Socialist Labor Party. He designed his major work, *The Co-operative Commonwealth*, to present socialist principles in plain language to an English-speaking audience, and that book encountered little competition as no adequate English translation of Marx's *Capital* existed for most of the 1880s. Gronlund certainly became well known in Britain. Two editions of *The Co-operative Commonwealth* were published in London; George Bernard Shaw edited the second.[56] When William Morris chaired a debate at London's Hall of Science in 1887, with the motion 'Is Socialism

---

[49] Pelling, *British Left*, pp. 51–52.

[50] Young, 'Changing Images,' p. 78.

[51] E. Bellamy, *Looking Backward, 2000–1887* (Cleveland: World Publishing Company, 1945).

[52] E. Sadler, 'One Book's Influence: Edward Bellamy's Looking Backward,' *New England Quarterly*, 17:4 (1944), p. 530.

[53] Archer, *No Labor Party*, pp. 209–10.

[54] Pelling, *British Left*, p. 64.

[55] J.H.M. Laslett 'State Policy Toward Labor and Labor Organizations, 1830–1939: Anglo-American Union Movements,' in Peter Mathias and Sidney Pollard (eds), *The Cambridge Economic History of Europe, Volume 8: The Development of Economic and Social Policies* (Cambridge: Cambridge University Press, 1989), p. 512; E.P. Thompson, *William Morris: Romantic to Revolutionary* (London: Lawrence and Wishart, 1955), p. 632.

[56] Pelling, *British Left*, p. 64.

Sound?,' one of the participants claimed that *The Co-operative Commonwealth* 'is justly one of the favourites of Socialists, and in some sense may be called their New Testament, as Karl Marx's book may be called their Old Testament.'[57] Gronlund also travelled across the Atlantic and his speeches had a significant effect on many early socialists, particularly in Scotland.[58] Doubtless his listeners were encouraged and flattered by the prediction at the conclusion of his work that 'for many reasons, either Great Britain or the United States – the universal colony – may be considered the place where the New Commonwealth will be first successfully established.'[59]

The popularity of these Americans in Britain illustrates the unique historical conjuncture that took shape during the 1880s. On the one hand, the speedy industrial development of the United States, and the social dislocations this development caused, stimulated the growth of the American labour movement. By 1886, that movement numbered upwards of 1 million workers and seemed to have caught up with its British counterpart for good. On the other hand, until the upswing of 1889 the British labour movement suffered from stagnating membership and faced mounting criticism from the representatives of new radical movements, particularly the small but growing British socialist parties. Many of these critics looked to the United States for answers. Through influential figures such as George, Bellamy and Gronlund, and through the powerful example of the Knights of Labor, whose methods seemed eminently suitable for an age of drastic technological change and the rise of powerful trusts and corporations, they found them.

During the 1880s, in other words, all the central tenets of American exceptionalism – the weakness of the American labour movement; its imitation of foreign, particularly British trends; and its tendency to lag behind those foreign trends – were turned on their head. The British and Irish Knights were a product of this unusual state of affairs. But the stagnation of the British labour movement, and the rapid advances of the Americans, did not create the Order's British and Irish assemblies on their own. To return to Lenin's formula, conditions were ripe for a transnational movement to flourish on foreign soil. Now we must explain why the Knights of Labor went abroad in the first place.

---

[57] A. Besant and G.W. Foote, *Is Socialism Sound?* (London, 1887), p. 13.
[58] Young, 'Changing Images,' p. 79.
[59] L. Gronlund, *The Cooperative Commonwealth* (Cambridge, MA: Belknap Press, 1965), p. 188.

The Internationalism of the Knights of Labor

In 1861, most Americans were completely absorbed by the terrifying prospect of civil war between the northern and southern states. Not Uriah Stephens. A Philadelphian tailor by trade, Stephens wrote to a friend in New York of a very different vision that had haunted him for some time. 'I do not claim to be gifted with the power of prophesy,' he began:

> But I can see ahead of me an organization that will cover the globe. It will include men and women of every craft, creed and color: It will cover every race worth saving. It will come in my time, I hope. Its groundwork will be secrecy, its rule obedience, and its guiding star mutual assistance. It will make labor honourable and profitable and lessen its burdens; it will make idleness a crime, render wars impossible, and obliterate national lines.[60]

Eight years later, Stephens created the Knights of Labor with six other garment cutters. His order never spanned the entire globe, ended war or did away with national borders. But the Knights came closer to his dream than he had any cause to expect.

The Knights have often been left out of the history of international working-class movements. Most scholarship concerns those movements based in Europe, whether the four revolutionary Internationals, the various international trade union federations, or the other trade unions, fraternal orders, cooperative congresses and political tendencies that made up the international labour movement. The idea of American exceptionalism also fails to account for an order that extended to three other continents and became one of the largest global working-class movements of its day.[61] The Order's international history, however, was no aberration. The Knights fit comfortably within wider nineteenth-century patterns and traditions of working-class internationalism on both sides of the Atlantic. We need to address these patterns and traditions in order to fully understand and contextualise the internationalism of the Knights of Labor.

The causes of labour internationalism have provoked debate and disagreement for nearly 200 years. The very idea of international solidarity, after all, is not always an automatic response to the problems that workers have always faced, particularly given the pervasive nationalism within industrial countries during the nineteenth and twentieth centuries. George Orwell even claimed that 'patriotism is usually stronger than class hatred, and always stronger than any kind of internationalism.'[62] In general,

---

[60] *Proceedings of the GA* (1897), n. pag.
[61] Weir, *Knights Down Under*, p. 206.
[62] G. Orwell, 'The Lion and the Unicorn,' in *Essays* (London: Penguin, 2000), p. 146.

working-class internationalism has always resulted from a combination of ideas and principles, whether sourced from Marx, Bakunin, Mazzini or some other thinker or set of traditions, and from material pressures, for example the desire to prevent foreign workers from undermining local wages. Mere ideological appeals for international solidarity seldom attract many workers without an appeal to self-interest as well; material interests alone seldom lead to international cooperation. John Logue even argues that the idea that international solidarity accords with workers' material interests no longer makes sense, except as a cultural trait that 'developed from concrete material self-interest grounded in the pattern of migration of skilled labor in the middle of the last century, at the time when modern trade union organization had its inception.'[63] This view, needless to say, is a contentious one.

As soon as workers began to define themselves or were themselves defined in opposition to other social classes, a process first powerfully expressed by the Chartists and which became increasingly apparent in continental Europe after the revolutions of 1848, they confronted the fact that production and trade were not constrained by national borders or national feeling. Their products competed with those made elsewhere in the world. The level of wages paid in other countries helped to determine theirs. And the movement of people across national borders raised the question of international working-class cooperation most powerfully of all. The preindustrial or artisanal patterns of migration that Logue mentioned above became important here. Nineteenth-century artisans maintained an older tradition of *compagnonnage*, whereby journeymen travelled from town to town and often country to country to practise their trade before settling down in a single place. Such traditions exposed them to craftsmen in other countries, to working conditions in other places and fostered an understanding that artisans in the same trade shared interests that transcended national borders.[64]

These movements were nothing next to the huge waves of migration stimulated by industrial development in Europe, North America and parts of Asia. That development generated an industrial core in western and central Europe, the eastern seaboard and Midwest of the United States and, towards the end of the century, in parts of Japan. Regions on the periphery of this development, especially eastern and southern Europe, urban China

---

[63] J. Logue, *Toward a Theory of Trade Union Internationalism* (Gothenburg: Gothenburg University Press, 1980), pp. 23–24.

[64] For an overview of these processes see M. van der Linden, 'Labor Internationalism,' in van der Linden (ed.), *Workers of the World: Essays toward a Global Labour History* (Leiden: Brill, 2008).

and rural Japan, saw little industrial development but were nevertheless transformed by the monetisation of their economies, the privatisation of their common lands and the general destruction, as David Montgomery writes, of 'long-established patterns of economic activity.' This destruction encouraged millions of men and women to seek employment in the industrial regions where, they knew, wages remained far higher than at home.[65] At the same time, millions of workers moved from one part of this industrial core to another in search of work, higher wages, new opportunities and, in the case of many radicals, freedom from political repression at the hands of European governments.

These migrations raised serious questions for local workers, especially those in trade unions. Until 1848 those workers were mainly concerned with asserting themselves as an independent social force. After that date, as Marcel van der Linden writes, workers began to practise what he terms 'sub-national internationalism,' where local groups of workers sought alliances with local groups in other countries to deal with the consequences of immigration. Trade unionists in one country financially supported strikes in another. They did so for idealistic reasons as well as to prevent defeated strikers from migrating elsewhere in search of work. Trade unionists also cooperated with their colleagues in other countries to prevent employers from recruiting foreign workers to break their own strikes.[66] These efforts at cooperation culminated in the meeting in September 1864 of mostly French and British workers at St Martin's Hall in London. The gathering, called to defend the cause of Polish national independence, instead began the International Workingmen's Association (IWMA), or First International.

London, the International's centre, as Susan Milner writes, became a 'minor International' in its own right during the middle decades of the nineteenth century and drew political refugees and migrant workers from across the Continent.[67] Trade unionists in the city hoped to draw on those international connections in order to reverse attempts by employers to import foreign workers to break strikes, force out union men and drive down standards. 'In the short term,' Milner argues, 'international links could be used by British workers as a means of creating solidarity and thus dissuading foreign workers from taking jobs in Britain during strike movements.' In the longer term, she adds, they 'saw the chance to spread the principles and methods of British trade unionism abroad, which would have the result of raising the standard of living in other countries, thus reducing the threat of

---

[65] D. Montgomery, *The Fall of the House of Labor: The Workplace, the State, and American Labor Activism, 1865–1925* (Cambridge: Cambridge University Press, 1989), pp. 70–82.

[66] Van der Linden, 'Labor Internationalism,' pp. 268–70.

[67] Milner, *Dilemmas of Internationalism*, pp. 21–22.

competition.'[68] Self-interest was not the only motivation here. In a number of major strikes, whether by Parisian bronze workers in 1867, or the building workers of Geneva and the silk workers of Lyon in 1868, the IWMA's ability to marshal international resources, particularly those of British trade unionists, proved crucial to the workers' victories.[69] The International also brought trade unionists into contact with socialists and anarchists, most under the banner of Marx and Bakunin respectively. Members of the IMWA, whatever their own political views, practised an internationalism based on their perceived material interests and political principles, and each informed the other.

The First International broke apart in the 1870s. Bitter and violent disagreements between Marx and Bakunin and their followers led to damaging factional fights. The repression unleashed across Europe against the International after the defeat of the Paris Commune reduced its numbers. The growth of national movements, first in Britain and then elsewhere, combined with the gradual integration of these movements into national political and industrial life, encouraged many trade unionists to abandon it.[70] But working-class internationalism was not only a European phenomenon: American workers had attempted to forge their own international connections over the course of the nineteenth century for much the same reasons. Tens of millions of immigrants arrived in the United States over the course of the nineteenth century, bringing Chartism and Owenism from Britain, socialism from Germany and anarchism from France. Like London in the middle of the nineteenth century, many American cities in the second half of the century resembled Internationals of a kind. But immigrant workers also competed with American workers and threatened to swamp the fledgling American labour movement. Even before the Civil War, the American Typographical Union established international connections in order to prevent English and Scottish printers from immigrating and thus flooding the American labour market.[71]

American workers' first major response to immigration came with the creation of the National Labor Union (NLU) in 1866. The crucial support of workers in Britain and elsewhere in Europe to the North during the Civil War made the idea of international cooperation more appealing. William Sylvis, leader of the NLU, saw the solution to the suffering of workers on

---

[68] Milner, *Dilemmas of Internationalism*, pp. 21–22.

[69] Braunthal, *International*, pp. 114–15.

[70] See, for instance, M. van der Linden, 'The Rise and Fall of the First International: An Interpretation,' from F. van Holthoon and van der Linden (eds), *Internationalism in the Labour Movement, 1830–1940, Vol. I* (Leiden: Brill, 1988), pp. 324–35.

[71] Yearley, *Britons*, p. 54.

both side of the Atlantic as 'the united and fraternal agency of our organs of labor.'[72] The NLU soon developed ties with the First International on the other side of the ocean. Sylvis sent A.C. Cameron, editor of the influential Chicago labour paper the *Workingmen's Advocate*, to the International's 1869 Conference at Basel.[73] Cameron's mission was to establish some kind of 'closer union' between American and European workers, as he told the International's General Council, that would regulate the flow of migrants across the Atlantic and enable the growth of the American labour movement. He and the delegates at Basel laid the groundwork for an Emigration Bureau to do just that.[74]

The collapse of both the NLU and the First International in the 1870s ended these tentative moves towards a transatlantic alliance. The Emigration Bureau, as Samuel Bernstein writes, 'very likely remained a paper body.'[75] Sections of the First International nevertheless survived in the United States throughout the decade and even into the 1880s.[76] Individual trade unions and trade unionists also maintained and expanded their transatlantic connections in the void left by the disintegration of the NLU. Organised ironworkers, cigarmakers, boilermakers and shipbuilders in the United States all sought to establish agreements with trade unionists in Europe, particularly Britain, concerning the mutual exchange of union cards, sending delegates to each other's conventions and even combining their forces in a single international union.[77]

All these activities, Clifton Yearley writes, 'seemed uninspired compared with the plans laid by the Knights of Labor.'[78] The Order's extension into Europe, Australasia and Africa went far beyond any previous American attempts to become a part of the international labour movement, and to play a leading role in it. But the Knights represented the continuation and,

---

[72] Yearley, *Britons*, pp. 45–50; W. Sylvis, *The Life, Speeches, Labors and Essays of William H. Sylvis* (Philadelphia, 1872), pp. 455–56.

[73] A.T. Lane, *Solidarity or Survival? American Labor and European Immigrants, 1830–1924* (Westport: Greenwood, 1987), p. 49.

[74] International Workingmen's Association, *The General Council of the First International, 1868–1870: Minutes* (Moscow: Progress Publishers, 1964), pp. 160–61; H. Katz, *The Emancipation of Labor: A History of the First International* (New York: Greenwood, 1992), pp. 60–63.

[75] S. Bernstein, *The First International in America* (New York: A.M. Kelley, 1965), pp. 33–34.

[76] For these sections see Bernstein, *First International*; T. Messer-Kruse, *The Yankee International: Marxism and the American Reform Tradition, 1848–1876* (Chapel Hill: University of North Carolina Press, 1998); Katz, *Appomattox to Montmartre*; H.C. Richardson, *The Death of Reconstruction: Race, Labor and Politics in the post-Civil War North, 1865–1901* (Cambridge, MA: Harvard University Press, 2001), pp. 85–89.

[77] Yearley, *Britons*, pp. 58–62.

[78] Yearley, *Britons*, p. 62.

ultimately, the culmination of American working-class internationalism. They also represented the continuation of European patterns of internationalism. The Knights formulated their own conception of international solidarity to match those of European socialists and anarchists, and they called this principle 'universal brotherhood.' Charles Lichtman, the Order's General Secretary at various points in its first 20 years, explained this principle in clear terms. 'The object we are working for,' he wrote in 1887, 'is to embrace all toilers, whether hand or brain, into one vast Brotherhood, and to endeavour to put an end to one trade fighting against another.'[79]

Terence Powderly put it even more simply in the same year. 'The motto of our organization, "An injury to one is the concern of all," he claimed, 'is worldwide in its application.'[80] The Knights decorated their assembly halls with symbols that underlined their commitment to brotherhood on an international scale. The globe placed outside the hall while the assembly was in session naturally symbolised 'the field of our operation' and signified 'Universal Organization.'[81] The Order's Great Seal, placed on most official documents, centred on a partial map of the world, and the pentagon that surrounded the map symbolised the 'five races of men,' one from each continent, who all looked to the Order for guidance.[82]

The idea of universal brotherhood had roots in both America and Europe. Uriah Stephens's desire to '[knit] up into a compact and homogenous amalgamation all the world's workers in one universal brotherhood' owed much to his experience of *compagnonnage* and to the fraternal orders, especially the Freemasons, which shaped his understanding of the roots of solidarity. Stephens felt that the Order's international mission would succeed when workers everywhere were 'guided by the same rules, working by the same methods, practicing the same forms for accomplishing the same ends.' As with Freemasonry and many other fraternal traditions, a kind of non-denominational Protestantism, based on the simple understanding of all men and women as equal in the eyes of God, lay behind the Order's brand of universal brotherhood.[83]

It also had roots in American political traditions, especially what labour historians now term 'labor republicanism.' That tradition emphasised the need for the unity of all producers to defend democratic and republican institutions from the parasitic and monopolistic forces that sought to corrupt and destroy them; like Marxist conceptions of class interest, labor republicanism had

---

[79] *Brisbane Courier*, 5 September 1887.
[80] *Reynolds's*, 2 October 1887.
[81] Knights of Labor, *Adelphon Kruptos* (Chicago, 1886), p. 13.
[82] Weir, *Knights Down Under*, p. 205.
[83] Powderly, *Thirty Years of Labour*, p. 89.

international implications as well.[84] The Knights, after all, recognised that the co-operative commonwealth they hoped to build was necessarily a global one. 'The cooperation of only a limited number of individuals will not result in the triumph of the cooperative principle all over the globe,' ran the report of the Order's Co-operative Board to the General Assembly in 1882, 'it would only improve the condition of those who were participants in the respective enterprises, for a short time.'[85] Clifton Yearley is right to argue that 'given the character of the order … it was almost inevitable that its members would want to sally into the international arena.'[86]

Material interests encouraged the Knights towards that arena too. These were not the narrow interests of the Order's leaders. The *New York Times* claimed that 'their only hope … seems to be in conducting a propaganda in new and foreign fields,' and an English trade unionist insisted that their foreign assemblies existed to 'feast and fatten men too idle to work,' but these accusations came in 1889, five years after the first foreign assemblies were launched. They also rest on the questionable assumption that easier ways of making money were not available to Powderly and the General Executive Board.[87] John Logue's claim that modern international trade union bodies work mainly to satisfy the desire of the officials who run them for international travel and other privileges does not apply here either, if only, as we will see in later chapters, because leading Knights refused to travel abroad even when foreign Knights begged them to.[88]

Instead, the Knights were led towards the international arena by their fears about the consequences of mass immigration, which reached unprecedented levels in the 1880s. More than half a million people entered the United States each year on average during that decade, more than twice as many as in the previous decade.[89] A growing proportion of immigrants also came from outside the traditional sources of immigration, western and northern Europe, coming instead from Asia and southern and eastern Europe, and the immigration question acquired a distinctly racial and ethnic cast. The Knights adopted a series of ambiguous and often contradictory positions on racial questions. Most Knights supported the legislative exclusion of all Asian and particularly Chinese workers from the United States, and many, including Powderly, extended their opprobrium to immigrants from

---

[84] Fink, *Workingmen's Democracy*, pp. 3–5.
[85] *Proceedings of the GA* (1882), p. 320.
[86] Yearley, *Britons*, p. 62.
[87] *New York Times*, 13 August 1889; *Walsall Observer*, 11 January 1889.
[88] Logue, *Theory of Internationalism*, pp. 27–29.
[89] *Report of the United States Immigration Commission 1911–12*, 41 vols (Washington, DC: Government Printing Office, 1911), III, pp. 4–5.

southern and eastern Europe. At the same time many Knights reacted with horror to outrages like the massacre of Chinese by white miners at Rocks Springs, Wyoming, in 1885. Some even formed assemblies of Chinese workers and voted at the General Assembly to admit them as members, and others organised many southern and eastern European immigrants into their assemblies.[90]

Certainly, the Order as a whole fiercely resisted any identification with the nativist movement, which enjoyed a revival in the 1880s.[91] Few Knights called for a blanket ban on immigration as a whole. Most called instead for a ban on Chinese immigration and on contract labour – that is, on workers brought in from overseas already under contract to a specific employer, who in return paid some or all of their travel costs. Employers frequently used contract labour to break strikes or circumvent closed shops at workplaces where unions were strong. Knights' opposition to this practice was led, as we will see later, by the glassworkers of Local Assembly 300. And while A.T. Lane writes that the Order's leadership widened the meaning of contract labour 'to embrace unskilled workers too, and in particular penurious and so-called degraded unskilled workers originating in Southern and Eastern Europe,' Knights organised these workers anyway.[92] They also insisted that they wished to regulate rather than end or curtail immigration. Powderly supplied a preface for a book in 1887 that claimed that 'there is no know-nothingism in wise adjustment of the supply of labor to the demand,' and this desire to make immigration manageable rather illegal pervaded the American labour movement of the day.[93]

---

[90] For the Knights and the racial and ethnic aspects of immigration see J. Gerteis, 'The Possession of Civic Virtue: Movement Narratives of Race and Class in the Knights of Labor,' *American Journal of Sociology*, 108 (2002), pp. 580–615. For the Knights and Chinese exclusion see Commons, *History of Labor*, pp. 252–68; Laurie, *Artisans into Workers*, p. 197. For Powderly deploring the condition of Hungarian miners in Pennsylvania see 'Testimony of T.V. Powderly,' *Testimony Taken by the Select Committee of the House of Representatives to Inquire into the Alleged Violation of the Laws Prohibiting the Importation of Contract Laborers, Paupers, Convicts, and other Classes* (Washington, DC, 1888), pp. 497–99, *U.S. Congressional Serial Set, 1817–1994*. For their willingness to organise them anyway see Ware, *Labor Movement in the United States*, p. xiv.

[91] For the Knights and nativism see J. Higham, *Strangers in the Land: Patterns of American Nativism, 1860–1925* (New York: Atheneum, 1963), pp. 53–54, T.J. Curran, *Xenophobia and Immigration, 1820–1930* (Boston: Twayne, 1975), pp. 102–05; K.G. Marsden, 'Patriotic Societies and American Labor: The American Protective Association in Wisconsin,' *The Wisconsin Magazine of History*, 41 (1958), pp. 287–94.

[92] A.T. Lane, *Solidarity or Survival? American Labor and European Immigrants, 1830–1924* (New York: Greenwood, 1987), p. 62.

[93] John Cameron Simonds and John T. McEnnis, *The Story of Manual Labor in All Lands and Ages: Its Past Condition, Present Progress, and Hope for the Future* (Chicago, 1887), p. 487.

We should not, in other words, associate the Knights of Labor with some kind of knee-jerk opposition to all immigrants or cast all the blame on them for later legislative limits on immigration. Regulation, not restrictionism, remained their aim from start to finish, and the Knights adopted two parallel methods to bring that aim to fruition. The first, of course, was through legislation. But to rest there, and to contrast, in the words of Janice Fine and Richard Tichenor, a 'nativist and restrictionist labor movement' in the late nineteenth century with 'an increasingly inclusive and pro-immigration one' in the late twentieth century, would seriously distort the historical record and leave out the second method adopted by the Knights of Labor.[94] That method was international action.

Like his American predecessors, Powderly entered into correspondence with the Scottish Lib-Lab MP and miners' leader Alexander MacDonald, almost as soon as he became Grand Master Workman in 1879. Powderly hoped that this correspondence would lead to a transatlantic alliance that could begin to regulate the flow of migrant workers across the ocean, and he urged the General Assembly in 1880 to 'do something whereby the benefits of a union between the workingmen of America and Europe may become so plain that a connecting link may be forged, binding them closely together.'[95] Powderly's overtures to MacDonald, and then to another miners' leader, Thomas Burt, in 1885, came to nothing; but he maintained his belief that the Knights should 'print circulars and documents concerning the status of the workingman here, and scatter them among our brethren in foreign lands.'[96] Other American Knights also saw the value of recruiting what were, in effect, anti-emigration agents abroad. J.F. Duncan, a Knight from Detroit, advised the Aberdeen Trades Council in 1886 to 'organize an assembly of knights of labour' so that masons from that city would not arrive in the United States and undercut wages and break strikes there.[97]

Knights also synthesised their desire to regulate immigration with their commitment to universal brotherhood, in what I have termed elsewhere 'brotherhood from a distance.'[98] That synthesis resembled very closely the goals of the British trade unionists who created and participated in the First International. In the short term, the Knights wished to regulate immigration

---

[94] Janice Fine and Daniel Tichenor, 'A Movement Wrestling: American Labor's Enduring Struggle with Immigration, 1866–2007,' *Studies in American Political Development*, 23 (2009), pp. 87–88.
[95] *Proceedings of the GA* (1880), p. 175.
[96] *Proceedings of the GA* (1885), p. 18.
[97] *Aberdeen Weekly Journal*, 13 May 1886.
[98] Steven Parfitt, 'Brotherhood from a Distance: Americanization and the Internationalism of the Knights of Labor,' *International Review of Social History*, 58:3 (2013), pp. 463–91.

through international action; in the longer term, they aimed to organise would-be immigrants in their home countries so that they could improve them, remove the material incentives behind migration in the process and ultimately extend the cooperative commonwealth all round the world. Charles Litchman expressed this logic in material terms in 1888. 'When the Knights of Labor and kindred organizations shall have obtained in foreign lands the same commanding position and influence enjoyed in the United States,' he wrote, 'the inequality of wages will disappear, not by levelling our wages down but by levelling their wages up.'[99] Powderly provided probably the most cogent explanation of this synthesis in the same year. In the Order's overseas assemblies, he wrote:

> The members are to be taught to reform existing abuses at home, so that emigration for the purpose of bettering their lot will not be necessary; they are to be taught that the right to enjoy life in the land of his birth is inherent in man. … To assist foreigners to improve their condition at home, it is not necessary to reduce our own people to a condition bordering on serfdom by loading us down with a helpless surplus population which can at best be used only to the advantage of monopoly.[100]

In this way Powderly reconciled universal brotherhood with material self-interest. The international expansion of the Knights of Labor would protect American labour and extend help to labour overseas at the same time.

The Order's first assembly in the Old World was the result of more mundane considerations than Powderly's lofty synthesis. An organiser, John Hughes, set up LA2886 in Cardiff during a visit to relatives in Wales.[101] The Cardiff assembly does not seem to have lasted very long or played any role in the subsequent history of the Order in Britain and Ireland. In the following year, however, other Knights, the glassworkers of Local Assembly 300, Window Glass Workers of America, placed that history on a solid foundation. LA300 was a unique branch of the Order with a misleading name. The assembly was based in Pittsburgh but organised skilled window glassworkers across the United States. According to Pearce Davis, it became 'the most powerful labor organization in the history of the United States.' The *New York Times* described its members as 'the very princes of the labor world.'[102]

---

[99] *Wichita Daily Eagle*, 13 September 1888.
[100] T.V. Powderly, 'A Menacing Irruption,' *North American Review*, 147 (August, 1888), p. 173.
[101] Frederick Turner to Powderly, 11 October 1883, Box 8, TVP.
[102] P. Davis, *The Development of the American Glass Industry* (Cambridge, MA: Harvard University Press, 1949), p. 126; *New York Times*, 18 November 1889.

It is easy to see why. LA300's members enjoyed an unbroken vacation through July and August, when the summer temperatures made glassblowing unsafe. They organised more than nine-tenths of eligible workers in the trade. They successfully maintained strict control over the proportion of apprentices to artisans in order to control the supply of skilled labour. They even managed to delay the introduction of new labour-saving methods into American window glass production.[103] Their average weekly wages approached the princely sum of $50.[104] Thanks to high weekly contributions and initiation fees, the assembly as a whole possessed enormous monetary reserves, with cash and stocks worth more than $100,000 in 1889.[105] For an order devoted to universal brotherhood and whose leaders regularly attacked craft prejudice, it is rather ironic that LA300, the very model of an exclusive (and successful) craft union, should have propelled the Knights of Labor across the Atlantic.

For that is exactly what the assembly did. The window glassworkers may have wrested control of the labour market from employers to a degree unthinkable elsewhere in the United States. But they remained vulnerable to developments in Europe. The widespread application of new machines and techniques there made European glass more competitive *vis-à-vis* American-made glass. These innovations also left many European glassworkers unemployed and desperate for work, and they became a potential source of recruitment for American employers who wished to use them to break strikes or start non-union glassworks outside the control and restrictions that LA300 imposed on the industry.[106] The assembly sent two representatives, James Michels and John Fetters, to Europe in 1880 'for the purpose of making an investigation into the condition of the window glass workers in Europe and, if possible … have the European workers form a union and establish closer communication between America and the old country, in order to protect the interest of all the window glass workers.'[107] Michels and Fetters returned without forming any unions and, in 1883, LA300 faced a series of prolonged strikes and lockouts as employers attempted to break their stranglehold over the window glass industry. They did so in part using European glassworkers, brought over already under contract. LA300 won these battles, with some assistance from the Order's General Executive

---

[103] Q.R. Skrabek, *Michael Owens and the Glass Industry* (Gretna: Pelican, 2006), pp. 38–39.

[104] *New York Times*, 18 November 1889.

[105] P.S. Foner, *History of the Labor Movement in the United States, Vol. II*, 2nd ed. (New York: International Publishers, 1975), p. 57.

[106] Fones-Wolf, 'Immigrants, Labor and Capital in a Transnational Context,' pp. 61–63.

[107] 'Proceedings of the Fifth National Convention of Window-Glass Workers,' p. 20, Box 110, TVP. Also quoted in Pelling, 'Knights in Britain,' pp. 314–15.

Board, largely because they had the money to organise or send back the Europeans imported to replace them.[108]

The assembly emerged in 1884 stronger than ever. For the next decade it established a unique 'double monopoly' with the American Window Glass Manufacturing Association whereby the assembly controlled the supply of skilled labour and employers collectively controlled the price and supply of window glass.[109] Yet the threat posed by imported glassworkers to the assembly's control of the labour market remained. LA300's leaders met that threat in two ways. First, they lobbied Congress to pass a contract-labour law, drafted by their lawyers in 1883, making the importation of workers already under contract illegal. They conscripted the Knights of Labor at large to support their proposed bill, and thanks to this support the bill became law in 1885 as the Foran Act.[110] Second, they returned to the course first charted by Michels and Fetters. F.M. Gessner, the assembly's secretary, opined at a meeting in 1884 that 'the question of foreign competition must be solved either by lower wages at home, or advanced wages and better organization abroad.' He added that 'from a business view, it is cheaper for us to organize the window glass workers' of Europe than it is to engage annually in $60,000 lockouts to resist a reduction of wages that at best only shifts, but does not finally, nor even satisfactorily settle the question of foreign competition.' Gessner asked the assembly to choose between 'temporary make-shifts, called strikes,' or 'a permanent cure by organization abroad.'[111]

LA300 chose the latter. At the end of April 1884, the assembly sent Isaac Cline and Andrew Burtt, its president and secretary, to Europe. They went, as Burtt wrote to Powderly, 'to endeavour to perfect the organization of Window Glass Workers on that side of the ocean.'[112] After several months of agitation throughout the Continent they met at Charleroi, in Belgium, with representative glassworkers from there, Britain, France and Italy, and created the Universal Federation of Window-Glass Workers. Cline became the first president of what *John Swinton's Paper* hailed as 'A World-Wide Union.'[113] Several days later the first convention of the Universal Federation took place at St Helens, home of Pilkington's, the world's largest glassworks.[114]

---

[108] Ware, *Labor Movement*, p. 197.
[109] Davis, *Development of the American Glass Industry*, pp. 126–32.
[110] Ware, *Labor Movement*, pp. 196–97.
[111] 'Report of the Secretary of LA300,' undated 1884, Box 12, TVP.
[112] Andrew Burtt to Powderly, 21 April 1884, Box 10, TVP.
[113] *John Swinton's Paper*, 15 June 1884.
[114] 'Fifth National Convention of Window-Glass Workers,' pp. 20–21; Pelling, 'Knights in Britain,' p. 315.

The Federation almost ended before it began, however. Delegates to its first convention adopted a constitution that allowed any member of the Federation to work in any other country upon the presentation of a clearance card. LA300 refused to accept that provision and approved changes that made it almost impossible for members of the Federation to move between different countries at all. 'That change,' according to an account several years later, 'came very near to breaking up the Federation.'[115] The international solidarity of American window glassworkers had very definite limits. The Universal Federation of Window-Glass Workers, as we will see in later chapters, existed only so long as it tightly regulated the flow of glassworkers from Europe to the United States. But LA300 decided to strike a conciliatory note and at its convention on 8 June 1884, the assembly resolved to send another representative to Europe to continue its work. Cline and Burtt selected A.G. Denny for the task.

In April 1884, when Burtt was about to leave for Europe to organise the glassworkers there, he wrote to Powderly 'as to the advisability of attaching them to the K of L, actively forming a nucleus from which an organization of all branches of labor under this head may be developed.'[116] Burtt and Cline made no moves in this regard. When Denny followed them in September, however, he went with the authority and financial assistance of the Order's General Executive Board as well as LA300.[117] He also kept in regular touch with the General Master Workman. When Denny asked Powderly for advice about adapting the Order's programme to British conditions, Powderly insisted that 'our cause must be attuned here and there in order to conform to existing circumstances,' and told Denny that 'you are on the ground and know best what to do.'[118]

Armed with this knowledge, Denny agitated among glassworkers in various parts of England and in November 1884, his agitation came to a successful conclusion with the creation of Local Assembly 3504. Built on lines identical to LA300, this new assembly had its headquarters in Sunderland and maintained four branches, called 'preceptories' as in the United States, at the four main English centres of window glass production: Pilkington's at St Helens; William Stock and Co. at Plank Lane, near St Helens; Chance Bros at Spon Lane in Smethwick; and Hartleys of Sunderland.[119] LA3504 duly appeared in the roll call of new assemblies in the *Journal of United Labor* in January 1885. When Powderly appeared and

---

[115] 'Fifth National Convention of Window-Glass Workers,' pp. 13–15.
[116] Burtt to Powderly, 21 April 1884, Box 10, TVP.
[117] *Proceedings of the GA* (1885), p. 55.
[118] Powderly to AG Denny, 18 November 1884, Box 94, TVP.
[119] Pelling, 'Knights in Britain,' p. 315.

spoke at a meeting of LA300 in April, its officials could proudly point to the Order's first major foothold in Britain.[120]

Conclusion:
Exceptionalism and the Rise of the British and Irish Knights of Labor

In 1882 Robert Layton, the General Secretary of the Knights of Labor and the editor of its official organ, the *Journal of United Labor*, was alerted to a report of the meeting of the Staffordshire potters at Hanley by one of the *Journal*'s readers. Layton was moved to write an article under the suggestive heading 'Can We Organize in England?' He answered in the affirmative. At the last General Assembly, Layton wrote, he 'did not then feel bold enough to assert that in Europe there was fast coming to the surface a strong feeling for organization into the Knights of Labor.' After the potters based their National Order on the Knights, and from a few 'indirect' sources of his own, Layton predicted that 'in a few years all Europe will be embraced within our folds.'[121]

The Knights made many grandiloquent predictions regarding their order's glorious future. Like all of these, Layton's never came to pass. But two years later the Knights opened their first assemblies in the Old World. They were able to do so because of a unique set of historical conditions that opened up during the 1880s and closed again soon afterwards. In that decade the American labour movement seemed to have shed its earlier backwardness and even, through the Knights of Labor, seemed more attuned to the problems of contemporary industrial society than the British trade unions. The Knights, despite their superficial resemblance to Robert Owen's Grand National Consolidated Trades Union, were the product of sweeping social and economic changes taking place on both sides of the Atlantic, from the threat posed by mechanisation to skilled labour, to the rise of monopoly capitalism. By contrast, the British labour movement remained stagnant for most of the 1880s. Its critics found in the Knights, and in radical Americans like Henry George, Edward Bellamy and Laurence Gronlund, the answers to pressing questions at home. During this unique decade, in other words, British and Irish workers became unusually receptive to ideas and institutions from the United States.

American workers were also unusually willing and able during the 1880s to export their own movement abroad. Following the basic pattern of working-class internationalism in Europe and North America over most of the nineteenth century, the Knights of Labor were guided by a concept of

---

[120] *JUL*, 10 January 1885; 'Minutes of LA300 Meeting,' 17 April 1885, Box 13, TVP.
[121] *JUL*, November 1882.

international solidarity – universal brotherhood. Like their predecessors in the First International and other international working-class associations, American Knights were also guided by their own material interests, in particular their desire to regulate immigration to the United States in order to protect the American labour movement and American standards of living. They reconciled their principles and interests on the grounds that by extending their order abroad they would protect the American labour movement while simultaneously helping to improve conditions for workers abroad. In the process they might even chip away at the material causes that led to mass immigration in the first place. Thanks to the window glassworkers of LA300, the Order actually began to put that synthesis into practice. Their Universal Federation, however much it was actually designed to keep foreign glassworkers out of the American labour market, brought organisation, financial assistance and other advantages to its European affiliates. Indeed, thanks to the window glassworkers of LA300, the Order established LA3504, its first lasting assembly in Britain and Ireland.

Virtually all of the elements of this story call the foundations of American exceptionalism into question. In the mid-1880s the American labour movement was far from weak. American Knights of Labor then outnumbered the British workers affiliated with the TUC. Nor was that movement backward. British radicals of the time looked to Americans like Henry George and Laurence Gronlund for the latest political doctrines, when they were not imbibing socialist and anarchist ideas from continental Europe. The Knights of Labor also fit comfortably into wider patterns of working-class internationalism, on both sides of the Atlantic, during the nineteenth century. Indeed, during the 1880s the classic picture of American exceptionalism was almost completely upended. In chapters 5 and 6 we will explore the consequences of that upending for American and British labour history.

In 1885, Robert Layton evidently thought himself sufficiently vindicated by the Order's expansion abroad to return to his earlier role as seer and prophet. 'Our name has become a household word in all parts of the world, and the day is not far distant when our banner will be planted in every civilized community,' he told that year's General Assembly. 'During the past year the Order has been firmly planted in England and Belgium, and before the next General Assembly meets I believe the principles of our Order will be inculcated in all the principal cities of those two countries.'[122] The next chapter gauges the extent to which Layton's prophecy came to pass across Britain and Ireland.

---

[122] *Proceedings of the GA* (1885), pp. 30–31.

2
The Rise of a Transnational Movement

On 5 May 1886, a crowded meeting of workers from various trades, from chain, anvil, tube, nut, bolt and vice makers to coal miners and ironworkers, met at the Boot and Slipper Inn in Smethwick, near Birmingham. The purpose of this meeting, as a newspaper report put it, was to consider 'a system of federation for all trades societies, or the advisability of joining the Knights of Labour in America.' The Reverend T.T. Sherlock opened with several introductory remarks. 'The object of the movement was to secure for the labourer his full hire,' he told the meeting. 'It was not pillage and confiscation but simple justice that they wanted.' The assembled workers began to applaud. As they did so two of the timber beams supporting the floor gave way with a crash. The applause was replaced by a surging mass of people who rushed the speaker's platform to escape from the collapsing scenery around them. No one, in the end, was injured or killed. The meeting reconvened in the open air, and Richard Juggins, one of the Black Country's most respected trade unionists, urged his listeners to 'follow the action of the Knights of Labour in America.'[1] They did not, or they did so in their own way. Juggins led the creation of the Midland Counties Trades Federation, an association of small trades around Birmingham and the Black Country that features in later chapters.

This was an inauspicious event for a movement that expected, as Robert Layton put it, to establish itself in every town and city in Britain within a matter of years. Yet it was hardly fatal. Knights had established LA2886 at Cardiff in 1883, LA3504 in 1884, and in the following year an assembly of dock labourers at Liverpool, which included the future Labour MP James Sexton, began, grew and then launched a disastrous, failed strike that brought the assembly to an end. In 1886, Robert Robertson and Charles Bird, two organisers with LA3504's Spon Lane preceptory, began to proselytise for

---

[1] *Birmingham Daily Post*, 6 May 1886.

the Order among local workers outside the glass trade. They were, ironically enough, initially constrained by a circular sent from the Order's General Secretary, which ordered all organisers to cease opening new assemblies for a period of 40 days. Leading Knights sent that circular to slow down their order's phenomenal growth, which they feared would result in new Knights leading a rash of strikes that they did not desire or have the money to wage successfully. At few other times in American labour history have trade union leaders so energetically prevented willing recruits from joining their movement.

Once Robertson received permission from Terence Powderly to ignore the circular, and received advice that 'in future when a document is sent to you from the general office you are to take the circumstances into account and be guided accordingly,' he and Bird commenced their agitation in earnest.[2] They attended a number of meetings like the one at the Boot and Slipper Inn during April and May, and Bird ended one of them with the promise 'that he had authority to initiate any body of men over 10, as members of the Knights of Labour.'[3] They also made their case at the Smethwick Salvation Army Barracks. A number of workers at Messrs Tangye's works in that suburb, a major producer of pumps and engines, soon invited them 'to a mug of ale and a chat,' as the *Birmingham Daily Gazette* later recalled, at the Boot and Slipper Inn. This time the floor remained intact. On 12 June 1886, Bird and Robertson took 13 workers from Smethwick and West Bromwich through the Founding Ceremony of the first long-lived assembly outside the glass trade, LA7952, and 50 more paid their initiation fee by instalments. The Knights, as the *Gazette* added, 'became the topic of the day at other factories, Messrs Tangye's men were continually invited to send the Organiser to such and such a workshop, and so the leaven spread.'[4] 'For now the stone has started to roll,' Robert Robertson wrote to Powderly, 'no knowing where it will go on to.'[5]

And so, nearly two years after A.G. Denny opened LA3504, the Knights of Labor began their quest to extend their order into all corners, and all trades and industries, of Britain and Ireland. This chapter explores how successful they were in that quest. It moves from conditions at a local level to events across the Atlantic, from the state of trade unionism in Birmingham to the strikes and political campaigns of the American Great

---

[2] Robert Robertson to Powderly, 22 March 1886, Box 19, TVP; Powderly to Robert Robertson, 6 April 1886, Box 95, TVP.

[3] For Knights at these meetings see *Labour Tribune*, 1 and 8 May 1886; for Bird, see *Smethwick Telephone*, 29 May 1886.

[4] *Birmingham Daily Gazette*, 18 February 1889.

[5] Robert Robertson to Powderly, 15 June 1886, Box 22, TVP.

Upheaval, and from the financial and human assistance that American Knights provided to those in Britain and Ireland to the ramifications of Irish and Catholic migration for the Order's prospects across the Atlantic. It ends with questions of race and empire, two interrelated themes that permeate the history of the British, Irish and American labour movements. Before we approach these themes, however, we first provide a brief chronology of the British and Irish assemblies.

The Knights were present for the longest period and in the greatest numbers in the area around Birmingham and the Black Country. In July 1887, a year after LA7952 opened its doors with 13 members, the assembly boasted 250. Eight other local assemblies now existed alongside it, all of them under the first district assembly (DA) in Britain and Ireland, DA208, based in Handsworth. Together they numbered nearly 800 members.[6] Only four months later that number had swelled to 18 assemblies with around 2,000 members.[7] A second district assembly, DA248 based in Cradley Heath, soon followed the first and between January and April 1888 the official membership figures for the two district assemblies rose from 2,382 to 3,184, in around 30 assemblies.[8] Some reports placed this membership as high as 6,000.[9] In February 1889, according to an expose in the *Birmingham Daily Gazette*, local assemblies ranged from 200 or less to nearly 900 members, and the newspaper estimated that around 7,000 Knights belonged to the two district assemblies.[10] Charles Chamberlain, an organiser for LA7952, claimed that this estimation was far too low, and that 'the list of Assemblies that was published corresponded to the one printed about twelve months ago ... Since that time we have more than doubled the number of our Assemblies.'[11] Chamberlain's estimate was probably too high. But Thomas Dean, the Master Workman of DA208, claimed in May 1889 that the Knights in Britain numbered 10,000 members in 50 assemblies.[12] That number seems warranted given that LA3054 alone organised more than 1,000 glassworkers at its various preceptories in 1886.[13]

The vast majority of Knights in May 1889 belonged to assemblies in Birmingham and the Black Country; but not all. The second major centre of the Order in Britain and Ireland was Rotherham, in South Yorkshire. Knights established LA1266 there in June 1888, particularly amongst local

[6] *JUL*, 13 August 1887.
[7] *JUL*, 10 December 1887.
[8] *Proceedings of the GA* (1888), pp. 4–5; *Reynolds*, 5 August 1888.
[9] *Halfpenny Weekly*, 9 June 1888.
[10] *Birmingham Daily Gazette*, 18 February 1889.
[11] *Smethwick Weekly News*, 2 March 1889.
[12] *Liverpool Mercury*, 27 May 1889.
[13] *John Swinton's Paper*, 14 February 1886.

stove-grate workers, and boasted two branches in the town in August 1889.[14] These assemblies were joined in the next year by three more in Rotherham itself, five others in the Sheffield and Rotherham area, and then by assemblies at Hoyland Nether and Platts Common, near Barnsley. All of them came together under DA256.[15] Assemblies at Derby and at Stanningley, near Leeds, operated at opposite fringes of the district. In 1888 the Knights also returned to Liverpool. LA647, composed of tinners, originally affiliated with DA208 but applied in 1890 to remain attached to the General Assembly; aside from this they remain outside the documentary record.[16] LA443 of Bootle did not. The assembly, based mainly but not exclusively on dock labourers, opened in May 1889.[17] Three months later the assembly boasted 250 members, and in early 1890 Knights in Bootle opened five new preceptories around Liverpool, planning to turn them in time into separate assemblies; however, for reasons we will explore later, LA443 soon fell into terminal decline and disappeared either at the end of 1890 or the following year.[18] Elsewhere in England, workers in Preston briefly formed their own assemblies in 1887 and styled themselves the 'K of L of Great Britain.' Preston's Knights quickly departed from the historical record, however.[19]

The Knights were never confined to England. Their first assembly in Britain and Ireland was based, after all, in Wales. But the historical record is silent on the subsequent activities of LA2886 after 1883, and it took six years for the next non-English assemblies to appear. The first assembly opened in Glasgow in July 1889. By October the city boasted seven, and a Scottish correspondent to the *Labour Tribune* noted that 'this looks like business.'[20] According to a telegram received by LA443 in December, the Scottish assemblies at that time boasted 3,000 members, 1,000 of them having joined in the previous month.[21] These assemblies came together under DA203 of Glasgow. At the same time, the Order also arrived in Ireland. In 1888 and 1889 two assemblies appeared in Belfast, LA418 representing bootmakers and shipyard workers, and LA1566 representing ropemakers. LA418 reached a membership of around 300 and LA1566 achieved similar numbers.[22] LA1601 in Derry joined them in 1889, and in March 1891 claimed around

---

[14] *Rotherham Advertiser*, 31 August 1889.
[15] Pelling, 'Knights in Britain,' p. 331.
[16] Garlock, *Guide to the Local Assemblies*, p. 582; *Proceedings of the GA* (1890), p. 8.
[17] *Bootle Times*, 1 June 1889.
[18] Bean, 'Knights in Liverpool,' p. 73.
[19] David Whittle to Powderly, 13 April 1887, Box 32, TVP.
[20] *Labour Tribune*, 12 October 1889.
[21] *Halfpenny Weekly*, 14 December 1889.
[22] Boyle, *Irish Labour Movement*, pp. 104–06.

800 members.[23] By that time the Belfast assemblies had collapsed, and the one in Derry faced serious and ultimately insurmountable problems. The Scottish assemblies also seem to have folded sometime in mid-1890 or 1891.

The end of 1889 marked the high point of the British and Irish assemblies. They extended the farthest around those countries and reached their peak total membership at that time. It is impossible to calculate accurately exactly what that membership was. In January 1890, one Knight provided the absurd figure of 200,000 throughout Britain and Ireland as part of a worldwide membership of 6 million; in May 1890, a Knight at Platts Common claimed that there were 18,000 Knights in Birmingham and the Black Country alone.[24] Thomas Dean's figure of 10,000 in total seems more accurate, and with the additional assemblies in Scotland and Ireland, not to mention the rapid growth of assemblies at Rotherham and Walsall, we might place the peak membership of the Order in Britain and Ireland between 10,000 and 15,000 in the early months of 1890.

This membership soon fell in dramatic fashion, for reasons we explore in later chapters. In August, 1891, Arthur Nadin of LA1266 claimed 5,000 members in England; in July of the same year, however, the *Smethwick Weekly News* claimed that DA208 numbered around 400, DA248 slightly more and DA256 rather less.[25] The latter figure seems closer to the mark, for the last two district assemblies came together in the British National Assembly in 1891, and when they entered their first return to the Registrar of Trade Unions and Friendly Societies, they had only 434 members between them.[26] DA208, which remained outside the National Assembly, was reduced to four local assemblies in February 1893 and only continued to decline afterwards.[27] The end of that year marked the point when, to all intents and purposes, the Knights of Labor no longer existed in Britain and Ireland. But the full story of that decline is reserved for later chapters; we return instead to the task of explaining the Order's growth from its first non-glass assembly to the end of the 1880s.

---

[23] McAteer, 'New Unionism in Derry,' p. 13. Several months later this figure stood at 700 (*JUL*, 30 July 1891).

[24] *Liverpool Echo*, 28 January 1890; *Sheffield and Rotherham Independent*, 21 May 1890.

[25] *Rotherham Advertiser*, 29 August 1891; *Smethwick Weekly News*, 11 July 1891. DA248, at least, claimed 1,000 members when they attended the Labour Electoral Congress in 1890 (Labour Electoral Association, *Report of the Labour Electoral Congress* (Manchester, 1890), p. 2).

[26] Pelling, 'Knights in Britain,' p. 330.

[27] Thomas Dean to Powderly, 8 February 1893, Box 77, TVP.

Disorganisation and the Great Upheaval

The early history of the British Knights was determined by the location of the four glassworks where LA3504 set up its preceptories, at Plank Lane, St Helens, Sunderland and Spon Lane. The first two, in Lancashire, were close together and potentially afforded an excellent base to recruit workers in the major industrial regions of the county. The assembly of dockers that James Sexton joined in Liverpool came about through the efforts of a visiting organiser who, Henry Pelling surmises, was likely on his way to or from one of these preceptories.[28] But the Plank Lane preceptory remained small and soon fell into disrepair and, as we will see in Chapter 4, the glassworkers at St Helens struggled to make any headway against their employer, Pilkington's. The Lancashire preceptories were in no shape to spawn assemblies in other trades.[29] Glassworkers in Sunderland found that the strong and rather parochial local labour movement that surrounded them did not permit the Knights to organise new assemblies, and still maintain friendly relations with other unions. 'As to the efforts for organisation we have done our best,' James Brown, the secretary of LA3504, later told General Secretary-Treasurer Hayes, 'but in the north of England they are all large trade organisations, the Boilermakers, Engineers, Shipwrights, National Labourers Union and Cetra and believe in their own principles and customs.'[30]

That left the preceptory at Spon Lane, near Birmingham. In the previous chapter we saw how the British labour movement, despite its pre-eminence amongst the trade union movements of the world, still organised only a small fraction of wage earners. That was particularly true in Birmingham and the Black Country, the area to the west of the city, which became one of the great industrial areas of Britain during the nineteenth century. Trade unions there remained weak even if, as John Benson argues, that difference was not as severe as historians have often claimed.[31] That weakness was partly conditioned by the characteristics of industrial development in the region. During the second half of the nineteenth century the iron and steel industries of the Black Country went into relative decline, and production remained concentrated to a greater degree than elsewhere in small units, often based in the family home and using outdated and

---

[28] Pelling, 'Knights in Britain,' p. 320.
[29] Pelling, 'Knights in Britain,' p. 319.
[30] James Brown to Hayes, 31 August 1892, Box 10, JHP.
[31] R.H. Trainor, *Black Country Elites: The Exercise of Authority in an Industrialized Area, 1830–1900* (Oxford: Oxford University Press, 1993), pp. 146–66; J. Benson, 'Black Country History and Labour History,' *Midland History*, 15:1 (1990), pp. 100–10.

inefficient equipment.[32] The chain makers – men, women and children, working in factories or in family workshops, and everywhere in abject poverty – became human symbols of that decline. *Commonweal* described them as the 'poorest paid slaves in the country.'[33] Not all Black Country workers were so poorly organised but their unions nevertheless remained weaker, and their employers more paternalistic, than in other major British industrial centres.

This disorganisation provided space for the Knights to grow, as T.R. Threlfall, a leading figure in the TUC, explained in 1894. 'It is a significant fact,' he wrote, 'that the society seemed to flourish best in those portions of the Black Country where trades unionism is weak.'[34] In 1886 there were movements afoot to end this weakness. 'Several orders of skilled workmen were casting about for a newer style of Trade Unionism,' as the *Birmingham Daily Gazette* later recalled, and 'artisans were ready for any organiser at that time.'[35] The meetings they held in April and May to create a federation for the district underlined this desire. They ended in the creation of the Midland Counties Trades Federation, a body that appears at greater length in Chapter 6, but some workers also gravitated towards Robert Robertson and Charles Bird as they attended the meetings, agitated at the Salvation Army Barracks and raised the Order's profile outside the premises of the Chance Bros Glass Works. That profile was raised most spectacularly due to events from abroad. The disorganisation of workers in Birmingham and the Black Country, and their attempts to remedy it, were contemporary to the struggles which collectively became known as the Great Upheaval, in which American Knights played a leading role.

In 1886, American workers engaged in 1,411 recorded strikes at 9,891 establishments with 499,489 participants, more than double the number of strikers in the previous year and far higher than the 129,521 strikers recorded in 1881.[36] American workers also engaged in boycotts and in a rash of unofficial, and thus unrecorded, strikes as well. Many of these struggles took place under the banner of the Knights of Labor, which nearly reached a million members in mid-1886. American workers also entered the political arena as an independent force in unprecedented numbers. They nearly

---

[32] E. Taylor, 'The Midland Counties Trades Federation, 1886–1914,' *Midland History*, 1:3 (1972), p. 26. For the iron industry see W.K.V. Gale, *The Black Country Iron Industry: A Technical History* (London: Metals Society, 1979); G.R.W. Medley, *The Geography of Industrial Decline: The Black Country Iron and Steel Industry, 1850–1900* (unpublished DPhil thesis, University of London, 1986).

[33] *Commonweal*, 26 February 1887.

[34] *Manchester Times*, 26 January 1894.

[35] *Birmingham Daily Gazette*, 18 February 1889.

[36] J. Brecher, *Strike!* (Boston: South End Press, 1977), p. 40.

elected Henry George as the Mayor of New York, and dozens of local labour parties sprang up in virtually every state, some of which won local elections. Anarchists and socialists held demonstrations throughout the United States. During one of them, at Haymarket Square in Chicago in May 1886, a bomb exploded among the police. A number of anarchists were charged with murder, on flimsy evidence, and some were sentenced to death. Middle- and upper-class Americans could be forgiven for thinking that they would soon face open and armed insurrection as well.

Most British newspapers reported on the Great Upheaval with an equal measure of fear and contempt. *The Times* hoped that Americans would put an end to this 'fooling with anarchy,' and hoped 'that our American kinsfolk will concede to us the right of putting an end summarily to any similar "fooling with anarchy" among the subjects of the British Crown.'[37] Reports that the Knights planned to open assemblies in Britain raised similar fears, even though trade unionists assured the London *Morning Post* that this remained 'a doubtful matter.'[38] The *Yorkshire Gazette* exclaimed that 'British industries are threatened with dire revolution!'[39] The *Halfpenny Weekly* later described the probable reaction to news of British assemblies in Liberal circles: 'a succession of huge strikes, resulting in the loss of our foreign trade, and labour candidates "splitting up the Liberal vote."'[40] British observers looked across the Atlantic and saw a level of violence and social conflict that far exceeded anything at home. Most were unaware that Terence Powderly and other leading Knights were desperately trying to dissociate their Order from that violence, and they feared that assemblies in Britain would bring the Great Upheaval with them.[41]

Those fears informed the coverage local newspapers gave to the British and Irish assemblies. Some of them, notably *Reynolds's*, the *Halfpenny Weekly* and the *Smethwick Telephone*, reported the Knights in a sympathetic way that reflected the liberal-radical views of their writers and editors. Others paid little attention to the Knights or simply reprinted articles on them from other publications. Most local newspapers did their best, however, to expose the Order as something alien and destructive. Subsequent chapters feature attacks on the assemblies from the *Smethwick Weekly News*, the *Birmingham Daily Gazette* and other papers determined to prevent them from exporting the Great Upheaval across the Atlantic.

---

[37] *The Times*, 13 October 1886.
[38] *Morning Post*, 28 September 1886.
[39] *Yorkshire Gazette*, 2 October 1886.
[40] *Halfpenny Weekly*, 9 June 1888.
[41] Laslett, 'Haymarket, Henry George,' pp. 68–82.

Workers in Birmingham and the Black Country, on the other hand, saw the Knights and the Upheaval in a rather different light. At the same meeting where the floor collapsed, in May 1886, the Rev. Sherlock described the presence of the Order's representatives as a 'pleasing feature,' and added that 'it was a splendid augury for the future when they had men to come right across the Atlantic to discuss what was the best means to carry on their trade organisations to a successful issue.'[42] Under the appropriate heading, 'Movement Among the Dry Bones,' one worker from Cradley told the *Labour Tribune* in September that:

> the working men of England could not do better than join the Knights of Labour ... Their programme, which I have before me as I write, seems to answer most of the requirements of the working-men, and there is some backbone in that society – something a man feels he can lean on in case of necessity.'[43]

Where many newspapers saw the Knights as harbingers of anarchy and violence, enough workers in Birmingham and the Black Country hailed them as a solution to their disorganisation.

A number of newspapers, from radical sheets like *Reynolds's* and *Commonweal* to mainstream journals in Birmingham, received inquiries from correspondents who wanted more information about the Order.[44] In April 1886, *Commonweal* printed the address of the Order's General Secretary, Frederick Turner, and directed future queries about the Knights to him.[45] In the correspondence pages of the *Labour Tribune* and other newspapers aimed at a working-class readership, workers in both Britain and America debated the merits of attaching themselves to the Knights from 1886 onwards.[46] The most notable inquiry, however, came in February 1886 from *Commonweal*'s American correspondent, H. Halliday Sparling, to the prominent American labour journal, *John Swinton's Paper*. 'I am continually being asked if there is a Lodge of the Knights of Labor in London,' Sparling wrote, 'and it makes me feel tired to keep on saying "No," or, "I wish there were." Is there no way of starting a Lodge, so as to show our British Trade Unionists *how* to combine?'[47] Swinton replied in the next issue. English soil, he claimed, was 'well prepared' for the Knights, for 'millions have been trained in trades unionism, and far broader ideas

---

[42] *Smethwick Telephone*, 8 May 1886.

[43] *Labour Tribune*, 4 September 1886.

[44] *Commonweal*, April 1886 and 17 September 1887; *Reynolds*, 21 August 1887, 15 and 29 July 1888; *Birmingham Daily Post*, 15 May 1888; *Birmingham Daily Gazette*, 9 July 1889.

[45] *Commonweal*, April 1886.

[46] See for instance, the *Labour Tribune*, 16 October and 20 November 1886; 1 January 1887.

[47] *John Swinton's Paper*, 28 February 1886.

than those of the Trade Unions are now leavening the democratic masses of England.' Swinton advised Sparling to contact Terence Powderly directly, and ended with an appeal for 'the Order [to] march to conquest in Great Britain and Ireland.'[48]

Others also greeted Sparling's letter with enthusiasm. George Schilling, a socialist and leading Knight from Chicago, argued in Swinton's paper that:

> [It is] only through a powerful labor organization like the K. of L., having its ramifications in every civilized country of the world, that national bigotry, vanity and the false hatred of the workers of one country toward their fellow-workmen of other countries, can be destroyed, and in its stead spring up that feeling of international fraternity among all producers, from which will yet be born the Universal Republic of Labor.

Schilling then suggested that 'in order to supply the want of our British fellow-workers, I *move that MICHAEL DAVITT be called upon to accept a commission as Organizer of the K. of L. on the other side of the Atlantic*, and espouse the cause of our Holy Order.'[49] Readers from Brooklyn, Newark, Providence and De Soto, Missouri, seconded Schilling's motion in the next issue of *John Swinton's Paper*.[50] Two years later, as we will soon see, Schilling's motion was enacted.

Yet the Knights never opened any assemblies in London. Sparling was no admirer of Powderly, as his American column in *Commonweal* made clear, and he probably wrote to Swinton to avoid contacting the General Master Workman directly. His exchange with Swinton ultimately led nowhere. Powderly commissioned an organiser, one James Russell Walker of Notting Hill, in December 1886. Another Londoner, William Beck, asked Powderly in 1887 for advice on starting assemblies in the city.[51] Neither Walker nor Beck met with any success. Jewish anarchists in London's East End did briefly organise a group called the Knights of Labor in 1888. They aimed, as William Fishman writes, 'to reverse the tide which had been removing the most gifted of their comrades to America.'[52] Yet no further references to that group have survived.

---

[48] *John Swinton's Paper*, 28 February 1886. Swinton could speak from personal experience, having recently visited Europe and met such luminaries of the contemporary political scene as Victor Hugo and Karl Marx over the course of his travels. See J. Swinton, *John Swinton's Travels* (New York, 1880), pp. 18–21, 41–45.

[49] *John Swinton's Paper*, 7 March 1886.

[50] *John Swinton's Paper*, 14 March 1886.

[51] 'List of Organizers, 1886–1888,' Reel 68, Terence V. Powderly Personal Papers Microfilm Collection, Library of Congress; Powderly to William Beck, July 22 1887, Box 97, TVP.

[52] W.J. Fishman, *East End Jewish Radicals, 1875–1914*, 2nd ed. (Nottingham: Five Leaves, 2004), p. 159.

The Knights, as Henry Pelling observed, remained 'completely unsuccessful' in London.[53] The assemblies around Birmingham relied on disorganisation, existing agitation among local workers and pre-existing assemblies to speed their growth; some Londoners showed interest in the Knights but not, evidently, with the same combination of favourable conditions and not with the same results. The assemblies that appeared towards the end of the 1880s largely followed the Birmingham example. When LA454 began in Walsall in 1888, Knights encountered the same diverse and small-scale industrial patterns as in the rest of the Black Country. Known as 'The Town of a Hundred Trades,' workers in Walsall's varied crafts and trades saw the Knights as a powerful ally in their own struggles.[54] Disorganised stove-grate workers in Rotherham speeded the growth of LA1266 and other assemblies in the town. LA443 in Bootle emerged in the context of widespread agitation among local tramwaymen and seamen and then among the assembly's main constituency, local dock labourers, who also saw American Knights as powerful allies against the transatlantic shipping companies.[55] The assemblies in Glasgow, Derry and Belfast also followed a similar pattern. Disorganisation and pre-existing agitation in each local setting combined with the idea that the Knights of Labor could solve their problems.

The Order's expansion around Britain and Ireland, and the consolidation and growth of its existing assemblies, also depended on a small but very enthusiastic cadre of leaders and organisers. Without the efforts of Robert Robertson and Charles Bird, the Spon Lane preceptory might never had spawned the assemblies that emerged around it. Richard Hill and Thomas Dean, recording secretary and Master Workman respectively of LA7952 and DA208, remained in those positions from 1886 right through to the end of those assemblies in 1894. Dean's speeches in Liverpool and Rotherham began and sped the growth of assemblies there, and Hill handled the bureaucratic side of the Order's business in the Birmingham area.[56] The *Journal of United Labor* was even moved to describe Zebulon Butler, a particularly vociferous Knight from Stourbridge, as its 'English Champion' for his defence of the Order in the press.[57] Jesse Chapman, a headmaster and the Master Workman of LA10227 in Smethwick, effectively coordinated organising efforts in the wider Birmingham region.[58] Charles Chamberlain,

---

[53] Pelling, 'Knights in Britain,' p. 324.
[54] H. Lee, *A Short History of Walsall* (Walsall: T. Kirby and Sons, 1927), p. 39.
[55] Bean, 'Knights in Liverpool,' pp. 70–71.
[56] *Liverpool Mercury*, 27 May 1889; *Rotherham Advertiser*, 21 December 1889.
[57] *JUL*, 26 September 1889.
[58] Pelling, 'Knights in Britain,' p. 321.

an organiser attached to DA208, became the public face of the Order in Birmingham and directed the growth of the assemblies there for a time in 1888 and 1889.

LA454 in Walsall and then LA1266 in Rotherham benefited from the oratorical talents of Haydn Sanders, a feature of later chapters.[59] LA443 in Bootle, a suburb of Liverpool, secured the leadership of Samuel Reeves, commonly described as the best-known socialist in the city and an effective agitator.[60] James Shaw Maxwell, a leading single-taxer in Scotland and prominent in the early Scottish Labour Party and the later Independent Labour Party, led the rapid if short-lived growth of DA203 in Glasgow. For a time, the first socialist member of the House of Commons, the colourful Scottish aristocrat Robert Bontine Cunningham Graham, affiliated himself with the Scottish Knights as well. Ben Turner and James Sexton, both later to become MPs and trade union leaders themselves, served part of their union apprenticeship in early British assemblies.[61] As we will see, the British Knights also briefly secured the services of Michael Davitt, the famed Irish nationalist leader. All these leaders feature in subsequent chapters.

They also attracted the sympathy of some influential local figures, particularly in the Black Country. The Rev. Sherlock advanced their cause at those early meetings in 1886. The Rev. Harold Rylett, a Methodist minister based in Dudley until he moved to Manchester in 1889, also proved sympathetic to the Knights.[62] Rylett became well known for his advocacy of Black Country chain makers. When John Burnett, the labour correspondent to the Board of Trade, visited the area in 1888, Rylett served as his guide.[63] A later biography of Rylett actually placed him as a leader of the Knights in Dudley and other parts of the Black Country.[64] And Sherlock and Rylett were not alone. An anonymous 'Minister of Religion,' perhaps one of them or a third party, defended the Knights in a letter to the *Birmingham Daily Post*.[65] The *Birmingham Daily Gazette* declared in 1889 that 'the Knights of Labour in and around Birmingham have some half-dozen public men – ministers of religion and the like – in their confidence,' and one of these

---

[59] K.J. Dean, *Town and Westminster: A Political History of Walsall* (Walsall: Walsall County Borough, 1972), esp. introduction.

[60] D.B. Rees, *Local and Parliamentary Politics in Liverpool from 1800 to 1911* (Liverpool: Edwin Mellen, 1999), pp. 67–71.

[61] J. Sexton, *Sir James Sexton: Agitator* (London: Faber and Faber, 1936), pp. 79–81; B. Turner, *About Myself, 1860–1930* (London: Cayme, 1930), pp. 130–31.

[62] *Smethwick Telephone*, 26 October 1889.

[63] *Birmingham Daily Post*, 11 October 1888.

[64] *Reynolds's*, 16 May 1897.

[65] *Birmingham Daily Post*, 21 May 1888.

anonymous well-wishers conducted an interview with the *Gazette* on the Order's behalf.[66]

The achievements of British and Irish Knights appear even more impressive when we consider the economic conditions that prevailed for most of the 1880s. Between 1877 and 1889, except for a brief upswing in 1882 and 1883, as A.E.P. Duffy writes, 'the general trade of the country had suffered from constant depression.' Many unions found their incomes falling while their expenditure on unemployed members increased, and 'the numbers represented at the TUC were falling sharply.'[67] These adverse conditions held back the Order's growth as well. Richard Hill told the *Journal of United Labor* in 1887 that 'our success would have been far greater but for the very indifferent state of trade in this part of our land.'[68] Yet the Knights reached 10,000 members just over three years after the first non-glass assembly appeared in the Black Country. Had the Great Upheaval coincided with the upswing in trade and trade unionism that occurred in Britain and Ireland at the end of the decade, their growth might have been even more explosive. But if the British and Irish Knights had a poor sense of timing, they also belonged to an international Order with resources and allies far beyond theirs, and whose leaders made sure that some of these resources and allies were used to speed the growth of assemblies across Britain and Ireland.

The Order as a Transnational Movement

In some ways, the Knights of Labor was destined to become an international and not simply an American order. Knights preached universal brotherhood with enthusiasm. They feared the consequences of uncontrolled immigration for the living standards and democratic rights of American workers. This combination, this brotherhood from a distance, gave them powerful incentives to organise abroad. In other ways, however, the Knights were an unlikely candidate for an international body. Their finances were always a mess. Robert Weir observes that one 'of history's frustrating ironies is that those federations that were chronically short of cash – such as the International Working Men's Association, the Knights of Labor, and the Industrial Workers of the World – were the ones to make the biggest efforts toward global organizing.'[69] Enthusiasm has never been a perfect substitute for money, the lubricant needed to pay organisers, support members on

---

[66] *Birmingham Daily Gazette*, 22 February 1889.
[67] A.E.P. Duffy, 'The Eight Hours Day Movement in Britain, 1886–1893,' *The Manchester School*, 36:4 (1968), pp. 207–08.
[68] *JUL*, 30 July 1887.
[69] Weir, *Knights Down Under*, p. 240.

strike and keep the bureaucratic wheels in motion. The Knights of Labor had a great deal of the first and a constant shortage of the second, and that always placed severe limits on their assistance to the assemblies that sprang up elsewhere in the world.

That, of course, was not the impression that many workers on both sides of the Atlantic had of the Order's finances. American workers between 1885 and 1887 assumed that the Knights, with their hundreds of thousands of members, drew on an equally impressive amount of money to back them up. The Order came to be seen as the source of virtually unlimited strike pay. Interested British workers, at a much greater distance, naturally made similar assumptions. The fact that the Knights arrived in Britain through the vehicle of LA300, an incredibly wealthy organisation that actually subsidised the Order at large for most of its history, encouraged those assumptions still further. So did the assistance granted to British Knights by the Order's General Executive Board. When Black Country assemblies engaged in their first disputes in 1886 and 1887, the Board sent them an unsolicited cheque for $100 and implied that more would follow if necessary.[70] Knights in Dudley still drew on this example in 1890 as proof of the benefits that the British assemblies derived from their connection to the United States. However, he claimed that the cheque had been for £200 – a useful symbol of the way that distance, and time, magnified the power and the financial resources of the American Knights in Britain and Ireland.[71] The idea of sending membership dues across the Atlantic was not universally popular in Britain and Ireland, and we will deal with financial questions at greater length in Chapter 7; but financial assistance from America attracted workers to the assemblies and provided them with the money needed to organise new ones.

American Knights certainly did what they could to make their British and Irish recruits feel part of an international movement. Despite pressing business and thousands of letters daily from Knights across the United States, Powderly and the other general officers maintained correspondence with their assemblies across the ocean, and usually replied to their letters promptly.[72] Powderly could provide little in the way of detailed advice for British and Irish Knights, and many of his suggestions, as we will see in later chapters, would have proved calamitous if followed; but the sheer fact of this correspondence proved to Knights in the Old World that they were not completely isolated from Knights in the New. The *Journal of United Labor*,

---

[70] *Birmingham Daily Gazette*, 18 February 1889. A note for future money figures: the contemporary exchange rate was about 4 US dollars to 1 pound sterling.
[71] *Stourbridge, Brierley Hill and County Express*, 1 March 1890.
[72] *Philadelphia Record*, 25 July 1886; *Philadelphia Press*, 27 July 1886.

the Order's official organ, fulfilled a similar function. Letters from Knights in Britain and Ireland regularly appeared in its pages. Frederick Shreeve, the recording secretary of Derby's LA395, recognised the *Journal*'s potential power as a means to weld the Order's various worldwide assemblies into a kind of imagined community, to use Benedict Anderson's term, and thus into a real international movement.[73] Shreeve 'earnestly ask[ed] some of our brothers in Great Britain to write to the Journal, for I feel convinced that it would cause brother members and others to read it with increased interest and to their own edification. As we are glad to hear good news from our brothers in America, so will they be glad to hear from us.'[74] The *Journal*'s editors certainly made great claims for its influence overseas. The doubling of the Order's English membership in 1888, they wrote, was 'a direct result of the missionary work carried on by the Journal in the hands of the Local Assemblies in that country.'[75]

The Order became an international movement without a bureaucracy to match, and in many ways this worked to the benefit of Knights in Britain and Ireland. Even in the United States, as Robert Weir observes, the seemingly clear hierarchical progression from local to district and state assemblies, and finally to the General Assembly and the general officers, became labyrinthine in practice. Local and district assemblies competed for jurisdiction between and within each other. These unclear jurisdictional boundaries encouraged internal conflict and drove many talented and committed members and leaders from the assemblies. The decisions reached at General Assemblies, or arrived at by the general officers, were only implemented when assemblies found it in their interest to do so.[76] American Knights never had the money, the inclination or the time, however, to replicate this bureaucratic nightmare on an international scale. British and Irish Knights never became entangled in the murky world of the Order's internal politics. The preoccupations of the general officers with American affairs also ensured that British and Irish Knights enjoyed a large measure of flexibility and independent action.

The only exceptions to this benign neglect, supplemented with occasional assistance, were the glassworkers. Isaac Cline, Andrew Burtt and A.G. Denny invested several months of their time to organise LA3504 as well as the Belgian assemblies and their Universal Federation. They and LA300's other

---

[73] B. Anderson, *Imagined Communities: Reflections on the Origins and Spread of Nationalism* (London: Verso, 1991).

[74] *JUL*, 10 October 1889.

[75] *JUL*, 24 January 1889.

[76] Robert Weir, *Knights Unhorsed: Internal Conflict in a Gilded Age Social Movement* (Detroit: Wayne State University Press, 2000), esp. ch. 4.

leaders stayed in direct contact with LA3504 throughout that assembly's existence, and worked with them and other European glassworkers through the Universal Federation. According to a report at LA300's convention in 1889, the assembly spent $15,000 building up the Federation and a further $1,000 per year to maintain it.[77] Through that Federation a number of English glassworkers were able to find positions in the United States, including Joseph French, the first secretary of LA3504, thanks in part to Powderly's intercession with James Campbell, the president of LA300.[78] Powderly's intercession with Campbell also allowed glassworkers at the St Helens preceptory to rid themselves of Joseph Norbury, their secretary, whose alcoholism threatened to undermine the difficult task of organising at the anti-union firm Pilkington Bros.[79] James Campbell, a strong advocate of temperance, initially resisted allowing Norbury to find work in the United States until the General Master Workman convinced him that 'if this man is not allowed to go to work the people on the other side may begin to think that they are allied to us only for our benefit and not theirs.'[80] English Knights certainly appreciated Powderly's help.[81]

Yet British and Irish Knights still felt their isolation from the Order at large. In 1887, Richard Hill wrote a letter to the general officers, read and debated at that year's General Assembly, which detailed the problems that arose from the distance between British assemblies and headquarters. It took nearly a month for letters to travel to and from the general officers, Hill wrote, and telegraphs were too short and expensive to effectively communicate problems. 'Besides hampering us in consultation,' he continued, 'the intervening distance makes it impossible for any representative from headquarters to come among us in case of trouble to mediate between labor and capital when local effort may prove fruitless, and so we are deprived of one of the most valued and most vital privileges of the Order.' He added that local disputes flared up too quickly for American Knights to mediate them by letter.

Hill proposed two alternative solutions. The first was to 'send over, for a year or two at any rate, some accredited member of the General Executive Board, or a representative specially appointed at the ensuing General Assembly.' This representative, Hill argued, could carry out 'missionary work at the various industrial centres of Great Britain ... could in cases of

---

[77] 'Fifth National Convention of Window-Glass Workers,' pp. 13–15.
[78] Joseph French to Powderly, 16 August 1887, Box 35, TVP; Joseph French to Powderly, 12 September 1887, Box 36, TVP.
[79] Joseph French to Powderly, 7 July 1887, Box 30, TVP.
[80] Powderly to Campbell, 21 February 1887, Box 96, TVP.
[81] Joseph French to Powderly, 16 April 1887, Box 32, TVP.

difficulty speak the final word of the General Executive Board, could be called upon without fear of consequences to plead our cause with employers.' Such a representative, he insisted, 'could do more in one year for the rooting and grounding of the Order in this country than we can do in five.' As an alternative, the Board could 'appoint a paid man among us beyond the reach of capitalistic vindictiveness for the organizing and mediating functions set forth above.'[82] In either case, Hill implied that the British assemblies needed American resources, and American representatives, to establish the Order there on a solid foundation. His suggestions gelled with the feelings of American Knights. Many, according to the *Washington Post* only days before the 1887 General Assembly convened, 'believed that with the aid of a man of executive ability and oratorical talent a continental contingent of the order might be established which would rival that of the United States.'[83] Upon reading Hill's letter, the Assembly authorised Powderly and the General Executive Board to appoint an American Knight to visit Britain and 'take any further action deemed advisable.'[84]

Powderly initially wanted Colonel John A. Price, a progressive manufacturer and public speaker and a native of his home town, Scranton, to perform that role, but Price declined.[85] Instead, the Knights found their man in the most prominent visitor to the 1887 General Assembly, Michael Davitt, who took part in the gathering as part of a wider tour around the United States to drum up support and money for the Irish cause. Even as the Assembly took place, newspapers opined that 'the order has in contemplation the securing the services of the Irish patriot in the task of developing the order in Europe.'[86] The *New York Sun* claimed that at the Assembly Davitt 'was made a member of the order and a Knight of Labor organizer,' that his Irish Land League would become 'a special district of the Knights of Labor' and that leading Knights were keeping this secret because of anticipated opposition from English and Scottish Knights.[87] Davitt denied these rumours and insisted that his visit to the United States was simply to advance the Irish cause and promote the sale of Irish wool.[88] The Irish Land League, for its part, certainly remained independent from the Knights

---

[82] *Proceedings of the GA* (1887), pp. 1770–72.
[83] *Washington Post*, 6 October 1887.
[84] *Proceedings of the GA* (1887), p. 1808.
[85] Jesse Chapman to Powderly, 12 May 1888, Box 44, TVP.
[86] *Washington Post*, 6 October 1887. Similar reports appeared in Britain too: for example, *Manchester Guardian*, 8 October 1887.
[87] *New York Sun*, 12 October 1887. The article did not explain whether the English and Scottish Knights were immigrants to the United States or were actually based in those countries.
[88] *Birmingham Daily Post*, 21 October 1887.

of Labor. But the idea was not new. George Schilling had proposed it to *John Swinton's Paper* a year earlier. *Reynolds's Newspaper* publicly appealed to Davitt to lead an organisation of unskilled English workers, modelled on the Knights, in July 1887.[89]

The opportunity for Davitt to work on behalf of British Knights came the following May. In that month Jesse Chapman, the Master Workman of Smethwick's LA10227, planned to hold a public meeting to celebrate the first anniversary of his assembly and raise the Order's public profile in Birmingham and the Black Country. Chapman asked Davitt to speak at the meeting and Davitt agreed, as Chapman told Powderly, 'almost gleefully.' Chapman asked the General Master Workman (GMW) to provide Davitt with 'a kind of socio-political programme of ideas upon which our energies as an Order in this country might expend themselves for a few years to come,' and which could form the basis of his speech.[90] Powderly did so, and on 8 May 1888, Davitt, the Revs. T.T. Sherlock and Harold Rylett, the English radical William Clarke and Richard McGhee, the Scottish single-taxer, gave speeches to an audience of more than 1,000 Knights and their families at Smethwick Public Hall. Chapman judged the meeting a 'magnificent success,' and it appeared in newspapers all over Britain and Ireland.[91] The meeting marked the British Order's transition from 'an organisation which has grown quietly and extensively in the Black Country during the last few years,' as the *Birmingham Daily Post* observed the day after, to an order that seemed to have a future in British social and political life. It also encouraged many workers to join the assemblies, partly because those who wished to hear Davitt speak had to become Knights to do so. According to statistics provided at the 1888 General Assembly, more than 1,200 workers joined DA208 and DA248 between January and August of that year.[92]

Michael Davitt served for a brief time as the Master Workman of DA208 after his speech at Smethwick, before his other duties and causes took him away. American Knights soon sent another prominent Irishman across the ocean, James Archibald, who lived in New York and headed the Order's National Trade District 210, representing paper hangers across the United States. Archibald came to visit relatives in Ireland in 1889; he also came to Britain and Ireland with a commission from Powderly to organise 'such worthy persons as may present themselves to him during his stay there.'[93]

---

[89] *Reynolds's*, 10 July 1887.
[90] Jesse Chapman to Powderly, 3 March 1888, Box 41, TVP.
[91] Jesse Chapman to Powderly, 12 May 1888, Box 44, TVP. The Dublin *Freemen's Journal*, for instance, carried more or less the entire address on 9 May 1888.
[92] *Proceedings of the GA* (1888), pp. 4–5.
[93] Circular from Powderly, 17 June 1889, Box 101, TVP.

Where Davitt's fame attracted workers to the assemblies, Archibald brought many workers into the Order through hard work and strong lungs. According to one report, between June and October 1889, he delivered no less than 70 speeches in various parts of the British Isles.[94] His visit to Liverpool spurred the early growth of LA443 there.[95] He gave the main address at the Order's first public meetings in Walsall and Rotherham.[96] He spoke to audiences in Scotland during the early days of the Glasgow assemblies.[97] His speeches also bolstered the morale and the numbers of assemblies around Birmingham.

James P. Archibald became a crucial figure at the very point when it seemed as though assemblies might appear in all the major industrial centres of Britain. His work played an equally crucial part in helping British Knights to reach their peak membership of around 10,000. General Secretary-Treasurer Hayes claimed at the 1889 General Assembly that the Order's extension into Scotland and Ireland and 'a large increase in membership in England' was 'largely due to the efforts of Brother James P. Archibald.'[98] Local Knights, as Henry Pelling writes, 'might have resented the attribution of their success so fully to Archibald, rather than to their own efforts,' but they certainly betrayed no resentment to Archibald himself.[99] He told Powderly that Thomas Dean and C.W. Butler, the Master Workmen of DA208 and DA248, 'vied so much with one another' for his attention that 'I feared I would be unable to please them both.'[100] Knights from all over Birmingham, the Black Country and South Yorkshire treated him to a lavish farewell dinner in September, where they praised Archibald's 'strong individuality, combined with and made more powerful by a magnetic temperament, distinctly manifestly unbounded sympathy and a high and lofty purpose,' and presented him with a marble timepiece inscribed with their thanks.[101] Archibald urged Powderly to write to Dean, Butler and Chapman to thank them for their hospitality, and he did so several months later.[102] He also

---

[94] *Bootle Times*, 28 September 1889.

[95] Bean, 'Knights in Liverpool,' pp. 70–71.

[96] In the three towns mentioned, reports of Archibald's speeches can be found in: *Bootle Times*, 6 July 1889; *Walsall Observer*, 31 August 1889; *Rotherham Advertiser*, 31 August 1889.

[97] J.R. Frame, *America and the Scottish Left: The Impact of American Ideas on the Scottish Labour Movement from the American Civil War to World War One* (unpublished PhD thesis, University of Aberdeen, 1998), p. 155.

[98] *Proceedings of the GA* (1889), p. 19.

[99] Pelling, 'Knights in Britain,' p. 327.

[100] James P Archibald to Powderly, 20 October 1889, Box 56, TVP.

[101] *JUL*, 14 November 1889.

[102] Powderly to J Chapman, 5 March 1890, Box 100, TVP; Powderly to C.W. Butler, England, 6 March 1890, Box 100, TVP; Powderly to Thomas Dean, 6 March 1890, Box 100, TVP.

told the *Birmingham Daily Post* near the end of his tour that 'my mission has been successful beyond my most sanguine expectations.'[103]

Archibald, as did Denny and Davitt before him, proved that it was possible to build a transnational working-class movement on British soil. The British and Irish assemblies only reached over 10,000 members and founded assemblies in most parts of Britain and Ireland due to their efforts and the money that American Knights brought with them. We might share Robert Weir's frustration that the most committed working-class internationalists tend to have the least money behind them. We can only speculate as to what might have been achieved if American Knights had been able to spare more money and manpower for the British and Irish assemblies. We can say, however, that with an investment of perhaps £1,000 in total and three organisers, Denny, Davitt and Archibald, the Knights became a movement of national significance in the home of trade unionism itself. That is not all. The last two named individuals, in particular, exposed a wider Irish-British-American nexus at the centre of the history of the British and Irish Knights. That particular transatlantic connection brought the Knights into contact with three major themes in British and Irish history: race, religion and empire.

Race, Religion and Empire

The Knights of Labor are justly recognised, for all their shortcomings, as the first major American working-class movement to organise extensively across the colour line. Drawing on the rich tradition of antebellum abolitionism, the still potent memory of the Civil War and the emancipation that came out of it, and the practical realisation that many employers set white against black workers to the detriment of both, Knights organised black workers as equal members. In the mid-1880s the latter accounted for a full 10 percent of the Order's total membership. That does not mean, of course, that Knights were colour-blind or even free of racial prejudice. Most black Knights, especially but not only in the South, organised in their own assemblies. Real unity between black and white Knights remained the exception rather than the rule, as Peter Rachleff documented in his study of black labour in Richmond, Virginia, and was usually a fleeting thing.[104] The Order's record on Asian workers, as we saw in Chapter 1, was almost uniformly bad. Yet the Knights represented the racial diversity of the American working class much more than their predecessors or, indeed, their successor, the American

---

[103] *Birmingham Daily Post*, 31 August 1889.
[104] Peter J. Rachleff, *Black Labor in the South: Richmond, Virginia, 1865–1890* (Philadelphia: Temple University Press, 1984).

Federation of Labor. The American labour movement would not match the proportion of black workers organised into the Order for at least half a century.

Scholars have only just begun to fully document the rich history of people of colour in Britain, which went back far before the nineteenth century. This history was larger and more significant, and British society much more racially and ethnically diverse, than earlier historians generally assumed.[105] The colour line that did (and does) prove so crucial in the United States, however, did not yet exist in Britain itself. British and Irish Knights were thus able to avoid that particular question in an immediate way. Their letters to the *Journal of United Labor*, their correspondence with headquarters, the reports of their meetings and speeches, and newspaper coverage of their activities do not refer to racial questions once. Knights in North America and the rest of the colonial world faced serious questions concerning Asian immigration, the status of indigenous peoples and other people of colour. Their responses to all these questions differed sharply from colony to colony, and between those colonies and assemblies in the United States. British and Irish Knights, by contrast, avoided any mention of them whatsoever.

At first glance, that fact precludes us from saying anything meaningful about the British and Irish Knights on the subject of race. Recent scholarship on that subject, however, suggests that race was at the heart of the formation and reformation of national and imperial identities among the British working class, even when nobody thought to say it aloud or in print. Over the course of the nineteenth century at least some British workers developed a national identity based on the exclusion of certain racial groups, particularly those of African and Asian descent, as Britain extended or expanded its control over large parts of the world. This exclusionary attitude even seeped at times into parts of the socialist movement, for all its protestations of internationalism and the fraternity of workers all over the globe.[106] Jonathan Hyslop suggests that white workers, primarily but not only of British descent, formed an 'imperial white working class,' bound together and defined as much by colour as class, which stretched from Britain to South Africa, New Zealand, Australia, Canada and perhaps the United States as well.[107] Marilyn Lake and Henry Reynolds further argue that white people

---

[105] For a local study of this history see Laura Tabili, *Global Migrants, Local Culture: Natives and Newcomers in Provincial England, 1841–1939* (London: Palgrave MacMillan, 2011).

[106] Racist attitudes were not, of course, uniform across the British socialist movement. See Kirk, *Comrades and Cousins*, especially ch. 3.

[107] Jonathan Hyslop, 'The Imperial Working Class Makes Itself "White": White Labourism in Britain, Australia, and South Africa before the First World War,' *Journal of Historical Sociology*, 12:4 (1999), pp. 398–421.

across the European empires, from all social classes, drew a global colour line that marked themselves off from their supposed racial inferiors at home as well as abroad.[108] Carl Nightingale has traced the concrete expression of that line through the rise of segregated cities all over the globe.[109]

Without the sources to interrogate them properly, these attitudes and actions must remain in the background of the Order's British and Irish history. Another racial or ethnic group that played a crucial role in the Order's history in Britain and naturally in Ireland, however – the Irish – provides us with a more solid point of connection between that history and questions of race and empire. Satnam Virdee, among others, casts Irish immigrants and their descendants as the original 'racialized other' in British labour history. They were, he writes, at once outsiders in British industrial life, increasingly caricatured over the course of the nineteenth century in crudely racial terms. But they were also militant insiders at various points within the British labour movement. From Bronterre O'Brien, the 'Chartist schoolmaster,' to James Sexton, the dockers' leader during the 'new unionism' of the early 1890s (and briefly a Knight himself), Irish immigrants played a crucial and leading (yet underappreciated) role in the nineteenth-century British labour movement, even as they were often excluded from what we might call the imagined British working-class community over the same period.[110]

Historians of American labour, by contrast, have never missed a chance to point out the enormous contribution of the Irish diaspora to working-class movements in the United States. Irish immigrants and their descendants comprised a disproportionately large fraction of trade union members all through the nineteenth century.[111] The Knights of Labor exemplified that trend. Terence Powderly often combined his duties as General Master Workman with agitation on behalf of a variety of Irish nationalist groups and, in this sense at least, he was not an atypical Knight.[112] Powderly wrote to Davitt, before the 1887 General Assembly, of his desire to 'have that body speak out in favour of Home Rule for Ireland.' The Assembly did not disappoint him. After Davitt spoke, the delegates clambered over one

---

[108] Marilyn Lake and Henry Reynolds, *Drawing the Global Colour Line: White Men's Countries and the International Challenge of Racial Equality* (Cambridge: Cambridge University Press, 2008).

[109] Carl Nightingale, *Segregation: A Global History of Divided Cities* (Chicago: Chicago University Press, 2012).

[110] Satnam Virdee, *Racism, Class and the Racialized Outsider* (London: Palgrave MacMillan, 2014), pp. 12–17.

[111] Sorge, *Labor Movement*, p. 249; K. Kenny, 'Labor and Labor Organisations,' in J. Lee and M. Casey (eds), *Making the Irish American: History and Heritage of the Irish in the United States* (New York: New York University Press, 2006), p. 359.

[112] Powderly, *The Path I Trod*, pp. 177–82.

another to introduce resolutions supporting Home Rule and praising Davitt himself in the most effusive possible terms.[113] It would be an overstatement to describe the American Knights as in some way an Irish movement, but the influence of Irish immigrants and the cause of Irish independence permeated the Order from Powderly on down.

The British assemblies certainly attracted many Irish immigrants, or workers of Irish descent, to their ranks. Although it is not possible to put a precise number on it without access to the membership rolls, there is no doubt that the Birmingham and Black Country assemblies contained a disproportionately large fraction of Irish workers.[114] Many of the other places where Knights at least briefly established a powerful local presence, from Liverpool to Glasgow to the west of Scotland, also contained large Irish immigrant communities.[115] Scottish-Irish radicals threatened to form assemblies of the Knights of Labor in 1888 unless Scottish Liberals supported Home Rule, and the Glasgow assemblies were led by at least one of those radicals, James Shaw Maxwell, while another, John Ferguson, addressed Knights at Derry in 1890.[116] The assemblies at Hoyland and Platts Common, near Barnsley, seem even to have been joint ventures between the Knights of Labor and local chapters of the Irish National League.[117] Organisers such as Archibald and Davitt, both born in Ireland, paid special attention to the concerns of Irish immigrants in their work for the Knights around Britain.

The greatest of all of these concerns was religion. The Knights had a long and stormy relationship with the Catholic Church, which banned secret orders like the Freemasons and initially proscribed the Knights of Labor. Uriah Stephens, after all, borrowed freely from Masonic practices, including Biblical references in the Order's early ritual and meetings with a Bible laid open in the centre of the hall. Stephens was a Baptist and possibly held bigoted attitudes toward Catholics. His Catholic successor, Terence Powderly, on the other hand, tried to secure good relations with the Church after Jesuits in Quebec, and then in parts of the United States, began to refuse the sacraments to members of the Knights of Labor in the

---

[113] Powderly to Michael Davitt, 6 April 1888, Box 99, TVP; *Proceedings of the GA* (1887), pp. 1835–42.
[114] Pelling, 'Knights in Britain,' p. 321.
[115] Young, 'Changing Images,' pp. 82–85; W. Kenefick, 'A Struggle for Recognition and Independence: The Growth and Development of Dock Unionism at the Port of Glasgow, c.1853–1932,' in Sam Davies et al. (eds), *Dock Workers: International Explorations in Comparative Labour History, 1790–1970* (Aldershot: Ashgate, 2000); E. Taplin, 'The History of Dock Labour: Liverpool, c.1850–1914,' in Davies et al. (eds), *Dock Workers*.
[116] Young, 'Changing Images,' p. 83; *JUL*, 13 February, 1890.
[117] *Mexborough and Swinton Times*, 21 November 1890.

early 1880s. He found two allies in Cardinal James Gibbons of Baltimore and Cardinal Henry Manning of London, both of whom successfully pressed the Order's case at the Vatican in 1886 and 1887.[118] Where religious matters were concerned, the Knights never caught a break. As soon as the Church withdrew its ban, a number of Protestant nativist organisations suggested that the Knights represented a front for Catholic conspiracies across the United States. But the Knights never had to face a hostile Church, although they continued to face opposition from individual clergy, at the same time as the enormous power of employers and the state.

Archibald made the rapprochement between the Knights and the Church a key theme of his speeches. At Walsall, 'he wished particularly to say that the Knights of Labour had the full approbation of the Holy Catholic Church, of which he was a member.'[119] At Smethwick, he asserted that 'the aims of their organisation were as legitimate as could be desired by the Catholic Church,' that Knights 'preached no heresy' and assured non-Catholic listeners that their order was truly ecumenical.[120] Archibald's message had an effect in some assemblies. Knights in Liverpool won the direct support of local clergy, and Dr Bernard O'Reilly, the Catholic Bishop of Liverpool, maintained what Ronald Bean describes as 'cordial' relations with the Knights of LA443.[121] In any case, religion did not divide the English assemblies. Knights in the Birmingham area found allies among Congregationalist and Methodists ministers like Sherlock and Rylett, even though many of them were Irish and Catholic. In Scotland, where sectarianism remained a potent force, the picture is less clear.[122] The history of the Sons of Labour, an order modelled on the Knights among Lanarkshire coal miners between 1888 and 1890, and explored in the following chapter, suggests that religious differences caused problems for the Scottish assemblies.[123]

The main attraction of the Order for Irish workers, however, was summed up by Michael Davitt in his speech at Smethwick in 1888. 'The Knights of Labor is not an American society, or an Irish society or an English society,' Davitt claimed:

> It is a society of all of these and more. By its aid here in England we are enabled to meet on common ground for the first time and to each of us is

---

[118] Ware, *Labor Movement*, pp. 73–102.
[119] *Labour Tribune*, 31 August 1889.
[120] *Smethwick Telephone*, 10 August 1889.
[121] Bean, 'Knights in Liverpool,' p. 71.
[122] Only one Scottish journal seems to have seen the Knights as tools of a wider Catholic conspiracy. See *The National Observer, and British Review of Politics, Economics, Literature, Science, and Art*, 15 March 1890 and 11 November 1893.
[123] Frame, *America and the Scottish Left*, pp. 129–55.

given the great privilege of taking a member by the hand and calling him brother regardless of his country, creed, or condition in life.[124]

Davitt thus advertised the assemblies as places where workers of all nationalities, Irish included, could find a home within a wider, truly international movement. The fact that the Order's headquarters lay in Philadelphia rather than London meant that the British imperial model, which subordinated Irish interests to English ones, would not be replicated by the Knights of Labor. Knights promised to bridge the main racial chasm in the nineteenth-century British working class by substituting internationalism for the British Empire, even if they could not always make good on this promise.

These powerful ideas certainly explain why the British assemblies attracted many Irish immigrants. What, then, about everyone else? There is no evidence that English workers viewed the Order as an Irish or Catholic front, and there is absolutely no evidence that the Order's enemies in the labour movement or the local press used the Irish question to attack the assemblies. Some newspapers did see American Knights as an unwelcome extension of Irish terrorism, yet others, such as *Reynolds's*, were attracted to the Knights precisely because they strongly supported Irish Home Rule.[125] It is possible, of course, that the Order's Irish connections limited its prospects without anyone ever having said so openly. The Scottish assemblies probably faced splits and attacks from the outside on national as well as religious grounds. On balance, however, it appears that the British-Irish-American nexus worked to the benefit of the British assemblies.

What we can be sure of is that sectarianism became a major issue for Knights across the Irish Sea. We have, after all, been discussing the Irish-American connection without even referring to Ireland itself. Partly that is due to the late appearance of assemblies there. As late as December 1889, the *Pittsburgh Dispatch* observed that 'efforts at organizing the K. of L. in Ireland have so far not been attended with conspicuous success.'[126] This was an odd state of affairs given the close association that existed between Ireland and the Order, especially after Michael Davitt spoke on behalf of the Birmingham assemblies in May 1888. But Davitt stated very clearly that he 'would not countenance the establishment of any society that might become opposed to the [Irish] National League,' and refused to organise

---

[124] *Freemen's Journal*, 9 May 1888. T.W. Moody does not mention the Knights in his work on Davitt and the British labour movement. See Moody, 'Michael Davitt and the British Labour Movement, 1882–1906,' *Transactions of the Royal Historical Society*, Fifth Series, 3 (1953), pp. 53–76.

[125] See, for instance, *The Times*, 7 June 1887; *Birmingham Daily Post*, 26 September 1887. *Reynolds*, 2 October 1887.

[126] *Pittsburgh Dispatch*, 7 December 1889.

any Irish assemblies.[127] It took the former Master Workman of an assembly in Columbus, Georgia, to convince workers in Belfast to form an assembly of the Knights of Labor in 1888.[128] Other assemblies in Belfast and Derry followed in 1889. Once formed, Davitt did speak at a meeting of Derry's LA1601 at the start of 1890, where he expressed his 'pride that the son of an Irish workingman should become the head of the greatest labor organization of the world.'[129]

Religion did cause problems for the Irish assemblies. When Michael M'Daid, an official of LA1601, lamented the poor attitude the local clergy displayed towards the Knights, Davitt reminded his audience that 'despite all the efforts that had been made, not a word of condemnation or of censure of the Order of the Knights of Labor had ever been uttered by the Holy Father.'[130] In Northern Ireland, however, a papal seal of approval alienated Unionists and Protestants as much as it attracted Irish Nationalists and Catholics. Protestant and Unionist members of Belfast's LA418 accused R.H. Feagan, its first secretary and a Catholic and staunch nationalist, of using the assembly for his own political purposes. They soon forced him to resign. The Knights of LA1601 were more successful in their attempts to negotiate what John Boyle describes as the 'religio-political battleground' of Derry, but as they found that sectarian rifts widened as they faced difficulties of other kinds.[131] Sectarianism did not destroy the assemblies in Belfast and Derry. The blame for their destruction rested with failed strikes, rival unions and financial problems, which appear in subsequent chapters. But sectarianism created unnecessary rifts among the membership and accelerated the decline of the Irish assemblies once it began to set in.

In England, in Scotland and in Ireland, then, the Knights grappled with racial, religious and imperial questions in different ways and with different results. In all three countries Irish immigrants, that original racialised other of the British labour movement, flocked to the Order's assemblies in their hundreds. Their presence seems to have caused no problems in England and some problems in Scotland, while religious sectarianism played a predictably important role in Ireland. On balance, the Irish connection served the British and Irish assemblies well. It is a pity that so little, aside from the name, survives of the Jewish émigré 'Knights of Labour' that briefly existed in London's East End, for Jewish immigrants rivalled the Irish for the title

---

[127] *Birmingham Daily Post*, 21 October 1887.
[128] Boyle, *Irish Labour Movement*, pp. 104–06.
[129] *JUL*, 13 February, 1890.
[130] *JUL*, 13 February, 1890.
[131] McAteer, 'New Unionism in Derry,' pp. 12–13; Boyle, *Irish Labour Movement*, pp. 104–06.

of the archetypal racial 'other' during our period. We can say, however, that the Knights promised to evade the unequal, imperial relationships between Britain and Ireland, and Irish immigrants and their host communities in Britain, by appealing to internationalism instead. The fact that the Order was American, without any direct connection to British imperialism, doubtless gave this appeal more credence. It would not be going too far to say that the Knights of Labor were the best placed, of any major working-class movement of their time, to attract and organise Irish immigrants in Britain and their compatriots in Ireland. That surely ranks as one of the main reasons behind their success.

Conclusion

On 19 November 1889, the General Assembly of the Knights of Labor convened in Atlanta, Georgia. The delegates began their deliberations at a time when the Order's American assemblies faced serious challenges, the greatest of which was a sharp decline in membership after the heady days of the Great Upheaval. Yet these same delegates represented an order whose international network of assemblies continued to extend into new countries and continued to grow in many existing ones. The *Atlanta Constitution*, understandably keen to highlight the significance of all major events that took place in the city, described the gathering as 'the general assembly of the world.' As the *Constitution* pointed out, the General Assembly brought 'two or three hundred delegates from all parts of the United States, Canada, England, Germany, France and Austria, Belgium and Australia.'[132] Terence Powderly oversaw an order in decline at home but advancing everywhere else. That contradiction forms a major part of the final chapter of this book.

The General Assembly at Atlanta also coincided with the high point of the Order's assemblies in Britain and Ireland. Knights had finally established a presence in England, Wales, Scotland and Ireland, and they found lodgement in important industrial commercial centres like Liverpool, Glasgow and Belfast, in other centres like Rotherham, Walsall, Derry and Derby, as well as their early bases in Birmingham, the Black Country, St Helens and Sunderland. In late 1889 or early 1890 they reached their peak membership of around 10–15,000. Thomas Dean told a meeting of DA208 in August 1889 that in England 'we have made some great steps in advance, but have also in some cases lost ground.' Dean urged his listeners to 'only practice what you teach and profess, and we must win, perhaps not

---

[132] *Atlanta Constitution*, 25 October 1889.

all at once, but in good time.'[133] A year later, in October 1890, Michael Davitt welcomed 'the growing feeling of international brotherhood among the workers of the world,' and gave as his main example 'the growth of responsive friendly feeling among American workingmen towards the working classes in England' through the Knights of Labor. 'Assemblies of the Knights of Labor are increasing day by day in these islands,' he wrote.[134] Davitt probably had little knowledge of the difficulties and reversals that began to chip away at their numbers after 1889. But the tone of cautious optimism that he and Dean both struck reflected a wider feeling among many Knights at the turn of the decade.

They had some reason for that feeling. Among English glassworkers, among craftsmen and unskilled workers in a variety of trades around Birmingham and the Black Country, and among workers in many different parts of Britain and Ireland towards the end of the 1880s, the Knights of Labor capitalised on important deficiencies in local labour movements. Their assemblies flourished where trade unions were weak, where agitation for new and improved organisations was strong, where Knights recruited capable and committed leaders, and where they won some wider local support. The struggles of the Great Upheaval increased the Order's appeal to British and Irish workers still further, even if the Upheaval also ensured that Knights received a hostile reception from most corners of the press.

The direct assistance of the American Knights also encouraged their growth. Financial aid remained relatively small but had an important psychological effect; indeed, many workers probably joined the assemblies because they imagined that the Knights had the money to match their million American members. Correspondence with the general officers and through the *Journal of United Labor* also maintained the important belief among British and Irish Knights that they remained an integral part of an international movement; and though Richard Hill insisted that they needed American boots on the ground, to borrow a contemporary phrase, Powderly ensured that Michael Davitt and, most crucially of all, James P. Archibald, arrived to augment the work of local organisers.

Their Irish and Catholic roots appealed particularly strongly to the many workers, in Britain as well as Ireland, who shared them. To paraphrase Davitt, the Order was very much an Irish as well as an American society, although it was also more than that. The Order's success among the Irish raises the possibility that global movements from abroad can, in the right circumstances, bring racially, nationally or religiously divided groups together

---

[133] *JUL*, 22 August 1889.
[134] M. Davitt, 'Labor Tendencies in Great Britain,' *North American Review*, 151 (October 1890), pp. 453–68.

in a way that local movements often cannot. American Knights, many of whom were themselves Irish or of Irish descent, had an advantage over their British rivals. They approached British workers from outside the Empire and outside the imperial framework that subordinated Irish to British interests. American Knights rejected that framework. They also retained the sympathy for Irish Home Rule or independence which many British trade unionists let go after the end of the Chartists.[135] This sympathy served them well as they formed assemblies throughout England and into Scotland and Ireland.

Many of these themes had an influence felt well beyond the British and Irish assemblies. Radicals and trade unionists did not need to become Knights to draw lessons and inspiration from the Order's record, whether in terms of politics or trade union methods, during the Great Upheaval. Other unions than the Knights also sought to profit from the disorganisation of workers in various regions and occupations, and often came into conflict with the assemblies. Irish immigrants numbered among the members and leaders of those unions and, indeed, we will see that unionised Irish immigrants fought the Knights as well as joined them. Knights in those assemblies, meanwhile, struggled to reconcile the Order's record during the Great Upheaval with its leaders' insistence on arbitration instead of strikes. These themes all feature in subsequent chapters. For now, we turn to questions of organisation, culture and gender.

---

[135] Virdee, *Racism, Class*, pp. 33–37.

3

Organisation, Culture and Gender

On 23 November 1885, about 120 members of Local Assembly 3504, the Alpha Assembly, sat down to their first anniversary dinner at the Rose and Crown Hotel, Sunderland. The lodge room of the hotel, as one newspaper described it, 'was tastefully decorated for the occasion, the four walls being draped and festooned with variegated bunting and national flags, prominent among which were the Union Jack and the Stars and Stripes.' After a 'very excellent repast, served up under the personal superintendence of Mr. Wingate, manager of the hotel,' the leaders of the assembly made a series of toasts, to the 'Alpha Assembly of the Knights of Labor,' 'The Mayor and Corporation,' 'Trade and Commerce' and then 'The General Assembly of the Knights of Labor in America.' The assembly's secretary, Joseph French, gave a short address on its history. The night was then given over to music and dancing, poetry and dialogue, and the anniversary ended with a hearty rendition of 'Auld Lang Syne.'[1]

Of the many intriguing symbols present that evening, the Union Jack and the Stars and Stripes are the most obvious. They are also the most pertinent to this chapter, which is concerned with the cultural practices and organisational methods of the British Knights of Labor, and the ways in which they adhered to and departed from the practices and methods that American Knights laid down for them. We see whether British Knights followed or deviated from the cultural and structural forms of their adopted order. We explore how other workers, not themselves affiliated with the Order, adopted its name and model for their own purposes. We finally address the reasons why British Knights failed to organise women workers, even though their counterparts organised them in large numbers in the United States. These three interrelated questions all point to wider questions of cultural and social similarities and differences between Britain and the United States – between

[1] *JUL*, 25 December 1885.

the Union Jack and the Stars and Stripes. They raise further questions about the nature of transnational labour movements, and of the attractions of these movements for workers in other, culturally distinct countries.

The Knights of Labor began its history in 1869 as a fraternal order. Its founder, Uriah Stephens, based its secrecy (later dropped), its titles (later altered), and its complex ritual and ceremonies (later simplified) on his experience of the Freemasons, Oddfellows and other fraternal orders. Indeed, Stephens, like later leaders, meant for his order to perform similar functions to those orders. The assemblies would educate their members in the principle of universal brotherhood. The assemblies would also become a schoolroom in which Knights would learn and debate the ideas of economics and political philosophy. Moral self-improvement would take place alongside collective struggle. Historians, like many of the Order's contemporaries, have generally viewed these practices as either harmful or irrelevant. Engels wrote off their titles and ritual as 'medieval mummeries.'[2] Even Terence Powderly later wrote that the Order's early rites were so long that they hampered recruitment and left little time at meetings for other business.[3] Most historians have agreed with them or else ignored the Order's ritual and other fraternal practices altogether.[4] Other historians claim that the emphasis on education served mainly as an excuse for Knights to avoid entering political and industrial struggles in earnest.[5]

Historians have also criticised the Order's hierarchical structure, from local to district assemblies and finally the annual General Assembly, as poorly suited to the needs of American workers in an age of nationwide corporations. They, and particularly John Commons, Selig Perlman and Gerald Grob – the so-called 'Commons school' – have done so mainly on the assumption that the Knights almost exclusively organised themselves into mixed assemblies, which brought together workers on the basis of geography rather than occupation, rather than in assemblies devoted to a single trade. In this view, the craft unions of the American Federation of Labor offered a more rational response to the requirements of advanced capitalism; this difference played no small role in the victory of the AFL and the decline of the Knights of Labor.[6] Many recent historians have taken issue with these claims, however. First, they point out that trade

[2] Friedrich Engels, 'Preface to the American Edition,' *Condition of the Working Class in England* (New York, 1887).

[3] Powderly, *The Path I Trod*, p. 48.

[4] Weir, *Beyond Labor's Veil*, p. 20.

[5] Philip S. Foner claims that 'to the leaders of the Order education became a substitute for action' (*History of the Labor Movement*. II, p. 76).

[6] See Commons, *History of Labor*; Perlman, *Theory of the Labor Movement*; Grob, *Workers and Utopia*.

assemblies remained as numerous and important as mixed ones throughout the Order's history. Second, they point out that the Order's model was well-suited to building powerful movements at a community level.[7] Some historians have gone even further and argued that the fraternal culture at the heart of the Order was not as harmful or irrelevant as others have claimed. Robert Weir, in particular, argues that fraternalism remained extremely popular throughout the late nineteenth century, and provided a kind of solidarity that often outlasted bonds based exclusively on material self-interest.[8]

Weir also argues that the Knights were so successful on the international stage because they remained willing to let foreign workers mould their Order to local conditions. In New Zealand, for instance, Knights enthusiastically practised their ritual and turned their assemblies into a powerful political lobby, even a nascent political party. Australian Knights developed their own elaborate regalia to heighten the drama of assembly-room ceremonial. Knights in South Africa created an equally elaborate series of titles, ritual and a system of degrees which they plagiarised directly from Freemasonry. Belgian coal miners, by contrast, found the ritual cumbersome and soon abandoned it.[9] Powderly allowed Knights in Britain and Ireland the same freedom of action. In 1884, he told A.G. Denny, LA300's representative to Europe, that:

> I will not attempt to lay down any rules or regulations for your guidance while in Europe ... The circumstances which surround the workingmen in Europe are, of necessity, different from those surrounding our people, and as a matter of course our cause must be attuned here and there in order to conform to existing circumstances.[10]

The main principle of the Knights of Labor, as Weir argues, remained the flexibility of its principles.

Yet British Knights held fast to the cultural practices and organisational structure of their order. Workers on both sides of the Atlantic, after all, shared important cultural traditions and one of these was an attachment to fraternal orders, which they joined in larger numbers than the trade unions. The ritual practised in British orders never reached the elaborate heights of their American counterparts, but both offered social insurance and some, like the Oddfellows, paid tens of hundreds of millions of dollars in sickness,

---

[7] Some notable examples include Oestreicher, *Solidarity and Fragmentation*; David Brundage, *Making of Western Labor Radicalism*; Faye Dudden, 'Small Town Knights: The Knights of Labor in Homer, New York,' *Labor History*, 28:3 (1987), pp. 307–27.
[8] Weir, *Beyond Labor's Veil*, ch. 1.
[9] Weir, *Knights Down Under*, ch. 6; *The Lantern*, 5 December 1891.
[10] Powderly to A.G. Denny, 18 November 1884, Box 94, TVP.

injury or death benefits over the course of the late nineteenth century.[11] Many British and some American trade unions offered similar benefits even if the Knights did not.[12] The ways in which the Knights melded the functions of a trade union with the secrecy and ritual of a fraternal order also had British precedents. As we saw in Chapter 1, the Grand National Consolidated Trades Union borrowed titles, ritual, oath-taking and other practices from the fraternal orders – as the Tolpuddle Martyrs found to their cost in 1834. The practices of the Knights of Labor fit comfortably within British working-class traditions.

The Order's record on questions of gender was an exception to that rule. Notions of Victorian respectability, the existence of separate public (male) spheres and domestic (female) spheres, and strong dichotomies between the feminine and the masculine, were equally powerful on both sides of the Atlantic in the late nineteenth century. Male workers in Britain and the United States all looked forward to a time when women would return to their rightful place as mistress of the home. Major differences, however, appeared in the 1880s when it came to the organisation of women already in the labour market. The American Knights of Labor pioneered the inclusion of women as equal members in the labour movement. The British trade unions preferred mainly to ignore the problem for as long as possible; alternatively, they tried to keep women out of employment altogether.[13] British and Irish Knights, faced with these mutually exclusive positions, chose exclusion rather than inclusion. That choice, however, rested not on the rejection of their order's stance on gender but on a misunderstanding of it. American Knights renegotiated rather than overturned Victorian ideas concerning the public and private spheres, and did so in an ambiguous way; British Knights failed to follow the nuances of their position.

---

[11] For the differences between English and American fraternalism see Weir, *Beyond Labor's Veil*, p. 25; M. Carnes, *Secret Ritual and Manhood in Victorian America* (New Haven: Yale University Press, 1989). For British fraternal orders and friendly societies in the nineteenth century, see S. Cordery, *British Friendly Societies, 1750–1914* (Basingstoke: Palgrave Macmillan, 2003); Gosden, *Self-Help*. For the revenues and expenditure of fraternal orders see Carnes, *Secret Ritual*, p. 5; Baernreither, *English Associations*, pp. 372–75.

[12] An overview of the ASE benefit scheme can be found in Jeffreys, *Story of the Engineers*. For the role of this benefit system in encouraging the international spread of the ASE see K.D. Buckley, *The Amalgamated Engineers in Australia, 1852–1920* (Canberra: Australian National University, 1970), pp. 6–7.

[13] For the Knights, see Levine, *Labor's True Woman*; B.M. Wertheimer, *We Were There: The Story of Working Women in America* (New York: Pantheon, 1977). For the British context see, for instance, N.C. Soldon, *Women in British Trade Unions, 1874–1976* (Dublin: Macmillan, 1978); S. Lewenhak, *Women and Trade Unions: An Outline History of Women in the British Trade Union Movement* (London: Benn, 1977); S. Boston, *Women Workers and the Trade Union Movement* (London: Davis-Poynter, 1980).

Important cultural themes, in other words, often became lost in translation. These misunderstandings and cultural differences were even sharper when British workers decided to make use of the name, model or methods of the Knights of Labor without affiliating with the Order itself. We saw in the first chapter that potters in Staffordshire borrowed freely from the Knights to create their own National order; over the course of the 1880s, coal miners in Lanarkshire, workers on Tyneside and Wearside, and even agricultural workers in Somerset did likewise. Their adaptations testified to the elasticity of the Order's model and to the many uses to which it could be put. Trade union, fraternal order, educational society, social insurance provider and political machine: in Britain and Ireland the Knights, and other organisations trading on their name or methods, became all of the above at various times in their history. We explore the limits of that flexibility through the organisation and culture practised by British and Irish Knights, through the organisations modelled on but not affiliated with the Order, and finally through the question of gender in the British and Irish assemblies.

Culture and Organisation in the British and Irish Assemblies

In 1885, James Sexton, later to become a dockers' leader and a Labour MP, joined a short-lived assembly of the Knights of Labor in Liverpool. 'We met,' he wrote in his autobiography,

> like conspirators hatching a second Guy Fawkes plot, gathering together in a gloomy cellar with only the flickering half-lights given by tallow candles thrust into the necks of pop bottles. The attendance was always small, and for a time we thought our proceedings were unnoticed, but something leaked out; it got to the ears of the bosses, and every individual who attended those subterranean conclaves soon became a man marked out for victimization.[14]

Not since the early days of the Knights of Labor in Philadelphia, when they announced their meetings in secret code on the walls of public buildings and kept the name of their order secret, had assemblies met in such a conspiratorial atmosphere. Then, Knights justified their secrecy on similar grounds to Sexton. Secrecy offered protection from victimisation at the hands of employers, especially through the infamous 'iron-clad' contract, which bound workers to never join a trade union, and made it more difficult for the Pinkertons and other private detectives to infiltrate their assemblies and identify their members.

---

[14] Sexton, *Agitator*, p. 80.

Later British assemblies also practised secrecy in a manner more reminiscent of the early days of the Order than of most American assemblies in the 1880s. In February 1889, the *Birmingham Daily Gazette* observed that 'their proceedings have hitherto been conducted in so secret a manner in England that few outsiders have even known of their existence … the desire to work without being known is conspicuous in the whole of the history of the English Knights.'[15] Like the early American Knights, they justified their secrecy on defensive grounds. One of the Order's supporters told the *Gazette* that while 'the best of the employers see the advantage of powerful combination amongst the workers, the majority do not, and they would discharge any of their men whom they knew to be taking a leading part in the Order.' This, he claimed, 'has happened in more than one instance in this district already.'[16] Knights insisted that this need for secrecy would disappear once they convinced employers that their intentions were benign. 'If our principles could be made a little clearer,' Charles Chamberlain told the *Smethwick Weekly News*, 'there would be no necessity for us to keep secret.'[17]

The British Knights soon underwent a similar evolution to their American counterparts, becoming more open and announcing their plans and activities to the public, but not for the reason Chamberlain gave. They had already held their first public meeting at Smethwick in May 1888, with Michael Davitt as their keynote speaker. With this coup the Knights developed a public profile. The next step came when the *Birmingham Daily Gazette* published a series of five exposés in February 1889, which revealed some of the Order's secrets and presented the Knights as a danger to the supposedly harmonious social relations of the city and surrounding area. Suddenly Charles Chamberlain made himself available for newspaper interviews where he had previously refused.[18] By August of that year Thomas Dean, the Master Workman of DA208, told its meetings that local assemblies should establish 'a channel for the dissemination of necessary information' with local journalists.[19] In 1889 and 1890 the Liverpool *Halfpenny Weekly* even ran a weekly half-page column that featured news from all the English assemblies.

As in the United States, not all British Knights regarded this greater openness as worthy of praise. 'Societies who show their weak points as well as their strength are often attacked where they are least able to stand,' one Knight from St Helens argued in 1888, 'whereas if they keep their own counsel the points their oppressors believe to be weak may be their

[15] *Birmingham Daily Gazette*, 18 February 1889.
[16] *Birmingham Daily Gazette*, 22 February 1889.
[17] *Smethwick Weekly News*, 2 March 1889.
[18] *Smethwick Weekly News*, 2 March 1889.
[19] *JUL*, August 1889.

stronghold.'[20] Another Knight from Handsworth complained to the *Journal of United Labor* of 'the infidelity of a great many of our members to the pledge they took at initiation wherein they promised to keep intact the things they saw and heard,' and insisted that 'if our secrecy tends to strength, then the fact remains that giving publicity to our affairs tends to weaken.'[21]

The British assemblies never became entirely open. Knights met almost exclusively at hotels and public houses to safeguard the identities of their members.[22] Haydn Sanders, of Walsall's LA454, explained in 1890 that 'people don't notice a man going to a lodge at a public-house on account of the other secret societies, such as Foresters, Oddfellows, Corks, &c., &c; whereas at a private meeting room anyone could ascertain easily.'[23] But Knights forged links between the assemblies and the pubs much earlier than that. When Robert Robertson and Charles Bird began their agitation among other workers in 1886 they had, after all, received their first break when local workers invited them to 'a mug of ale and a chat' at the Boot and Slipper Inn.[24] The connection between ale and organisation survived as long as the assemblies themselves.

American Knights, on the other hand, generally advocated temperance and wished to sever any ties between the labour movement and the saloon.[25] Many American assemblies built their own halls to make that separation clear. Some British Knights also called for temperance, and Richard Hill made the evils of drink the subject of his second letter to the *Journal of United Labor*.[26] Sometimes they had good reason for that stand. Glassworkers at St Helens were obliged to send their secretary, Joseph Norbury, to the United States after his drinking problems held back their organising work at Pilkington's.[27] But British Knights lacked the infrastructure of their American cousins. Pubs offered private lodge rooms specially designed for the meetings of various societies, and British Knights had no alternative but to use them.[28]

[20] *Manchester Guardian*, 10 January 1888.
[21] *JUL*, 20 September 1888.
[22] When the *Birmingham Daily Gazette* published a list of all the extant assemblies and the times and places of their meetings, all of them met at one of these two institutions (*Birmingham Daily Gazette*, 18 February 1889).
[23] *Walsall Observer*, 11 January 1890.
[24] *Smethwick Weekly News*, 23 February 1889.
[25] Norman Ware argues that for Powderly, temperance was second only to the land question as the most important issue facing American workers (Ware, *Labor Movement*, p. 89).
[26] *JUL*, 13 August 1887.
[27] Joseph French to Powderly, 7 July 1887, Box 30, TVP.
[28] Cordery, *British Friendly Societies*, p. 181.

British and Irish Knights did, however, keep the Order's assembly structure intact. They organised local and district assemblies with the numbers assigned to them in Philadelphia, elected officials with the same titles and roles as in the American assemblies, and continued to do so even after they formed the British National Assembly in 1891, a subject explored at greater length in later chapters. Apart from the glassworkers of LA3504, all the British assemblies were mixed, although some were dominated by a single trade. Hollowware turners in Wolverhampton, stove-grate workers around Rotherham and dockers in Bootle all dominated their own assemblies.[29] Even when British Knights broke with the American model they claimed an American precedent. LA3504, for example, copied their American colleagues in LA300 and organised separate 'preceptories' at each of the major glassworks. LA443 of Bootle experimented with a similar structure, except that they designed their preceptories as temporary bodies that would in time become full assemblies in their own right.[30]

So far as we can tell, the British and Irish Knights also adhered to the ritual and fraternal culture of their order. The rulebook of the British National Assembly outlines a number of ceremonies, from the initiation of new members to the opening of new assemblies, which are indistinguishable in content from those laid down in the *Adelphon Kruptos* or *A.K.*, the Order's book of ritual.[31] Newspaper reports mention opening and closing ceremonies at assembly meetings.[32] In the course of debates with trade unionists in Walsall, Haydn Sanders referred to 'giving the pledge of S.O.M.A.,' an acronym that stood for the Knights' watchwords, Secrecy, Obedience and Mutual Assistance; one of his critics heaped scorn on the 'tinselled lances and toy globes' that Knights received in return for the money they sent to headquarters. Globes and lances, as we saw in Chapter 1, were crucial symbols in the Order's assembly halls.[33] James P. Archibald, moreover, arrived in Britain and Ireland with instructions from Powderly to secure 'uniformity of method in the way of making signs, giving passwords and gaining admittance to Assemblies in session so that the secret work may be alike all over the jurisdiction of the Order.'[34] Taken together, this evidence suggests that British and Irish Knights conformed to the practices outlined in the *Adelphon Kruptos*.

[29] *Birmingham Daily Gazette*, 18 February 1889; *Rotherham Advertiser*, 29 March 1890; Bean, 'Knights in Liverpool,' p. 69.
[30] *Halfpenny Weekly*, 11 January 1890.
[31] *Preamble of the British National Assembly of the Knights of Labour* (London, 1891), pp. 43–55.
[32] For one example at Rotherham see the *Rotherham Advertiser*, 23 January 1892.
[33] *Walsall Observer*, 28 December 1889 and 11 January 1890.
[34] Circular from Powderly, 17 June 1889, Box 101, TVP.

They certainly agreed with American Knights on the importance of education. The Order, its *Declaration of Principles* proclaimed, would 'make individual and moral worth, not wealth, the true standard of individual and National greatness'; and one American leaflet even claimed that education was its fundamental principle. Leading American Knights certainly saw their assemblies as schools in which members would become educated enough to play an active and intelligent part in political and industrial life.[35] Knights in many American assemblies did their best to turn this dream into something approaching fact. The *Journal of United Labor* and other working-class newspapers addressed questions of deep political and economic significance, and simultaneously provided readers with the practical knowledge necessary to become an accomplished worker at their chosen trade. Many local assemblies created libraries and reading rooms. These were as likely to contain the works of leading thinkers like Marx and John Stuart Mill as cheap paperback novels. Some assemblies even created Labor Temples that, as Philip S Foner writes, 'became the center of all social and cultural life' in their communities.[36]

Most British assemblies lacked the time or the resources to go this far. They did, however, make education one of their prime concerns. Richard Hill informed the readers of the *Journal of United Labor* in 1887 that 'at present we are having a course of lectures on [cooperative enterprise] and kindred subjects, for the purpose of educating our brothers to the required standard for active work.'[37] Jesse Chapman, of LA10227, expressed his agreement with Powderly as to 'the wisdom of formulating and enforcing an Educational Policy for the Order in lieu of that baneful wage-squabble idea which, worse luck, still finds lodgement in many members' minds.'[38] English assemblies, at least, gave generously to the periodic Special Educational Funds which paid for the Order's roving lecturers.[39] This educational work also concerned the history of their order. Robert Robertson asked Powderly in 1886 for as many pamphlets on that subject as could be sent.[40] Five years later Arthur Nadin, the secretary of Rotherham's LA1266, told the GMW

---

[35] Ware, *The Labor Movement*, pp. 14–15; Foner, *History of Labor Movement*, II, pp. 75–76.
[36] Foner, *History of Labor Movement*, II, p. 76.
[37] *JUL*, 10 December, 1887.
[38] Jesse Chapman to Powderly, 12 May 1888, Box 44, TVP.
[39] In August 1888, LA7952 contributed the princely sum of $72.10, nearly double any of the Order's other assemblies anywhere in that month (*JUL*, 23 August 1888). LA647 of Liverpool, LA10356 of Smethwick and LA9086 of Cradley Heath also sent sums of more than $10, while LA913 of West Bromwich and LA583 of Aston sent smaller sums, the latter assembly in two instalments (See, respectively, *JUL* 26 July, 9 August, 13 September, 20 September and 1 November, 1888, and 28 March, 1889.)
[40] Robert Robertson to Powderly, 15 June 1886, Box 22, TVP.

that he had 'long felt the want of some further knowledge of the history of our noble order than I at present possess,' and asked Powderly for a copy of Michael Davitt's speech at Smethwick in 1888.[41] Powderly replied by sending Nadin a copy of his own book, *Thirty Years of Labor*.[42]

Local assembly meetings discussed ideas and current affairs. At one meeting of LA10227, for example, Jesse Chapman debated with J.W. Mahony, described by one newspaper as a 'Radical Fair Trader,' on the twin subjects of free trade and protectionism. Chapman defended the former while Mahony defended the latter.[43] On one occasion the members of LA7952 heard a lecture on the House of Lords.[44] The Master Workman of LA583 led the assembly in a debate on the topics of overproduction and overpopulation, and concluded that 'the remedy is to study till you understand, then combine to get rid of the monopolies of land and capital.'[45] Other assemblies engaged in discussions ranging from the rise of the Knights in New Zealand to the fate of Jewish people driven out of Russia by pogroms and state repression.[46] 'Lectures on political economy have been and are frequently given in the various assemblies in this district,' their supporters told the *Birmingham Daily Gazette*, and 'discussions upon economic questions are very frequent.'[47]

In 1889, Knights in the Birmingham area entertained ambitious plans that would extend their commitment to the principle of education even further. 'They hope somehow and somewhere,' the *Birmingham Daily Gazette* reported, 'to raise £10,000 wherewith to build a Knights' hall in Smethwick. The lower floor would be let to shopkeepers; the floor above would contain library, reading room, lecture hall, sanctuary, and whatnot.'[48] These plans never materialised. The Knights of Derry's LA1601, however, built on their growth in 1889 and 1890 by renting a hall in the town, and to meet their expenses they sublet it to other local societies. They established a reading room in the hall containing newspapers and non-gambling games, and held weekly concerts by local musicians.[49] In Derry, Knights created institutions that briefly became the centre of local working-class cultural life and rivalled those of some American assemblies.

---

[41] Arthur Nadin to Powderly, 20 May 1891, Box 67, TVP.

[42] Powderly to Arthur Nadin, 3 June 1891, Box 103, TVP; Arthur Nadin to Powderly, 21 June 1891, Box 67, TVP.

[43] *Smethwick Telephone*, 14 June, 1890. For the description of Mahony see *Midland Counties Express*, 14 June 1890.

[44] *Smethwick Telephone*, 25 October 1890.

[45] *Smethwick Telephone*, 8 November 1890.

[46] *Smethwick Telephone*, 21 February 1891; *Smethwick Telephone*, 13 June 1891.

[47] *Birmingham Daily Gazette*, 22 February 1889.

[48] *Birmingham Daily Gazette*, 23 February 1889.

[49] Boyle, *Irish Labour Movement*, p. 106.

This life revolved around more than lectures and debates. Like the glassworkers at their first anniversary dinner, the British assemblies celebrated their successes, marked important days of the year and promoted the solidarity of their members outside the workplace through a variety of social events. They followed the American Knights here too. Robert Weir has explored the ways in which Knights used sport, games, music, poetry and other leisure activities to bring their assemblies together in play as well as work.[50] These social occasions often presented the rougher aspects of working-class life, and the austere Powderly informed the *Journal of United Labor* in 1883 that he would no longer attend picnics after one experience where, in the middle of giving a lecture on the labour question, his audience left *en masse* to the beer tent and to watch boys attempt to climb greased poles or catch greased pigs.[51]

British Knights never held picnics, perhaps due to the vagaries of British weather. No pigs or poles, greased or otherwise, appeared at their gatherings. But every assembly seems to have enjoyed anniversary balls and suppers. Even in Scotland, where little evidence of the assemblies survives, Knights engaged in at least one 'annual festival' attended by such prominent figures in the labour movement as Keir Hardie and J. Bruce Glasier.[52] Knights in Bootle ushered in the year 1890 with their first annual ball. After a concert, Knights and their wives and friends danced to a quadrille band playing 'all the latest dance music.' The band only stopped to bring in the New Year, 'after which,' the secretary told the *Halfpenny Weekly*, 'dancing was resumed and carried on with great spirit until 5 am.'[53] Assembly meetings also became cultural events at times. In one case the members of LA7952, after hearing a pacifist lecture, listened to a poem entitled 'The Lifeboat' which, according to one account, 'was given with pathos, spirit, and fire by a young lady friend.'[54]

These occasions served a wider purpose than leisure alone. Knights inserted educational material into their dinnertime speeches, as when Joseph French regaled the 1885 supper of LA3504 with a short history of their assembly.[55] They also drew on culture to advance their assembly's wider agenda. The leaders of Derry's LA1601, for example, hoped to form an Alpha band, uniting musicians from both Protestant and Catholic groups, in an attempt to break down the sectarianism that divided the town.[56] This was more than

---

[50] Weir, *Beyond Labor's Veil*, ch. 7.
[51] *JUL*, July 1883.
[52] *Glasgow Herald*, 28 December 1889.
[53] *Halfpenny Weekly*, 11 January 1890.
[54] *Smethwick Telephone*, 8 November 1890.
[55] *JUL*, 25 December 1885.
[56] Boyle, *Irish Labour Movement*, p. 106.

wishful thinking: the Derry Trades Council succeeded in bringing together Protestant and Catholic workers in this way in the early 1890s.[57]

These occasions also demonstrated the cultural ties between the British Knights and their American order, and they did not all require the presence of the Union Jack and the Stars and Stripes. Knights in Barnsley celebrated the opening of an assembly with that most stereotypically English of customs, the tea party.[58] Knights in Bloxwich, near Walsall, settled down to a 'dinner of good English beef and plum pudding' at the opening of LA1713.[59] Even the practice of toasts owed much to the best traditions of British convivial culture. But British Knights also borrowed from the songs and sayings of their American cousins. Their toasts often concerned the experiences and principles of their order in the United States. And at the farewell dinner that Knights in Yorkshire and the Midlands put on for James P. Archibald, a highlight of the evening came when one of the Master Workmen sang 'If We Will, We Can Be Free,' a song written by Tom O'Reilly, a Powderly loyalist and leading American Knight. 'The chorus,' one Knight informed the *Journal of United Labor*, 'was heartily rendered by the Knights assembled.'[60] This represented an attempt to make Archibald feel at home; it also, however, demonstrates that Knights were aware of their own order's cultural achievements and were prepared to make use of them.

In song as well as in their secrecy, their ritual, their focus on education and in their use of social occasions towards that end, the British and Irish Knights very closely resembled the American Knights. They made some changes, of course. Their assemblies were initially as secret as those in the early days of the American Order, though like the Americans the British and Irish Knights soon moved in a more open direction. Their need for secrecy, as well as the availability of suitable lodge rooms and the absence of any alternative, led them to meet at public houses. They may not have followed every dot and comma of the Order's ritual – and there is no way to tell if they did – but they never abandoned it. Their determination to follow all the practices of their order, as far as possible, becomes even clearer when compared with those organisations that used the name or the methods of the Knights for their own distinct purposes.

---

[57] McAteer, 'New Unionism in Derry,' p. 15.
[58] *Sheffield and Rotherham Independent*, 21 May 1890.
[59] *Walsall Free Press*, 7 December 1889.
[60] *JUL*, 14 November 1889.

Appropriating the Knights of Labor

In November 1886, agricultural workers marched in a torchlit procession to Montacute, near Yeovil in Somerset, accompanied by two bands of musicians.[61] Their procession was reminiscent of the glory days of the 1870s. Then, many of the agricultural labourers of Britain, led by Joseph Arch, had confounded the prevailing wisdom that they were incapable of organised action and had created the National Agricultural Workers' Union, which organised torchlit processions like this one. One of the three speakers at their meeting, George Mitchell, embodied another link with that past. Mitchell had served as Arch's chief lieutenant in the Union before it fell into disrepair at the end of the 1870s.[62]

One newspaper claimed that the procession and meeting represented an extension into the countryside of the socialist agitation among the unemployed of London.[63] Mitchell was flanked not by socialists, however, but by an Australian trade unionist and a minister of religion. It might be thought that Mitchell wished his listeners to breathe new life into their old union. But he and his fellow speakers had another organisation in mind. After introducing resolutions that called for land for the agricultural labourers, and Home Rule for all the various nationalities that made up the United Kingdom, the speakers then turned to their main objective: 'a union of the working classes to be known as the Knights of Labour.'[64] Should anyone doubt the provenance of the phrase, they added that this new union would work, as *The Times* reported, 'for the purpose of assisting each other in sickness, old age, &c.,' and with 'lawyers, bankers, gamblers, dealers in strong drink, and all non-producers not to be admitted.'[65] The Knights of Labor would become the vehicle for the rejuvenation of trade unionism in the English countryside.

The *Bristol Mercury* attached 'very little importance' to this new movement, and was soon proved right.[66] Mitchell's new union soon disappeared off the edges of the historical record. The fact that he chose to call it the Knights of Labour, however, captures the interest, explored in the previous chapter, which the Order generated in Britain and Ireland. We have already seen the how the Staffordshire potters based their new order on the Knights; workers in Preston also began their own short-lived Knights of Labor assemblies in

---

[61] *The Times*, 15 November 1886; *Ipswich Journal*, 16 November 1886.
[62] R. Groves, *Sharpen the Sickle: The History of the Farm Workers' Union* (London: Porcupine, 1949), pp. 61–63.
[63] *Ipswich Journal*, 16 November 1886.
[64] *Ipswich Journal*, 16 November 1886.
[65] *The Times*, 15 November 1886.
[66] *Bristol Mercury and Daily Post*, 16 November 1886.

1887.⁶⁷ Nor was this power limited to the British Isles. Assemblies of Knights emerged in Australia and New Zealand in 1887 and 1888 before the first organiser, W.W. Lyght, set foot in either place.⁶⁸ South African workers created their own assemblies in 1890 on very different lines to Knights elsewhere, and took nearly a year to establish any contact with Philadelphia. An Italian founded three assemblies based on his experiences of the Order as a migrant worker in the United States. The Knights of Labor was an order that workers joined; it was also a model and a name that workers appropriated for themselves.

In the coal mining towns of Lanarkshire, in the west of Scotland, the most important of those British appropriations took place. Conditions in the Lanarkshire coalfields resembled the American Order's early years in the coal mining districts of Pennsylvania, where employers had ruled through private detectives and collusion with the local authorities, and where the Molly Maguires, the secret organisation which used violence against the mine owners in an attempt to force them to the negotiating table, had been crushed through a close alliance between the coal masters and local law enforcement.⁶⁹ The Lanarkshire Coal Masters' Association was not as ruthless as its Pennsylvanian equivalents, but employers missed no opportunity to dismiss men suspected of union activism.⁷⁰ They exerted a tremendous effect over the social and political life of the pit towns, as one miner explained in 1889:

> First, if a man votes with his conscience, the manager turns him out of the 'pet'; second, the landlord turns him out of the 'hoose'; third, the minister turns him out of the 'kirk'; so if a man's got 'weans' he thinks twice before he votes with his conscience.⁷¹

The miners' union also lay in tatters after a failed strike in August 1887, when mounted police and soldiers shepherded strike-breakers through the picket lines.⁷² Coal mining trade unionism in Lanarkshire seemed ripe for a new departure.

---

⁶⁷ David Whittle to Powderly, 13 April 1887, Box 32, TVP.

⁶⁸ There is some evidence that an assembly existed in Adelaide as early as 1887 (*Burra Record*, 15 February 1887). There is even stronger evidence that trade unionists in Brisbane hoped to either create assemblies directly affiliated with Philadelphia or independently create their own between 1886 and 1888 (For the first, see W. Lane to Powderly, 12 May 1886, Box 21, TVP; for the second, see *Brisbane Courier*, 5 September 1887). The pre-Lyght history of the New Zealand Knights can be found in Weir, *Knights Down Under*, pp. 1–10.

⁶⁹ Foner, *History of the Labor Movement*, II, pp. 455–63.

⁷⁰ Campbell, *Scottish Miners*, p. 36.

⁷¹ *Labour Tribune*, 2 March 1889.

⁷² F. Reid, 'Keir Hardie's Conversion to Socialism,' in Asa Briggs and John Saville (eds), *Essays in Labour History, 1886–1923* (London: Macmillan, 1971), pp. 39–40.

Its leaders looked to the United States. In Scotland, as James D. Young observes, 'American labour organizations still provided the leaders of the advanced thought of the age with an ideological pivot.'[73] In 1887 they looked especially to the Knights of Labor. Keir Hardie had already drafted a programme for the Sons of Labour, based on that of the Knights, in the July issue of his journal, *The Miner*. In the following year this name reappeared as the title of a new organisation in the Lanarkshire mining towns. Its founder, William Bulloch, had attempted to revive trade unionism in the coalfields for some time and had experimented with another new organisation at Kilsyth in March.[74] In April 1888, Bulloch opened Mother Lodge No. 1 of the Sons of Labour at Maryhill. Another lodge soon opened at Lambhill and by the end of July 1800, Blantyre miners met to draft a constitution for their new order, 'on the lines of the Knights of Labour.'[75] By January 1889, reports claimed that the Sons of Labour numbered 14,000 members throughout Lanarkshire.[76] This estimate may have been optimistic, but as late as March of that year, the *Dundee Courier* reported that 'the "Sons of Labour" are prosecuting their cause with vigour amongst the mining districts throughout the West of Scotland, and week by week report considerable accession to their members.'[77] Yet the Amalgamated Order of the Sons of Labour, as it became known, came to an end in 1890. Lanarkshire's coal miners soon returned to a more orthodox trade unionism.[78]

There are no signs that the Sons of Labour ever affiliated themselves with the Knights in Britain or the United States. One knowledgeable source claimed that Bulloch was less the founder than the 'introducer of the order into Scotland'; a newspaper report mentioned that local seamen had received a £25 cheque from 'the Sons of Labour in the neighbourhood of Birmingham,' suggesting that they were the same in all but name.[79] Yet the Sons of Labour registered as a trade union with the Registrar of Trade Unions, listing their headquarters in Airdrie, and never referred to the Knights in their rulebook.[80] The Knights' records contain no reference to their almost namesake. The two orders had much in common, however.

[73] Young, 'Changing Images,' pp. 84–85.
[74] See, for instance, *The Miner*, August and November 1887, and January and February 1888; for the Kilsyth Miners and Labourers' Association, see *The Miner*, April 1888.
[75] Campbell, *Scottish Miners*, p. 36; *The Miner*, June 1888; *Glasgow Herald*, 31 July 1888.
[76] *Birmingham Daily Post*, 4 January 1889.
[77] *Dundee Courier*, 22 March 1889.
[78] For a more detailed history of the Sons of Labour see Frame, *America and the Scottish Left*, pp. 129–56.
[79] *Labour Tribune*, 23 February 1889; *The Scotsman*, 14 February 1889.
[80] *Rules of the Amalgamated Order of the Sons of Labour*, National Archives of Scotland, FS7/75.

Early newspaper reports concerning the Sons of Labour referred to either lodges or local assemblies, based at individual collieries.[81] Sometimes these assemblies met as 'Trades Councils of the Sons of Labour' when discussing specifically industrial questions; at other times, they organised 'general assemblies,' which denoted a meeting of any large body of its representatives and not an annual gathering as it did for American Knights.[82] In 1889, representatives held general assemblies in February, April and June.[83]

The rulebook of the Amalgamated Order suggests that the Sons of Labour evolved over the course of their short history. That document placed the Amalgamated Order's administration in the hands of a district assembly, to which local assemblies at all the various collieries became subordinated. The leadership of the local assemblies was vested in a Master Workman, and each assembly elected a Worthy Foreman, secretary and treasurer, as the Knights did with their assemblies. But the rulebook also dictated the election of an Agent, under the control of the district assembly, who would 'receive for his services such remuneration as the members of the Association shall decide.' The Amalgamated Order held the Agent responsible for the day-to-day organising work while the Master Workman presided over meetings.[84] The Sons of Labour, in other words, appeared to be a curious hybrid between the organisation of the Knights and the demands of a conventional coal miners' union.

The leaders of the Amalgamated Order emphasised certain features of both and discarded others. They certainly adopted a strict veil of secrecy to avoid what one miner described as 'the victimisation which is practiced by employers [and] prevents the very best men in the mines from taking part in union work.'[85] There is one reference to ritual, from an unconvinced miner at a meeting in Maryhill – but only one, and from the absence of any ceremony in the rulebook or in other sources, we must assume that the Sons of Labour placed little weight in fraternal rites.[86] The same applies to education which, William Bulloch claimed in May 1888, was 'another of the higher

---

[81] *Glasgow Herald*, 19 April 1889.

[82] For 'Trades Councils,' see for instance *Glasgow Herald*, 8 February 1889; *Glasgow Weekly Mail*, 9 February 1889.

[83] *Glasgow Herald*, 8 February, 19 April and 25 June 1889.

[84] *Rules of the Amalgamated Order of the Sons of Labour*, p. 4.

[85] *Labour Tribune*, 16 February 1889. Even those titles which the Lanarkshire miners borrowed from the Knights, such as the office of Worthy Foreman, which dealt mainly with the ritualistic and ceremonial elements of assembly-room culture, were given other functions. In the Amalgamated Order, for instance, the Worthy Foreman acted as no more than a deputy to the Master Workman (*Rules of the Amalgamated Order of the Sons of Labour*, p. 4).

[86] *Glasgow Herald*, 17 May 1889.

duties of a local assembly or lodge.'[87] No further references to educational activities have survived. On the other hand, the Sons of Labour envisaged a system of benefits from the very beginning. Each member was entitled to a funeral benefit and, according to one report, also in case of sickness.[88] Taken together, it seems clear that from this merger of the Knights and local union traditions, the leaders of the Sons of Labour hoped to make their Amalgamated Order the vanguard of a new and improved industrial miners' union in the west of Scotland and, perhaps, the rest of the country. Where the British and Irish Knights tried to transplant the American Order wholesale, the coal miners of Lanarkshire took what they wanted from that model as a way to quickly revive organisation in the county.

Workers in northeastern England, by contrast, used the Order's name to construct their own benefit society. Glassworkers in Sunderland had proved less successful than their colleagues at Spon Lane in spreading their order beyond the glass trades. But at the end of 1888 a new organisation appeared in Sunderland which called itself the Knights of Labour. Initially, the leaders of this new organisation insisted that 'this society would be governed by the rules and regulations of the American societies from the head branch,' which they erroneously located in New York, and at a subsequent meeting 'referred to what their brothers in the States intended doing for them.'[89] Some of the leading figures of this order had the same surnames as the leaders of LA3504, and though this is not conclusive proof of links between the two organisations it nevertheless suggests that some connections existed at first.

In its first few months the new organisation certainly adopted some of the rhetoric of the American Order. 'As an order they had a higher mission to serve than the forming of a mere political party,' their first president claimed, and 'by far the highest motive that concerned them was the education of the masses to that point where they would fully see, not only their wrongs and degradation, but a full and final solution of the labour problem.'[90] At a meeting of one of their early branches they intended 'to see that a man could secure a fair day's payment for a fair day's work,' and noted the poor wages of workers employed on the Wear.[91] The object of their branches, they claimed, was 'to unite together all working men to form an organisation to assist one another in case of sickness and strikes.'[92] Their first plan, in November

[87] *The Miner*, May 1888.
[88] *Rules of the Amalgamated Order of the Sons of Labour*, pp. 9–10; *Dundee Courier*, 1 February 1889.
[89] *Sunderland Daily Echo*, 21 and 27 November 1888.
[90] *Sunderland Daily Echo*, 11 December 1888.
[91] *Sunderland Daily Echo*, 18 December 1888.
[92] *Sunderland Daily Echo*, 21 November 1888.

1888, stipulated that for an entrance fee of 4d and weekly contributions of 3d, members received 6s per week in strike benefits, sickness benefits of 10s per week for the first 24 weeks and 5s thereafter, and £5 in funeral benefits.[93]

With that plan in mind, this new northeastern order grew quickly. By July 1889, the All-England Royal Order of the Knights of Labour, whose name soon changed to the British United Order, boasted 18 branches and 4,000 members.[94] By June of the following year that number reached 12,000.[95] But with this growth they soon abandoned everything of the Knights except their name, and became indistinguishable from any other English friendly society. They kept titles and ritual, which these societies shared with the Knights, but their titles, from Grand National Presidents to Grand National Secretaries, could have been borrowed from any number of fraternal orders.[96] The British United Order of Oddfellows was their most likely model – one of their members had served as its Grand Master, and they became a British United Order themselves.[97] They made no attempt to compete with or even complement local trade unions. Instead they began to compete with more traditional forms of local social insurance, usually based around collections made at public houses.[98] The appointment of a medical officer to oversee sickness payments, and an auditor to ensure the accuracy of the necessary bookkeeping, became in consequence the most important decisions facing the lodges of the British United Order.

The Order registered as a friendly society at the beginning of 1890.[99] Their members joined marches with other friendly societies in church parades,[100] in celebration of the opening of a new park in South Shields[101] and in galas which brought together all friendly societies in the local area.[102] They organised benefit concerts for the death of at least one member.[103] At the 'Annual Moveable Delegation' of the British United Order in June 1890 – a term that owed nothing to the American Knights – the leaders themselves admitted, implicitly at least, that their order differed in name

---

[93] *Sunderland Daily Echo*, 21 November 1888.
[94] *Sunderland Daily Echo*, 9 July 1889.
[95] *Sunderland Daily Echo*, 2 June 1890.
[96] For the initiation of new members at a branch meeting in Monkwearouth, in *Sunderland Daily Echo*, 4 December 1889; for the opening ceremony of a new branch, see *Sunderland Daily Echo*, 29 December 1888.
[97] *Sunderland Daily Echo*, 8 July 1889.
[98] *Morpeth Herald*, 9 and 30 November 1889.
[99] *Sunderland Daily Echo*, 11 February 1890.
[100] *Shields Daily Gazette*, 20 July 1889.
[101] *Shields Daily Gazette*, 16 June 1890.
[102] *Shields Daily Gazette*, 7 August 1890.
[103] *Shields Daily Gazette*, 1 October 1889.

only from any other local, rival society based on social insurance. Balance sheets and the ratio of contributions to payments, and nothing else, dominated all discussion.[104] It only took just over a year for them to take the final step and replace their name with a more suitable English one. In 1891, the lodge at Shildon restyled itself, appropriately enough, as the Independent Order of St George.[105] Other branches soon began styling themselves as 'late Knights of Labour.'[106] Finally, in 1892, most of the lodges reorganised themselves as the Durham Conquerors Friendly Society though they did, initially at least, keep the phrase 'late Knights of Labour' in brackets at the end.[107]

That did not immediately mean the end of this group of Knights in the northeast. As late as 1897, a friendly society calling itself the Knights of Labour marched in a procession alongside friendly societies in South Shields.[108] This may have been the Independent Order of the Knights of Labour, created in Jarrow in 1889, which was organised along industrial lines; or else some lodges maintained their name and continued for some time without any notice from the press. As far south of Sunderland as Hull, a 'Knights of Labour Recreation Club' briefly flourished in 1893 and showed signs of affiliation with the British United Order, or at least its remnants.[109] Like the Sons of Labour, those orders showed that the Knights of Labor were as flexible an instrument as Robert Weir has claimed. Their many changes to the Order's model further illustrate how closely the Order's British and Irish assemblies followed it. Actual Knights in Britain and Ireland did *not* dine *à la carte* from the Order's menu of official guidelines, practices and methods. Yet they did depart in one crucial respect from their American brethren: and that departure concerned the place – or the absence – of women in their respective assemblies.

Gender and the British and Irish Knights

As we saw in the previous chapter, scholars rightly recognise the Knights of Labor as the first major experiment in multiracial organising in American labour history. They carried that effort into the realm of gender too. Female and black workers each represented around 10 percent of the Order's total American membership in the mid-1880s. The Knights took that record

---

[104] *Sunderland Daily Echo*, 2 June 1890.
[105] *Northern Echo*, 22 October 1891.
[106] *Sunderland Daily Echo*, 30 October 1891.
[107] *Sunderland Daily Echo*, 10 October 1892.
[108] *Shields Daily Gazette*, 20 September 1897.
[109] See *Hull Daily Mail*, 2 May and 21 August 1893.

with them when they expanded abroad, with mixed results. Knights in New Zealand welcomed women and fought for female suffrage, and made repeated and relatively successful attempts to organise Maori workers. On the other hand, Knights in South Africa seem to have been exclusively male and prohibited black workers from joining their assemblies.[110] The other non-American assemblies fell somewhere in between these two poles. Knights could use their order to include; they could also use it to exclude.

American Knights took the inclusion of women to unprecedented heights. More than 400 assemblies included women, two-thirds of them separately and the rest mixed with men, and all women became members on an equal standing with men. The Knights boasted around 65,000 female members in 1887, about 10 percent of the total membership. To put this in perspective, women made up around 10 percent of the total American workforce at this time.[111] Female Knights also rose to positions of leadership. Elizabeth Rodgers became Master Workman of Chicago's District Assembly 24, composed of around 50,000 members, while at the same time raising ten children.[112] Eleven female delegates attended the Richmond General Assembly in 1886. That convention created a Department of Women's Work, headed by Leonora Barry, an Irish-born widow and seamstress who toured the country lecturing and investigating the conditions of women workers. In the words of one contemporary, she became 'to the women of the Order, what Terence Powderly is to the men.'[113] The Knights also allied themselves with advocates of temperance and women's rights. Famous early feminists like Susan B. Anthony and Elizabeth Cady Stanton joined the Order.[114] Powderly developed close ties with Frances Willard, whose Women's Christian Temperance Union (WCTU) became a significant body in the United States and opened branches throughout the English-speaking world.[115]

These achievements put them well ahead of their British and Irish sisters. Women joined some trade unions and attended Trades Union Congresses from the 1870s onwards, but their representatives there often faced contempt and hostility from the male delegates.[116] The Women's Protective and

---

[110] Weir, *Knights Down Under*. Some scholars have even seen the South African Knights as contributors to the emergence of apartheid within the South African labour movement. See Simons, *Class and Colour in South Africa*, p. 45.

[111] Levine, *Labor's True Woman*, p. 106.

[112] *Belfast News-Letter*, 28 September 1886; Montgomery, *Fall of the House of Labor*, p. 147.

[113] Quoted in Levine, *Labor's True Woman*, p. 105.

[114] Weir, *Beyond Labor's Veil*, p. 7.

[115] For the WCTU and its international branches see Tyrell, *Woman's World*.

[116] S.O. Rose, 'Gender and Labour History,' in M. van der Linden (ed.), *The End of Labour History? International Review of Social History Supplement 1*, 38 (1993), p. 155.

Provident League – whose founder, Emma Paterson, had been inspired to create the league through her experience of women's trade unionism on honeymoon in New York in 1873 – tried to alter this picture, and enjoyed some small success in the nineteenth century.[117] But they could not compete with the record of the Knights of Labor. One correspondent to the *Women's Union Journal*, the organ of the Women's Protective and Provident League, urged her sisters to heed the Order's example. 'The men and women of that noble order work side by side,' she wrote. 'They do not try to crush the women and also what is quite as important the women don't crush the men in the way of working for less wages while doing the same work.' She suggested that they get more information from the Knights themselves, adding that 'some help may be gained even if we do not follow quite in their footsteps.'[118]

The Order's advanced position on the inclusion of women, and the relatively backward position of the British trade unions, should have given the young British and Irish assemblies ample reason to organise sisters as well as brothers. Yet they failed to follow in the footsteps of their own order. When James P. Archibald told an audience of Knights at Cradley Heath that 'he hoped assemblies of women would be formed, for by their elevation the men would become more successful, and homes would be made happier,' they responded with applause. But they did nothing more than repeat demands that women should receive equal pay for equal work.[119] The only evidence we have for women Knights in Britain comes from George Barnsby, who remarks that an assembly in Lye had 'a separate female section.'[120] The only other women present at assembly meetings were the friends or the wives of male members.[121] Ironworking Knights at Lye actually went on a number of strikes to expunge female labour from their industry.[122] Even when they supported the organisation of women in public, they did not suggest their order as a possible home. James Brown of LA3504 voiced his support for female trade unionism in 1891, but only as part of the

---

[117] R.M. Jacoby, *The British and American Women Trade Union Leagues, 1890–1925: A Case Study of Feminism and Class* (New York: Carlson, 1994), pp. 9–10; Soldon, *Women in British Trade Unions*, esp. chs 1–2; H. Goldman, *Emma Paterson: She Led Woman into a Man's World* (London: Lawrence and Wishart, 1974).

[118] *The Women's Union Journal*, 15 November 1887.

[119] *Preamble of the British National Assembly*, p. 52.

[120] G. Barnsby, *Socialism in Birmingham and the Black Country* (Wolverhampton: Integrated Publishing Services, 1998), p. 83.

[121] In one suggestive passage, 'only members of the Order and their wives' were admitted to hear a speech from Henry George at Smethwick in 1888. See *Smethwick Telephone*, 8 December 1888.

[122] T. Brake, *Men of Good Character: A History of the National Union of Sheet Metal Workers, Coppersmiths, Heating and Domestic Engineers* (London: Lawrence and Wishart, 1985), p. 169.

Female Workers' Union of Great Britain.[123] Nor can we argue simply that the Knights organised exclusively in male-dominated trades, which they did, for that leaves open the question of why they failed to target industries where women were numerous. American Knights practised gender inclusion; British and Irish Knights most certainly did not.

This difference would be easier to explain if the British and Irish Knights did not follow their order's example in most respects. Paradoxically, they did their best to follow that example on gender questions too. While the Knights went further when it came to organising women than any of their contemporaries, they were, of course, hardly the avant-garde of a gender-neutral, post-patriarchal utopia. Many American Knights, Susan Levine writes, 'did not accept their sister Knights willingly.'[124] Knights only admitted women as members from 1881, and then only due to local initiatives which the next General Assembly accepted as a *fait accompli*. Even those who were more willing to organise women workers usually still viewed them as only temporary sojourners in the workforce who would, as the conditions of life improved, return to their 'natural' place in the home. As Levine argues, even female Knights, along with many nineteenth-century feminists, 'believed in a particularly feminine sensibility, one that upheld the values of hearth and home and that could at the same time infuse the public world with a more moral, humane, and cooperative character.' For Levine, the great achievement of the Knights was that they viewed women as productive citizens not only during their short stay in the labour market, but also through their domestic functions, and reconciled the private, feminine domestic sphere with the public sphere of the labour movement.[125]

That complicated brew failed to survive the journey across the Atlantic, and visiting American Knights did not make it any easier to understand. At the same time that Archibald called on Knights in Cradley Heath to form female assemblies, he told them that it 'was revolting to see women forging red hot iron in that country, and he hoped the day would not be far distant when it would be illegal for women to do such work.'[126] When Leonora Barry visited Cradley Heath in 1889, on her way to the Paris Exposition as part of a delegation of representative American workers, she 'considered it a disgrace to civilization that women with babies should be engaged in making chain, and that their children should be practically reared in the chainshops.'[127]

---

[123] *Sunderland Daily Echo*, 15 April 1891.
[124] Levine, *Labor's True Woman*, p. 111.
[125] Levine, *Labor's True Woman*, p. 121.
[126] *Midland Counties Express*, 12 September 1889.
[127] *Dudley Herald*, 10 August 1889.

Chain makers agreed that the solution to problems in their industry lay in the prohibition or restriction of women from their trade.[128]

British Knights took a very similar view. Ironworkers at Lye opposed female labour on very similar grounds to the chain makers: local ironmasters employed women on their machines and thus directly threatened the livelihood of their male co-workers.[129] Samuel Reeves adopted the same logic at a meeting of Bootle's LA443 in December 1889. 'At the present time,' he claimed, 'male labour in many branches of the trade was being rapidly supplanted by females.' If women were not given equal pay to men or, preferably, were removed from paid employment altogether, Reeves argued that the very world of gender relations would be turned completely, and disastrously, upside down. 'In a large number of industries,' he explained, 'the husbands had to remain idle while the wife was forced to become the bread-winner.'[130] Men must exclude women from the labour market before the reverse became true. And Reeves was only echoing Archibald's claim, made at a meeting at Bootle two months earlier, that 'in many of the industries in America – particularly in the weaving sheds and shoemaking – women were driving their fathers, husbands, and brothers from the field, and were taking their places.'[131] As with other questions of culture and organisation, British and Irish Knights followed what they thought their American representatives were saying on the subject of gender. Archibald and Barry, after all, seemed to echo the views of local trade unionists who wished to exclude women workers from the labour market altogether, rather than recruit them as members.

Wider differences between the American and British assemblies also encouraged different outcomes when it came to female membership. The American Knights emerged from, and remained closely linked to, an American reform tradition that made some room for the concerns of women.[132] Women played a major part in the work of the Grangers, a reformist society devoted to the interests of farmers, from the 1860s onwards.[133] The second congress in 1868 of the National Labor Union, a predecessor of the Knights, publicly called for women to 'join our labor

---

[128] Blackburn, *Sweated Labour*, p. 63.
[129] Brake, *Men of Good Character*, p. 169.
[130] *Halfpenny Weekly*, 7 December 1889.
[131] *Bootle Times*, 28 September 1889.
[132] One recent synthesis of the tradition which, though it tends to overemphasise the egalitarian tendencies of American reformers compared with the distinctly non-egalitarian tendencies of the immigrant socialists, does demonstrate the links between women's rights and wider reform, is Messer-Kruse, *The Yankee International*.
[133] C.M. McConnaughy, *The Woman Suffrage Movement in America: A Reassessment* (New York: Cambridge University Press, 2013), p. 139.

unions or form protective unions of [your] own,' and the women's suffrage movement formed close links with the NLU before it collapsed at the beginning of the next decade.[134] The Knights built on these precedents, ensuring that they were willing from the outset to consider the possibility of female members, and could count on active support in this regard from significant women's organisations such as the WCTU.[135]

British Knights swallowed their order more or less whole, but they remained cut off by the width of the Atlantic from this reform tradition and its implications for female membership. As Robin Miller Jacoby argues, at this time women trade unionists had fewer middle-class allies in Britain than the United States, leaving them more isolated within the wider labour movement. Electoral calculations played an important role here. American feminists operated in a political system with universal male suffrage and naturally appealed to working-class women, and the labour movement in general, in order to win female suffrage. In Britain, with limited male suffrage, many feminists were more inclined to seek suffrage for women with the same property qualifications as men and so had less need of working-class women as allies than in the United States. The infrastructure of interlocking organisations and causes that brought women's suffrage, temperance and women themselves into the heart of the American Knights of Labor did not exist to anywhere near the same extent in Britain and Ireland.[136] Many British trade unions, for their part, kept organisations like the Women's Protective and Provident League at arm's length and often tended to view women workers as part of an unorganisable residuum.

In the absence of this reform tradition, and the institutional infrastructure that made it so (relatively) successful, it is not surprising that Knights in the British Isles ended up emphasising certain aspects of their order's gender stances and downplaying others.

These differences also ensured that they interpreted other inheritances from their order in particular and male-only ways. British and Irish Knights faithfully adopted the secret and fraternal forms of the Knights of Labor in their own assemblies, and nineteenth-century fraternalism was very much a masculine affair on both sides of the Atlantic. Many fraternal orders, particularly those of lower-class origins like the Oddfellows, had begun on the basis of 'conviviality,' which essentially meant group (male)

---

[134] Wertheimer, *We Were There*, p. 161; Foner, *History of Labor Movement*, I, pp. 382–88.

[135] Even as late as 1893, for example, Willard and Powderly continued to exchange correspondence and promote an exchange of newspaper columns and fraternal delegates between their two organisations. See particularly Frances Willard to Powderly, 25 August 1891, Box 68, TVP; Frances Willard to Powderly, 8 August 1893, Box 80, TVP.

[136] Jacoby, *Women Trade Union Leagues*, p. 2.

drinking. Even after the temperance movement challenged these traditions from the mid-nineteenth century, fraternalism still provided an alternative male social world, free of both the saloon – in situations where the public consumption of alcohol was no longer socially accepted – and the feminised, domestic world of the home. 'The fraternal order,' Mary Ann Clawson writes, 'provided a way for men to comply with the norm of temperance without acceding to the attack on the male social world that it could imply.'[137] Indeed, these orders played a vital role in the construction, maintenance and development of masculinity in the nineteenth century on both sides of the Atlantic.[138] 'Friendly societies,' Simon Cordery concludes, 'contributed to the nineteenth-century move toward excluding women from public space.'[139]

A joke that appeared in newspapers during the 1890s, on both sides of the Atlantic, made this gender segregation very clear. A woman's hopes to bring friends over in the evening are soon dashed by the very active fraternal life of her husband. 'No my dear, I must attend the meeting of the Ancient Order of Foresters to-night,' he says to Monday evening. Tuesday is reserved for the Ancient Order of United Workmen; Wednesday the Oddfellows; Thursday the Knights of Labour; Friday the Royal Templars of Temperance; Saturday a special meeting of the Social Circle; and Sunday, the Grand and Ancient Order of Christian Fellowship. The woman then delivers the punchline. "'But you have forgotten another society, John,'" she says, "'of which you were once a member." "What's that?" he asks. "Your wife's."'[140]

The Knights of Labor reflected the masculine assumptions behind this fraternal tradition. Like men in other fraternal orders, some male American Knights resented a female presence in their assemblies and claimed that women, supposedly natural gossips, would inevitably betray the secrets of the Order's ritual and ceremonies.[141] From the standpoint of female American Knights, fraternal culture was both unfamiliar and uncongenial. Even Robert Weir, who bucked the historiographical trend with his argument that fraternalism 'built community' and encouraged solidarity in a way that material self-interest could not, points out that the Order's fraternal culture never attracted women.[142] Female assemblies, by contrast, removed virtually

---

[137] M.A. Clawson, *Constructing Brotherhood: Class, Gender, and Fraternalism* (Princeton: Princeton University Press, 1989), p. 164.
[138] See especially Clawson, *Constructing Brotherhood*; Carnes, *Secret Ritual and Manhood in Victorian America*.
[139] Cordery, *British Friendly Societies*, p. 181.
[140] *Northeastern Gazette*, 28 November 1892.
[141] Weir, *Beyond Labor's Veil*, p. 52.
[142] Weir, *Beyond Labor's Veil*, pp. 62–66.

all ritual from their meetings.¹⁴³ In the face of these powerful social norms it is surprising that as many women flocked to the Knights as they did. Among friendly societies and fraternal orders, the Knights were unique even in their own, home context.

Prospective female Knights in Britain and Ireland faced an additional problem. In Britain, probably more than in the United States, friendly societies and fraternal orders maintained close connections with public houses and hotels, which in turn provided private lodge rooms for their use. A meeting of a fraternal order was already considered a masculine space; the hotel and the public house was a masculine space in its own right. The pub, as Geoffrey Best writes, remained 'a power base distinct from that of the home' and, in the words of Valerie Hey, even served as 'female substitutes' that offered men 'plentitude, availability, warmth, food, and companionship, [and] a servicing of male needs.' These included sexual needs, and the association of female patrons with prostitution further marked out pubs and hotels as places that respectable women should avoid.¹⁴⁴ These trends slowly began to change. Towards the end of the nineteenth and the beginning of the twentieth century, wives began to join their husbands at the pub or husbands drank at home.¹⁴⁵ But in the late nineteenth century pubs remained, as Hey entitled one of the chapters of her work, 'masculine republics on every street.'¹⁴⁶

British Knights met at these places to keep their identities hidden from hostile employers. By doing so, however, they made it virtually impossible for respectable women to attend their meetings, except as the wife of a member at certain social occasions. The very air of these spaces also choked off any desire of any women to enter them, literally and metaphorically. News reports described the 'tobacco-laden atmosphere' in which meetings of the British assemblies were held.¹⁴⁷ Female American Knights certainly complained about the prevalence of smoking and tobacco chewing among their male counterparts. They, at least, had the option of all-women assemblies and alternative meeting places to escape these habits; aside from a single adjunct to an assembly in Lye, women had no such option in Britain and Ireland.¹⁴⁸

In time the British and Irish assemblies may have found ways to encourage women to join their ranks. It took 12 years, after all, for the American

---

[143] Weir, *Beyond Labor's Veil*, p. 55; Levine, *Labor's True Woman*, pp. 117–19.
[144] G. Hunt, *The Pub, the Village and the People* (unpublished PhD thesis, University of Kent, 1989), p. 54; V. Hey, *Pub Culture and Patriarchy* (London: Tavistock, 1986), p. 30.
[145] J. Benson, *The Working Class in Britain, 1850–1939* (London: Longman, 1989), pp. 101–02.
[146] Hey, *Pub Culture and Patriarchy*, ch. 1.
[147] *Walsall Observer*, 10 May 1890.
[148] Levine, *Labor's True Woman*, p. 117; Weir, *Beyond Labor's Veil*, p. 55.

Order to admit its first female member. But Knights across the Atlantic were denied that luxury. Had they grown further they might have become able to forge alliances with women trade unionists and the wider women's movement. They might then have managed to build local centres, as they hoped to do in Birmingham and briefly did at Derry, which in time could have provided an alternative to the male-only spaces of the lodge rooms. But this is only conjecture. Knights in Britain and Ireland took what they saw to be their order's message and methods, compared them with local practice, and ended up with assemblies of men and men only.

British and Irish Knights also lacked the powerful stimulus of social conflict that led American Knights to encourage female membership. Their immersion in an American reform tradition where women's issues were given some credence does not explain why they organised so many women in such a short space of time in the mid-1880s. In those years the Great Upheaval became a social explosion that surpassed its predecessor in 1877. And social upheavals of that kind create spaces where women can emerge as independent actors in ways considered unthinkable at other times. The French and Russian Revolutions, the Paris Commune, the struggles of the 1960s and the protests on Tahrir Square, among others, all bear this point out. So does the Great Upheaval. The women who joined the American Knights of Labor benefited from this temporary loosening (certainly not an abandonment!) of gender divisions in the public sphere. The masculine bonds which restricted female membership in the Order also loosened for a time, although they strengthened again, of course, as the Upheaval subsided and the Order declined.

This powerful intersection between class struggle and gender relations has a British precedent too. Robert Owen's Grand National Consolidated Trades Union, as we saw in Chapter 1, resembled the Knights in its aim to organise all workers under a single banner and its reliance on some level of secrecy, oath taking and fraternal rites. It also set out with enthusiasm to organise women workers into its ranks. Like the Knights it rose and fell in the midst of a social upheaval which in time produced the Chartists.[149] The judgement of J.L. Hammond concerning the Grand National is reminiscent of the Knights: that union, he wrote, organised 'classes like agricultural labourers and women workers for whom combination seemed impossible except under some unusual stimulus of despair or excitement.'[150] Throughout

---

[149] G. Phillips, 'The British Labour Movement Before 1914,' in D. Geary (ed.), *Labour and Socialist Movements in Europe before 1914* (Oxford: Oxford University Press, 1989), pp. 30–31.

[150] J.L. Hammond, *The Age of the Chartists, 1832–1854: A Study of Discontent* (London: Longmans, 1930), p. 265.

the nineteenth century, in other words, *large-scale* and *integrated* female participation in the labour movement remained an exception to a set of very powerful rules. Only in the fires of mass struggle – Hammond's 'unusual stimulus of despair or excitement' – would these rules lose some of their power, and only for a brief time. The American Knights and the British Grand National, in their own times, showed that these rules could be overcome, however briefly.

The British Knights went through no such upheaval. Even in the upsurge of British trade unionism in 1889–91 they played only a minor role. They remained bound to the masculine characteristics of their order even as Knights in America temporarily qualified – but did not entirely drop – them. But the fact that they never had their Great Upheaval should not distract us from the fact that the British Knights missed an obvious chance to make a far greater contribution to the British labour movement – and to boost their own numbers – than they eventually did. Viewed through the lens of their British and Irish history, the American Knights of Labor, for all of their faults and shortcomings, appear even more impressive and unique in their attitudes towards women in the workplace than when viewed from a solely American perspective.

Conclusion:
Lost in Translation?

In 1888, the *Journal of United Labor* carried an unusual story from across the Atlantic. A Bishop Burrows of London, called on to deliver his 1887 Christmas sermon, addressed his congregation as 'fellow citizens' and promised to start with a scriptural injunction from the Epistle of James: 'Go to now, ye rich men, weep and howl for your miseries that shall come upon you.' In the course of a dramatic speech the bishop attacked the Church, declared that he had been living in a fool's paradise and announced his intention to renounce his bishopric, his palace, his seat in the House of Lords, his £10,000 stipend, 'devote his life to the cause of suffering humanity' and henceforth preach socialism on Trafalgar Square. Terence Powderly hailed the bishop's conversion as an outstanding symbol of the righteousness of labour's cause; numerous enquiries reached London from Americans anxious to read more sermons from the infamous and presumably now ex-bishop. Yet Bishop Burrows, much to the consternation of his admirers across the Atlantic, was none other than Herbert Burrows of the Marxist Social-Democratic Federation. His sermon was a small literary effort in *Justice*, the SDF's weekly newspaper. The result, as the *New York Times*'s English correspondent related, was that 'a great deal of amusement has been caused in Socialist circles here.' *Justice*, for its part, commented on the degree of American confusion and gleefully added that the sermon would 'shortly be republished with notes and additions.'[151]

There are few better symbols of transatlantic misunderstandings than this one. And as we have seen in this chapter, these misunderstandings could run across the ocean in both directions. A transnational order like the Knights, with its many contradictory stances and practices across a wide range of cultural, economic and political issues, was in greater danger of being misunderstood than most. That is not to say that British and Irish Knights did not do their best to adapt themselves to their new order as much as the other way around. They took the Order's secrecy more seriously than most American assemblies. They left the titles and the ritual of assembly room practice intact. They relished the educational goals of their order and did their best to follow the American example and turn their assemblies into centres of local working-class social and cultural life. They followed the cultural prescriptions of the Order as far as they could and yet they departed so far from that order when it came to half of the human race.

That departure occurred partly because the American Knights emerged from a tradition favourable to the organisation of women that the British and Irish Knights did not share. It also occurred because American Knights did not – perhaps could not – adequately explain to their brothers in the British Isles the many complexities and contradictions that attended their own stance on gender questions. Left largely to their own devices, British and Irish Knights took what they could and reconciled it with local custom. This was true when it came to economic questions, it was true when it came to fraternal culture and it was true when it came to meeting at hotels and pubs. In each case they understood what they could of their order's positions and ended up excluding women altogether.

As a series of misunderstandings, this far outdid the prank that 'Bishop Burrows' inadvertently played on Powderly and the *Journal of United Labor*. That only cost the General Master Workman a few blushes. The absence of women in the British and Irish assemblies cost them the chance to play the role that many local radicals, feminists and trade unionists thought and hoped they would play – to advance the cause of female trade unionism on a par with the relative triumphs of their American brothers and sisters. But perhaps that is too harsh a verdict. The uniqueness of the Knights on gender as on racial issues was so much a product of the environment in which it rose and fell. The American Knights provided the institutional form for one of the great social upheavals of the late nineteenth century. The British and Irish Knights remained a graft from a successful American Order. In the light of these differences we find yet another reason to suppose that

---

[151] *Justice*, 20 October 1888; *New York Times*, 5 August 1888.

principles and contexts are important, but material conflicts and struggles are just as, if not more, important when it comes to practical and not merely rhetorical support for gender equality, or some moves towards it.

Not all British workers in this story found that misunderstandings became a problem. Coal miners in Lanarkshire took what they knew and wanted from the Knights of Labor's model and used it to build the Sons of Labour. Half secret fraternal order, half conventional coal miners' union, the Sons of Labour allowed the Lanarkshire miners to revive some kind of organisation after their strike was defeated in 1887. The Knights also lent their topical name to the British United Order in Sunderland and then the wider northeast, which initially looked as if it might ape the practices of its namesake but quickly became a run-of-the-mill English benefits society. When the name lost its appeal they soon found a suitable English one instead. These examples, and even George Mitchell's attempt to build a copy of the Knights of Labor among the agricultural workers of Somerset, demonstrate the flexibility of the Order which Robert Weir emphasises so strongly. Indeed, it could function well enough even if it was misunderstood or if its methods were only partially followed; even if it led to the *de facto* exclusion of women as a body. The next chapter, which looks at the Knights and industrial relations broadly conceived, further develops these arguments and sees how Knights interpreted the industrial methods and aims of their order in the workplace as well as in the lodge room.

4
The Knights in Industry

A.J.P. Taylor wrote of Napoleon III that, 'like most of those who study history, he learnt from the mistakes of the past how to make new ones.'[1] The early leaders of the Knights of Labor also drew a number of very important lessons from the history of the American labour movement in the 1870s. The strikes, protests and occasional riots in the United States during that decade ended with the destruction of many trade unions and the decimation of many others after their repression by employers, their hired private detectives, local police, state militias and, especially in 1877, the United States Army. Even when workers won their strikes, their gains often failed to make up for the wages lost during them. Uriah Stephens, Terence Powderly and most other leading Knights concluded that strikes were best avoided wherever possible. Arbitration and negotiation with employers, they argued, would settle the wage disputes of the future. Over time, workers would educate and then emancipate themselves from the wage system altogether through a network of cooperative enterprise.[2]

The struggles of the 1880s put these lessons to a severe test. The staggering growth of the Knights of Labor from 100,000 members in 1885 to nearly 1 million in 1886 came about as the result of widespread strikes, especially the victory of Knights over Jay Gould, the most notorious speculator of the day, in a strike against his Southwestern railroad system in 1885. American workers entered the assemblies to strike and win, or they struck first and joined the Knights afterwards. Many Knights conducted boycotts, a tactic adapted from the struggles of the Irish Land League at the beginning of the decade, to bring their employers to heel without leaving work. During the Great Upheaval, American workers seldom

---

[1] A.J.P. Taylor, 'Men of 1862,' in C.J. Wrigley (ed.), *AJP Taylor: From Napoleon to the Second International* (London: Faber and Faber, 1993), p. 279.
[2] Ware, *Labor Movement*, p. 117.

had the patience or the desire to submit their grievances to arbitration. American employers also remained unwilling to deal with organised labour unless the threat of successful strike action left them no choice. They desired mainly to wipe out the labour movement altogether, and their attacks on the assemblies were a major cause of the Order's decline. Only the leaders of the Knights of Labor seemed interested in replacing conflict with conciliation. At the same time, the Order's experiments in cooperative enterprise generally failed because of either a lack of capital or the obstruction of rival corporations. Powderly recognised these contradictions when he wrote to a friend that as a

> Teacher of important and much-needed reforms, [the Order] has been obliged to practice differently from her teachings. Advocating arbitration and conciliation as first steps in labor disputes she has been forced to take upon her shoulders the responsibility of the aggressor first and, when hope of arbitrating and conciliation failed, to beg of the opposing side to do what we should have applied for in the first instance. Advising against strikes we have been in the midst of them.[3]

Like Napoleon III, the General Master Workman found that the lessons of previous decades did not always solve the problems of the present.[4]

The Knights applied the same lessons in Britain and Ireland. They preached arbitration as the solution to industrial conflict, and if that failed they practised the boycott instead of strikes wherever possible. They also planned cooperative establishments that would slowly emancipate local workers from their dependence on employers. Most of these tactics were already part of the landscape of British industrial relations. Formal arbitration procedures and informal negotiations between workers and management had existed for some time in major British industries, and Britain was the home of the cooperative movement. British workers had not yet adapted the boycott from Irish agrarian struggles to industrial conditions, as American Knights had, but the tactics of the Land League were well known across Britain and Ireland. Yet Knights found the same contradictions awaiting them there as in the United States, between their desire for arbitration and the unwillingness of many employers and workers to submit to it, and between their attempts to build cooperative enterprises and their lack of the funds necessary to make them successful.

These contradictions shaped the Order's British and Irish history. The glassworkers' assembly, LA3504, faced stern opposition from management at the largest British glass manufacturer, Pilkington Bros in St Helens,

---

[3] Quoted in Ware, *Labour Movement*, p. 375.
[4] See, for instance, Foner, *History of the Labor Movement*, II, pp. 75–88.

which curtailed the growth of the assembly and contributed to its downfall. At Hartley's in Sunderland, and Chance Bros in Spon Lane, Knights established cordial relations with management but as economic conditions in the glass industry worsened over the course of the 1880s, those relations also worsened and the assembly collapsed after several long and fruitless strikes. Employers were not the only opponents of arbitration. Dockers in Liverpool, hollowware turners in the Black Country and stove-grate workers in Rotherham all left the assemblies after Knights insisted that they submit to arbitration rather than embroil the Order in costly and risky strikes. The British and Irish Knights also failed to take account of changing economic circumstances, and the changing expectations of British workers, towards the end of the 1880s. In the depressed economic conditions that prevailed during the middle of the decade, when the prospects for a successful strike remained slim, an order that practised arbitration, often quite successfully, could prove popular. As economic conditions improved, and workers consequently developed a more militant attitude towards industrial relations, they flocked instead to organisations – particularly the 'new unions' – more willing to lead them on strike.

Conflict and competition between the Knights and the new unions is explored in more depth in Chapter 6. We deal here with the ways in which the Knights implemented or failed to implement their preferred industrial tactics, with the role that employers played in the successes and failures of the British and Irish Knights and with the effects that both had on the growth and then the decline of the Order in Britain and Ireland. This chapter also builds on the previous one. There we saw how British and Irish Knights faithfully followed the cultural and organisational prescriptions of their order, although misunderstandings and contextual differences meant that they never organised women as American Knights did. Here we find that British and Irish Knights were equally faithful to the instructions of their American leaders when it came to industrial relations, even when doing so was unpopular among their own members or among workers they hoped to organise. Both cases, moreover, provide insights into the reasons why British and Irish workers joined the Knights and why they followed its prescriptions so closely, even at the cost of their own success.

Arbitration, Boycotts and Cooperation

The British National Assembly of the Knights of Labor, as its framers made clear in 1891, sought 'no conflict with Capital.' They assured employers that the Assembly would not sanction 'any unreasonable or unjust demands made by any of its members,' but that 'if conflict becomes necessary, in defence of their interests, the responsibility will be carried on as long as necessity or ability exists.'⁵ These lines stated perfectly the attitude of the American Knights of Labor, or at least the attitude of most of its leaders, towards individual employers. Their desire to substitute negotiation for conflict was based on more than an understanding of the defeats of the 1870s: they wished to see reason replace force as the decisive factor in industrial relations. Workers, they felt, never possessed the strength and resources available to employers; as Knights educated themselves in political and economic principles, and as the growth of Bureaus of Labor Statistics across the United States provided workers and employers with the empirical evidence needed to negotiate fairly, reason would become a more powerful ally than force. This was an article of faith for Terence Powderly and his associates. It also became a guiding principle, almost a dogma, of Knights on the other side of the Atlantic.

Arbitration had a long history in British industry. After the repeal of the Combination Acts legalised trade unions in 1824 and 1825, unions and employers in a number of trades slowly began to meet to fix wages and hours, and to settle other grievances before they resulted in open conflict. The joint board of workers and employers, formed in the Nottingham hosiery trade in 1860 with an equal number of representatives from each side and a chairman from outside to break any deadlock, became the model for formal arbitration in a growing number of trades.⁶ The boot and shoemaking, cotton spinning, iron foundry and coal mining industries all established joint boards of employers and employees in the 1870s and 1880s.⁷ Trades Union Congresses in the latter decade passed resolutions declaring, in one example, that these boards were 'very necessary and would bring about a better understanding between them and secure settlement of vexed questions affecting the interests of both.'⁸ Liberals agreed that arbitration and conciliation remained the best method of resolving any industrial dispute.⁹ Even socialists, who might have been expected to want and support as many strikes as possible, generally regarded them as unhelpful distractions from more important tasks. They argued that the money and energy spent on strikes was much better spent on agitation for socialism; the logic of market forces, they added, meant that any gains made through strikes were only temporary, and only complete social transformation could ensure workers a higher standard of living.¹⁰

---

⁵ *Preamble of the British National Assembly*, p. 2.
⁶ I.G. Sharp, *Industrial Conciliation and Arbitration in Great Britain* (London: Allen and Unwin, 1950), pp. 1–7.
⁷ V. Gore, 'Rank and File Dissent,' in Wrigley, *History of British Industrial Relations*, p. 51.
⁸ Quoted in Sharpe, *Industrial Conciliation*, p. 4.
⁹ Kirk, *Class, Continuity, and Change*, p. 189.
¹⁰ V. Rabinovitch, *British Marxist Socialism and Trade Unionism: The Attitudes, Experiences*

When the Knights arrived in Britain and Ireland, arbitration was already a common and popular means of settling disputes.

The Knights preferred and practised arbitration from the very beginning until the very end of their history. When English glassworkers created LA3504 they immediately formed committees to meet and negotiate with their employers. Managers at Hartley's in Sunderland and Chance Bros in Spon Lane, they claimed in 1885, 'have at different times treated our committee with great kindness.'[11] Managers from Pilkington's in St Helens were not inclined to meet with any committee of organised employees; but the *St Helen's Examiner* still stressed that 'arbitration is advocated in preference to strikes as a mode of settling disputes' among local Knights.[12] Assemblies outside the glass trades adopted the same stance, particularly in the Black Country, where some form of arbitration took place in most of the small trades that dominated the region. Trade unionists in the chainmaking industry, as Sheila Blackburn writes, saw conciliation boards as 'infinitely preferable' to strike action.[13] The Midland Counties Trade Federation sent 82 deputations to negotiate with employers in 1888 and 160 in 1889.[14] The emphasis that Powderly placed on arbitration as opposed to conflict was particularly well-suited to the regions in Britain and Ireland where the Knights of Labor established their longest and largest presence.

The Black Country assemblies had strong grounds for preferring talking to strikes. 'All our Assemblies are of mixed trades, no trade or branch even having a large representation,' Richard Hill, the recording secretary of LA7952, told the General Assembly in 1887. 'While being exposed at many points,' he continued, 'we are much more liable than an ordinary trades-union to the outbreak of industrial hostilities.' The 'hitherto undisciplined character of our army,' composed mainly of unskilled workers with no prior experience of trade unions, represented another danger.[15] With the assemblies in danger of becoming embroiled in a series of costly strikes, none of which they had the numbers or resources to wage effectively, the need for successful negotiation became doubly important. In 1887 and 1888, the *Birmingham Daily Gazette* reported in 1889, 'nearly every employer of labour in West Bromwich has been politely asked for an "interview"

---

and *Activities of the Social-Democratic Federation, 1884–1901* (unpublished PhD thesis, University of Sussex, 1977), p. 247.

[11] Quoted in T.C. Barker, *The Glassmakers: Pilkington, The Rise of an International Company, 1826–1976* (London: Wiedenfeld and Nicholson, 1977), p. 180.

[12] Quoted in *JUL*, 25 April, 1886.

[13] Blackburn, *Sweated Labour*, p. 63.

[14] E. Taylor, *The Working Class Movement in the Black Country, 1863–1914* (unpublished PhD thesis, Keele University, 1974), pp. 278–79.

[15] *Proceedings of the GA* (1887), pp. 1770–72.

by "representatives of the employees."' Even the *Gazette*, which always opposed the Order's presence in the Birmingham area, admitted that Knights approached employers 'most courteously and sensibly,' that 'a dozen petty complaints have been quietly investigated and settled by this means' and that 'the employers are continually conferring on moot points to mutual advantage.'[16] In January 1890, *Reynolds's* claimed that Black Country Knights had engaged in 'only three strikes in four years, while hundreds of disputes have been settled.'[17]

A dispute at the Brades Steel Works at Oldbury in the beginning of 1889 illustrates the methods that Knights used to settle grievances. Brades employed 250 people, of whom 180 belonged to the Order. Knights claimed that 80 of them had for some time worked ten and a half hours, instead of the customary nine and a half, and 24 of them sent a respectful letter to George Heston, the manager of the works, asking that their hours be reduced. They signed their names in a circle to prevent Heston from singling out any of them as a leader. When Heston failed to reply, they sent another letter, which also received no reply. The Knights met in their local assembly and satisfied themselves that they had done all they could to peacefully solve the dispute. They then waited on the leaders of the district assembly, which called a special meeting and resolved to send one final letter before considering more drastic action. These attempts to exhaust every possible alternative to a strike won the Knights praise from the *Smethwick Weekly News* which, like the *Birmingham Daily Gazette*, usually attacked the assemblies. The Knights, claimed the *News*, 'have no desire to resort to extreme measures, but are willing to exhaust all the resources of civilization in bringing about a good understanding.'[18]

Knights elsewhere in the Black Country followed the same pattern. In Walsall, Haydn Sanders, the socialist town councillor and the Master Workman of LA454, claimed that 'he had no desire to set men and masters against each other' and added that 'strikes were always best avoided.'[19] Though known best for his polemical turn of phrase, as we will see in the following chapter, Sanders was also a capable negotiator. Thanks to his leadership, local bridle bit makers won a 5 percent increase in addition to a further 10 percent over the preceding year, all without needing to strike, while the cased hame, solid hame and awl blademakers, representing other local saddlery trades, also presented their claims and in the latter case managed to negotiate a more favourable list of prices from their employers

---

[16] *Birmingham Daily Gazette*, 18 February 1889.
[17] *Reynolds's*, 5 January 1890.
[18] *Smethwick Weekly News*, 9 March 1889.
[19] *Walsall Observer*, 4 January 1890.

without needing to take industrial action.[20] Indeed, as trade improved in 1888 and 1889, Sanders's ability to arbitrate effectively with employers brought workers in many small trades into the Order as a body and rapidly swelled the membership of LA454.[21] At the same time, Knights in Smethwick and West Bromwich negotiated concessions for workers in the tinplate and vice making trades.[22] In Wolverhampton, a Knight became one of three workers to sit on a Board of Conciliation convened by the town's Trades Council.[23]

Far from the harbingers of industrial strife, British Knights appeared moderate in their demands and devoted to industrial peace. 'The Knights of Labour are not Socialists,' their supporters told the *Birmingham Gazette* in 1889. 'They do not look upon employers as enemies.'[24] The press, claimed one Knight in Dudley, had convinced him that the Knights were all 'Socialists and dynamiters' until he found out for himself that 'they respected the rights of the masters as well as those of the men, fair play all round being their motto.'[25] But socialists, as we have seen, also had their reasons for preferring to avoid strikes wherever possible, and Sanders was not the only socialist Knight to counsel arbitration instead. Samuel Reeves, a major figure in Liverpool's socialist movement and a leading figure in Bootle's LA443, gave a lecture in October 1889 entitled 'Arbitration v Strikes, or Why I Became a Knight of Labour.' 'The object of the Knights of Labour,' he stated in another speech, 'was to put an end to strikes.'[26] The commitment of British and Irish Knights to arbitration cut across ideological lines.

They also experimented with the boycott as an alternative to strike action. American Knights, many of whom were first- or second-generation Irish immigrants, had adapted this tactic from the Irish Land League's struggles against uncooperative landlords and their agents, and used it against employers who refused to deal with organised labour. The long lists of boycotted companies that appeared in the *Journal of United Labor* during the 1880s testifies to the popularity of the boycott as a means for workers to force employers to grant concessions or recognise their union without sacrificing wages and risking their jobs to go on strike. Newspapers in areas where the British Knights were active certainly feared that they would introduce the boycott into British industrial life. When Knights registered their new British National Assembly under the Trade Union Acts in 1891,

---

[20] *Halfpenny Weekly*, 30 November 1889; *Walsall Observer*, 14 December 1889, 25 January 1890.
[21] *Walsall Observer*, 4 January 1890.
[22] *Stourbridge, Brierley Hill and County Express*, 1 March 1890.
[23] *Wolverhampton Chronicle*, 2 April 1890.
[24] *Birmingham Daily Gazette*, 22 February 1889.
[25] *Stourbridge, Brierley Hill and County Express*, 1 March 1890.
[26] *Bootle Times*, 1 February 1890.

the *Smethwick Weekly News* announced that 'the Registrar of Friendly Societies will shortly be asked to legalise boycotting.'[27]

That was hyperbole, of course, but British Knights did boycott several firms in the Birmingham area. In 1888 they boycotted the *Birmingham Mail* after receiving criticism from that newspaper. In the same year they boycotted the Mayor of West Bromwich, who owned the only grocery stores in the area that did not give in to the local early closing movement and allow their employees half a day's rest per week. According to the colourful account provided by the *Birmingham Daily Gazette*, the assemblies agreed to commence the boycott. Then:

> The interdict was conveyed from inn to inn; each Master Workman read it out in the presence of the Venerable Sage and the Unknown Knights before the Silent Globe and the Knightly Lance, and members all were warned to have neither truck, nor faith, nor sale, nor barter with, of, or from the interdicted one.[28]

Knights in Preston also threatened to boycott *Commonweal*, the organ of the Socialist League, unless it was sold locally through one of their members in the stationery business. 'An injury to one is the concern of all in our order,' they concluded, 'and we are not anxious to purchase if our brother Mr. Hall is to be the injured party.'[29]

In all these cases the Knights were unsuccessful. They claimed to have reduced the circulation of the *Birmingham Mail* by 30,000 during their action, yet it was claimed simultaneously that 'the *Mail* was to be found in the very sanctuaries of the Order.'[30] According to the *Birmingham Daily Gazette*, the Mayor of West Bromwich never even realised that his stores were subject to a boycott until it appeared in the newspapers. The wives of local Knights also joined the boycott but only for a time. One, claimed the *Gazette*, told an assistant that 'she had gone elsewhere till her John had forgotten about that Knights of Labour stuff,' and then promptly returned to shop at the mayor's stores.[31] Their boycott ended after the mayor's employees wrote to the *Gazette* in his defence, and after the hero of many local Knights, Henry George, described the boycott as 'ridiculous' during a visit in May 1889.[32] The editors of *Commonweal* also gained a reprieve as the Preston Knights disappeared before they could put a boycott into effect.

---

[27] *Smethwick Weekly News*, 11 July 1891.

[28] *Birmingham Daily Gazette*, 23 February 1889.

[29] Letter from James Riley, 18 June, 1887, 2572, Socialist League Archives, International Institute of Social History.

[30] *Birmingham Daily Gazette*, 23 February 1889.

[31] *Birmingham Daily Gazette*, 23 February 1889.

[32] *Birmingham Daily Gazette*, 23 and 28 February and 15 May 1889.

In all these cases the Knights lacked the numbers and discipline to make their boycotts effective. Where American Knights mustered tens or hundreds of *thousands* of workers to sanction uncooperative employers, British Knights mustered only tens or hundreds. When they and their wives continued to patronise the offending firms it is not surprising that the Mayor of West Bromwich had to learn of his boycott from the press. The only kind of embargo that Knights practised with any success was at the workplace, when Knights refused to cooperate with non-union workers until employers removed them. In a workshop at Rotherham, for instance, where the Order organised 90 of the 100 workers, Knights opposed the continued employment of a man who agreed to replace another worker for less than the prevailing wage. After pressuring their employer, the boycotted man was dismissed.[33] In any boycott wider than an individual workshop, however, the fears of the *Smethwick Weekly News* remained unfounded.

The Knights of Labor always maintained that workers would never receive a fair share of the fruits of their labour until they abolished the wage system and replaced it with a cooperative commonwealth. To bring that day closer, Knights were encouraged to form cooperative enterprises of their own that would, with time, remove private firms from the industrial landscape. The General Executive Board of the Knights of Labor bought a coal mine at Cannelburg, Indiana, as a symbol of the new order and spent more than $20,000 on it over the next two years. After the local railroad refused to extend a siding to the mine the whole scheme collapsed, and the Knights sold it at a loss in symbolic as well as financial terms. Most of the Order's cooperative enterprises were more local affairs, however. When many assemblies built their own assembly hall they established grocery or general stores on the ground floor. Others began cooperative workshops. Where the Cannelburg experiment ended in dismal failure, some of these local ventures survived and prospered for as long as the assemblies that created them.[34]

British and Irish Knights certainly wanted to emulate the cooperative achievements of their American cousins. Richard Hill told the *Journal of United Labor* in 1887 that 'co-operation, productive and distributive, is now under consideration,' and added that members were now studying the subject with great interest.[35] Soon afterwards, as Charles Chamberlain told the *Smethwick Weekly News* in 1889, Knights established a special voluntary fund for members who wanted to invest in a future cooperative

---

[33] *Smethwick Weekly News*, 11 July 1891.

[34] S.B. Leikin, *The Practical Utopians: American Workers and the Cooperative Movement in the Gilded Age* (Detroit: Wayne State University Press, 2005), pp. 66–67.

[35] *JUL*, 10 December 1887.

venture.³⁶ That venture, as we saw in the previous chapter, was to have been a dedicated assembly hall in Smethwick with a library, reading rooms and a ground floor leased to shopkeepers on the American model. They also hoped to create a cooperative workshop of some kind, and in 1889 these plans came together in the shape of the Smethwick and District Knights of Labour Co-Operative Society.³⁷ In Walsall, Haydn Sanders promised saddle tree workers on strike that the Knights would provide £100 towards a cooperative saddle tree works designed to free them from wage slavery altogether.³⁸

These plans all failed for a very simple reason: not enough money. An order that struggled to mount an effective boycott against a local grocer could hardly be expected to raise the £10,000 that Knights estimated they needed for their hall, library and shop space. Even as Chamberlain told the *Smethwick Weekly News* about the special cooperative fund, he admitted that 'we have not gone in for this much up to the present.'³⁹ The unskilled workers and struggling craftsmen that Knights organised in the Black Country could not provide the capital needed to make cooperation work, and the recent failure of another cooperative society in Smethwick made them even more cautious with their limited savings.⁴⁰ The Walsall assembly rose and fell too quickly to give anything like £100 to the saddle tree workers. Knights in Derry came the closest to building a cooperative enterprise when they mortgaged a hall that they used as a library and for meetings and cultural events. Even there they were only able to keep the hall afloat by leasing it to other societies. Elsewhere, Knights lacked the numbers, the money or sufficient time to do anything more than talk about cooperation. Chamberlain argued that 'so far as we fail to put that principle into operation we shall fail as an organisation.'⁴¹ Judged by this impossible standard, the Order in Britain and Ireland was a miserable failure.

Its record on cooperation, as with arbitration and the boycott, also leads to other conclusions. These tactics were, of course, already part of the British and Irish labour movements' repertoire. Craftsmen in the Black Country, for instance, did not need Powderly's advice to seek arbitration with their employers. The impulse to form cooperative enterprises did not begin with the arrival in Britain of the Knights of Labor. The boycott

---

36 *Smethwick Weekly News*, 2 March 1889.
37 *Birmingham Daily Gazette*, 23 February 1889. This society is mentioned once in the *Report of the Chief Registrar of Friendly Societies, For the Year Ending 31st December 1890*, Part A, p. 133, in HCPP. The society only appears in this one report.
38 *Walsall Observer*, 4 January 1890.
39 *Birmingham Daily Gazette*, 23 February 1889; *Smethwick Weekly News*, 2 March 1889.
40 *Smethwick Weekly News*, 2 March 1889.
41 *Smethwick Weekly News*, 2 March 1889.

was an Irish innovation that the Knights reimported into Britain. But the fact remains that in each case British and Irish Knights tried to follow the industrial tactics that their American leaders prescribed for them as closely as possible. When Michael Davitt commented on the growth of the British assemblies in 1890, he observed that 'the workingmen enrolled in such branches can be more or less influenced in their strike policies by the orders of General-Master Workman Powderly.'[42] Indeed, British Knights were more likely to follow Powderly's instructions regarding strikes than most American workers who joined the Order during the Great Upheaval. As in the previous chapter, we find that British Knights remained truer to the principles of their order, as defined by its leaders, than many in the land of its birth. As in the previous chapter, we might also conclude that British Knights adapted themselves to their order at least as much as the other way around. In so doing, however, they found themselves entangled in the same contradictions that plagued American Knights. The first of these concerned those employers who did not share their desire for arbitration and peaceful industrial relations.

Employers and the Knights

The Knights of Labor, as we saw in the previous chapter, were born in an atmosphere markedly hostile to organised labour. The upheavals of the mid-1880s, when the Knights of Labor rose to the peak of their strength, only convinced employers further of the need to identify and remove labour organisations from their own concerns, and as the Great Upheaval began to subside it was replaced by a fierce counter-attack from employers who sought to reverse the gains made by organised labour in the middle of the decade. Where earlier scholarship attributed the decline of the Knights of Labor mainly to internal conflict, inept leadership and internecine conflict between the Knights and the trade unions, recent historians have placed greater emphasis on this 'employer counter-offensive' as the most salient cause of the Order's disintegration in the late 1880s and early 1890s. In these conditions, naturally enough, arbitration remained unworkable.

Employers in Britain and Ireland never became as hostile to organised labour as their American counterparts, and seldom employed the surveillance and repression that American employers regularly directed against the unions. Indeed, British Knights sometimes established cordial relations with employers. One manager, after conceding a wage increase at his firm, 'told the representative of the Knights of Labour who arranged the matter, that if that was an example of how they did their business they would always have his

---

[42] Davitt, 'Labor Tendencies in Great Britain.'

sympathy and support.'[43] At the Brades Steel Works and at the great pump and engine-making works of Messrs Tangye in West Bromwich, Knights and managers soon consulted with each other to prevent grievances from flaring up into strikes. We have already seen that even hostile newspapers like the *Birmingham Daily Gazette* and the *Smethwick Weekly News* were willing to praise the Knights for their determination to exhaust all other possibilities before going on strike. Most employers, however, remained unwilling to meet with the Knights or, alternatively, to grant the concessions the Knights requested. In Britain and Ireland, as in the United States, Knights found that arbitration often worked only after they convinced employers that a strike, or the credible threat of a strike, awaited them if negotiations failed.

Knights learned this lesson very early in the Black Country. In 1887 and 1888, even as the Order's representatives met with local employers to establish a basis for future negotiations, the Knights conducted several strikes in the area to convince employers, as well as any potential members, that 'the leaders meant "business."'[44] The Knights fought these battles without admitting that they led them, but word spread that the assemblies stood prepared to use forceful means if reason failed.[45] Even Messrs Tangye, which soon developed a friendly relationship with the assemblies, only agreed to negotiations with the Knights after they organised most of the workforce and declared their intention to strike if their demands were not met.[46] Knights in Derry led a strike by workers at the distillery of Messrs Watts, and won wages increases for both skilled and unskilled employees, the reinstatement of overtime wages, sick pay and free coal for the workers. The leading partner in the firm also promised to 'visit personally each department of the firm, inquire into the men's grievances, and remedy them as far as possible.'[47] Arbitration in Derry emerged directly out of conflict.

This strategy carried substantial risk. The first assembly of dockers in Liverpool in 1884 and 1885, as James Sexton later explained in his autobiography, secretly planned a strike that would force the shipping companies and other employers on the waterfront to deal with the Knights. Their strike, as Sexton wrote, 'was a lamentable, woeful, total failure.' They lacked sufficient savings to continue it for more than several days and employers placed its leaders on a blacklist. Many of them never found employment on the docks again.[48]

[43] *Stourbridge, Brierley Hill and County Express*, 1 March 1890.
[44] *Birmingham Daily Gazette*, 18 February 1889.
[45] *Birmingham Daily Gazette*, 18 February 1889.
[46] *Birmingham Daily Gazette*, 18 February 1889.
[47] *JUL*, 20 November 1890.
[48] Sexton, *Agitator*, pp. 80–81.

Many other British employers remained opposed to organised labour as well. The Sons of Labour, as we saw in the previous chapter, faced Lanarkshire coal masters who worked together to blacklist union activists. Knights in Preston predicted that 'when it becomes known to the employers that we have started it [the Order] here we shall be left to their mercy, which will cause a few thousands of us to be thrown out of work.'[49] Knights at the Hoyland Silkstone Colliery, near Barnsley, were ordered in 1890 to sever their connection with the Order or lose their jobs.[50] Charles Chamberlain told an interviewer in March 1889, that 'when a little dispute took place some time ago one of our lodge rooms was watched night after night for more than a month.'[51] British and Irish Knights never faced the Pinkertons, *agent provocateurs* and violent repression that plagued the American assemblies. But the blacklisting and surveillance that some British employers did employ against organised labour constrained the Order's growth in Britain and Ireland on occasion. The most significant example of this concerned the glassworkers of LA3504, the oldest and largest assembly in the country, whose growth was restricted by opposition from employers which ultimately led to its demise in 1893.

The Knights established LA3504 at a crucial period in the English window glass industry. The three main firms, Chance Bros at Spon Lane, Pilkington's at St Helens and Hartley's at Sunderland, had established a cartel in the 1860s to regulate the prices and output of window glass and their own respective market share. In the next two decades, however, their cartel broke apart. First, they faced growing competition from Belgian glass manufacturers, who could not be induced to join the cartel; instead they flooded the English market with Belgian glass, reducing prices and profits for the English manufacturers. Second, Pilkington's invested more heavily in new plants than its two major English competitors, and as the cartel collapsed it soon dominated the domestic production of window glass.[52]

To continue this growth, the managers at Pilkington's brooked no compromise with organised labour. In 1878 they broke up the Sheet Glassmakers' Association after a failed strike and rehired the Association's members at a lower rate of pay. When Knights arrived in St Helens to hold the first convention of the Universal Federation of Window-Glass Workers in 1884, Pilkington's resolutely opposed them. One of their employees chaired a public meeting called by the Knights; the company dismissed him

---

[49] David Whittle to Powderly, 13 April 1887, Box 32, TVP.
[50] *Sheffield and Rotherham Independent*, 10 October 1890.
[51] *Smethwick Weekly News*, 2 March 1889.
[52] N. McCord, *North East England: An Economic and Social History* (London: Batsford Academic, 1979), p. 143.

the following day. Joseph French, the secretary of LA3504, told Powderly in 1887 that Pilkington's was 'continually discharging our members for no other reason than that they belong to our Society.'[53] When the Universal Federation held subsequent congresses at St Helens in 1886 and 1888 to encourage organisation at Pilkington's, the company kept a note of the employees who attended meetings called by the Knights and asked the Chief Constable of the town to protect their property against sabotage by the Order's representatives.[54]

This simple and effective policy made arbitration impossible. When French tried to set up a meeting anyway, managers told him that 'the Firm would not discuss the matter with any one only their own men.' Powderly suggested an alternative strategy: the boycott. 'Get the manufacturers who do treat their men properly to join with you in putting a stop to the sale of the St Helens glass,' he advised French, 'and by that means, bring Mr Pilkington to a recognition of the claims of humanity.' French demurred. 'You must consider Pilkingtons are the largest producers in the world,' he explained to the General Master Workman, 'and besides that they have large retail warehouses in very near all the large towns in the United Kingdom so you will understand at once that that line of action is out of the question.' French wanted instead to organise a strike to bring Pilkington's to the negotiating table.[55] Powderly, however, was not keen on the idea and French eventually proved unable to muster anything like the number of workers needed to launch an effective strike. Pilkington's also operated a staggered contract system, where workers finished their contracts and applied for new ones in small batches and not all at once, which made it more difficult for large numbers of employees to strike without breaking their contract. James Brown, who replaced French as the secretary of LA3504, told Beatrice Potter (soon Webb) that this system presented the main obstacle to organisation at Pilkington's.[56] In short, opposition from the company ensured that the St Helens preceptory failed to established a permanent presence there, let alone negotiate with management.

This failure was a severe setback for LA3504, as Pilkington's was by far the largest window glass manufacturer in England. Henry Pelling concludes that 'the failure at St Helens was indeed decisive for the whole English [glass] Assembly.'[57] At Chance Bros and Hartley's, where relations

[53] Joseph French to Powderly, 30 March 1887, Box 32, TVP.
[54] Barker, *The Glassmakers*, pp. 179–80.
[55] Joseph French to Powderly, 3 May 1887, Box 33, TVP.
[56] James Brown to Beatrice Potter, 30 November 1891, Webb Collection. E.-A, 43.398, British Library of Political and Economic Science.
[57] Pelling, 'Knights in Britain,' p. 317.

between management and the Knights were initially cordial, Knights also found that economic difficulties put serious strains on their goodwill towards the end of the 1880s. Those firms suffered from a competitive disadvantage against Pilkington's as they had failed to invest in new plant and production techniques. Competition from Belgian glass manufacturers, and the McKinley Tariff of 1890, which protected American industries against imported goods including glass, further reduced their market share at home and abroad.[58] To maintain profitability these firms had to increase their investment in new machinery, squeeze more out of their workers or both.

The end of the decade saw two minor strikes at Hartley's as the firm sped up production without a corresponding increase in wages.[59] The major test of amicable relations between the Knights and the firm, however, came in 1890 when Hartley's introduced the new continuous tank system, which had greatly improved productivity at Pilkington's. At the beginning of the following year the company then imposed a 10 percent wage reduction on skilled glassworkers. They went on strike in response.[60] In July 1891, Chance Bros followed suit with a new piecework wage system. Glassworkers there claimed the new system reduced their weekly pay by as much as 20 or 25 percent and introduced greater uncertainty about their earnings. Chance Brothers countered that 'glass is being sold at St Helens and elsewhere cheaper than they can make it, and in order to compete with these places they have suffered a considerable loss.'[61] The company refused to prove that assertion to their employees. Representatives from the Spon Lane preceptory then travelled to the United States to consult with the glassworkers of LA300 and the Order's General Executive Board. When they returned, and after they failed to broker a last-minute settlement with management, the company locked out its workers at the end of July.[62]

The entire membership of LA3504 was now on strike. Knights in Sunderland only had to pay strike pay for skilled glassworkers, as unskilled workers at Hartley's belonged to the National Labour Union. Knights at Spon Lane, however, had to subsidise the unskilled workers thrown out of employment during the strike themselves, as James Brown complained

[58] McCord, *North East England*, p. 146; Pelling, 'Knights in Britain,' p. 320.
[59] *Sunderland Daily Echo*, 20 and 22 June 1888, 6 December 1888.
[60] *Sunderland Daily Echo*, 2 February 1891. Catherine Ross instead claims that the firm cancelled a 10 percent wage increase agreed to the previous year – but in any case, the effect was the same. See C. Ross, *The Development of the Glass Industry on the Rivers Tyne and Wear, 1700–1900* (unpublished PhD thesis, Newcastle University, 1982), p. 515.
[61] *Smethwick Weekly News*, 18 July 1891.
[62] *Smethwick Weekly News*, 18 July 1891.

to General Secretary-Treasurer John Hayes in September.⁶³ The financial problems caused by the strike also opened rifts between the Spon Lane and Sunderland preceptories. Workers at Chance Brothers, as Robert Robertson informed Hayes in September, 'thought after so long a struggle of twenty nine weeks for Sunderland and we nine we should have got assistance before now, as we paid to Sunderland Bros while we were at work ten per cent of our wages to assist them.'⁶⁴ James Brown added that 'the Spon Lane men are continually asking how it is we receive nothing from the General Assembly.'⁶⁵ Glassworkers at Chance Bros found that the Smethwick Local Board even refused to let them hold a boxing display to raise money for the strikers.⁶⁶ The firm refused to resolve the dispute through arbitration, and rumours began to circulate at the end of 1891 that individual strikers were returning to work.⁶⁷ Some Knights at Spon Lane remained on strike as late as February 1892, but the strike, and the Spon Lane preceptory, came to an end soon afterwards.

The dispute at Hartley's ended on more favourable terms. In November 1891, the Knights and the firm agreed to arbitration and there were signs that they might re-establish friendly relations. But then both sides were faced with a very different kind of disaster. After only two weeks back on the job, a fire destroyed most of the works and Hartley's went into receivership. The glassworkers were again thrown into unemployment. Brown told Hayes in August 1892 that 'we are doing our best to keep the members of our Assembly together so as to be ready for anything that may turn up in our own trade so as we will be able to get the best terms we can.'⁶⁸ A new firm restarted part of the works at the end of 1892, raising Brown's hopes, but it closed again for good in 1894.⁶⁹ The history of LA3504 ended with it. 'It is very easy to see how our Assembly has gone down,' Brown wrote in August 1892. 'It was through a few giving in at Spon Lane during the strike and the others fell away.'⁷⁰

Terence Powderly might have predicted that the glassworkers' strikes would end badly. He boasted in his autobiography that he never ordered a strike in his 15 years as General Master Workman and helped to end

---

⁶³ Ross, *Development of the Glass Industry*, pp. 515–17; James Brown to Hayes, 17 September 1891, Box 10, John W. Hayes Papers (JHP), Catholic University of America History Research Center and University Archives.
⁶⁴ Letter from Robert Robertson to Hayes, 14 September 1891, Box 10, JHP.
⁶⁵ Letter from James Brown to Hayes, 17 September 1891, Box 10, JHP.
⁶⁶ *Smethwick Telephone*, 14 November 1891.
⁶⁷ *Smethwick Weekly News*, 12 December 1891; *JUL*, 17 December 1891.
⁶⁸ James Brown to Hayes, 31 August 1892, Box 10, JHP.
⁶⁹ Ross, *Development of the Glass Industry*, pp. 517–18.
⁷⁰ James Brown to Hayes, 31 August 1892, Box 10, JHP.

many of them.[71] But unless Knights managed to find employers who were willing to allow labour organisations at their concerns, and who were as willing as the Knights to submit their disputes to reason rather than force, arbitration remained impossible. British and Irish Knights occasionally encountered such magnanimous employers. More often, they found that the friendliness of management was directly linked to their own ability to strike and win if necessary. Messrs Tangye in West Bromwich and Messrs Watts in Derry became enthusiastic negotiators after they faced a strike, or the credible threat of one. When employers remained implacably opposed to organised labour, or when economic circumstances forced them to abandon their earlier goodwill, Knights were only left with the option to strike. The glassworkers found this to their cost. But employers were not the only ones to view the Order's methods with suspicion. As trade improved at the end of the 1880s, the Knights found that many workers could become as implacably opposed to arbitration as the managers of Pilkington's.

Arbitration and the Workers

The Knights of Labor arrived in Britain and Ireland amidst a severe depression in trade that lasted, with only brief patches of growth, until 1888. Successive Trades Union Congresses reported a falling away in membership. The Amalgamated Society of Engineers, an established union in a trade crucial to British industry, found that as many as one-eighth of its members were out of work. With so many unemployed workers ready to replace those who walked out, strikes remained infrequent and it is no surprise that the TUC placed its hopes on arbitration as an alternative. From 1888 until the end of the decade, however, trade began to improve. As unemployment fell, the number of strikes rose from 517 in 1888 to 1,211 in 1889, and the number of strikers increased from 119,000 in 1888 to around 400,000 in 1890.[72] These were the years of the New Unionism, when a rash of new organisations representing hitherto unorganised, and particularly unskilled, workers became a powerful presence within the British labour movement and engaged in a series of large, bitter and often successful strikes. Between 1886 and 1890 the outlook of many British workers changed from resignation to militancy, from an understanding that arbitration remained their best hope, where possible, to the belief that strikes were the fastest and most effective way to wring concessions from their employers.

The British and Irish assemblies began at the height of the depression, between 1884 and 1886. Their penchant for arbitration and their unwillingness

[71] Powderly, *The Path I Trod*, p. 105.
[72] Cronin, 'Strikes,' p. 89.

to countenance strikes were doubly popular in the Black Country. Workers there were not noted for engaging in strikes. Poor trade in the 1880s only accelerated the long-term industrial decline of the region. In these conditions, where low wages ensured that a strike inevitably led to great and immediate hardship for the workers and their families, trade unionists avoided industrial conflict wherever possible. The Knights conducted several strikes, as we have seen, to prove to workers and employers that 'they meant business,' but they and their rivals in the Midland Counties Trades Federation both went to extreme lengths to secure settlements through arbitration.

As trade improved, and as workers' expectations grew, however, Knights found that their pacific approach to industrial relations was not always so popular. The hollowware turners at Kenrick's in West Bromwich provided one example of workers refusing to submit to arbitration. Kenrick's occupied a similar position in the iron hollowware industry to Pilkington's in the glass trade. The firm organised other manufacturers into the Association of Cast Iron Hollow Ware Manufacturers, a cartel designed to maintain high prices and the existing market share of its members. Kenrick's also epitomised the paternalistic attitudes of many employers in Black Country. The firm gave money to local schools, hospitals, cricket and football clubs. Part of West Bromwich became known as 'Kenrick's village' even though the company contributed little to its construction.[73] Kenrick's extended the same paternalism into labour relations. Managers enrolled workers into a number of welfare schemes and went through most of the nineteenth century without a single strike.[74] But the introduction of new machinery from 1884 onwards threatened to disturb that industrial peace, as it threatened the position of turners and other skilled workers on the factory floor and stimulated resentment among them. In 1888 the company made some of them redundant, including Charles Chamberlain, a leading local Knight, and all 100 turners and many of the 800 other workers at Kenrick's turned to the Order for help.[75]

The Knights became involved soon after the redundancies took effect. Hollowware turners from across England and Scotland had already met in West Bromwich at the beginning of 1888 to draw up a price list to present to their employers, which they did in July. Neither side initially acted on these demands, but in January 1889 the Knights, anxious to demonstrate the strength of their Black Country assemblies, presented a version of the

---

[73] Trainor, *Black Country Elites*, p. 146.

[74] W.G. and C.L. Staples, *Power, Profits, and Patriarchy: The Social Organization of Work at a British Metal Trades Firm, 1791–1922* (Lanham: Rowman and Littlefield, 2001), p. 11.

[75] R. Church, *Kenricks in Hardware: A Family Business, 1791–1966* (Newton Abbot: David and Charles, 1968), p. 286.

existing list to employers and insisted that they accept it without delay. The employers initially refused to do so, and even issued notices that the turners would be locked out. Yet the Knights seemed to have convinced them and the local press that in the event of a strike the turners could draw on enormous resources from the Order's British and American assemblies. One report claimed that local assemblies boasted more than £100 in reserve funds, and that the General Assembly was prepared if necessary to raise as much as £20,000 for strikes that they approved.[76] Charles Chamberlain reiterated this theme in an interview with a local journalist in March. 'If a strike took place in the hollowware trade tomorrow,' he claimed, 'the Americans would send us £500 as a first instalment straight off.'[77]

Faced with these numbers, the hollowware manufacturers decided on arbitration instead. Where the newspapers previously worried over a 'Threatened Gigantic Strike,' they now reported the meetings of the turners and their managers. By mid-March, both sides put forward a detailed list of their grievances and positions. They also agreed on an arbitrator, Nigel C.A. Neville, the stipendiary magistrate of Wolverhampton, who made his decision on 2 April. The turners did not receive Neville's award with much enthusiasm. Half of them had their wages reduced rather than increased, and as the award was retroactive to 29 January they actually owed money to their employers. The turners went on strike against the award and only returned to work when the Knights demanded that they honour their pledge to abide by the results of arbitration.[78]

The dispute flared up again in December 1889 when the Association of Cast Iron Hollow Ware Manufacturers unilaterally decided to grant a 10 percent increase on the prices listed in Neville's award. Only a day before the arbitrator's list was due to expire, on 29 January 1890, the turners and employers met one final time to attempt a last-minute settlement, and failed. When the employers suggested further arbitration the workers, as their secretary reported, 'unanimously decided to cease work the next day, January 29th, and try to obtain by that means that which they thought they were justly entitled to.'[79] Yet the Knights remained opposed to a strike. Rumours circulated that they would refuse to give money to striking turners. 'They have gone in the face of the constitution, and landed themselves in

[76] *Smethwick Weekly News*, 23 February 1889. This article also provides a detailed list of their grievances and demands.

[77] *Smethwick Weekly News*, 2 March 1889.

[78] *Report on the Strikes and Lock-outs of 1890, By the Labour Correspondent to the Board of Trade*, pp. 188–89. Found at HCPP.

[79] *Report on the Strikes and Lock-outs of 1890, By the Labour Correspondent to the Board of Trade*, pp. 188–89. Found at HCPP.

the position of being on strike without being entitled to strike pay,' one Knight claimed in the *Halfpenny Weekly*.[80] Nevertheless, the Birmingham and Black Country assemblies voted to 'forgive the turners for their stupid act of insubordination' and to raise £50 for their strike.[81]

That strike, however, collapsed after turners at firms in Wolverhampton, Coseley and Manchester returned to work. Turners at Kenrick's admitted defeat soon afterwards, and by 22 March 1890, they were all back at work.[82] The Knights, writes R.A. Church, 'refused to countenance the turners' militancy.'[83] The turners soon refused to countenance the Knights as well. Some of them remained in the assemblies until the end of the year, but most never forgave the Knights for their equivocation and left the assemblies for good.[84] Managers at Kenrick's further increased the mechanisation of their works and soon dispensed with the need for turners altogether. They also redoubled their welfare schemes in order to prevent any re-emergence of trade unions and strikes at the firm.[85] Tranquillity soon reigned again at Kenrick's; Knights found that their commitment to arbitration could provoke severe and ultimately disastrous opposition from their own members.

American Knights had already discovered, amidst the Great Upheaval two years earlier, that once workers began to see strikes as a quick way to settle disputes, and saw other workers fighting and winning strikes of their own, no amount of speeches, articles, resolutions or even orders could stop them. A similar wave of strikes began in Britain in 1888, intensified in 1889 and reached a crescendo in 1890. British and Irish Knights initially welcomed the new optimistic mood. In Walsall they led subscription drives to raise money for the London Dock Strike in 1889, supported striking fibre drawers in Sheffield, and helped local bit filers, saddle tree makers, awl blademakers and other saddlery workers to negotiate with employers and, if necessary, backed them if they were forced to strike.[86] Knights in Derry, as we have seen, quickly expanded after winning victories over employers like Messrs

---

[80] *Halfpenny Weekly*, 22 February 1890.

[81] *Halfpenny Weekly*, 22 February 1890. DA248 of Cradley Heath and DA256 of Rotherham raised £25 and £15 respectively towards the strike (*Halfpenny Weekly*, 8 March 1890).

[82] The trustee of LA7952, for example, was a turner in October 1890 (*Smethwick Weekly News*, 4 October 1890).

[83] Church, *Kenricks in Hardware*, p. 289.

[84] The trustee of LA7952, for example, was a turner in October 1890. *Smethwick Weekly News*, 4 October 1890.

[85] Church, *Kenricks in Hardware*, p. 293; Staples and Staples, *Power, Profits, and Patriarchy*, p. 11.

[86] *Walsall Observer*, 31 August 1889, 4 and 25 January 1890; *Birmingham Daily Post*, 20 July and 2 September 1889; *Sheffield and Rotherham Independent*, 24 September 1889; *Halfpenny Weekly*, 1 March 1890.

Watts. In the opening years of the new unionism the ranks of the Knights of Labor swelled along with the rest of the British labour movement. But their industrial tactics soon caused them problems, as they had at Kenrick's, among two large bodies of workers, dockers in Liverpool and stove grate workers in Rotherham, who had initially seemed destined to become major players in the Order's British and Irish history.

The leaders of LA443 took their commitment to arbitration very seriously. From the earliest days of the assembly they cultivated ties with the master stevedores and shipping companies active on the Bootle docks. In December 1889, a meeting of the assembly discussed the demands they should place on employers, and 'it was unanimously resolved that the employers be asked to appoint a time when the matter can be settled by arbitration.'[87] Most dock employers looked on their demands with some favour and in January 1890, the Knights followed up on these initial attempts at negotiation with a full set of rules to govern work on the docks.[88] These rules governed everything from the working day, which was to be nine hours, to overtime pay, from 6 p.m. to 6 a.m. and with double time on Sundays and a number of public holidays.[89] Two leading master stevedores and two shipping companies accepted these rules, in the words of the secretary of LA443, 'without a murmur.'[90]

But the negotiations carried out by Knights in Bootle did not take place in a vacuum. Their assembly began at the same time as a new union, the National Union of Dock Labourers (NUDL), formed in Glasgow at the beginning of 1889, expanded southward into Merseyside. Later chapters examine conflict between these two organisations in more detail, but we can say here that in Bootle they represented two very different approaches to the question of dealing with employers. In May, almost immediately upon arriving in Liverpool, the NUDL considered sending its members on strike. Thomas Dooling, one of the leaders of LA443, told local Knights in response that 'on no consideration were the members to strike. They must seek arbitration, and should they fail in this attempt then their American brothers would help them.'[91] NUDL leaders, for their part, publicly attacked the working rules that Knights presented to employers as the product of agitators with no practical knowledge of work on the docks, and they refused to recognise the agreements that Knights had made with the stevedores and shipping companies.[92] Against this, LA443 promised

---

[87] *Halfpenny Weekly*, 14 December 1889.
[88] *Halfpenny Weekly*, 1 February 1890.
[89] A full copy of these rules can be found in *Liverpool Weekly Courier*, 1 February 1890.
[90] *Halfpenny Weekly*, 1 February 1890.
[91] *Bootle Times*, 31 August 1889.
[92] *Liverpool Echo*, 27 January 1890.

to uphold their agreements and to establish 'mutual respect and confidence between employers and employees.'[93]

These disagreements reached a head at the beginning of 1890 as both organisations expanded on the Liverpool docks. When NUDL leaders insisted that none of their members should unload cargoes alongside non-union workers, Knights in Bootle were faced with a stark choice: support that union or abide by their agreements with employers. They chose the latter course. Individual Knights, if not the assembly at large, agreed to offload ships that NUDL members refused to handle. They gained short-term advantages from this course. Stevedores began to give Knights preferential treatment over other workers. But as their currency rose among employers, their reputation within the rest of the local labour movement, and among many dockers, began to plunge. Dockers in Liverpool, meanwhile, clamoured for a strike like the one their comrades had recently won in London. The NUDL offered to lead one, and their leaders' plans for a strike in March were only delayed until the next month thanks to obstruction from the Knights. This delay gave employers time to recruit large numbers of strike-breakers and when the dockers did strike, they went down to defeat.

Ironically, the strike was settled by a man strongly associated with the Knights: Michael Davitt. Davitt advised the dockers to negotiate with their employers and, if that failed, to seek assistance from American Knights, who could mount a transatlantic boycott of anti-union shipping and so bring employers back to the negotiating table.[94] This advice was indistinguishable from that given by Thomas Dooling in August 1889. The Knights, however, would not be the ones to benefit from it. The NUDL survived for a time. The Bootle assembly, now tainted by its association with strike-breaking, did not survive the year. Knights disregarded the change in *zeitgeist* at their peril. Eric Taplin concludes that with their almost fanatical devotion to arbitration at any cost, they managed to alienate themselves even from those dockers who might otherwise have supported them.[95]

The case of the stove grate workers of Rotherham illustrated other dangers. In 1889 they joined the Order in large numbers, and from their first assembly, LA1266, they soon created ten others. In March 1890, they decided to demand a 10 percent wage advance on the grounds that their earnings had not increased even after the introduction of new, more productive machinery in recent years.[96] When employers refused to negotiate with them or with a

---

[93] *Halfpenny Weekly*, 1 February 1890.
[94] Bean, 'Knights in Liverpool,' p. 74.
[95] E. Taplin, *Liverpool Dockers and Seamen, 1870–1890* (Hull: University of Hull, 1974), p. 80.
[96] *Reynolds's*, 11 May 1890.

deputation the Knights sent from Birmingham, they handed in their notice and struck work.[97] Haydn Sanders travelled up to Rotherham from Walsall to direct the strike while claiming, in public at least, that he remained determined to settle the dispute through arbitration. The employers refused to negotiate with him too.[98] As the strike went on, new assemblies continued to open in Rotherham, and in May the strike ended with employers conceding their demands.[99]

This battle was the largest and most prominent strike that the Knights ever carried out in Britain and Ireland. It was also their most notable industrial victory. Yet this victory ended not with the Order's expansion throughout the stove grate industry, but with the formation of a new union, the Stove-Grate Workers Union, headed by none other than Haydn Sanders. We will explore the wider ramifications of that new union in later chapters. But we can say here that even as many stove grate workers expressed their thanks to the Knights for their assistance during the strike, many of them also wondered if the Knights would help in future disputes. Their suspicions were probably well founded. While it is unlikely that the Knights completely refused to support the strikers, as one writer claims, many of them received no or little strike pay.[100] A new union, uniting stove grate workers across Britain, was better placed to provide financial support when strikes broke out than an order that seemed unable, or unwilling, to do so.

British Knights attempted to solve this problem when they finally created a National Assembly in 1891. They proposed to increase the contributions of their members in order to 'build up a fund which would attract recruits, and enable any serious dispute to be properly fought.'[101] After they registered the National Assembly they planned to test that new plan with a strike of vice makers at Lye. But these steps came too late to halt their decline. The judgement the *Smethwick Weekly News* passed on the Order's Black Country assemblies in 1891 could equally have applied to assemblies in Liverpool, Rotherham and elsewhere. 'The thousands who joined two years ago, expecting half-crowns for shillings,' it claimed, 'ceased to subscribe when they found that the Knights, apart from their mysteries and secret codes, were a hum-drum set who rather disliked strikes.'[102]

In the depressed conditions of the mid-1880s that dislike did not cause the Knights many problems. At the end of that decade it lost them recruits. Newly

---

[97] *Rotherham Advertiser*, 22 February 1890.
[98] *Leeds Mercury*, 12 April 1890.
[99] *Rotherham Advertiser*, 29 March, 26 April and 17 May 1890.
[100] Brake, *Men of Good Character*, p. 330; *Reynolds's*, 11 May 1890.
[101] *Smethwick Weekly News*, 11 July 1891.
[102] *Smethwick Weekly News*, 11 July 1891.

militant workers lacked the patience to wait on the results of negotiation. Nor were they willing to accept the compromises that arbitration entailed. The Knights, those that stayed in the assemblies at least, held onto their faith in arbitration until the very end of their history. In Rotherham they gained at least one small victory through negotiations at an axle turning shop in 1892.[103] But these minor victories counted for little next to the hundreds, if not thousands, of workers who left the Knights because they would not or could not support their strikes.

Conclusion

Thanks to their name, the Knights of Labor became the butt of many jokes in British newspapers. 'Judging by the strikes they are always organizing,' claimed the London magazine *Fun*, 'days of idleness seem the natural outcome of Knights of Labour.'[104] The *Taunton Courier* jibed that 'an assembly of the Knights of Labour in New York has disbanded in order that its members may go to work.'[105] These jokes, however, were completely unrepresentative of the Order's history in Britain and Ireland. The Knights preached arbitration and strained every nerve to practise it. Some employers refused to submit to arbitration, notably Pilkington's, and then, as their position in the window glass industry deteriorated, Hartley's and Chance Bros too. Knights were forced into strikes they did not want and when they ended, with some help from a fire in Sunderland, LA3504 was destroyed. The hostility of employers never became as damaging to British and Irish Knights as it did to American Knights but it ended the glassworkers' assembly – the strongest assembly, composed of the most skilled and highly paid workers, that ever existed in Britain and Ireland.

In other cases, Knights called strikes in order to bring employers to, or back to, the negotiating table. But their preference for arbitration proved so strong, and their unwillingness to walk out so great, that they appeared to some, particularly dockers in Liverpool and hollowware turners in West Bromwich, to be friendlier to employers than to workers on strike. That preference survived through all the fluctuations of the economic cycle and the swings in militancy, strikes and trade union membership that accompanied it. Indeed, Knights preached and tried to practise arbitration even when doing so put them at odds with the desires of the workers they wanted to represent. With the rise of the new unionism, their lukewarm attitude to strikes cost them an excellent chance to establish a permanent

---

[103] *Sheffield Daily Telegraph*, 14 May 1892.
[104] *Fun*, 7 March 1888.
[105] *Taunton Courier*, 31 August 1887.

presence on the Liverpool docks, and meant that even when they won an impressive victory in Rotherham, stove grate workers preferred to form their own union rather than rely on an order that seemed unwilling or incapable of financing a serious dispute. Efforts to change those perceptions came too late to save the assemblies.

The sheer fact that Knights persevered with this course for so long, even when it was not always in their interests to do so, tells us something about the British and Irish workers who joined the Knights of Labor. In the previous chapter we saw how they made as few changes as possible to the cultural practices and organisational style of their adopted order. Their attitude towards industrial relations was no different. As well as following Powderly's dictates regarding arbitration and strikes, British and Irish Knights attempted a number of boycotts and even tried to amass enough capital to start a cooperative enterprise of their own. They lacked the numbers and the savings to make either effective, but in both cases they remained true to the industrial prescriptions of their order. Arbitration and cooperation, if not the boycott, were already popular in the British labour movement – but the consistency with which British and Irish Knights followed them suggests that their main inspiration came from Powderly and the General Executive Board. If we compare their record with that of most American Knights, whose propensity to strike with or without the sanction of their leaders infuriated Powderly and his associates, we find that the orders of the General Master Workman were more closely followed in Britain and Ireland than in the Order's American home.

British and Irish Knights never explained why they remained so 'pure' in this sense, and we can only speculate as to why. The most likely explanation is that they established and joined the assemblies because they saw the Order as superior to any local alternative. They doubtless hoped to emulate the achievements of American Knights who had briefly become, in 1886, the largest and most successful labour organisation in the world. Having already adopted that order it seemed natural to keep, as far as possible, to all of the practices, methods and principles that their American leaders laid down for them. Better to keep them all rather than change something that, for all they knew, was a crucial ingredient in the Order's American victories. And why, indeed, join a transnational organisation if you wish to change it completely, unless you wish only to trade on its name? The Sons of Labour and the British United Order, as we saw in the previous chapter, went down that road and the assemblies, had they wished, could have done the same.

But the British and Irish Knights did not. Their adherence to the principles of their order won them recruits in the 1880s; that same adherence lost them members in the following decade. Powderly repeatedly encouraged the British and Irish Knights to adapt their order to suit local conditions;

they became amongst his most faithful followers instead. It is often said that the most virulent nationalists come from border regions or from outside the nations they claim to represent, from Napoleon, a Corsican, to Hitler, an Austrian. The history of the Knights of Labor in Britain and Ireland suggests that in a transnational movement, the most enthusiastic followers of the official line might also be found on the periphery of the movement rather than at its centre.

5

The Knights and Politics

In February 1887, representatives of ironworkers throughout the Black Country met at Brierley Hill to discuss whether they should attend a conference organised by trade unionists in the north of England. A delegate from the Corngreaves works in Cradley Heath suggested that they form assemblies of the Knights of Labor instead. The representatives then debated the relative merits of each organisation and argued over the costs that each would impose on their members. One delegate then introduced a new theme into the discussion. 'He objected,' one newspaper reported, 'to the introduction of politics in trade matters.' Many of his colleagues voiced their agreement. 'The Knights of Labour,' he continued, 'were always interfering in politics.'[1] After his speech, the meeting then voted to attend the conference instead of joining the Knights. The speaker's fears were also confirmed by the Order's history in Britain and Ireland. Over the course of that history the Knights of Labor certainly interfered in politics.

American Knights always remained ambivalent about the Order's political role. Terence Powderly saw it as something 'more and higher' than a political party.[2] Partisan loyalties had often divided the American labour movement in the past, most notably the Order's predecessor in the 1860s and 1870s, the National Labor Union. Powderly and other leading Knights enjoined their members to keep party politics out of the assemblies, and counselled further education in the principles of philosophy and political economy instead. Practical political concerns found their way into the Knights of Labor anyway. The glassworkers of LA300 paid Ralph Beaumont to lobby the Houses of Congress for legislation in the working-class interest. Knights pioneered the practice of 'rewarding friends and punishing enemies' whereby they encouraged members to vote for candidates who endorsed the

[1] *Birmingham Daily Post*, 1 March, 1887.
[2] *Proceedings of the GA* (1879), p. 57.

Order's programme, which later became the stated policy of the American Federation of Labor. The Knights never officially aligned themselves with a political party until the mid-1890s, when the last surviving assemblies briefly cast their lot with the Populist Party. All the Order's leaders, however, dabbled in partisan politics at some stage. Uriah Stephens resigned as Grand Master Workman to run for Congress as a Greenback-Labor Party candidate; Powderly, his successor, became Grand Master Workman while already serving as the Mayor of Scranton, Pennsylvania.[3]

The assemblies also led an unprecedented political mobilisation of American workers during the Great Upheaval. In 1886 and 1887, American workers created dozens of new, independent labour parties in almost every state of the Union, or wrested control of their local Democratic or Republican parties from the political elites that controlled them.[4] The most famous campaign centred on the mayoralty of New York, where Henry George ran in 1886 as a candidate of the new United Labor Party. He polled nearly 70,000 votes, only 20,000 less than the Democratic candidate Abram Hewitt and more than the Republican candidate, one Theodore Roosevelt. Many workers believed that Hewitt, and the infamous Tammany Hall machine that supported him, only defeated George thanks to widespread electoral fraud.[5] And New York was not the only place where the old political order appeared on the verge of collapse. The newly minted United Labor Party won more than a quarter of the vote for the mayoralty of Chicago, the People's Party won the mayoralty of Milwaukee and similar results poured in from virtually every state in the Union. A small number of Knights even won election to the House of Representatives.[6]

That political mobilisation subsided towards the end of the decade, along with the membership of the American Knights of Labor; yet their enthusiasm infected Knights all over the planet. Anarchists, single-taxers and advocates of working-class politics in Australia seized on the Order as a vehicle for their propaganda.[7] South African Knights attempted to form a political movement that would end the symbiotic relationship between De Beers and the governance of the Cape Colony, and they hoped to vote out of office the chief symbol of that relationship, Prime Minister and De Beers director Cecil Rhodes.[8] Knights in Belgium became active in the

[3] For discussions of the Knights in politics see especially, amongst others, Ware, *Labor Movement*; Fink, *Workingmen's Democracy*; Hild, *Greenbackers, Knights of Labor, and Populists*.

[4] For a series of local case studies see Fink, *Workingmen's Democracy*.

[5] R. Weir, 'A Fragile Alliance: Henry George and the Knights of Labor,' *American Journal of Economics and Sociology*, 56:4 (1997), p. 421.

[6] Foner, *History of the Labor Movement*, II, p. 129.

[7] Weir, *Knights Down Under*, pp. 227–28.

[8] *Manifesto of the Knights of Labour of South Africa*.

agitation and protests for universal male suffrage throughout the 1880s and 1890s. The Order's New Zealand assemblies enjoyed the greatest political victories of all. More than a dozen Knights entered the colonial legislature and John Ballance, the Premier of the colony between 1890 and 1893, joined an assembly as well. The assemblies became powerful political machines, and their lobbying was instrumental in the passage of landmark legislation, from female suffrage to laws mandating compulsory arbitration and conciliation, that earned New Zealand world recognition as a pioneer in social legislation.[9] Few Knights across the world followed Powderly's injunction to keep their order out of politics.

British and Irish Knights never built political machines on anything like the scale of their American cousins. They never came close to equalling the legislative record of Knights in New Zealand. But they did become part of one of the great stories of British labour history: the birth of the British Labour Party as an independent force, distinct from the Liberal Party. Labour historians have constructed a compelling narrative to explain that story. As the franchise widened to include working-class electors in the second half of the nineteenth century, British trade unionists forged an alliance with the Liberal Party. As many as 12 Lib-Labs were returned to Parliament in 1885. In the following year Henry Broadhurst became the first trade unionist to serve as a junior minister in a British government. The rise of the British socialist movement, however, combined with the extension of trade unionism beyond the skilled trades hitherto organised within the TUC – the 'new unionism' – encouraged a growing number of trade unionists to consider the possibility of organising independently of the Liberals. Keir Hardie's independent campaign for the Mid-Lanark by-election of 1888, the creation of the Scottish Labour Party later that year, the formation of the Independent Labour Party in 1893 and the birth of the Labour Representation Committee in 1900 remain the key events and institutions that marked the road from the Lib-Labs to the Labour Party.[10]

A number of historians have recently subjected that account to severe criticism. Some dismiss the significance of British socialists in this process. Others insist on the continued power of working-class Liberalism (and

---

[9] See Weir, *Knights Down Under*; W.B. Sutch, *The Quest for Security in New Zealand, 1840 to 1966* (Oxford: Oxford University Press, 1942), p. 68.

[10] The classic text for this interpretation remains Pelling, *Origins of the Labour Party*. An excellent synthesis of this brand of scholarship can be found in J. Lovell, 'Trade Unions and the Development of Independent Labour Politics, 1889–1906,' in B. Pimlott and C. Cook (eds), *Trade Unions in British Politics: The First 250 Years*, 2nd ed. (London: Longman, 1991). An overview of the historiographical debates on working-class politics in the late nineteenth and early twentieth century can be found in Kirk, *Change, Continuity and Class*, esp. chs 6 and 8.

working-class conservatism) well into the twentieth century. Still more, and particularly the contributors to Alastair Reid and Eugenio Biagini's landmark collection of essays *Currents of Radicalism*, see the Labour Party as the natural outgrowth of the Lib-Lab movement rather than a divergence from it.[11] Where the writers of the classic interpretation of the British Labour Party saw ruptures with existing patterns of working-class politics, revisionists see their continuation. Continuity and change, however, need not be placed in such stark opposition; out of necessity, the new arises out of the old. The British Labour Party emerged from the Lib-Lab politics of the nineteenth century; it also emerged from opposition to the Lib-Lab pact. Knights in Britain and Ireland became involved in both trends.

This chapter explores the political history of the British and Irish Knights of Labor. It looks firstly at the political affiliations that Knights brought with them into the British and Irish assemblies, so far as we can discern them. It then charts the political record of the assemblies at a municipal level. Finally, this chapter explores the engagement of British and Irish Knights with politics at a national or parliamentary level. In all these cases, as we will see, the Knights became active in many of the landmark events, institutions and currents that ultimately led to the British Labour Party.

The Politics of the Knights of Labor

At the 1886 General Assembly in Richmond, Terence Powderly later wrote, 'Protectionists, Free Traders, Single Taxers, Socialists, Anarchists, Bellamyites, and Blatherskites as well as some trade-unionists, had stated openly that it was their intention to capture the Knights of Labor at Richmond and make use of it as a field for their propaganda.' It was Powderly's aim, he wrote, 'to hold the Knights of Labor organization for Knights of Labor.'[12] That task was fruitless as well as impossible. Like any large, broadly representative labour movement, the American Knights were composed of many competing political factions, particularly but not only the ones that Powderly named. The Order's programme outlined a series of principles, from land reform and the nationalisation of the railway and telegraph lines to their vague aspiration to 'make industrial and moral worth, not wealth, the true standard of individual and national greatness,' which all the factions at various points claimed as their own. That heterogeneity caused problems, as political tendencies struggled for control over the Order, but it also allowed the Knights to become the first national working-class movement in the United States.

[11] Reid and Biagini, *Currents of Radicalism*.
[12] Powderly, *The Path I Trod*, p. 142.

The Knights of Labor established their assemblies in Britain and Ireland just before, and particularly during, the mass working-class political action in the United States that formed part of the Great Upheaval. That political action, particularly the Henry George campaign in New York, and to a lesser extent the other political campaigns that took place across the United States in 1886 and 1887, became major news on the other side of the Atlantic. Respectable opinion, as measured in the editorial pages of *The Times*, condemned George's movement as 'fooling with anarchy.'[13] *Reynolds's Newspaper* saw the George campaign as the beginnings of a rejuvenation of radicalism on both sides of the ocean: 'There was St. George; there was George Washington; there is Henry George ... the platform of the Labour Party on which Mr. George stands ought to be carefully weighed by the working men of this country.'[14] Friedrich Engels welcomed the arrival of the American working class as an independent political force, and hoped that they would soon leave figures like Powderly and George 'out in the cold with small sects of their own.'[15] Even in 1891, Eleanor Marx and Edward Aveling made a prediction that sounds strange to modern ears. 'The example of the American working men will be followed before long on the European side of the Atlantic,' they wrote. 'An English or, if you will, a British Labour Party will be formed, foe alike to Liberal and Conservative.'[16]

The years of the Great Upheaval, as Henry Pelling writes, 'constitute one of the few periods when the state of political organization of the working class as such in America could be regarded as more complete than that of the British workers.'[17] To most British observers that unusual state of affairs was strongly associated with the Knights of Labor. *The Times* commented before the New York mayoral election that if George won, Powderly and the Knights would be to blame.[18] Many Liberals, as one newspaper remarked in 1888, feared that the Order's introduction into Britain would lead to independent labour candidates and a split in the Liberal vote.[19] *Reynolds's* saw the George campaign as the Knights' first step to 'tak[ing] possession of the political machinery of the country.'[20]

---

[13] *The Times*, 13 October 1886.
[14] *Reynolds's*, 24 October 1886.
[15] Engels to Florence Kelley Wischnewetsky, 28 December 1886. Found at *Marxists Internet Archive* (MIA): https://www.marxists.org/archive/marx/works/1886/letters/86_12_28.htm
[16] Eleanor Marx and Edward Aveling, *The Working-Class Movement in America* (London, 1891). Found at MIA.
[17] Pelling, *British Left*, p. 62.
[18] *The Times*, 17 October 1886.
[19] *Halfpenny Weekly*, 9 June 1888.
[20] *Reynolds's*, 24 October 1886.

British and Irish workers of various different political backgrounds were drawn to this example, and to the Knights themselves. Some came from the radical and working-class wing of the Liberal Party, who admired and agreed with the emphasis that Knights placed on arbitration and negotiation instead of strikes, and on education and moral self-improvement. Jesse Chapman, the Master Workman of LA10227, became the secretary of the Smethwick Liberal Association in 1890 and turned it in a radical direction.[21] The Revs Harold Rylett and T.T. Sherlock both supported the Knights in their early days in Birmingham and the Black Country, and were also strongly associated with the radical wing of the Liberal Party there. David Ben Rees describes William Newcomb, one of LA443's early leaders, as a 'typical Liberal/Labour social reformer.'[22]

Socialists also entered the assemblies. In 1881, Friedrich Engels insisted that the trade unions were condemned to fight a losing struggle for higher wages and shorter hours unless they also fought the wage system itself. 'At the side of, or above, the Unions of special trades,' he wrote, 'there must spring up a general Union, a political organisation of the working class as a whole.'[23] Socialists in the Social Democratic Federation (SDF), and in the Socialist League, which split from the SDF at the end of 1884, adopted a similar attitude. Some wanted to dispense with trade unionism altogether and focus all energies on political agitation, while others insisted that the trade unions, or some new general union, must organise all workers and not simply the crafts then grouped together in the TUC.[24] The Knights of Labor, who loudly proclaimed their opposition to the wage system, and whose members inaugurated the great American political movements of the mid-1880s, appeared to many socialists to be precisely the kind of 'political organisation of the working class as a whole' that they wanted to create. Marx and Aveling even described the Order's opposition to the wage system as 'pure and unadulterated Socialism.'[25] The SDF's organ, *Justice*, and

---

[21] *Smethwick Telephone*, 12 July 1890 and 9 January 1892.

[22] Rees, *Local and Parliamentary Politics*, p. 67. Some scholars argue that Newcomb was never directly a member of the Knights of Labor. See E. Taplin, 'Liverpool Tramwaymen,' in H.R. Hikins (ed.), *Building the Union: Studies in the Growth of the Workers' Movement, Merseyside, 1756–1967* (Liverpool: Liverpool Trades Council, 1973), p. 58. Rees and Bean, however, both state that he was (Rees, *Local and Parliamentary Politics*, p. 67; Bean, 'Aspects of 'New Unionism' in Liverpool, 1889–91,' in Hikins (ed.), *Building the Union*, p. 108).

[23] F. Engels, 'Trade Unions: Part 1,' in *The British Labour Movement: Articles from the Labour Standard*, (London: Martin Lawrence, 1934), pp. 20–21.

[24] For the attitudes of British socialists towards the trade unions see, amongst others, Crick, *Social-Democratic Federation*; Thompson, *William Morris*; Rabinovitch, *British Marxist Socialism*.

[25] Marx and Aveling, *The Working-Class Movement in America*.

the Socialist League's *Commonweal*, both printed the Order's *Declaration of Principles*. H. Halliday Sparling of the Socialist League, as we saw in Chapter 2, even asked *John Swinton's Paper* for advice on how to organise assemblies, although he and other British socialists, along with Engels, regularly condemned Powderly and the Order's leaders as opportunists.

J.T. Tanner, one of the SDF's most prominent voices in Birmingham, briefly associated himself with Knights there.[26] Samuel Reeves, a fellow SDFer and Liverpool's best-known contemporary socialist, led Bootle's LA443.[27] Charles Chamberlain appeared on SDF platforms in Birmingham that called for the eight-hour day.[28] Chamberlain, along with Tanner, Haydn Sanders and James P. Archibald, appeared at the SDF's ninth annual convention held at Birmingham in 1889.[29] Knights in the short-lived assembly at Preston maintained contact with the Socialist League and many of its members subscribed to *Commonweal*.[30] Haydn Sanders, who one enemy claimed had at turns been a 'flaming Bradlughite, a Freethinker, a Malthusian, a Spiritualist, a Liberal, a Radical, a Socialist or soloist, and goodness knows what else besides,' also settled on the Socialist League in 1887.[31] He formed the League's first branch in Walsall and, in addition to his agitation around the Black Country, he became 'responsible for the first socialist propagandist effort in north Wales to be recorded in print.'[32] As we will see, Sanders and other socialists in Walsall were responsible for the creation of LA454.

[26] In one meeting of the Birmingham Trades Council, Tanner described Henry Broadhurst as a sweatshop operator; at another, he described him as a traitor to the labour cause, after which he was briefly expelled from the Council (see *Birmingham Daily Post*, 8 April and 6 May 1889). Yet John Corbett writes that 'he deserves to be remembered' alongside John Burns and Tom Mann as one of the outstanding leaders of the 'New Unionism' (J. Corbett, *The Birmingham Trades Council: 1866–1966* (London: Lawrence and Wishart, 1966), p. 51). Tanner is described as a member of the Knights in *Birmingham Daily Post*, 17 June 1889.

[27] Rees, *Local and Parliamentary Politics*, pp. 67–71. In 1894, Reeves was president of his local branch of the Independent Labour Party (*Liverpool Mercury*, 23 July 1894).

[28] *Birmingham Daily Post*, 30 October 1888.

[29] *Pall Mall Gazette*, 6 August 1889.

[30] James Riley to the Socialist League, 18 June 1887, 2572, Socialist League Archives, IISH.

[31] *Walsall Free Press*, 19 January 1889. Sanders was able to appear on SDF platforms in 1889 mainly because, though the split between them and the Socialist League was rather pronounced in London, there were often no barriers between them elsewhere in the country; indeed, Sanders is listed in Martin Crick's work on the SDF as one of the Federation's members elected onto municipal bodies in 1889 (Crick, *Social-Democratic Federation*, p. 56).

[32] For examples of Sanders reports, see *Commonweal*, 7 May, 4 June, 16 and 23 July, 3 September, 8 October, 1887. For his Wales trip see *Commonweal*, 22 October 1887. For his role as secretary see Haydn Sanders to the Socialist League, 22 August 1887, 2632, Socialist League Archives, IISH; M. Wright, *Wales and Socialism: Political Culture and National Identity, c.1880–1914* (unpublished PhD thesis, University of Cardiff, 2011), p. 39.

Other Knights became attracted to the Fabian Society. That organisation, composed mainly of intellectuals, fused socialist principles with the English radical Liberal tradition, and early Fabians welcomed the Order's growth and hoped that it might soon incorporate all the American trade unions within its folds.[33] Arthur Nadin combined his role as recording secretary of Rotherham's LA1266 and organiser for that town's DA256 with his position as district secretary of the Rotherham branch of the Fabian Society. Samuel Reeves left the SDF at the turn of the decade and became a leading Fabian in Liverpool.[34] Finally, in Scotland the first openly socialist MP, the colourful aristocratic radical Robert Bontine Cunningham Graham, briefly aligned himself with the assemblies around Glasgow.[35]

Some followers of Henry George and his single tax also joined the British and Irish Knights. The strong association between George and the Order, even though their relationship remained fraught and broke down soon after the 1886 mayoral election in New York, undoubtedly encouraged single-taxers to enter the British assemblies.[36] So did the willingness of Knights to include land reform in their *Declaration of Principles*. A supporter of the Knights told the *Birmingham Daily Gazette* in 1889 that 'there is not an assembly in the neighbourhood of Birmingham which is not thoroughly familiar ... with the main principles advocated by Mr Henry George in his work on "Progress and Poverty."' Further, he added, 'that book is practically the text-book of the Knights of Labour in this country.'[37] One of the most strident single-taxers in the Black Country, Zebulon Butler, became a Knight and his many letters to local newspapers defended both George and the Order.[38]

Links between the Knights and the single tax were even closer in Scotland than in England. Irish immigrants appreciated George's advocacy on behalf of the Irish Land League, radicals who defended the Highland crofters supported George's land reform proposals, and both filled the Scottish assemblies.[39] James Shaw Maxwell, the future Master Workman of Scotland's DA203, was a devotee of Henry George who stood in 1885 as a

---

[33] A.M. McBriar, *Fabian Socialism and English Politics, 1884–1918* (Cambridge: Cambridge University Press, 1966), pp. 1–29.

[34] *Sheffield and Rotherham Independent*, 19 February 1891; Rees, pp. 67–71.

[35] For a biography of Cunninghame Graham see C. Watts, *R.B. Cunninghame Graham* (Boston: Twayne, 1983).

[36] Weir, 'A Fragile Alliance,' pp. 421–39.

[37] *Birmingham Daily Gazette*, 22 February 1889.

[38] For Butler's support of George, both in terms of his New York electoral campaign and the single tax, see especially *Labour Tribune*, 6 and 20 November 1886. For his participation in Liberal groups see *Dudley Herald*, 25 January and 24 May 1890.

[39] Aspinwall, 'The Civic Ideal,' p. 75.

parliamentary candidate for the Scottish Land Restoration League, a body created after George visited Glasgow in 1884.[40] Richard McGhee, another prominent Scottish single-taxer and one of George's closest British friends, received an organisers' charter from assemblies in the Black Country.[41]

The British and Irish assemblies never became the province of any one of these political tendencies. Radical Liberals, Lib-Labs and single-taxers, often the same people, comprised most of the Order's members in the Black Country, aside from Walsall. There, and to an extent in Liverpool and Rotherham, leading Knights tended towards socialism. Socialists and single-taxers, again often the same people, dominated the Scottish assemblies. In Ireland, so far as we can see, most Knights were single-taxers and Irish Nationalists, which generally meant that they stood on the radical wing of the Liberal Party. These disparate political views could coexist within the Knights of Labor because the Order's programme offered something to all of them, and because they all shared one central demand: the need for more working-class representation at all levels of government. Whether British and Irish Knights worked for that goal through the Liberal Party, one of the socialist groups, an organisation of their own making, or independently of all existing parties, the principle of electing workers to represent workers remained the central theme of their history in the political arena. Naturally enough for an order whose bedrock was the local assembly, the Knights concentrated most of their political energies on municipal affairs.

The Knights and Municipal Politics

Local government in Britain changed immeasurably over the course of the nineteenth century. After the 1835 Municipal Corporations Act, which reformed and regularised the governance of towns and boroughs throughout England, councils and local authorities gradually obtained an increasingly wide range of powers concerning local issues from public health and education to the provision of parks, libraries and swimming pools.[42] As workers slowly gained voting rights towards the end of the century, they looked as much to local as to national government for ameliorative measures

---

[40] Wood, 'Irish Immigrants and Scottish Radicalism,' pp. 72, 76; D. Howell, *British Workers and the Independent Labour Party, 1888–1906* (Manchester: Manchester University Press, 1983), pp. 136–41; I. McLean, *Keir Hardie* (London: Allen Lane, 1975), p. 35.

[41] A. Armstrong, *From Davitt to Connolly: 'Internationalism from Below' and the Challenge to the UK State and British Empire from 1879–95* (Edinburgh: Intfrobel Publications, 2010), p. 105; Newby, *Ireland, Radicalism and the Scottish Highlands*, p. 163.

[42] D. Fraser, *Power and Authority in the Victorian City* (Oxford: Blackwell, 1979), esp. ch. 6.

and political representation. Electing one of their number as a councillor or a member of a school board was, after all, cheaper and more likely than electing them to Parliament. Local bodies could also deliver tangible and immediate improvements to the lives of working-class communities, from better street lighting to relief work for the unemployed, that need not wait on a parliamentary majority. As Shelton Stromquist writes, 'local stories provide the building blocks for national political narratives.' But these local stories also 'embodied a politics of local autonomy and grassroots democracy that was tied directly to workers' lives and their immediate, concrete needs.'[43] Historians of British labour have uncovered many such local stories in towns and cities across the United Kingdom, all of them showing the growing awareness of trade unionists and political activists, from Fabian advocates of 'municipal socialism' to SDFers like John Burns, that the conquest of municipal power was both a stepping stone to the House of Commons and an end in itself.[44]

Assemblies of the Knights of Labor emerged in Britain and Ireland as the movement for working-class representation in local government, independent of the Liberals and Conservatives, began in earnest. Annie Besant's election to the London School Board in 1888, and John Burns's election to the London County Council in 1889, both on a socialist ticket, provided famous contemporary victories for that principle. Numerous trade unionists also sat on councils and school boards across the United Kingdom as Liberals or Conservatives. But in the 1880s their achievements were all outdone by the political campaigns of trade unionists, Knights particularly, across the Atlantic. Indeed, the Knights fought the vast majority of those struggles at a municipal level, against urban elites who controlled their local branches of the Democratic and Republican parties. As Leon Fink and other recent scholars have made clear, the Order's emphasis on organising workers along geographical as much as occupational lines might have complicated industrial relations at times, but helped them to build local political movements.[45] The Knights arrived in Britain and Ireland as the representatives of a movement with an enviable record

---

[43] S. Stromquist, '"Thinking Globally, Acting Locally": Municipal Labour and Socialist Activism in Comparative Perspective, 1890–1920, *Labour History Review*, 74:3 (2009), p. 235.

[44] See, for instance, S. Pollard, *History of Labour in Sheffield* (Liverpool: Liverpool University Press, 1959); K. Laybourn and J. Reynolds, *Labour Heartland: The History of the Labour Party in West Yorkshire During the Inter-war Years, 1918–39* (Bradford: Bradford University Press, 1987); P. Thompson, *Socialists, Liberals and Labour: The Struggle for London, 1885–1914* (London: Routledge, 1967); C.J. Wrigley, 'Liberals and the Desire for Working Class Representatives in Battersea 1886–1922,' in K.D. Brown (ed.), *Essays In Anti-Labour History* (London: Macmillan, 1974), pp. 126–58.

[45] Some notable examples include Fink, *Workingmen's Democracy*; Oestreicher, *Solidarity*

of winning municipal contests and with an internal structure well suited to local political action.

The British and Irish assemblies needed to attract a sufficiently large membership, however, before they could exert any meaningful political influence. The first mixed assembly, LA7952, only began in June 1886 and the first district assembly, DA208, only appeared the following year. British Knights were thus unable to seize immediately on the publicity generated by their American cousins for their own political ends. Indeed, many assemblies, such as those in Wales, Ireland and Liverpool, never held sufficient members for long enough to mobilise them for political action or, especially in the Irish case, never managed to overcome the sectarianism that plagued Northern Ireland and made politics there so problematic. The British Knights only began their first political venture in Smethwick and West Bromwich, where they organised around 2,000 workers, at the end of 1888.[46] At a meeting of LA7952 in December, an unnamed delegate urged Knights to make 'a new departure,' by which he meant a break with the Liberal Party. The following speaker came straight from campaigning for Annie Besant's election to the London School Board, and suggested that the Knights 'put a definite programme before the labour party in this country, and make their power felt.'[47] With Besant's example fresh in their minds, and with one of their Master Workmen, Jesse Chapman, serving as the headmaster of a local school, the Knights decided on the West Bromwich School Board as their first target for political action.[48]

The new Board was due to be appointed, or elected if there were more candidates than vacancies, in the middle of 1889. At the beginning of that year the Knights chose two candidates for the Board, both on an independent labour ticket: Charles Chamberlain, one of their local organisers, and a Mr Cox, who was a member of the Amalgamated Society of Engineers, not the Knights, but sympathised with the Order's goals.[49] As it turned out, they never even had to test their political strength. The Mayor of West Bromwich wanted to avoid the costs involved in organising an election, and after he, Chamberlain and Cox conducted negotiations with the existing members of the Board, they decided to appoint Chamberlain to join them. His politely phrased assertion that if it came to an election the Knights were confident that they could elect two members of the Board instead of one, probably had

---

and Fragmentation; Brundage, *Making of Western Labor Radicalism*; Dudden, 'Small Town Knights,' pp. 307–27.

[46] *West Bromwich Free Press*, 23 February 1889.
[47] *Smethwick Weekly News*, 1 December 1888.
[48] Pelling, 'Knights in Britain,' p. 321.
[49] *Smethwick Weekly News*, 2 March 1889.

an effect – and the Knights ended their first political campaign in victory without even going to the polls.⁵⁰

Chamberlain told one interviewer that he would sit on the Board 'with the simple object of watching the interest of the working classes … [and to] see that a strict economy was practised, but not at the expense of efficiency.' He also promised to 'work thoroughly in harmony' with the other members of the Board.⁵¹ Chamberlain certainly kept that last promise. He also maintained a good attendance at Board meetings. Yet the minutes of those meetings contain no instance where he proposed or seconded a motion, and his only legacy to the Board was that it chose another worker, William Rathbone, to replace him.⁵² Chamberlain also dismissed as 'premature' the suggestions of one interviewer in March 1889 that 'the Knights had determined to have a representative on every public body in the borough.' There were, he said, 'few members of their Order who had the necessary property qualification for the West Bromwich Guardians, and even those who had could not leave their work to attend the meetings either of the Guardians or the Town Council, which were always in the day time.'⁵³

Knights in Smethwick and West Bromwich soon abandoned direct political action of their own. They tried instead to build up a voting bloc that could help elect candidates representing other bodies, such as the local Ratepayers Association.⁵⁴ In one case, an aspiring councillor in nearby Birmingham actually targeted the Knights as a potential source of hundreds if not thousands of votes. Jack Tanner, an SDF member and firebrand on the Birmingham Trades Council who ran in every council election between the mid-1880s and '90s – and usually came dead last – stood in the Rotton Park Ward in 1889 on an SDF ticket. He evidently hoped that the Knights, 'said to be strongly posted in that quarter,' would catapult him onto the city council. Tanner's hopes were dashed; but the idea of the assemblies as potentially significant voting blocs survived his defeat.⁵⁵

---

⁵⁰ Several newspapers carried detailed transcripts of this meeting. See, for instance, *West Bromwich Free Press*, 23 February 1889; *Midlands Advertiser*, 23 February 1889; *Birmingham Daily Post*, 19 February 1889.

⁵¹ *Smethwick Weekly News*, 2 March 1889.

⁵² West Bromwich School Board Minutes, 3 February 1891, Sandwell Local Council Archives.

⁵³ *Smethwick Weekly News*, 2 March 1889.

⁵⁴ *Smethwick Weekly News*, 29 March 1890.

⁵⁵ Incidentally, Tanner pressed within the SDF for dispensation to run on a wider platform during the 1880s, but the national leadership insisted that all SDF members running for election must do so on the Federation's ticket. See Crick, *Social-Democratic Federation*, p. 54; *Birmingham Daily Post*, 17 June 1889.

Knights in Wolverhampton worked with other trade unionists through the Wolverhampton Trades Council to elect working-class representatives to the council. The Order's assemblies, as Jon Lawrence writes, strengthened 'the position of the "advanced" wing of the local labour movement' when it came to political action, and they supported the chairman of the Trades Council, W.F. Mees, who remained an ardent supporter of working-class representation on municipal bodies.[56] Knights on the Trades Council, immediately upon joining that body in August 1889, called for 'labour candidates' to run for local election independently of the Liberals and Conservatives. They hoped that these candidates would demand the 'recognition of Unionist principles by public bodies,' pay municipal employees higher wages and thereby set an example to workers in the private sector.[57] As neither Liberals nor Conservatives showed any interest in fielding working-class candidates, two local trade unionists, both nominated and supported by the Knights on the Trades Council, ran for the Wolverhampton Town Council in 1890 and were only narrowly defeated. The following year, however, a working-class representative was returned unopposed to the council, along with two representatives on the School Board.[58] Having strengthened those factions in the Wolverhampton Trades Council that made these victories possible, the local assemblies soon fell into decline and played no further role in the political life of the town.

Knights in other parts of Britain also ran their own municipal campaigns. In Sunderland, James Brown, the head of LA3504, stood for the town council in 1889 as a candidate of the Labour Electoral Association (LEA), an organisation that championed trade unionists for public office and features later in this chapter. Brown promised to steer clear of partisan rivalries, to press for a union rate of wages for all Council employees and to encourage public works, especially a new bridge, that would provide employment in his ward.[59] Despite support from the Sunderland Trades Council, Brown was not elected.[60] At a subsequent meeting of the Sunderland branch of the LEA he 'announced his intention to come forward time after time until he won'; the branch immediately put him forward as a candidate for the

---

[56] J. Lawrence, *Speaking for the People: Party Language and Popular Politics in England 1867–1914* (Cambridge: Cambridge University Press, 1998), p. 116; R.A. Wright, *Liberal Party Organisation and Politics in Birmingham, Coventry and Wolverhampton, 1886–1914, with Particular Reference to the Development of Independent Labour Representation* (unpublished PhD thesis, University of Birmingham, 1977), pp. 135–36.

[57] *Wolverhampton Express and Star*, 30 August and 27 September 1889.

[58] *Midland Counties Express*, 20 September 1890; Wright, *Liberal Party Organisation*, pp. 136–37.

[59] *Sunderland Daily Echo*, 22 October 1889.

[60] *1890–1 Report of the Sunderland Trades Council* (Sunderland, 1890), p. 2.

Board of Guardians.[61] He was unsuccessful. In 1891 Brown ran again for the town council and again he lost, despite the support of the local Liberal Association, after a Radical candidate siphoned off much of his potential vote.[62] Brown was both persistent and unlucky. In any case, enthusiasm like his was needed for the cause of working-class political representation, which faced the opposition of well-established and well-organised Liberals and Conservatives and was bound to suffer numerous defeats before it could hope to win victories on a regular basis.

The Knights came closest to realising that principle, and to building a successful local political movement of their own, in Walsall. That town was not the most promising context for the development of independent labour politics. The economy of Walsall was characterised by many small trades and industries and a correspondingly low level of trade union organisation well into the twentieth century.[63] Liberals dominated local politics and few contested elections took place before 1910.[64] One of the exceptions to that trend occurred in October 1888 when a socialist, Haydn Sanders, won election to Walsall Town Council. Walsall became, as the *Walsall Observer* remarked with some chagrin, 'the only town in the kingdom, we believe, in which a Socialist has been elected.'[65] Sanders's election rested on several unusual developments. Local authorities had broken up his meetings during earlier election campaigns in 1888, and Sanders finally won in October on a platform that defended free speech and assembly as much as it advanced socialist principles. The *Walsall Observer* also hinted darkly that he received the votes of local Conservatives who wished to upset the Liberals.[66]

After his election Sanders did his best to antagonise the politicians and journalists of the town. He harangued his fellow councillors at length on subjects ranging from the poor state of housing and the hours and wages of municipal employees to, as the report of one meeting put it, 'fleecers, bondholders, shareholders, light men and dark men, fleabites, and other "relevant" matters.'[67] On at least one occasion he was expelled from the council for repeatedly speaking over other councillors, whom he described at a meeting of the Birmingham Trades Council as 'bald-headed, pot-bellied

---

61 *Sunderland Daily Echo*, 29 November 1889.
62 *Sunderland Daily Echo*, 23 October 1890; 14 October, 3 and 4 November 1891.
63 Dean, *Town and Westminster*, pp. 2–5.
64 C.R.J. Currie, M.W. Greenslade and D.A. Johnson, *A History of Walsall, Being an Extract from the Victoria County History of Staffordshire, Volume XVII* (Walsall: Staffordshire Libraries, 1976), p. 217.
65 *Walsall Observer*, 3 November 1888.
66 *Walsall Observer*, 3 November 1888.
67 *Walsall Free Press*, 16 March 1889.

old town councillors, who were fonder of guzzling than of justice.'[68] The *Midland Counties Express* deplored his 'radicalism and unsavoury behaviour,' and the *Walsall Observer* admitted that Sanders had succeeded 'in perplexing almost beyond endurance the journalists of the town.'[69] Sanders also made enemies in the local labour movement, some of whom exchanged angry letters with him through the pages of local newspapers. But he also won the admiration of many others in Walsall for his willingness to raise many serious local issues at council meetings. Sanders, claimed one, was 'a man whom I have learned to respect and admire for his earnest endeavour to improve the condition of his fellow-men.'[70] If nothing else, the socialist town councillor from Walsall proved successful in shaking up the consensual political atmosphere that dominated the town.

He and his socialist supporters also looked to build on their victory. 'Having been deprived of all public speaking places in the borough,' the *Halfpenny Weekly* later reported, 'the Socialist party turned their attention to the next best work that lay to their hands. They finally hit upon and decided to start the Knights of Labour.'[71] Where Jack Tanner had looked to the Knights as a ready-made constituency for his own election campaign, Sanders and his supporters founded LA454 to create their own political constituency. That assembly grew rapidly and by the end of November 1888, *Reynolds's* described the Knights as 'a force in the town and district' of Walsall.[72] They decided to test their political strength at the next council elections in 1889, and selected two candidates to run as representatives of the Knights of Labor in separate wards: Frederick Eglington, president of the Bit Makers' Union, an organisation affiliated with the Order, and W.H. Sanders, father of Haydn, who owned a small lockmaking concern and shared his son's penchant for radical and labour politics.[73]

The election campaign polarised the town. 'On the one hand we have an active Socialistic and trades' unionist propaganda, leaving no stone unturned to catch every possible vote,' the *Walsall Advertiser* explained, 'and on the other hand two candidates, estimable men in themselves; but who, as far as I can learn, have not even gone to the trouble of issuing an address to the electors.'[74] This was not entirely true. Differences between Liberals, however radical, and Conservatives miraculously collapsed as they faced this

---

[68] *Walsall Free Press*, 15 June 1889; *Birmingham Daily Post*, 7 May, 1889.
[69] *Midland Counties Express*, 2 November 1889; *Walsall Observer*, 23 February 1889.
[70] *Walsall Observer*, 2 March 1889.
[71] *Halfpenny Weekly*, 4 January 1890.
[72] *Reynolds's*, 24 November 1888.
[73] *Walsall Observer*, 12 and 19 October 1889; *Justice*, 19 October 1889.
[74] *Walsall Advertiser and Newspaper*, 2 November 1889.

new challenge, and the local press abandoned any pretence of neutrality.[75] 'In view of the disaster of last November,' editorialised the *Advertiser*, 'it behoves every burgess to interest himself in the matter, and to see that the character of the Council is maintained.'[76] Newspapers repeated rumours that the campaign was causing splits amongst local Knights.[77] Libellous leaflets circulated through the town. One, which claimed to quote Benjamin Dean, a local miners' leader, questioned Eglington's working-class credentials; another accused W.H. Sanders of embezzling the proceeds from a concert held to raise money for a local hospital. Both accusations were false. Dean later denied any involvement in the attacks on Eglington, and Sanders won a court action against his libellers, but in both cases they were vindicated too late to influence the election.[78]

One of the Knights was nearly elected nevertheless. W.H. Sanders received only two-thirds of the votes of the second successful candidate in his ward, but Eglington polled 706 votes against the 771 and 767 received by the two successful candidates in his.[79] Haydn Sanders certainly regarded that outcome as a sign that working-class representation was gaining momentum in Walsall. 'If they made as much progress in the next twelve months as they had done in the last,' he told one meeting immediately after the election, 'they "would make the bosses sit up."'[80] Walsall Knights quickly set about creating an institutional framework for future campaigns. In January 1890, Eglington and J.T. Deakin, a local socialist, created the Walsall Labour Representative Wages Fund to subsidise Sanders's activities as a town councillor and as an agitator for the Knights of Labor.[81] That fund was probably based on the Battersea Labour League, which provided financial assistance to John Burns, the famed socialist agitator, during his time on the London County Council.[82] At least several bodies of workers contributed generously to the fund in the early months of 1890 after Sanders satisfactorily resolved their disputes. The leading English socialist H.H. Champion even spoke at a meeting organised by the Knights to publicise and raise money for the fund.[83]

As in West Bromwich the Knights failed to keep this momentum going. In mid-1890, Sanders left Walsall for Rotherham to lead a strike by Knights

---

[75] *Halfpenny Weekly*, 23 November 1889.
[76] *Walsall Advertiser*, 19 October 1889.
[77] *Walsall Free Press*, 26 October 1889; *Walsall Observer*, 26 October 1889.
[78] *Walsall Free Press*, 7 December 1889. The defendants in the libel case were ordered to pay £25 and costs. See *Walsall Observer*, 22 March 1890.
[79] *Walsall Observer*, 2 November 1889.
[80] *Walsall Advertiser*, 9 November 1889.
[81] Walsall Labour Representative Wages Fund, Walsall Local History Research Centre.
[82] Shepherd, 'Labour and Parliament,' p. 206.
[83] *Walsall Free Press*, 8 March 1890.

in the stove-grate industry there and vacated his seat on the council. His many local enemies were delighted. 'We may breathe freely,' the *Walsall Advertiser* remarked, 'in the hope that our Town Council – fast drifting into a bear garden – will resume its former peace and dignity now that its *enfant terrible* has taken his departure.'[84] Without his oratorical skills and energetic campaigning style the Walsall Knights quickly faded as a political force in the town. In November 1890, J. Hykin, like Eglington a Knight in the bit trade, did win election to the town council but his victory was due to the newly reconstituted Walsall Trades Council rather than to the assemblies.[85] The Knights were the first to make independent working-class representation an important political issue in Walsall, and the first to seriously apply that principle in practice; but they remained too dependent on a single charismatic individual, and their assemblies rose and fell too quickly, to make a more lasting impression on the political life of the town.

Sanders took his political activism with him to his new home in Rotherham. With the help of local Knights and the members of the new National Union of Stove-Grate Workers, which was established after the successful conclusion of their strike and elected Sanders as its president, he won election to the Rotherham School Board in November 1890. Knights continued to support Sanders even as he neglected them in favour of the Rotherham Trades Council and the Stove-Grate Workers' Union. A meeting of DA253 in September 1891, pledged the assembly to 'use every endeavour' to support his upcoming candidature for Rotherham Town Council.[86] Sanders failed to win election.[87] Rotherham's Knights supported him during the next council election in 1892. By this time, however, their assemblies were in severe decline, and Sanders was again unsuccessful.[88] With that anticlimactic defeat the last municipal campaign waged by British Knights came to an end.

What had those campaigns achieved? Knights in Smethwick and West Bromwich made a promising start but failed to build on it. In Rotherham they never made any impression at all. Knights persisted (unsuccessfully) in attempts to elect trade unionists to the council in Sunderland, and they played an important, if brief, role in the wider (and more successful) movement to elect trade unionists onto local bodies in Wolverhampton. The only place where British Knights built a political movement of their own that came close to winning an election was in Walsall. Superficially, at least,

---

[84] *Walsall Advertiser*, 31 May 1890.
[85] *Walsall Observer*, 8 November 1890.
[86] *Rotherham Advertiser*, 26 September 1891.
[87] *Leeds Mercury*, 3 November 1891.
[88] *Rotherham Advertiser*, 29 October 1892.

the movement led by Haydn Sanders and the Walsall Knights resembled that of John Burns and the Battersea Labour League in the same period. Both possessed a charismatic, popular and controversial leader. Both fought for the election of working-class candidates to local government. And both established mechanisms to pay for successful candidates and coordinate their future election campaigns.[89] At this point, however, the analogy breaks down. The Walsall Knights already possessed one sitting councillor when they began their agitation and never succeeded in electing another; the Battersea Labour League helped elect John Burns to the House of Commons. Where that League continued to shape local politics into the twentieth century, the Walsall Knights remained a significant political force for little more than a year. Once Haydn Sanders left for Rotherham, their influence soon disappeared.

For an order whose American assemblies had won majorities on numerous local bodies across the United States, and not just isolated councillors or School Board representatives, this was a disappointing record. But it was also understandable. As the British assemblies grew between 1886 and 1889 they remained too small to play any meaningful role in local politics; after 1890 their decline left them unable to play any such role in the future. British Knights had influence over municipal affairs only in 1889 and 1890, and only in areas where the assemblies became large enough to influence an election result. Within these restrictions, they did their best to bring the issue of working-class representation to the centre of political debate in several important industrial towns.

The Knights and National Politics

We saw at the beginning of this chapter that two main roads led to, and converged upon, the British Labour Party. On the one hand, that Party emerged from the Lib-Lab tradition, and its emphasis on working-class representation in the House of Commons and in town and borough councils across Britain and Ireland. On the other, the Labour Party arose out of the rejection by a growing number of workers of any electoral alliance between trade unionists and the Liberals, an alliance in which the unions were consigned to a junior role, and out of a related desire for workers to organise independently of all the existing parties. The Knights, as we have seen, contributed in a minor way to the growth of independent labour politics at a municipal level. Paradoxically, they played a more important

---

[89] See Wrigley, 'Liberals and Working Class Representatives'; W. Kent, *John Burns: Labour's Lost Leader, a Biography* (London: Williams and Norgate, 1950); Kenneth D. Brown, *John Burns* (London: Royal Historical Society, 1977).

role in the development of that politics on a national stage. Not all of their attempts to influence parliamentary politics ran in that direction: in some cases, Knights worked for the election of more conventional Liberal politicians. But British Knights also participated in the LEA, a leading Lib-Lab organisation, and attempted to steer it towards independence from the major parties. They were active in many of the major events and movements that accelerated the growth of independent labour politics in the late nineteenth century. Their narrative also divides rather cleanly along national lines. English Knights generally concerned themselves with Liberal and Lib-Lab politics while Scottish Knights generally took the independent course. In both cases, and in their different ways, all of them were part of the political ferment in trade union circles that eventually culminated in the British Labour Party.

British Knights recognised that their assemblies needed to become involved in parliamentary as well as municipal politics. 'As the ends aimed at by the Order in England can only be obtained by legislation,' one of their supporters told the *Birmingham Daily Gazette* in 1889, 'it is the duty of all, regardless of party, to assist in nominating and supporting such candidates for Parliament and other representative bodies as will support the measures the Order considers necessary for the attainment of its objects.' They did not consider it sufficient for these candidates to have impeccable working-class credentials. Their ideal candidate 'had a good intellectual grip of the Labour problem, and he would have to prove that he had grit enough in him to withstand the corrupting social influences which are so powerful in Parliament.'[90] And while one of Haydn Sanders's enemies on the Sheffield Trades Council claimed that he held 'a great aspiration to become a paid MP' – although MPs were not paid until 1908 – British Knights generally recognised that they would not initially find their ideal parliamentary candidate from within their own assemblies, and looked for other ways to achieve their political objectives.[91]

Knights in Birmingham and the Black Country reached for what Norman Ware described as the most characteristic political weapon of the American Order: the lobby.[92] Their supporter, when interviewed in the *Daily Gazette*, explained that 'it is certain that the Order will insist upon the adoption by all the candidates who seek its support of a much more drastic programme of social legislation than either political party has yet announced.'[93] When pressed to provide an example of the issues that Knights would present to

[90] *Birmingham Daily Gazette*, 22 February 1889.
[91] *Rotherham Advertiser*, 23 July 1892.
[92] Ware, *Labor Movement in the United States*, p. 358.
[93] *Birmingham Daily Gazette*, 22 February 1889.

parliamentary candidates he raised the question of mining royalties. These were, in effect, rents that large landowners charged mine owners who extracted minerals from their lands.[94] It was also an issue, as one Knight claimed at an assembly meeting in West Bromwich, that Liberals, with the notable exception of the Rev. Harold Rylett, failed to address in their lectures or manifesto.[95]

They now searched for a parliamentary candidate willing to accept some if not all of their programme. Thanks to Jesse Chapman, the Master Workman of LA10227 and the secretary of the Smethwick Liberal Association from 1889 onwards, they settled on H.G. Reid, a Gladstonian Liberal. In October 1890, Chapman ensured that the Liberals nominated Reid as their candidate for the 1892 general election in the Handsworth parliamentary division, where the oldest and largest local and district assemblies in Britain were located.[96] LA7952 officially endorsed Reid's campaign the following month.[97] By July, Knights throughout the area followed suit along with the other large local labour organisation, the Midland Counties Trades Federation.[98] Most observers expected Reid to win the election. But he went down in a surprise defeat to the Liberal Unionist candidate, Henry Meysey-Thompson, even as the general election saw a large swing from the Conservatives and Liberal Unionists to the Gladstonian Liberals.[99] Superstitious Knights must have wondered if they were cursed to lose even their most promising electoral campaigns.

English Knights never abandoned the idea of the lobby or electing MPs favourable to their cause. The constitution of the British National Assembly, hammered out by delegates from assemblies in Rotherham and the Black Country in the summer of 1891, charged its new Executive Council with taking 'such action as it thinks advisable to secure the attention and support of Members of Parliament to all measures or bills introduced into the House of Commons in the interests of Labour,' and with supplying to the district and local assemblies sufficient information on all these measures and bills 'as may enable the members to understand the issue of every question involved.'[100] By the time the British National Assembly was formed, however, the assemblies had lost most of their members and were struggling to survive, let alone lobby Parliament for new legislation.

[94] *Birmingham Daily Gazette*, 22 February 1889.
[95] *Smethwick Weekly News*, 1 December 1888.
[96] *Smethwick Weekly News*, 1 November 1890.
[97] *Smethwick Telephone*, 6 December 1890.
[98] *Smethwick Weekly News*, 4 July 1891.
[99] *Smethwick Telephone*, 23 July 1892.
[100] *Preamble of the British National Assembly*, pp. 3, 23–24.

English Knights fared better with the LEA. The LEA emerged out of a decision by the TUC of 1887 to promote the election of trade unionists to all levels of government. T.R. Threlfall, a compositor who served as the TUC's president in 1885 and also served on the Southport Town Council, became its secretary and moving spirit. Threlfall represented Lib-Lab traditions within the labour movement and, as David Howell observes, the Association 'operat[ed] typically under Lib-Lab auspices.'[101] But the LEA also supported working-class candidates for political office regardless of their party affiliation, and Threlfall worked especially hard to recruit the Knights for his association. Knights also appreciated the fact that he publicised their activities through his weekly column on labour affairs in the Liverpool *Halfpenny Weekly*, which in 1889 and 1890, before the paper ceased publication, became the main clearing house for news on the Order's British activities.[102] In February 1890, Threlfall invited the Order's British assemblies to attend the next congress of the LEA in April.[103]

The congress was attended by six delegates representing local and district assemblies from Birmingham, Liverpool and the Black Country, and a seventh Knight as a delegate from the Wolverhampton Trades Council.[104] The most prominent of them were Sanders of Walsall, Reeves of Liverpool, Thomas Dean of Smethwick and Zebulon Butler of Dudley.[105] Henry Pelling writes that 'they presumably attended for the sake of converting the Association to a more radical policy, as other Socialists had done at earlier conferences, though without success.'[106] But the main theme that the Knights, socialists or otherwise, consistently pressed at the congress was the need for independent labour representation. Sanders argued that 'their experience of Liberals and of Tories showed that they must expect nothing of those parties, except on the same line as a traveller was kindly disposed to a pack of wolves that were following him.'[107] Reeves called for 'no compromise with either the Liberal or the Conservative party' lest workers be 'dragged at the chariot wheels of either party'; radical Liberals, he added, often proved to be 'the most determined sweaters.'[108] Instead of calling on the LEA to adopt socialist principles, Reeves argued for 'putting

---

[101] *Report of the Labour Electoral Congress* (1890), p. 1; Howell, *Independent Labour Party*, pp. 144–45.
[102] *Halfpenny Weekly*, 18 May 1889; Pelling, 'Knights in Britain,' p. 327.
[103] *Halfpenny Weekly*, 22 February 1890.
[104] For the Wolverhampton delegate, see *Wolverhampton Chronicle*, 2 April 1890.
[105] *Report of the Labour Electoral Congress* (1890), p. 2.
[106] Pelling, 'Knights in Britain,' p. 327.
[107] *Report of the Labour Electoral Congress* (1890), pp. 22–23.
[108] *Report of the Labour Electoral Congress*, (1890), pp. 16–17, 25.

forward a Labour candidate with a substantial programme.'[109] Zebulon Butler, the single-taxer from Dudley, put the same case in a different way. 'A fair representation of Labour in the House of Commons,' he told the congress, would involve 'the classes … represented by nine members, and the masses – the producers and workers – by the remainder.'[110]

Finally, it seemed, the English assemblies had combined their forces to push forward the cause of independent labour politics within one of the major political organisations of the British labour movement. They received a sympathetic hearing from the other delegates at the congress. But, as with all of their other political ventures, they lost their momentum at the very point when it began to build. Sanders and Reeves, their two most significant political leaders, left the Knights between the LEA's congresses in 1890 and 1891. Other leading Knights were more concerned to halt the decline in the Order's membership over that time than to attend a political convention, and only two Knights, representing DA248 of Cradley Heath, attended the next congress of the LEA in 1891.[111] Neither said anything that made it into the official proceedings. No Knights ever attended any subsequent congress of the LEA. Once again, the speed with which the English assemblies rose and fell ensured that their political influence was concentrated in only two years, 1889 and 1890 – and as with their municipal campaigns, that was too short a period to leave a lasting impression on the LEA.

A very different story unfolded in Scotland, however. The Scottish labour movement, as James D. Young argues, had long found inspiration from political institutions and movements in the United States.[112] Early efforts by Scottish workers to enter politics on an independent basis in the 1860s and 1870s, for instance, were based on what American workers were doing at the time. The miners' leader, Alexander MacDonald, wrote back glowingly of American labour politics while on holiday there in 1868.[113] In the 1880s, as we have seen, Scottish radicals became profoundly influenced by the theories and personality of Henry George. As the events of the Great Upheaval thrust the Knights into global prominence, important figures in the Scottish labour movement also began to see the Order as a profitable example to follow. And Keir Hardie, whose candidacy for Mid-Lanark in 1888 on an independent labour ticket is widely considered one of the great precursors to the Independent Labour Party, and then to the British Labour Party itself, was at the forefront of them.

---

[109] *Report of the Labour Electoral Congress*, (1890), p. 17.
[110] *Report of the Labour Electoral Congress*, (1890), p. 20.
[111] *Report of the Labour Electoral Congress* (1891), p. 4.
[112] Young, 'Changing Images,' pp. 69–89.
[113] Marwick, *Short History of Labour*, p. 75.

In the July 1887 issue of his journal, *The Miner*, Hardie presented a lengthy analysis on the subject of 'Labour Representation.' He began with a rhetorical question: 'Do either of the existing parties fairly represent [the workers] aspirations and desires?' Hardie's answer was a resounding 'No.' The Conservatives offered them nothing. Liberal Unionism existed simply 'to keep Mr Gladstone out of office.' Gladstonian and Radical Liberals promised no more than a series of minor adjustments. Even their working-class representatives, Hardie argued, 'are content to follow in the train of the Liberal party, whithersoever it may lead.' The LEA was a promising beginning, with its aim 'to promote the return of working men to Parliament,' but, Hardie added, 'what difference will it make to me that I have a working man representing me in Parliament if he is a dumb dog who dare not bark, and will follow the leader under any circumstances?'

With the help of Robert Chisholm Robertson, another coal miners' leader, Hardie drafted the programme of the Sons of Labour, a document modelled on the *Declaration of Principles* of the American Knights of Labor.[114] The only major difference between these documents, as J.H.M. Laslett argues, was that Hardie anticipated a greater role for the state than most American Knights were prepared to contemplate.[115] It was with this basic programme in mind that Hardie made the fateful step of running as an independent labour candidate at the Mid-Lanark by-election in April 1888, after being disowned by the local Liberal Association there. A direct line thus connected the Knights of Labor with that most famous event in the origins of independent labour politics in Britain.

Nor was Hardie alone in seeing the Knights and their programme as directly applicable to Scottish labour politics. The Knights, after all, were closely aligned with movements seeking Irish Home Rule, a cause that appealed to the many Irish immigrants concentrated in western Scotland. The Order's programme explicitly called for the nationalisation of land. This plank fit well with the concerns of supporters of the Scottish Land Restoration League and reflected the sympathies of many working-class Scottish radicals for the single tax theories of Henry George. John Ferguson, an Irish Nationalist based in Scotland and with single tax sympathies of his own, began to call in 1888 for the introduction of the Knights of Labor into western Scotland unless the Liberals brought about land nationalisation and an eight-hour working day, itself another demand strongly associated with the Order. In this he was supported by James Shaw Maxwell, another single-taxer with close ties both to the Land Restoration League and the Scottish labour movement.[116]

---

[114] W. Stewart, *J. Keir Hardie* (London: Cassell and Co., 1921), p. 64.
[115] Laslett, *Colliers Across the Sea*, p. 170.
[116] Young, 'Changing Images,' p. 83.

Their threats were not immediately carried out. But all these figures, Hardie included, gave their political ambitions an institutional form, the Scottish Labour Party, in September 1888.[117] All of them were present at the meeting on 25 August that brought into being this new body – which James J. Smyth claims marked the moment when 'Labour politics, as we understand them even today, first emerged.'[118] The Party, after all, possessed one sitting MP in the form of Robert Cunninghame Graham, the aristocratic Liberal-turned-socialist who became closely aligned with the Scottish Knights as well. And while the coal miners of Lanarkshire turned the programme of the Sons of Labour into an order centred on organisation at the workplace and based explicitly on the Knights, the Scottish Labour Party slowly grew. In 1889 the Sons of Labour quickly rose and then just as quickly declined in Lanarkshire. In the same year assemblies of the Knights of Labor, directly affiliated with the American Order, began to appear in Glasgow and Ayrshire.

The relationship between the Knights and the Scottish Labour Party was close from the outset. In September 1889 the Party opened a branch in Glasgow.[119] Three months later the Knights in that city held their first annual 'festival.'[120] Both events were held at the same venue. Many of the notable attendees at both meetings were also the same people. Shaw Maxwell acted as the chairman of each, and Hardie was present to support the Knights just as he helped lead the Party meeting. A Mr Burns, representing the Order, was also on hand to participate in the birth of the Party's Glasgow branch. From the very beginning, then, Scottish Knights cast in their lot with local struggles for independent working-class political representation. And there were other links between the two organisations. In February 1890, Shaw Maxwell wrote to Powderly, asking him to draw up a letter explaining the Order's support for the eight-hour day. This was, Shaw Maxwell assured him, in support of a bill promoted by Cunninghame Graham in the House of Commons that would enforce an eight-hour day for miners. 'A statement from you to him that it is the general wish of the workers of America would greatly strengthen his hands,' he claimed.[121] In this way Scottish radicals tried to conscript the American Order in support of British labour politics.

---

[117] *The Miner*, September 1888.
[118] J.J. Smyth, 'The ILP in Glasgow, 1888–1906: The Struggle for Identity,' in A. McKinlay and R. Morris (eds), *The ILP on Clydeside, 1893–1932: From Foundation to Disintegration* (Manchester: Manchester University Press, 1990), p. 20.
[119] *Glasgow Herald*, 28 September 1889.
[120] *Glasgow Herald*, 28 December 1889.
[121] Shaw Maxwell to Powderly, 27 February 1890, Box 59, TVP.

The leaders and friends of the Scottish Knights did operate in some respects like their English comrades. In the 1890 election for Partick, a parliamentary seat in northwestern Glasgow, Cunninghame Graham quickly recognised, as Knights in other places had in their turn, that the Order's assemblies could give the right candidate a decided electoral advantage.[122] In this case he hoped to use this advantage to the wider benefit of his young party. A three-way series of negotiations soon commenced between Cunninghame Graham for the Scottish Labour Party, Shaw Maxwell for the Glasgow Knights of Labor and Edward Marjoribanks, the Gladstonian chief whip. The first two, according to a report in *The Times*, issued a manifesto to the voters of Partick that

> The Scottish labour party advises its adherents in the Partick Division, especially the organisation of the Knights of Labour, to record their votes for the Liberal candidate in consequence of an interview with Mr. Marjoribanks in which he assured their representatives that Greenock and two other labour seats to be subsequently agreed upon, should be left to the labour party to try the fortune of labour candidates.[123]

Marjoribanks denied making such an agreement. The sheer fact that he considered it 'was the worst bit of electioneering he ever did in his life,' according to one Glasgow newspaper, for it allowed the Liberal Unionist candidate to triumph over the Gladstonian one.[124]

Yet again an attempt to use Knights as bargaining chips in the parliamentary process ended in failure. Cunninghame Graham soon departed the House of Commons as well, after losing on a Scottish Labour Party ticket in an 1892 election for the seat of Glasgow Camlachie. Ironically, it was the same Irish nationalists who had encouraged the development of the Knights in Scotland, as a way to pressure the Liberals into a firmer stance in favour of Home Rule, who abandoned their support for labour and socialist candidates when the Liberals signalled their desire to put Home Rule back at the top of the agenda.[125] Irish nationalism temporarily made and then unmade the fortunes of the Knights and of the wider working-class political movement in Scotland. In the course of those two years, moreover, the Scottish assemblies quickly disappeared along with their political significance. Yet their erstwhile leaders continued to agitate for independent labour politics.

---

[122] Cunninghame Graham often appealed directly to the Knights in this election. See, for instance, *The Scotsman*, 28 January 1890; *Glasgow Herald*, 28 January 1890.

[123] *The Times*, 1 March 1890.

[124] *Glasgow Weekly Mail*, 8 March 1890.

[125] I.G.C. Hutchinson, 'Glasgow Working-Class Politics,' in R.A. Cage (ed.), *The Working Class in Glasgow, 1750–1914* (London: Croom Helm, 1987), p. 133; Laslett, *Colliers Across the Sea*, pp. 171–72.

Shaw Maxwell, who continued for some time to keep in contact with American Knights, although he moved from Scotland to London in 1891, became the first secretary of the Independent Labour Party in 1893.[126] Hardie quickly became the ILP's president, and most branches of the Scottish Labour Party followed them into the new body.

The creation of the ILP, in October 1893, also provides a bridge between the stories of the English and Scottish Knights. By then, few Knights remained in a shrinking number of assemblies, all of them concentrated around Rotherham, Birmingham and Cradley Heath. They would all be gone within a year. But former Knights, particularly Samuel Reeves in Liverpool and Haydn Sanders in Rotherham, were amongst the first to welcome the new party. Sanders even claimed, at an ILP meeting in 1894, that 'the Labour party had existed as an independent organisation in Rotherham, at all events since his advent into the town,' and that 'even if they had not adopted the term "Independent," they had carried out the programme of the Independent Labour Party with more or less success.'[127] Reeves became the President of the Liverpool branch of the Independent Labour Party in the same year.[128]

We should not, of course, attribute too much to the Knights in these cases. But as with the stirrings of independent labour representation in Scotland in 1887, with Keir Hardie's Mid-Lanark campaign in 1888, with the creation of the Scottish Labour Party in the same year and with the development of the Independent Labour Party in 1893, the influence of the Knights of Labor, and the presence of their leaders and supporters, was undeniable. English Knights also participated in Lib-Lab movements which promoted working-class political representation and, as revisionists have argued, operated in their own way to bring the Labour Party a little closer. The Knights of Labor, in other words, were present and active in some of the defining movements and moments in the early political history of the British labour movement.

Conclusion:
The Knights of Labor and Anglo-American Labour Politics

In 1894, at the annual convention of the American Federation of Labor at Denver, Colorado, the delegates of the affiliated unions set down to vote on a political programme. This programme was drafted by Thomas Morgan, an Englishman by birth and the socialist head of the Chicago Trades and

---

[126] *JUL*, 5 March 1891.
[127] *Rotherham Advertiser*, 24 February 1894.
[128] *Liverpool Mercury*, 23 July 1894.

Labor Assembly. Morgan had presented its preamble and 11 planks, which contained proposals for independent political action by the American trade union movement along broadly socialist lines, at the 1893 convention. Morgan explicitly praised the British labour movement for its action in the field of independent labour politics and called for American trade unionists to follow the 'British road.' In the year between the two conventions, the AFL's affiliated unions overwhelmingly approved Morgan's programme, with only the Bakers' union rejecting it outright and a small number of others rejecting plank ten, the demand for 'the collective ownership by the people of all the means of production and distribution.' On the other hand, AFL President Samuel Gompers and his allies remained thoroughly opposed to the programme. He and his supporters managed through skilful management of the proceedings, and by convincing enough delegates of the dangers to the trade union movement of political action, to turn the majority against it. At the opening of the convention most delegates pledged themselves to support Morgan's proposals. By the end, they voted against it by 1,173 to 735.[129]

The AFL never came so close to endorsing independent political action again. That is not to say, however, that the AFL stayed out of politics altogether, as early historians of the movement often suggested. A formidable body of scholarship now insists that the AFL, even Gompers himself, sought not to remain aloof from politics but to engage in politics without committing the Federation to supporting an independent party. AFL leaders lobbied governments at local, state and federal level for favourable legislation and particularly, as legal scholars have explained, to protect themselves from a hostile judiciary.[130] They presented demands to the Democratic and Republican parties at election time and called for AFL members to elect those congressmen, senators and state representatives who most pledged themselves to those demands, and called them to vote against representatives who appeared hostile to the trade unions. Eventually, just as the Knights aligned themselves did with the Populist Party, the AFL aligned itself with

---

[129] J. Greene, *Pure and Simple Politics: The American Federation of Labor and Political Activism, 1881–1917* (Cambridge: Cambridge University Press, 2006), pp. 61–64.

[130] The main texts on the state, particularly the judiciary, and the AFL include W. Forbath, *Law and the Shaping of the American Labor Movement* (Cambridge, MA: Harvard University Press, 1991); C. Tomlins, *The State and the Unions: Labor Relations, Law and the Organized Labor Movement in America, 1880–1960* (Cambridge: Cambridge University Press, 1985); M Dubofsky, *The State and Labor in Modern America* (Chapel Hill: University of North Carolina Press, 1994); G. Friedman, *State-Making and Labor Movements: France and the United States, 1876–1914* (Ithaca: Cornell University Press, 1998); R. Archer, 'Unions, Courts, and Parties: Judicial Repression and Labor Politics in Late Nineteenth-Century America,' *Politics and Society*, 26:3 (1998), pp. 391–422.

the Democrats during the Wilson administration, from 1912 onwards. It is no exaggeration to say that the AFL leaders followed to a great extent the political methods of those who once led the Knights of Labor.

But Gompers in particular also claimed other precedents, as Neville Kirk has observed. Just as Morgan called for the AFL to follow what he saw as the British model of independent labour politics, Gompers insisted that the AFL should follow its own 'British road.' This, Gompers claimed, was based upon the parliamentary lobbying practised by the Parliamentary Committee of the TUC and not, as Kirk notes, the political activities of the TUC's Lib-Lab MPs. A focus on lobbying, Gompers felt, would protect the American labour movement, as it had the British, from the dangers of partisan politics – the same dangers which he claimed had fatally undermined the Knights and their predecessors, the National Labour Union. Gompers, in his selective reading of Anglo-American labour history, at least partially based the future of the American labour movement's political strategies on the basis of the British labour movement's past.[131]

The other side of this parallel was equally striking. In the 1880s, and even into the 1890s, those British trade unionists and radicals who sought to substitute independent working-class action for Lib-Lab politics looked in part to the United States for their inspiration. In particular, they looked to the political struggles of the Knights of Labor. The fact that Powderly and other leading Knights tried to keep the Order aloof from partisan politics, or that many complexities attended the political history of the American Knights, were not so important to British workers and radicals. They saw only that the victories and near-victories of independent labour parties across the United States in the middle years of the 1880s were profitable examples to follow. Gompers found in the British experience a justification for his retreat from independent political action. Many British workers and radicals found in the Knights more justification to hasten its arrival.

British Knights, as the ironworker at Brierley Hill feared, often interfered in politics. They first engaged in political struggles at a municipal level. In Wolverhampton, in Sunderland, in West Bromwich, in Walsall and in Rotherham they brought the principle of working-class representation on town councils and the School Board to the electors, even if they generally met with defeat. At a national level, they attempted to bring the weight of their numbers to bear in two parliamentary divisions, though they were unsuccessful in both cases. They participated at the LEA, but decline prevented them from becoming an influential part of that body. Most importantly of all, the struggles of American Knights during the Great Upheaval helped inspire Keir Hardie's political programme for the Sons

[131] Kirk, *Comrades and Cousins*, ch. 1.

of Labour, the same programme that he ran with in his unsuccessful, but highly significant, campaign in 1888 at Mid-Lanark. Most of the leading figures in the Scottish Labour Party were also Knights, and these same figures were instrumental in the creation of the ILP. The long road to the Labour Party was paved, at least in part, by the hands of Knights of Labor.

British trade unionists created the Labour Representation Committee in 1900. The formal establishment of the Labour Party followed six years later. The British assemblies of the Knights of Labor had disappeared before either, and in no way were they directly involved in the meetings and conventions in which they were formed. But in their own struggles at all levels of politics they formed part of the movement, based around the principle of working-class representation, independent of Liberals and Conservatives, out of which both bodies emerged. The future of American labour politics drew in part on an understanding of the British past; the future of British labour politics drew in part on an understanding of the American past. Nor was this the only transatlantic parallel to attend the history of the Knights of Labor in Britain. In the next chapter, as we will see, the Knights played a similar role in the history of the British trade unions themselves, and with similar consequences for labour on both sides of the Atlantic Ocean.

6

The Knights and the Unions

No account of the Great Upheaval is complete without the story of the Knights of Labor and the trade unionists of the American Federation of Labor. Amidst the titanic industrial and political struggles between capital and labour, the American labour movement, divided mainly into these two camps, fought its own internecine war until the Knights were driven off the field and the Federation, weakened but intact, was left to lead organised labour into the twentieth century. The outcome of this struggle still shapes the way we understand American labour history. John Commons, Selig Perlman and Gerald Grob, among others, argued that the AFL's victory represented the triumph of rational trade unionism, concerned solely with narrow economic interests, over the utopian dreams of the Knights of Labor.[1] Norman Ware and most subsequent historians see that victory as a retreat, however necessary it might have been, from the powerful and wide-ranging organisation of American workers that the Knights briefly maintained in the mid-1880s. Black and women workers suffered most from that retreat.[2] The American labour movement would not achieve the proportion of workers organised by the Knights until the 1930s. Indeed, the Knights organised proportionally more workers than the American labour movement does today.[3]

The labour civil war of the mid-1880s should not obscure other trends in the history of the Knights and the unions, however. They were not always

---

[1] The most vehement explanation of this thesis can be found in Grob, *Workers and Utopia*.

[2] See, for instance, Ware, *Labor Movement*, p. xii. For the effect of the Order's decline on women workers see Levine, *Labor's True Woman*. For its effect on black workers see, for instance, E. Arnesen, 'Following the Color Line of Labor: Black Workers and the Labor Movement Before 1930,' *Radical History Review*, 55 (1993), pp. 53–87.

[3] J. Kaufman, 'Rise and Fall of a Nation of Joiners: The Knights of Labor Revisited,' *Journal of Interdisciplinary History*, 31:4 (2001), p. 555.

or necessarily enemies. In the first decade and a half of the Order's history, the Knights established cordial ties with many trade unionists. The Knights became an attractive option for many of the latter during the 1870s as poor trade and failed strikes decimated the unions. Some trade unionists became Knights. Whole unions even joined the Order as a body. Cooperation was as much a part of the story as conflict, even if conflict ultimately proved more decisive. Equally decisive was the absence of any meaningful rival to the Knights until the revival of the trade unions in the mid-1880s.[4]

The same considerations governed the Order's growth outside North America. Belgian Knights exploited the absence of trade unions in the glass and coal industries of the Charleroi basin.[5] Knights in New Zealand grew rapidly in the aftermath of a large failed strike in 1890, and 'the early 1890s was the era of KOL activists,' as Robert Weir writes, 'for the simple reason that they didn't have a lot of competition.'[6] Australian Knights, by contrast, faced a relatively powerful trade union movement. Though some trade unionists flirted with the Order during the Great Upheaval, Australian unions consistently fought against the assemblies that opened there from 1888 onwards.[7] The strength of the local labour movement remained a powerful determinant of the Order's success or failure in any given country or region.

In this respect British and Irish Knights faced an uphill task at best. In August 1886, the *Omaha Daily Bee* claimed that extending the Order into Great Britain 'will be very difficult, if not impossible. The trade-union spirit in Great Britain is very strong, and British workingmen are very stubborn.'[8] Certainly, as we saw in Chapter 1, the British trade union movement, for all its problems, remained the most powerful in the world. Its affiliated unions would make formidable adversaries. But Knights had solid grounds for optimism. The TUC only organised around 4 or 5 percent of the British labour force for most of the 1880s.[9] The Knights, committed to organising all workers regardless of skill, gender, race or national origin, could potentially

---

[4] Ware, *Labor Movement*, p. xviii.

[5] Watillon, *Knights of Labor in Belgium*, pp. 21–29.

[6] Weir, *Knights Down Under*, p. 18.

[7] Trade unionists in Brisbane wrote to Powderly in 1886 and then held meetings with a view to forming assemblies there (W. Lane to Powderly, 12 May 1886, Box 21, TVP; *Brisbane Courier*, 5 September 1887). The Melbourne Trades Council twice kept the Knights from affiliating while the wider movement in the various Australian colonies prevented the Knights from attending what became the first congress of the Australian Labor Party (*Melbourne Argus*, 11 July 1891; *Melbourne Argus*, 15 April 1893; Weir, *Knights Down Under*, p. 228; Churchward, 'American Influence on the Australian Labour Movement,' pp. 265–66).

[8] *Omaha Daily Bee*, 8 August 1886.

[9] Hinton, 'Mass Labour Movement,' p. 20.

find support from some sections of this unorganised mass – even, perhaps, without upsetting unions affiliated with the TUC.

The changes that took place at the end of the decade further complicated this picture. The end of the 1880s and the beginning of the 1890s, as we saw in Chapter 4, saw the rise of the new unionism. Strikes and trade union membership skyrocketed. New unions like the National Union of Gas Workers and General Labourers and the Dock, Wharf, Riverside and General Labourers' Union spearheaded the extension of trade unionism into unskilled occupations. New unionists like Tom Mann, John Burns, Ben Tillett and Will Thorne gave the new movement a younger and more radical image. Historians agree that the upswing in trade and the fall in unemployment at the end of the 1880s encouraged workers to strike and organise in large numbers.

Agreement ends there. The classic view of the new unionism saw it emerge out of a small but growing socialist movement that, despite its small numbers, provided most of the new unions' leadership and gave these institutions a distinctly radical edge. In this view the new unionism represented a new departure in the British labour movement. Cheap organisations, catering to unskilled workers and more ready to strike, grew in importance at the expense of traditional unions with their high dues, benefit plans and reluctance to engage in industrial action. Revisionists argue that the socialists played a negligible role in the new unions. They point out that the established unions benefited most from the upswing in trade. Still more assert that the new unions, and many of the new unionists, came to resemble the old unions and old unionists more than the other way around. Revisionists even argue that the new unionism represented a quantitative advance in the membership of the trade union movement but not a qualitative change at all. Others point to previous movements among unskilled labourers in the 1870s as proof that the new unionism was not all that new.[10]

These are useful cautions to keep in mind. They continue to inspire historical debate. They should not stop us, however, from seeing the new unionism as at least the beginnings of a qualitative change in the British

---

[10] For a short précis of these arguments see J. Lovell, *British Trade Unions, 1875–1933* (London: Macmillan, 1977), pp. 10–16; Kirk, *Change, Continuity and Class*, ch. 6. For this 'classic' view, see, for instance, E.J. Hobsbawm, 'The New Unionism in Perspective,' in *Workers: Worlds of Labour* (New York: Pantheon, 1984); G.D.H. Cole, *A Short History of the British Working Class Movement* (London: Allen and Unwin, 1948). For revisionist accounts see A.E.P. Duffy, 'New Unionism in Britain, 1889–90: A Reappraisal,' *Economic History Review*, 14:2 (1961), pp. 306–19; H. Clegg, A. Fox and A.F. Thompson, *A History of British Trade Unions Since 1889, Vol. 1, 1889–1910* (Oxford: Oxford University Press, 1964). For a précis of the revisionist arguments see D. Matthews, '1889 and All That,' pp. 24–58.

labour movement. The TUC that entered the twentieth century was a very different animal from that of 1880 or even 1888.[11] And the Knights of Labor became a part of that change. The influence of their American struggles and victories in the mid-1880s helped generate debate among trade unionists keen to revitalise their movement, and provided them with ideas to speed this revitalisation along. The British and Irish assemblies became part of the new unionism themselves. Their attempts to organise unskilled workers and create local federations in several towns and regions provided models for other new unions, and other new unionists, to follow.

The story of the Knights and the new unionism also returns us to a central question from Chapter 1: American exceptionalism. Chapter 1 rejected exceptionalist arguments that see the American labour movement as always and inevitably smaller and backward compared with the labour movements of Europe. This chapter builds on the arguments of Kim Voss, who claims that the relative weakness of the American labour movement in the twentieth century resulted from the defeat of the Knights of Labor in the nineteenth.[12] American exceptionalism was not something inherent, she argues: it was *made*. The story of the Knights in Britain and Ireland provides a new twist on top of this one. The decline of the American Knights caused the labour movement there to retreat; in Britain and Ireland the Knights encouraged the labour movement to advance. American exceptionalism was made by Knights on both sides of the Atlantic.

British and Irish Knights left that powerful legacy to the British labour movement. Their encounters with actual trade unions, however, mirrored the failures of American Knights in the 1880s and 1890s. Knights in some places made alliances with other trade unionists, and in some cases small unions willingly absorbed themselves into the assemblies. More often the Knights and the unions came into conflict. On the one hand, they faced craft unions that resisted any attempts to let their members join the Knights. On the other, they faced new unions of unskilled workers that, despite all the affinity that they might otherwise have shared with the assemblies, also competed with them for members. The Knights were driven out from some industries and displaced by rival unions in others. This chapter, in other words, addresses the deep historical significance of the Order in Britain and Ireland; it also points us towards the reasons behind its decline. As in Belgium, New Zealand, Australia and the United States, the history of the Knights of Labor in Britain and Ireland was powerfully shaped by the trade unions.

---

[11] See, for instance, B.C. Roberts, *The Trades Union Congress, 1868–1921* (London: George Allen and Unwin, 1958).

[12] See Voss, *Making of American Exceptionalism*.

The Knights and the Crafts

The Knights of Labor arrived in England in 1884 as the saviour of local trade unionists. The glassworkers had seen their union crumble in the previous decade, and LA300 and its Universal Federation offered them the chance to revive trade unionism in the industry and build alliances with fellow craftsmen in Europe and North America. A.G. Denny, LA300's European organiser, met with Thomas Burt, the Lib-Lab MP and leader of the Durham Miners' Association, and reported to Powderly that Burt 'was very favourably impressed with the K of L as far as he understood it.'[13] Burt and Henry Broadhurst, the secretary of the TUC's Parliamentary Committee, both praised the Knights in public for their work among the glassworkers.[14] At the Labour Electoral Congress in 1890, however, a Knight from Cradley Heath gave a very different view of their relationship with the trade unions. 'The Knights of Labour, of whom he was one,' he told the Congress, 'held out the hand of fellowship to other bodies, but it did not seem to be accepted.'[15] In just six years the Knights went from saviours to enemies.

During that time more than 10,000 British and Irish workers became part of upwards of 50 assemblies. The Knights naturally focused most of their attention on the great majority of workers that no trade union organised. They became most successful in regions like the Black Country where, as we saw in Chapter 2, unions remained weaker than in other major industrial centres. But their growth, gradual as it was, soon brought them into contact with trade unions that claimed the Order's members for themselves. One Knight from Smethwick told the *Labour Tribune* in December 1886 that, 'in stating that we are opposed to trade unions,' one of the Order's critics 'has made a mistake. One half of its members are trade society men.'[16] These comments aroused suspicion from the trade societies involved. Eric Hobsbawm wrote in his study of British general unions that 'they avoided the competition with the "crafts" which wrecked the Knights of Labor in the more mechanized USA of the late 1880s.' More precisely, the British general unions organised 'labourers' and left 'artisans' to the craft unions while the Knights tried to organise them all, and faced opposition from the 'crafts' as a result.[17] The British Knights, like their American cousins, also faced damaging and, for some assemblies, fatal opposition from the 'crafts.'

---

[13] A.G. Denny to Powderly, 29 December 1884, Box 12, TVP.
[14] Pelling, 'Knights in Britain,' p. 315.
[15] *Report of the Labour Electoral Congress* (1890), pp. 22–23.
[16] *Labour Tribune*, 4 December 1886.
[17] E.J. Hobsbawm, 'General Labour Unions in Britain, 1889–1914,' *Economic History Review*, 1:2 (1949), p. 139.

The Knights began to establish assemblies outside the glass trade in 1886, at a propitious time in the history of trade unionism in the Black Country. The many small trades in the area, from chain making to ironworking, were represented by a loose patchwork of small organisations. In that year, as the *Birmingham Daily Gazette* later recollected, 'several orders of skilled workmen were casting about for a newer style of Trade Unionism.'[18] Well-known local trade union sympathisers, like the Rev. T.T. Sherlock and the Rev. Harold Rylett, chaired meetings that brought together workers who wanted to unite these small organisations into a meaningful alliance. As we saw in Chapter 2, Robert Robertson and Charles Bird attended these meetings and urged listeners to make the Knights the basis of their proposed federation.[19]

These meetings offered Black Country Knights the chance to become the standard-bearers for craftsmen all across the region. They enjoyed some local support. T.T. Sherlock claimed that their presence 'was a splendid augury for the future.'[20] Richard Juggins, the foremost trade unionist in the Black Country, expressed his sympathy for the Knights and announced his intention 'to unite all trades together so as to form one strong Union, on a similar basis to the Knights of Labour in America.'[21] His preference for arbitration over strikes also fit well with the industrial philosophy of the Knights. One American newspaper even reported in May that the Order had brought about federation in the Black Country.[22] Yet these reports proved premature. Juggins and others flirted with the Knights but ultimately built their own organisation, the Midland Counties Trades Federation (MCTF), instead.[23] The MCTF, writes Eric Taylor, represented a 'late flowering of craft unionism' in the Black Country, and aimed to give the various small craft unions in the area parity with employers.[24]

Knights viewed the new Federation as an ally at first. They told one meeting of Black Country workers in April 1886 that while they hoped that all English societies would join them, they 'would not in any way interfere with the objects

---

[18] *Birmingham Daily Gazette*, 18 February 1889.

[19] *Smethwick Telephone*, 29 May 1886.

[20] *Smethwick Telephone*, 8 May 1886.

[21] *Labour Tribune*, 17 April 1886. One contemporary pamphlet listed Juggins as the most respected trade unionist in the area. See Sunday Chronicle, *Chains of Slavery: A Visit to the Strikers at Cradley Heath* (Manchester, 1886), p. 15.

[22] *John Swinton's Paper*, 30 May 1886.

[23] Taylor, *Working Class Movement in the Black Country*, pp. 274–75; E. Taylor, 'The Midland Counties Trades Federation, 1886–1914,' *Midland History*, 1:3 (1972), pp. 26–40.

[24] E. Taylor, 'A Craft Society in the Age of General Unions: The Chainmakers and Strikers Association of Saltney, Pontypridd and Staffordshire 1889–1914,' *West Midlands Studies*, 5 (1970), p. 28; Blackburn, *Sweated Labour*, p. 58.

of federation for the Unions of this country; for, with that, co-operation would be the more easy.'²⁵ Assemblies in Wolverhampton, Lye, Stamber Mill and Wollescote, as well as others from outside the Black Country, all affiliated with the MCTF.²⁶ The Dudley vice makers, for instance, belonged to both bodies in 1889.²⁷ Leaders from both organisations sometimes worked together to settle disputes which involved members of each.²⁸

But this *entente cordiale* soon broke down. In May 1889, chain makers accused the Knights of using aggressive tactics against them. Juggins 'disclaimed any understanding' between the Knights and the Federation.'²⁹ In June, reports surfaced that the Knights were trying to force out workers affiliated with the Federation unless they switched to their side.³⁰ These reports reflected the Knights' desperation as they found that even when they worked with the MCTF that body drew hundreds of potential members away from the assemblies. George Barnsby argues that the Order's 'ultimate failure in the Black Country was due to there being a British organisation able to do everything that the Knights could do – the Midland Counties Trades Federation.'³¹ That was not true in the short term, of course. As early as 1888 the Knights operated two district assemblies and more than 30 local assemblies in the Black Country alone.³² There were enough disorganised workers available for both organisations to grow. In the long run, however, both the Knights and the MCTF strove to unite the workers of the Black Country under a single banner. The Knights missed their chance to hold that banner in 1886 before the MCTF became an established fact.

The Federation slowed the growth of the assemblies without the need for much open conflict. The Amalgamated Society of Engineers, on the other hand, wrenched their members from the assemblies in the space of a year. The ASE remained one of the most powerful trade unions in Britain, indeed the world, with its overseas branches scattered across North America, Australasia, France and other parts of the world where British engineers plied their trade. The ASE also had a history of cooperation with trade unionists from the United States. A young Terence Powderly, then a junior

---

[25] *Labour Tribune*, 17 April 1886.
[26] Barnsby, *Socialism in Birmingham*, p. 80.
[27] *Birmingham Daily Post*, 4 December 1889.
[28] See for instance, the example of the fireclay trade, where different crafts in the industry were affiliated with each body (*Birmingham Daily Post*, 24 December 1889), or the block-chain trade (*Smethwick Weekly News*, 21 September 1889, *Dudley Herald*, 7 September 1889).
[29] *Midland Counties Express*, 4 May 1889.
[30] *Midland Counties Express*, 8 June 1889.
[31] Barnsby, *Socialism in Birmingham*, p. 85.
[32] A list of assemblies from the end of 1888 can be found in *Birmingham Daily Gazette*, 18 February 1889.

official of the Machinists' and Blacksmiths' Union, had worked with the Engineers in the 1870s to promote transatlantic cooperation between the two unions through the pages of their journals.[33] In the 1880s the ASE's General Council began to cede some autonomy to the Australasian and North American branches. The North American branches let their members become Knights and retain their membership in the Engineers, with all the unemployment and sickness benefits that membership entailed.[34] Their leniency in regard to the Order probably stemmed from the enthusiasm that accompanied its growth in the mid-1880s. That enthusiasm infected skilled as much as unskilled workers, and the ASE's American officials probably worried that if they refused to allow dual membership it would be theirs that engineers would discard.

The General Council in Britain was not inclined to leniency, and stuck rigidly instead to the ASE rules that forbade any member from joining another trade society. The secretary of the new National Labour Federation on Tyneside, himself an Engineer, was informed in 1887 that the General Council would expel anyone who remained a member of both organisations. They extended the same threat to members of the Birmingham No. 4 branch, which asked the Council in September 1887 if it might join the Knights.[35] Hundreds of engineers defied these instructions, according to Jesse Chapman, the Master Workman of LA10227.[36] Their minor rebellion, however, was soon dealt with. The ASE's Monthly Report for April 1888 instructed branch secretaries to tell 'every member who has violated one of the fundamental principles of the Amalgamated Society of Engineers, by joining another trade society, that he cannot retain his membership in our Society whilst he belongs to the "Knights of Labour," and that he must immediately give up one (ours) or the other.'[37] Knights in the engineering

---

[33] Yearley, *Britons*, pp. 56–57.

[34] In 1885 the General Council ruled against members in Montreal joining the Knights (Meeting 22 May 1885, *Minutes of the Executive Council of the Amalgamated Society of Engineers, November 1884–July 1885*, Warwick Modern Records Centre [MRC], MSS.259/ASE/1/1/53). In 1887, John Hewitt, a delegate to the General Council, noted that 'the Local Executive Council's decision, directing our members to sever their connection with the "Knights of Labour," does not apply to our members belonging to the American and Canadian Branches' (ASE, *Abstract Report of the General and Local Councils' Proceedings, From January 1st to June 30th, 1888*, pp. 17–19, MRC, MSS.259/ASE/11/1).

[35] ASE, *Abstract of the Council's Proceedings, From June 30th, 1887, to December 31st, 1887*, pp. 61–62, MRC, MSS.259/ASE/4/1/19. Note: the ASE's Executive Council generally met in London and handled day-to-day issues, while the General Council met several times each year and generally handled larger issues.

[36] Jesse Chapman to Powderly, 3 March 1888, Box 41, TVP.

[37] ASE, *Monthly Report of the Amalgamated Society of Engineers for April, 1888*, p. 34, MRC, MSS.259/ASE/4/1/20.

trades attempted to defend themselves. They visited all the Birmingham branches and, according to Chapman, met with 'very marked success among the men – many, when matters are fairly explained to them, taking up our side with enthusiasm.'[38]

But the General Council overcame all opposition from the local rank and file. Knights sent a deputation headed by Richard Hill, the recording secretary of LA7952 and DA208, to plead their case at the triennial meeting of the General Council in May 1888; the Council, with some dissenting votes, refused to spare any time for their petition. The General Council then reaffirmed the decision of the Executive Council and gave ASE members six months to sever their ties with the Knights or face expulsion. Knights protested to no avail.[39] The Monthly Report for December 1888 reminded members that the six months had now elapsed, and judging by the silence on expulsions for joining another society in subsequent reports, the engineers followed the orders of their General Council and abandoned the assemblies.[40] The Knights lost hundreds of members in the engineering trades as a consequence.

Knights achieved greater success for a longer time among the ironworkers of the Black Country. Edward Trow, an ironworkers leader originally from the Black Country but based in Darlington, viewed the Black Country ironworkers in 1888 as 'a dead letter so far as unionism was concerned.'[41] This was an exaggeration. Ironworkers in the Black Country held onto a semblance of local unions, and some became early recruits to the Order's assemblies.[42] In March 1887, as we saw in the previous chapter, their representatives held several meetings to discuss the prospects of forming a new association with ironworkers in the north of England. At the first meeting, the delegate from an ironworks at Corngreaves, near Cradley Heath, called for all of them to form assemblies of the Knights of Labor and claimed that workers from Corngreaves would not accept any alternative.[43] His advice and threats did not go unchallenged. Other delegates claimed that affiliation with the Order

---

[38] Jesse Chapman to Powderly, 12 May 1888, Box 44, TVP.

[39] ASE, *Abstract Report of the General and Local Councils' Proceedings, From January 1st to June 30th, 1888*, pp. 17–19, MRC, MSS.259/ASE/11/1; Jesse Chapman to Powderly, 12 May 1888, Box 44, TVP.

[40] ASE, *Monthly Report of the ASE for December, 1888*, p. 34, MRC, MSS.259/ASE/4/1/20.

[41] *Ironworkers Journal*, January 1888; E. Taylor, 'Edward Trow,' in J. Bellamy and J. Saville (eds), *Dictionary of Labour Biography, Vol. III* (London, 1976), pp. 187–92.

[42] At the Royal Commission on Labour in 1892, the Associated's president, William Aucott, referred to the Knights as the main predecessor to his own union ('Minutes of Evidence from 1892 Royal Commission on Labour, Group A, Volume II,' p. 311. Found at: HCPP).

[43] *Stourbridge, Brierley Hill, and County Express*, 3 March 1887.

would prove expensive and that the Knights were obsessed with politics. One remarked, to general laughter, that 'he had greater faith in getting some of his money back from the North than from America.'[44]

The sceptics won out. The delegate that Corngreaves sent to the next meeting made it clear that his predecessor spoke only for himself.[45] Delegates from the Black Country soon helped to lay the groundwork later in 1887 for Edward Trow's new union, the Associated Iron and Steel Workers of Great Britain, which represented part of a wider trend towards national unions in the iron and steel industries.[46] Trow and other leaders of the Associated immediately set out to recruit those ironworkers who had already joined the Order. His *Ironworkers Journal*, and the West Bromwich *Labour Tribune*, which aligned itself with the Associated Iron and Steel Workers, raised questions about the future of the assemblies in Britain and the United States. Both carried stories on 'the reported decadence of the Knights of Labor.'[47] The first letter to appear in Trow's journal came in May 1888, and was obviously published with local rivalries in mind. The writer, an English ironworker living in the United States, reported his disillusionment with American Knights, claimed that ironworkers in the Order received less than those in rival unions and were led by workers with no direct knowledge of the ironworkers, and ended with praise for Trow's new union.[48] In November, the *Labour Tribune* reported on 'a numerous migration from the ranks of the Knights of Labour to the [British] A.A.I.S.W.,' and provided the story with an easily digestible moral. 'It is the duty of every ironworker first and foremost to support his own society,' the *Tribune* explained. 'He can support whom he pleases afterwards.'[49]

With these favourable winds from the press, the Associated Iron and Steel Workers slowly won ground from the Knights in the Black Country. The *Labour Tribune* was almost certainly premature to suggest a 'numerous migration' between the two. Even in 1892 the president of the Associated, William Aucott, commented that 'a large number of those men [the Knights] are now joining us.' Aucott also claimed in 1892 that 'relations with them are friendly.' But that can only have been the friendliness that comes after the defeated party has forgiven the victors. The Knights were that defeated

[44] *Birmingham Daily Post*, 1 March 1887.
[45] *Stourbridge, Brierley Hill, and County Express*, 12 March 1887.
[46] The British Steel Smelters' Association, the Amalgamated Steel and Iron Workers of Scotland and the National Steel Workers' Association all arose between 1886 and 1888. See T.H. Burnham and G.O. Hoskins, *Iron and Steel in Britain, 1870–1930* (London: Allen and Unwin, 1943), p. 238.
[47] *Ironworkers Journal*, September 1888; *Labour Tribune*, 25 August 1888.
[48] *Ironworkers Journal*, May 1888.
[49] *Labour Tribune*, 17 November 1888.

party, even if their defeat at the hands of Aucott's organisation was not as abrupt or comprehensive as it had been in their conflict with the ASE. Trow and his fellow trade unionists lacked the power of the ASE General Council or the means to force ironworkers to leave the assemblies. Their main drawcard remained their ability to secure representation on the Joint Boards of Arbitration and Conciliation that traditionally governed the iron industry, something that the Knights, as Aucott told the 1892 Royal Commission on Labour, either never attempted or achieved.[50] As with the Midland Counties Trades Federation, the Knights found themselves displaced and then replaced by a new body that first competed with them and then gradually took many of their members.

The case of the iron plate workers was perhaps the most discouraging example of all. During the 1880s, the Knights organised about 450 iron plate workers around Lye and helped them win a number of concessions from employers. We saw in earlier chapters that these concessions included barring female labour from the works; Knights also helped the iron plate workers to get 'a unified list of prices.' In 1890, however, the Knights faced new competition from the new National Amalgamated Iron Plate Workers Society, which brought together workers in the trade from London, Liverpool, Manchester, Bristol, Walsall and other parts of the Black Country. Iron plate workers from Lye, as Ted Brake writes, 'were understandably loath to desert those who had helped them in their hour of need.' But gratitude towards the Order did not stop them deserting their assemblies and joining the new Society after a few months.[51]

In each of these confrontations the Knights soon emerged the clear losers. They nearly burst onto the Black Country scene as a federation organising craftsmen throughout the region, only for the Midland Counties Trades Federation to occupy that position instead. They won support from engineers until the ASE very effectively forced Knights in that trade to choose their side. For all their protests, the engineering Knights chose the ASE. Knights made inroads among the ironworkers of the Black Country until the Associated arrived and soon took their members. Even among iron plate workers at Lye, whose affiliation with the Knights brought them nothing but victories, the rise of the Iron Plate Workers Society soon cost the assemblies some 450 more men. George Barnsby's claim that the Order could not compete with 'a British organisation able to do everything that the Knights could do,' rings true in each of these cases.[52] These organisations need not even battle with the Knights to displace them. The crafts,

[50] 'Minutes of Evidence,' p. 311.
[51] Brake, *Men of Good Character*, p. 167.
[52] Barnsby, *Socialism in Birmingham*, p. 85.

Hobsbawm suggested, eventually wrecked the American Knights; in Britain they hamstrung many assemblies in a short space of time.

'There is no room for an organization of the Powderly type here,' the *Smethwick Weekly News* concluded in December 1888. 'The ground is occupied, the English trades unions are not going to dissolve themselves to make room for a new order.'[53] The experiences of Black Country Knights certainly bore out the second half of that statement. But there were those who made radically different predictions about the future of the British Knights of Labor. In February 1889, a correspondent for *Reynolds's Newspaper* claimed that the Knights of Labor would soon eclipse the TUC itself. That view seems pure fantasy when we consider the Order's first five years in the Black Country; but method lay behind his apparent madness. The TUC, he explained, had 'selfishly ignored the cause of unskilled labour,' a mass of workers that far outnumbered all the trade unionists in Britain, for much too long. The Knights seemed much more likely to organise them than the Parliamentary Committee of the TUC.[54] If the trade unions thwarted the Knights among skilled workers, in other words, the Knights might do better on the other side of the skill divide. And the *Reynolds's* correspondent made his startling prediction just as the rise of a new movement, the 'new unionism,' placed the issue on unskilled labour squarely on the trade union agenda. The Knights and the new unionism were very closely related. The former, indeed, played an integral role in the origins and the development of the latter.

The Knights and the New Unionism

When Michael Davitt appeared at the General Assembly of the Knights of Labor in 1887, he told the delegates that 'the spectacle which the Knights of Labor organization presents to European workingmen gives pride and pleasure and hope to your less powerful and less favoured brethren across the Atlantic.'[55] Less than a year later, the strike of female workers at the matchworks of Bryant and May began a groundswell of trade union action that became known as the new unionism. The 1889 strikes of gasworkers and dockers in London became the great symbols of the new movement, and at all subsequent Trades Union Congresses the leaders of the older, established unions faced severe challenges to their leadership from 'new unionists' like John Burns, Tom Mann and Ben Tillett. These events were related. The pride and pleasure and hope that Davitt mentioned in 1887 formed part of the context from which the new unionism emerged in 1888 and 1889.

---

[53] *Smethwick Weekly News*, 1 December 1888.
[54] *Reynolds's*, 24 February 1889.
[55] *JUL*, 15 October 1887.

Contemporary observers certainly associated the Knights with the rise of the new unions. 'The "New Unionism," Sidney Webb wrote to a London newspaper in 1890, 'is doing for England the work of the Knights of Labour in America.'[56] The *Birmingham Gazette* observed at the end of 1889 that 'the labour movements which were initiated by the [1889 London] dock strike are clearly following on the same lines as those which the Knights of Labour marked out.'[57] Historians have elaborated further. J.H.M. Laslett argues that 'the K of L acted as part catalyst, and part actor in the movement towards trades amalgamation and general unionism.'[58] Logie Barrow and Ian Bullock agree that the Knights briefly played an important role in the agitation for federation, a heading under which amalgamation and general union schemes usually fell.[59] Henry Pelling writes that the Order 'contributed in several ways to build up interest in unionism, especially among the unskilled.'[60] Ronald Bean has shown how Knights in Liverpool played crucial roles in the development of new unionism in Liverpool, while James D. Young has underlined the important role that the Knights played, along with other American figures and institutions, among the workers of Scotland.[61]

The Knights of Labor did not create the material conditions that led to the upswing in trade, or to the fall in unemployment that made hitherto unorganised workers more likely to act and organise. But strike waves are more than simply a function of economic conditions and especially of unemployment.[62] James Cronin writes that in the 1870s and 1880s the extension and expansion of the British trade union movement remained hindered by the lack of 'a new set of political ideas, by novel strategic thinking or what might be termed a new philosophy of labour.' The growth of British socialism went some way towards providing this new philosophy. Many trade unionists learned lessons from the economic downturns of the period which became, as Cronin argues, a 'great teacher of labour.'[63] And from across the Atlantic, the Knights provided an alternative philosophy to the prevailing methods of the TUC. These and other strands combined to give the new unionism intellectual as well as material foundations.

---

[56] *Pall Mall Gazette*, 7 February 1890.
[57] *Birmingham Daily Gazette*, 20 December 1889.
[58] Laslett, 'Haymarket, Henry George,' p. 72.
[59] L. Barrow and I. Bullock, *Democratic Ideas and the British Labour Movement, 1880–1914* (Cambridge: Cambridge University Press, 1996), pp. 67–70.
[60] Pelling, 'Knights in Britain,' pp. 329–30.
[61] R. Bean, 'Knights of Labour in Liverpool,' pp. 68–78; Young, 'Changing Images,' pp. 69–89.
[62] Hobsbawm, 'New Unionism in Perspective,' p. 155.
[63] Cronin, 'Strikes,' p. 87–88.

The Great Upheaval gave a powerful jolt to radicals and trade unionists in Europe. Socialists were accustomed to seeing the Americans as laggards in the revolutionary movement. Now their struggles appeared, in the words of Jules Guesde, as 'the tocsin for the social revolution … in all the civilized world.'[64] Engels even predicted that the Americans would soon take their place in the vanguard of the international revolutionary movement.[65] British trade unionists were also accustomed to seeing the American labour movement as a smaller and derivative version of their own. Yet in 1885 they saw the Knights defeat the infamous robber baron Jay Gould in a strike against his Southwestern railroad system – possibly the greatest victory ever won by a working-class movement against any corporation in the world. Now it seemed that British trade unionists had something to learn from the Americans instead of, as in the past, the other way around.

American Knights offered them two interrelated lessons in particular, both of which became central to the new unionism: organising unskilled workers and forming them and skilled workers into a single, grand federation of all trades and industries. Both causes animated British socialists and some radicals and trade unionists in the 1880s.[66] The TUC of the 1880s, however, almost exclusively represented the skilled crafts and largely refused to lead a movement to organise workers outside the crafts. The Congress also failed to act on a number of schemes for federation that delegates proposed over the course of the decade.[67]

Both causes had a rich British pedigree. 'Ideas of federation,' write Logie Barrow and Ian Bullock, 'were part of something older and looser: of those aspirations for united action by all working people – however labelled – unionised or not.'[68] Robert Owen's Grand National Consolidated Trades Union in the 1830s, the United Kingdom Alliance of Organised Trades and the plans of the British and Irish sections of the First International for an 'international trades union' in the 1860s, each provided precedents for organising skilled and unskilled workers together. Yet Barrow and Bullock note that the supporters of both causes in the 1880s and 1890s tended to look for more recent precedents than these.[69] And while the President of the 1886 TUC, Frederick Maddison, may have doubted 'whether a system such as that instituted in America by the Knights of Labour would be congenial to

---

[64] Quoted in Laslett, 'Haymarket, Henry George …,' p. 69.
[65] Engels, 'Preface to the American Edition.'
[66] Rabinovitch, *British Marxist Socialism*, pp. 89–90.
[67] See, for instance, *Report of the 1886 Trades Union Congress*, p. 46; *Report of the 1887 Trades Union Congress*, pp. 36–37, all from TUC Online Reports, found at: http://www.unionhistory.info/reports
[68] Barrow and Bullock, *Democratic Ideas*, p. 58.
[69] Barrow and Bullock, *Democratic Ideas*, pp. 57–61.

the majority of our societies,'[70] the Order provided many radicals and trade unionists with proof that federation and the organisation of unskilled labour worked in practice as well as in theory.

The staff of *Reynolds's Newspaper* consistently urged their readers to follow the Order's example. In May 1886, 'Dodo' called the attention of unionists to 'the programme of the Brotherhood of the Knights of Labour.' It was, he claimed, 'worth studying':

> In England we can hardly be said to have a pure labour movement. We have a skilled labour movement, the chief manifestations of which is the trades unions. The unskilled labourers are still more numerous. America is now showing them a glorious example.[71]

Dodo's colleague 'Demos' agreed, in an open letter to Michael Davitt in July 1887, that 'an organization on the pattern of the American Knights of Labour seems to offer itself at once as the framework best suited to a Labour Union in this country.'[72] In August he added that the man who led a great movement of unskilled labourers would become 'one of the most powerful men in England.' He would, Demos claimed, 'be the English Powderly.'[73]

Reynolds's was not alone. Socialists wanted to build a single organisation of all British workers and found a powerful model in the Knights. *Justice* and *Commonweal*, the two main socialist publications and the organs of the Social Democratic Federation and the Socialist League, respectively, praised the Order even if they also attacked the moderation, even anti-radicalism, of Powderly and its other leaders.[74] Some trade unionists also found the Order's message appealing. An anonymous trade unionist wrote in the magazine *Fortnightly* that 'eager spirits' saw the labour movement as either too limited in its goals or too exclusive in its membership. 'In the opinion of the first,' he explained, 'social revolution is to supersede the union and render it unnecessary.' In the second case, he added, 'a new form of organisation is required, which, like the Knights of Labour of America, shall be all embracing and gather to its protecting folds the skilled artisan, the unskilled labourer, and the female toiler.'[75]

We can see the influence of the Knights on individual trade unionists, whether radical or moderate, well known or unknown. Ben Turner, a future Labour MP, cotton trade union leader, and widely regarded as moderate, saw the Knights as 'the first definite attempt to have a working

---

[70] *Report of the 1886 Trades Union Congress*, p. 24, from TUC Online Reports.
[71] *Reynolds's*, 16 May 1886.
[72] *Reynolds's*, 10 July 1887.
[73] *Reynolds's*, 7 August 1887.
[74] See *Justice*, 18 April 1885; *Commonweal*, December 1885.
[75] Trade Unionist, 'Trade Unions,' *Fortnightly*, September 1887.

class Trades Union covering the white races of the world.' This message, he claimed, inspired his attempts in the 1890s to broaden the membership of his union 'and take in as members all grades of textile workers other than cotton operatives.'[76] Michael Davitt, after his appearance at the General Assembly in 1887 and his subsequent work for Knights around Birmingham, went on to publish a short-lived paper, the *Labour World*. He also settled a strike on the Liverpool docks in 1890 and then tried to kick-start the new unionism in Ireland with the creation of a general union, the Irish Democratic Labour Federation.[77] Anonymous trade unionists in Wales hoped, in 1887, to build 'one federated society of working-men ... after the fashion of the Knights of Labour.'[78] The socialist J.L. Mahon published *The Labour Programme* the same year. That document called for a 'general workmen's union' that would 'gather together all kinds of disorganised workers' and form them into a 'workable system of Labour Federation.'[79] Mahon's text never mentioned the Knights but his proposed union mimicked the Order in all important respects.

We can find the Order's imprint on trade unions too. The first of these was the National Labour Federation (NLF), founded on Tyneside in November 1886. The NLF organised unskilled workers across the northeast, and A.E.P. Duffy argues that it was the first of the new unions, several years before the Gasworkers and Dockers in London.[80] Its creators, writes M. Searle, were inspired by the victory of New York tramwaymen, in a strike organised by the Knights, 'into thinking that the "all-grades" approach could herald a breakthrough on Tyneside.'[81] The Order's role in the eight-hour movement encouraged them further.[82] The Federation's executive committee acknowledged these debts in a letter to Powderly on 6 December 1886, only days after the Federation was formed. J. Ramsey, the founding president, asked Powderly for 'an outline of the working of your society, your code of Rules, number of members and your rate of increasing your plan of

---

[76] Turner, *About Myself*, pp. 131, 130; D.E. Martin and B. Turner, 'Ben Turner,' in D. Howell and K. Gildart (ed.), *The Dictionary of Labour Biography, Vol. XIII* (Basingstoke: Palgrave Macmillan, 2010), pp. 251–57.

[77] L. McNeil, 'Dissecting Davitt: (Ab)using the Memory of a Great Irishman,' in F. Lane and A.G. Newby (eds), *Michael Davitt: New Perspectives* (Dublin: Irish Academic Press, 2009), p. 187.

[78] *Labour Tribune*, 26 March 1887.

[79] J.L. Mahon, *A Labour Programme* (London, 1888), pp. 78–80.

[80] Duffy, 'New Unionism,' pp. 307–08.

[81] M. Searles, 'The Origins of New Unionism on Tyneside,' *North East Labour History*, 25 (1991), p. 37.

[82] A.E.P. Duffy, 'Eight Hours Day Movement in Britain, 1886–1893,' *The Manchester School*, 36:3 (1968), pp. 210–12.

action, when engaged in a strike or dispute, and any other information you may consider likely of service to us in our future operations,' adding that 'it is your enterprise and achievements that makes your practical experience of such value to us in our attempts to benefit the class on whose behalf both societies are working.' Ramsey then informed Powderly that as well as taking inspiration from the American Knights, the new Federation had appointed a local Knight to its executive board.[83]

The NLF soon became little more than a vehicle for socialist agitation on Tyneside.[84] When the new unionism reached its height in 1889, however, the Order's influence remained important. Henry Pelling argues that the Knights and their 'conception of a general union which refused no applicant for membership … was an example to the Gasworkers,' whose membership actually consisted of labourers of all kinds, and especially to its president, Will Thorne.' Thorne's thinking was powerfully shaped by Eleanor Marx, who had in turn been inspired in the direction of a general union like the Gasworkers by what she and her partner, Edward Aveling, saw of the Knights on a trip to the United States in 1886.[85] The leaders of the National Union of Dock Labourers, on the other hand, which organised dockers in Liverpool, Glasgow and other northern cities, had in some cases been Knights themselves. Richard McGhee actually arrived in Glasgow in 1889 as an organiser for the Black Country assemblies before he decided to begin the NUDL instead.[86]

Many new unionists sought to build on the rise of the new unions and create federations that would link them with the rest of the labour movement. In 1889 and 1890, as Hobsbawm observes, 'all manner of federations and centralized "general staffs" had been suggested.'[87] The founders of these bodies also drew inspiration from the Knights. John Williams, a socialist long active among London's unskilled labourers, told participants in the London Dock Strike in September 1889 that 'his purpose was to form a federation to consist of labourers and mechanics.

---

[83] J. Ramsey to Powderly, 6 December 1886, Box 27, TVP.

[84] Searles, 'Origins on Tyneside,' p. 30.

[85] Pelling, *Origins of the Labour Party*, p. 85; D.E. Martin, 'William James Thorne,' J.M. Bellamy and J. Saville (eds), *Dictionary of Labour Biography, Vol. I* (London: MacMillan, 1972), pp. 314–19. Indeed, Marx and Aveling had incurred the wrath of German-American socialists for suggesting while there that they swallow their contempt for Terence Powderly and his supporters and convert the Knights of Labor to a socialist position. See Y. Kapp, *Eleanor Marx: The Crowded Years, 1884–1898* (London: Lawrence and Wishart, 1976), pp. 145–49, 167–87; R. Holmes, *Eleanor Marx: A Life* (London: Bloomsbury, 2014).

[86] W. Kenefick, *Red Scotland! The Rise and Fall of the Radical Left, c.1872 to 1932* (Edinburgh: Edinburgh University Press, 2007), p. 32.

[87] Hobsbawm, 'General Unions,' p. 136.

Let all classes of workmen drop distinctions, so that when the mechanics struck the labourers would stop work, and when the labourers struck they would not go out without the mechanics.' Williams added that 'they must be like the Knights of Labour, now so powerful in the United States as to be able to dictate terms to employers and boycott those firms that are against the strikers. It had been the object of his life to form a union of this kind.'[88] He soon helped to build the National Federation of Labour Union, which remained, according to Victor Rabinovitch, 'one of the most ambitious attempts at general federation' attempted during this period. Rabinovitch further claims that the model for the NFLU came from the Knights' branches in Britain, which had a large proportion of socialists among their ranks. Williams's own words, however, suggest that the Order's American example loomed even larger.[89]

The power of that example soon waned. Opponents of the new unionism seized on the Order's American decline as proof that organising unskilled workers and building grand federations were both doomed to failure. When H.H. Champion debated the new unionism in 1890 with George Shipton, the most outspoken of the 'old' unionists, he claimed that 'federations have met with a good deal of success in America'; Shipton responded that federations 'have been tried over and over again, and have failed, the collapse of the greatest organisation of the kind, that of the Knights of Labour, proving the truth of this assertion.'[90] The same Order that once helped to inspire the new unionism now became a liability to that movement. By this point, of course, British trade unionists no longer needed inspiration from foreign movements like the Knights. Their own new unions and federated bodies proved that it was possible to organise unskilled workers in large numbers. Even then, however, the Order held some lingering appeal for many trade unionists who came of age in the 1880s. Logie Barrow and Ian Bullock argue that the Knights of Labor remained a precedent when debates over federation grew even more intense at the very end of the 1890s.[91] The industrial unionists and syndicalists of the early twentieth century, as Larry Peterson writes, looked to Robert Owen's Grand National and the Knights of Labor as their predecessors.[92]

But the Knights were more than just a precedent: the British and Irish assemblies became part of the new unionism themselves. Like most

---

[88] *The Times*, 6 September 1889.
[89] Rabinovitch, *British Marxist Socialism*, p. 308.
[90] *Newcastle Weekly Courant*, 7 June 1890.
[91] Barrow and Bullock, *Democratic Ideas*, pp. 67–70.
[92] L. Peterson, 'One Big Union in International Perspective: Revolutionary Industrial Unionism, 1900–1925,' *Labour/Le Travail*, 7 (1981), p. 41.

other trade unions, they benefited from the upswing in trade at the end of the 1880s, especially in their main base in the Black Country. Knights in Walsall, in particular, briefly established a powerful federation of the town's small crafts between 1889 and 1890, and claimed to organise 40 distinct trades.[93] While other trade unionists dreamed of great national federations, the Knights pushed for comprehensive unity on a local level. Walsall's Haydn Sanders explained the concept when he lectured among workers at Rotherham. The Order's 'power of application and strength did not depend upon support from any other town or country,' he told one meeting in September 1889. He 'assumed there were 30,000 working men in the Sheffield and Rotherham district and showed what a power they would have if united. By contributing twopence per week there would be a sum realised of nearly £700 per week.'[94]

As the Knights spread into new corners of Britain and Ireland at the end of the 1880s they particularly encouraged the development of the new unionism, and especially the organisation of unskilled workers, in three places. The first was Glasgow. The agitation surrounding the Sons of Labour, with its close plagiarism of the Knights in neighbouring Lanarkshire, led to the formation of assemblies in Glasgow and on the west coast of Scotland. Though few sources concerning the Scottish assemblies have survived, we do know that the Knights helped to revive trade unionism among dockers at Ardrossan in Ayrshire, as well as in Glasgow itself.[95] The second was Derry. Historians have usually confined their study of the new unionism in Ireland to three bodies: the Gasworkers, the NUDL and the National Amalgamated Union of Labour. Yet the Knights arrived in Derry in 1889, more than two years before the Gasworkers and the NUDL. In that time LA1601 reached 800 members. Its first recording secretary claimed that the assembly was 'comprised of all classes of industry in this city,' including unskilled workers at a distillery and what the replacement secretary called 'outside labourers.'[96] Most of LA1601's members were those in that last category who, as the secretary explained to Powderly in 1891, 'found this organization for the purpose of getting an increase of their pay.'[97] Knights in Derry briefly managed to build a powerful local federation that crossed lines of skill as well as the all-important sectarian lines that then, as now,

---

[93] *Halfpenny Weekly*, 30 November 1889.

[94] *Rotherham Advertiser*, 28 September 1889.

[95] C. Levy, *Ardrossan Harbour, 1805–1979* (Glasgow: Workers Educational Association, 1988), pp. 46–47; Marwick, *A Short History of Labour*, p. 67.

[96] *JUL*, 13 February and 20 November 1890; William Stewart to Hayes, 14 August 1891, Box 9, JHP.

[97] William Stewart to Powderly, 2 October 1891, Box 69, TVP.

permeated all facets of life in Northern Ireland. They became both the standard-bearers of the new unionism and the precursors of other new unions in the town.[98]

The Knights proved most instrumental in the development of the new unionism on Merseyside. Their short-lived assembly in 1885 had anticipated later attempts to organise on the Liverpool docks. In 1889 the Knights re-established themselves in the city and, as in Derry, they predated all the new unions with the exception of the Sailors' and Firemen's Union. Not long after establishing LA443 in May, they led the agitation for trade unionism among the city's tramwaymen, an agitation that soon mushroomed into a wider movement to organise unskilled workers. James P. Archibald, the Order's American organiser, spoke at one of their early meetings.[99] John Higgins, one of LA443's leaders, became the first chairman of their new union although he stepped down from that role after only several days.[100] William Newcomb, the tramwaymen's subsequent leader, was also closely associated with local Knights.[101] And Samuel Reeves, Liverpool's most prominent Knight and the Inside Esquire of LA443, remains known as 'a pioneer of the New Unionism.'[102]

As in Walsall, Rotherham, Derry and elsewhere, Knights in Liverpool saw LA443 as the first step towards a citywide federation that would number upwards of 50,000 members. They soon attracted interest from local railwaymen and plasterers.[103] Most of all, they sparked a revival of trade unionism along the waterfront. In 1889, LA443 found many recruits among workers at the Bootle docks. They soon found that rival trade unions were more successful at corralling the city's unskilled workers into more permanent bodies than theirs. The NUDL soon occupied the ground that Knights had cleared. But the latter remain important as pioneers and, as Brian Towers writes, 'their espousal of the unorganised industrial worker fed into the emerging pressure from industrial workers for union representation.'[104]

American and British Knights each contributed to the new unionism in distinct and important ways. The Americans had four main effects on the British labour movement during the 1880s. First, Knights showed,

---

[98] McAteer, 'New Unionism in Derry,' pp. 12–13.
[99] Bean, 'Knights in Liverpool,' p. 70.
[100] Taplin, 'Liverpool Tramwaymen,' p. 58.
[101] Rees, *Local and Parliamentary Politics*, p. 66.
[102] Rees, *Politics in Liverpool*, p. 67; R. Bean, 'Samuel Reeves,' in *Dictionary of Labour Biography, Vol. I* (London: MacMillan, 1972), pp. 282–85.
[103] Bean, 'Knights in Liverpool,' pp. 72–73.
[104] B. Towers, *Waterfront Blues: The Rise and Fall of Liverpool's Dockland* (Lancaster: Carnegie, 2011), p. 116.

through their organising of unskilled as well as skilled workers in a single federation, that British and Irish trade unionists could build a broader and more united movement than that then represented by the TUC. Second, they showed that such a movement could indeed work and win great victories against powerful employers. Third, they directly influenced a number of individuals who became new unionists. Fourth, they directly influenced the creation of bodies like the National Labour Federation, the National Federation of Labour Union and other similar federations as well as, to a lesser extent, ones like the Gasworkers, the NUDL and the London Dockers' Union.

The Knights of Labor did more than simply influence the development of the new unionism in Britain and Ireland. In some towns and cities they were the new unionism, or at least the first expression of it. They were, to quote Laslett, 'part-catalyst and part-actor' in the rise of general unionism; they also played this same role in the new unionism as a whole. They might not have provided the critical factor in that movement. Their presence does not require the complete rewriting of nineteenth-century British labour history. But they were definitely a part, and an important and discernible one, of the new unionism. Even if that had been their only contribution to the history of the British labour movement, it would have been enough to ensure that the British and Irish Knights of Labor did not rise and fall without trace. It also supplied one of the central ironies of their history. Just as the crafts had stymied the progress of the British and Irish assemblies in the 1880s, the new movement that the Knights inspired then helped to bring about their downfall in the 1890s.

The New Unionism and the Knights

Knights in the Black Country had found over the course of the 1880s that many skilled workers, even those initially attracted to the assemblies, soon deserted them in favour of rival unions. Their dream of becoming more than a transient collection of small and disparate trades diminished with each new defection. But the upswing in trade at the end of the decade, and the new unionism that the Knights of Labor part-inspired and part-led, seemed to offer new avenues for growth and new constituencies for their brand of all-embracing trade unionism. If the old unions checked their progress, then the new unionism appeared to be a salvation. Knights in Derry, Liverpool and Glasgow also epitomised the ways in which the revival of trade and trade unionism revived the fortunes of the British Knights of Labor. They were not alone. In the first months of the new decade the Order approached its peak membership and reached into more parts of Britain and Ireland than it had or ever would again. Yet trade worsened again in the next several years. The tide of the new unionism receded with it, and the Knights became one of the many casualties of the ensuing retreat. But their fall was not simply an index of the swings of the business cycle. Knights in Britain and Ireland found that the new unionism gave rise to new movements and new organisations that, for all the intellectual debt they owed to the Knights, were as likely to compete with the assemblies as to cooperate with them.

The years of the new unionism, of course, were not just the story of newly organised unskilled workers fighting unprecedented numbers of strikes. Most of the increase in union membership during the period occurred in the skilled trades, and 'old' unions like the ASE benefited as much if not more from improved economic conditions as the Dockers or the Gasworkers. The Midland Counties Trades Federation, that ally-cum-enemy of Knights in the Black Country, organised as many as 14,000 workers in 1891.[105] The Order's growth in some places reflected these trends too. LA454 in Walsall, for instance, grew more as a local alternative to the MCTF than anything else. They were able to do so because of rifts between that Federation and local unions. The bit filers and forgers, in particular, accused the Federation of failing to support them during a strike even though, as Richard Juggins made clear, they had severed their connection with the Federation some months earlier. The Knights, as Richard Juggins and the MCTF's other leaders suspected, used these rifts to attract craftsmen in Walsall to LA454 instead.[106]

They were not entirely successful. Some local trade unionists were none too happy to see their organisations absorbed into the Knights of Labor. In 1889 and 1890 the newspapers of Walsall often printed letters from trade unionists attacking LA454 and particularly its Master Workman, Haydn Sanders. Samuel Welsh, the president of the Coach Harness Furniture Trade Society, whose members were targeted by the Knights as potential recruits, became Sanders's most vehement critic. The Knights, he claimed in one long screed, operated with 'money obtained by means of delusive promises incapable of realisation [which] is wastefully expended in providing residences and exorbitant salaries for domineering officials.' He implored his fellow trade unionists in other letters to resist the incursions of the Knights.[107] Some did. The head of the local miners, Benjamin Dean, often criticised the Order.[108] These men and their organisations, however, remained too weak to defeat the Knights as the Engineers

---

[105] Taylor, *Working-Class Movement in the Black Country*, pp. 282–83.
[106] *Midland Counties Express*, 13 July 1889.
[107] *Walsall Observer*, 11 January 1890.
[108] *Walsall Free Press*, 2 November 1889.

and other craft unions had done. They could only slow and not stop the growth of the Knights as a (briefly) powerful force in Walsall's industrial and political life.

The Walsall experience acts as a caution against any too-neat compartmentalisation of the old and new unions, or the old and new unionism. The new unions and not the old, however, determined the fate of the British assemblies in the 1890s. The Knights were generally inclined to treat them as allies. They participated in the early growth of the National Labour Federation on Tyneside in 1886, and in the same year they spoke on behalf of seamen busy organising the Sailors' and Firemen's Union.[109] In 1889, as the new unionism began to peak, the assemblies also raised money for the London dock strike, for bedstead workers on strike in Birmingham and for seamen on strike in Glasgow.[110] Haydn Sanders acted as secretary of the local Gasworkers Union at the same time as he led LA454, and Sam Reeves agitated for unskilled workers throughout Liverpool as well as for the Knights and for his own trade, the iron core moulders.[111] The seamen, at least, reciprocated this support for a time. Knights worked relatively closely with them in the early months of LA443 in Bootle.[112] Seamen in Glasgow appreciated the Order's help so much that when James Shaw Maxwell went to open a new assembly at Ardrossan, on the Ayrshire coast, he was accompanied by a representative of the Sailors' and Firemen's Union.[113]

The Knights also found a vehicle to secure further cooperation with other unions through the trades councils. These bodies, which brought together trade unionists from all the different unions in a given town or city, had emerged as early as the 1860s and were, in the words of their first historian, 'pioneers of Trade Union solidarity.'[114] In the 1880s they remained the only official bodies, apart from the TUC, where representatives of the various trade unions formally met. As the new unionism began in earnest, many trade unionists looked to the trades councils as forums where delegates from both new and established unions could combine forces and even extend trade unionism among new and disorganised bodies of local workers.[115] Knights

---

[109] *Sunderland Daily Echo*, 1 December 1886.
[110] *Walsall Observer*, 7 September 1889; *Birmingham Daily Gazette*, 9 December 1889; *Edinburgh Evening News*, 9 February 1889.
[111] *Walsall Observer*, 16 November 1889; Rees, *Politics in Liverpool*, p. 67.
[112] Bean, 'Knights in Liverpool,' p. 71.
[113] *The Scotsman*, 20 January 1890.
[114] C. Richards, *A History of Trades Councils: 1860–1875* (London: Labour Research Department, 1920), p. 20.
[115] A. Clinton, *The Trade Union Rank and File: Trades Councils in Britain, 1900–40* (Manchester: Manchester University Press, 1977), pp. 81–82.

became involved publicly on the trade councils of Dudley, Wolverhampton, Sunderland, Walsall and Rotherham. In the first two places they formed an important part of the council.[116] James Brown of LA3504 even served as the secretary and then the treasurer of the Sunderland Trades Council in the early 1890s.[117]

Knights in Walsall and Rotherham actually set up the trades councils in these towns with some help from other trade unionists. Where Knights elsewhere sought nothing more than the cooperation and friendship of the local labour movement, Knights in these towns used the trades councils to put their ideas of local federation into practice. The trades councils would go beyond simply bringing together existing unions in the area. 'If the trade has no organisation,' said Haydn Sanders, explaining the new Walsall Trades Council to a meeting in October 1889, 'then it is hoped the trades' council will be the means of forming one.'[118] Knights in Rotherham even claimed that their new body, founded in 1891, represented an advance over all previous trades councils. 'Under the old order of things,' one claimed in 1892, 'beyond their power to exchange opinions, advise each other in time of strike, and allow the members to collect at the shop gates of the various unions federated with the different councils, little could be done.' Workers in Rotherham, however, went for a 'new idea, viz., of having a Trades Council, whose members paid one penny per week, and got 5s in return for it while on strike.'[119]

These trades councils allowed the Knights to bury past disagreements. Haydn Sanders and Samuel Welsh, among others, put aside their polemic to bring the Walsall Trades Council to life.[120] But these trades councils also outgrew the Order that helped create them. The Walsall Trades Council assumed the political role that LA454 had developed in 1889 and, as we saw in the previous chapter, quickly replaced the assembly as the local champion of working-class representation.[121] The trades councils also became substitutes for the local federations that Knights hoped to build. Haydn Sanders had advanced an identical plan to the one adopted by the Rotherham Trades Council three years earlier – but through the vehicle of the Knights of Labor. The Walsall and Rotherham Trades Councils represented the extension of the Order's own aims, a local federation

---

[116] For their importance see *Birmingham Daily Post*, 17 August 1894; Lawrence, *Speaking for the People*, p. 116.

[117] *1890–1 Report of the Sunderland Trades Council* (Sunderland, 1891), p. 2; *1892 Report of the Sunderland Trades Council* (Sunderland, 1892), p. 1.

[118] *Walsall Observer*, 5 October 1889.

[119] *Rotherham Advertiser*, 12 March 1892.

[120] *Walsall Observer*, 22 February and 8 March 1890.

[121] *Walsall Observer*, 8 November 1890.

comprised of and appealing to workers of all occupations and grades of skill – but by other means. The very success of the trades councils left the assemblies without a clear role in their local labour movement.

The situation was even worse in the larger centres, where more established trades councils excluded the Knights and left them isolated from the rest of organised labour. The Glasgow United Trades Council enforced this isolation very early on in the history of the city's assemblies, despite their mutual commitment to organising unskilled workers in the city.[122] At a meeting in March 1890 one delegate moved that, as the Knights represented no particular trade, they 'could not, according to the constitution of the Council, be admitted.' His resolution was held over until the Knights addressed the Council in person. Two weeks later, however, the United Trades Council approved the resolution by 34 to 16.[123]

The Liverpool Trades Council proved even less sympathetic, despite the fact that Samuel Reeves sat on it as a delegate for the local core moulders' union.[124] Indeed, it was generally known as one of the more conservative trades councils and one that looked with suspicion upon the new unionism in all its iterations. And Knights in Liverpool became early standard-bearers for the new unionism. Members of the Liverpool Trades Council, one paper reported, regarded the Knights as 'itinerant agitators who, not understanding local conditions, frequently do a great deal of harm by gratuitously meddling in labour disputes.'[125] The same article contrasted the 'intelligent, respectable artisans' of the Council with the Order's 'band of intermeddling strangers.'[126] Unlike their Glaswegian counterparts, delegates to the Liverpool Trades Council did not even put the question of admitting the Knights to a vote. They also failed to respond to letters from LA443 over the course of 1890.[127] The assembly's fate was sealed in one brief line in the Council's minutes in October. 'Knights of Labour write and send rules,' it read, and recommended no

---

[122] The Glasgow Trades Council, like Scottish trades councils generally, supported the new unions. See W.H. Fraser, 'Trades Councils in Nineteenth Century Scotland,' in I. McDougall (ed.), *Essays in Scottish Labour History*, p. 9; *Annual Report of Glasgow United Trades Council, 1889–90* (Glasgow, 1890), p. 14.

[123] *Glasgow Weekly Mail*, 15 March 1890; *Glasgow Weekly Herald*, 29 March 1890.

[124] *1890–1 Report of the Liverpool Trades Council* (Liverpool, 1891), p. 20. Reeves actually became the president of the Trades Council later in the decade; his immediate predecessor was James Sexton, another former Knight. See 'Souvenir: Trades Union Congress, Liverpool, 1906,' Liverpool Trades Council Archives, Liverpool Record Office, 331 TRA 5/4.

[125] *Liverpool Weekly Courier*, 8 February 1890.

[126] Liverpool *Weekly Courier*, 8 February 1890.

[127] Knights of Labour, LA 443, Bootle, to the Liverpool Trades Council, August 26, 1890, Liverpool Trades Council Archives, Liverpool Record Office, 331 TRA 2/84.

further action.[128] By that point the Bootle assembly was on the verge of dissolution anyway.

Knights in Derry, as in Liverpool, spearheaded the local rise of the new unionism. And, as in Liverpool, the Derry Trades Council became an enemy of the Knights – but for the opposite reason. The Council, writes Shane McAteer, took an early interest in organising unskilled and female workers, and in bridging the sectarian divide that cut the town in two.[129] But the Knights never figured in their plans. Instead, the Derry Trades Council chose to put its weight behind the Gasworkers Union, when they arrived in the town in 1891, and against LA1601. The Council and the Gasworkers both accused the Order of working illegally, as it was not yet registered under the Trade Union Acts. They also accused the Knights of refusing to support strikes by their members, and further claimed that American Knights were unable to give them financial support. In this way they forced Derry Knights to support a strike they could not afford, and to make matters worse, bureaucratic mishaps in Philadelphia meant that LA1601's appeals for financial assistance to the General Executive Board went unanswered.[130] The Knights seemed to prove the propaganda of their opponents. At the same time, according to one local Knight, the Derry Trades Council even 'resorted to the device of getting a number of their tools enrolled in the Assembly.'[131] These crippling financial burdens and the opposition of powerful forces in the local labour movement played no small part in the reduction of LA1601's numbers from 800 to 100 over the course of 1891.[132]

The fights between the Knights and the Gasworkers Union in Derry suggested wider differences between the assemblies and the new unions, first and most importantly in their approaches to industrial relations. Most new unions emerged out of strikes. This was true even if, as revisionist historians have made perfectly clear, the leaders of most new unions, irrespective of whether they were socialists, soon favoured arbitration over strikes and became less militant than many of their members. British and Irish Knights, as we saw in Chapter 4, practised arbitration even when it jeopardised the very future of the assemblies. The second major difference lay in the public image of the respective organisations. The Knights, even when they

---

[128] Minutes of the Liverpool Trades Council, October 1, 1890, *Liverpool Trades Council Archives*, Liverpool Record Office, 331 TRA 1/2.
[129] McAteer, 'New Unionism in Derry,' pp. 12–15.
[130] William Stewart to Hayes, 14 August 1891, Box 9, JHP; William Stewart to Powderly, 25 October 1891, Box 69, TVP.
[131] *JUL*, 30 July 1891.
[132] McAteer, 'New Unionism in Derry,' p. 19.

publicised their meetings, maintained a higher level of secrecy than other trade unions. The new unionists generally took the opposite course. They, as Ken Coates and Tony Topham write, 'readily abandoned the clandestinity of the Knights of Labour ... in favour of the open, bands-and-banner-waving public demonstrations of the new unions.'[133]

Secrecy and arbitration often aided the growth of Knights in Britain, as in the early years of the Order in America and other parts of the world. Secrecy became valuable when trade unionists suffered victimisation; arbitration prevented risky and costly strikes that destroyed whole assemblies in depressed, or even in favourable, economic conditions. When trade remained poor, as for most of the 1880s, these strategies ensured steady if often slow growth. But when trade improved, as at the end of that decade, they made it difficult for the Order to expand as quickly as the other new unions. Eric Hobsbawm observes that, before trade unions became 'recognized and institutionalized,' their growth occurred in discontinuous leaps 'because if unions are to be effective they must mobilize, and therefore seek to recruit, not numbers of individuals but groups of workers sufficiently large for collective bargaining.'[134] Thanks to their ritual, the Knights could steadily initiate small numbers of workers at a time but not large numbers all at once. To make matters worse, the main opportunity to recruit in large numbers came through the momentum that accompanied a strike, which Knights refused to countenance in most cases. The new unions, then, could 'recruit in lumps,' as Hobsbawm puts it. Knights in Britain and Ireland could not, or at least did not; or they did not do so enough. This was an unfortunate turn of events for an order whose American assemblies grew so quickly after they relaxed their secrecy and struck in large numbers, even against the wishes of Powderly and most of its other leaders.

These drawbacks caused the most damage in Liverpool. Knights there harboured hopes of a network of assemblies 50,000 members strong and received early support from the local Sailors' and Firemen's Union. Their negotiations with stevedores and shipping companies had won them a number of concessions, as we saw in Chapter 4, and their numbers grew steadily over the course of 1889. Yet their willingness to secure these concessions through the unloading of cargoes boycotted by the NUDL soon caused them problems. Dockers in Liverpool hoped to emulate the victory of their counterparts in London. The NUDL seemed willing to lead them; the Knights seemed more interested in winning the trust of employers on the waterfront.[135]

---

[133] Coates and Topham, *Making of the Labour Movement*, p. 112.
[134] Hobsbawm, 'New Unionism in Perspective,' p. 155.
[135] Taplin, *Dockers and Seamen*, p. 79.

The attacks of some Knights against rival trade unionists seemed to confirm these suspicions. John Higgins had, before the establishment of LA443, described the Sailor's Union as a fraud; in January 1890, an anonymous Knight described the NUDL as nothing more than a front for the Sailor's Union.[136] Conflict between the Knights and the NUDL came to a head at an 'uproarious' meeting of LA443 at the end of that month.[137] The local secretary of the Sailor's Union accused Higgins, the chairman, of defaming his union and accused the Knights of scabbing on the NUDL. Sam Reeves attempted to maintain order and distance the assembly from these charges, but 'disorderly scenes' and 'several violent altercations' between Knights and NUDL members ensued. Higgins then read a telegram from Knights in Glasgow, claiming that 15,000 workers joined assemblies there in a single day. 'A Glasgow telegram sent from the Bootle Exchange,' one man said to general laughter; others shouted 'they are all swindles.' The meeting soon ended with members of the rival organisations engaging each other, as one report of the meeting described it, in 'verbal warfare' that continued late into the night.[138]

The Knights lost this war. John Havelock Wilson, the president of the Sailor's Union, and Edward McHugh, the general secretary of the NUDL, very pointedly praised the American Knights but deplored the behaviour of their followers in Liverpool.[139] The NUDL led Liverpool dockers on strike in April. The strike failed, but by the middle of the year its branches in the city numbered upwards of 15,000 workers.[140] Dockers were hardly likely to return to an order now stained by strike-breaking and by the suggestion that it had collaborated with employers. The Knights, writes Eric Taplin, 'had proved to be "a transient organisation," no more than an irritant to the more militant unions of the waterfront.'[141] When representatives of the Sailors' and Firemen's Union again appeared at meetings of LA443 in the final months of 1890, they were not there to offer forgiveness but to entice Knights to their own union.[142] The assembly's fate was soon sealed. And it was sealed by a union whose co-founder, Richard McGhee, had once worked as an organiser for the Black Country assemblies, and whose future leader, James Sexton, had served his trade union apprenticeship in that early, ephemeral assembly of Liverpool dockers in 1885. Former Knights ended the Knights of Labor in Liverpool.

136 Bean, 'Knights in Liverpool,' p. 75; *Liverpool Echo*, 28 January 1890.
137 *Liverpool Mercury*, 31 January 1890.
138 *Liverpool Weekly Post*, 1 February 1890.
139 *Liverpool Weekly Post*, 8 February 1890.
140 Bean, 'Knights in Liverpool,' p. 77.
141 Taplin, *Dockers and Seamen*, pp. 79–80.
142 Bean, 'Knights in Liverpool,' p. 77.

Stove grate workers in Rotherham, as we saw in Chapter 4, went one better. Unlike Knights in Bootle, Knights in Rotherham supported the stove grate workers' strike in April 1890. Yet when the strike was won they responded to the Knights with the creation of their own union and took Sanders with them to serve as its president. 'As time went on,' Henry Pelling observes, 'mention of the Knights of Labor became less and less common in his utterances.'[143] In one stroke the Knights lost the services of their most vociferous and capable agitator. Though Sanders initially claimed that steps would be taken to affiliate the new union with the Knights, this never happened.[144] Some officials in the Stove-Grate Workers Union remained Knights for some time, and its secretary, Arthur Nadin, and one of its presidents, Thomas Guest, remained Knights until the very end.[145] But the new union blunted the growth of the Rotherham assemblies and then slowly reversed it. Former Knights may have ended the Liverpool assembly, but members in good standing were responsible for the decline of the assemblies in Rotherham.

Few events have a single cause, and conflict with the trade unions was only one of a number of causes behind the decline of the British and Irish assemblies. We have already explored some of them and in the next and final chapter we explore others. But conflict between the Knights and the trade unions became a crucial part of the Order's history, and the new unions became opponents of the Knights as implacable as the old. One trend also tied the Order's battles with the old and new unions together. In each case, the Knights were supplanted by organisations with a national or wide regional remit. The Midland Counties Trades Federation, the Amalgamated Society of Engineers, the Associated Iron and Steel Workers of Great Britain, the National Amalgamated Iron Plate Workers Society, the National Union of Dock Labourers, the National Union of Gas Workers and General Labourers, and the National Union of Stove-Grate Workers all fell under these headings. The Knights represented an alternative current that concentrated instead on building powerful local federations of all workers. The rise and growth of the trades councils during the years of the new unionism proved that this current was not dead. The trend towards centralised, national unions, however, was much stronger. The TUC emphasised that trend in 1895 when its representatives voted to exclude trade council delegates from the Congress.[146]

---

[143] Pelling, 'Knights in Britain,' pp. 323–24.
[144] *Sheffield Daily Telegraph*, 20 May 1890.
[145] For a meeting of Knights at Hoyland that included both men, see *Rotherham Advertiser*, 30 January 1892. In 1892 Guest was the Master Workman of LA1266, the largest assembly in Rotherham. See *Rotherham Advertiser*, 23 January 1892.
[146] Clinton, *Rank and File*, pp. 95–96.

Powerful national unions of skilled workers defeated the Knights in the 1880s. Their assemblies contributed to the rise of the new unionism and were then beaten by powerful new national unions of unskilled workers in the 1890s. At a local level their plans for town- or citywide federations increasingly resembled those of local trades councils, including those they supported or helped to create. Those plans became surplus to requirements even when the trade councils welcomed the Knights rather than excluding them. Where the national unions supplanted the Knights, the trades councils made them redundant. The economic downturn towards the middle of the new decade did not make the assemblies' identity crisis any easier. The new unions that survived that downturn generally managed to establish themselves in a particular industry or set of industries. The Knights of Labor could not become the Knights of Glass after LA3504 was crippled in strikes at Hartley's and Chance Bros; and the unions had forced them out of every other major industry in which assemblies had once operated. They never, Henry Pelling writes, 'found a raison d'etre in Britain comparable to that of the "new unions" which managed to survive the depression of the early 1890s.'[147] When the depression ended, the assemblies were not there to see it.

Conclusion:
The Knights of Labor and the British Labour Movement

In 1886 the Knights of Labor burst onto the world stage and became the largest labour organisation in the world. With their 1 million members they outnumbered the trade unions of Britain, the traditional home of trade unionism. Few had predicted it. Many commented on it. For a brief moment the centre of gravity in the international trade union movement shifted from Western Europe, and Britain above all, to the United States. The American labour movement failed to hold this unusual position for long. Four years later the Knights were reduced to a fraction of their former numbers and the American Federation of Labor, now the larger organisation, remained well below the Order's peak figure of 1 million members. Things had also changed on the other side of the Atlantic. The rise of the new unions in Britain and Ireland, and the increase in membership of the old, had restored Britain to its accustomed place at the top of the trade union world. Grave structural changes in both movements accompanied these see-sawing membership figures. The American labour movement retreated from the expansive goals and membership of the Knights to the craft unionism that would guide the leaders of the Federation for some time to come. The British labour movement advanced into hitherto unorganised industries and occupations,

---

[147] Pelling, 'Knights in Britain,' pp. 328–29.

without falling into a full-scale war between the new and old unions like the one that had overtaken the Order and the Federation in the 1880s.

The Knights of Labor naturally played a decisive role in the American side of that story. Their defeat, Kim Voss points out, heralded the beginning of American exceptionalism in all matters relating to the working-class movement. Craft unionists like Samuel Gompers, writes Norman Ware, may have saved the labour movement from complete destruction, but their determination to avoid the kind of repression that employers and the state dealt to the Order also led to undue caution, and the Federation failed to retake the mechanised industries that the Knights had once held.[148] The Knights not only failed to maintain their assemblies and their hopes of a nationwide federation of all American workers. They also encouraged the next generation of trade union leaders to adopt an unduly defensive posture, even as their colleagues on the other side of the Atlantic and Pacific oceans began to assert themselves and build comprehensive trade union movements. Under Gompers's and his successors' leadership, the American labour movement began to fall further behind its counterparts in Europe and Australasia, regardless of whether we measure this gap in terms of proportional union representation or in terms of political influence.

But the Knights of Labor also played an important role in the British side of the story. Their growth and victories during the Great Upheaval illuminated many of the shortcomings of the TUC in the mid-1880s and encouraged many trade unionists to remedy them. Their calls for a federation of all wage earners, skilled or not, resonated with many British and Irish trade unionists, who became impatient with the slow pace of change within the TUC. The American Knights heavily influenced a number of trade unions and trade unionists, and their British and Irish assemblies played their own powerful roles in the development of the new unionism in several important centres, Liverpool and Glasgow most of all. The new unionism required the right material conditions, in this case the upswing in trade at the end of the 1880s, to emerge in the way that it did. But its leaders also required a set of ideas and theories, backed up if possible with some kind of practical evidence, to guide their thinking and plans. The Knights provided a successful and powerful alternative to the entrenched practices of the TUC at a time when such alternatives were very thin on the ground.

These are, of course, broad generalisations that need some qualifications. The AFL was never simply a bastion of craft privilege. The Federation also soon faced rivals like the Industrial Workers of the World who were anything but 'moderate.' The 'old' British unions, far from disappearing with the arrival of the 'new,' actually grew in the 1890s and beyond. The new

---

[148] Ware, *Labor Movement*, p. xii.

unions increasingly resembled them. Eric Hobsbawm even speculates that had there not been a renewed upsurge of trade unionism just before the First World War, the general and new unions that survived into the twentieth century may have become de facto 'craft' unions of unskilled workers along the lines of the Teamsters and the Hod-Carriers in the United States.[149]

But with these qualifications in mind we can take Voss's arguments even further. American exceptionalism is, after all, a relative term that depends as much upon the state of labour movements outside the United States as on the American labour movement itself. It would be stretching things to say that the British and American labour movements swapped places between 1886 and 1890, with the British labour movement in 1890 assuming the position held by Knights in 1886 and the American labour movement retreating to the British position of four years earlier. But each movement travelled along these lines, one advancing, the other retreating. In the previous chapter we saw this pattern take shape when it came to working-class politics. In this chapter the same pattern arose in terms of organisation at the workplace. Both cases point to one simple conclusion. The making of American exceptionalism began with the decline of the Order in America; it also began thanks to the influence and work of Knights in Britain and Ireland.

The British and Irish assemblies never benefited from the wider historical changes of which they were part. The Knights were caught between the 'crafts,' who so successfully resisted and reversed the Order's incursions and advances in the 1880s, and the rise of the new unions in the 1890s. In the first case the British and Irish assemblies met the same problems as Knights in the United States, even if their relations with the ASE or the ironworkers never became as hostile as those between American Knights and the AFL. In the second case they were undone by a new movement whose commitment to organising unskilled workers resembled their own order more than anything else. In both cases the local federations of workers from all crafts and none, which they began to build in the Black Country, South Yorkshire, Merseyside, Clydeside and Northern Ireland, were supplanted from two different directions. The national unions, representing skilled or unskilled workers, took their members in specific trades and industries. The trades councils fulfilled the role that Knights hoped their assemblies would play at a community level. Knights in Britain and Ireland were caught between these pairs of scissors, and it is not surprising that in this predicament many assemblies began to decline or disappeared altogether. In the next and final chapter, we look at this decline in greater depth. Having examined the rise of a transnational movement, we now turn to its fall.

---

[149] Hobsbawm, 'General Labour Unions,' p. 135.

7
The Fall of a Transnational Movement

On 31 December 1889, the members of LA443 in Bootle met with their wives and friends to bring in the New Year. As the band played, and as the partiers danced, the assembly seemed secure and the new decade seemed to promise only better things to come. LA443 planned to open new preceptories in various parts of Liverpool, and these would in time become assemblies themselves. Knights elsewhere in Britain and Ireland approached the new decade with similar optimism. New recruits swelled the ranks of the Scottish assemblies. Knights secured a strong foothold in Belfast and Derry. The assemblies in the Black Country seemed to be overcoming earlier problems with local trade unions, and LA454 of Walsall in particular led a powerful local political and industrial movement. Assemblies in Rotherham, even in Derby, grew rapidly in size and number. The total membership of the British and Irish assemblies at this time stood between 10,000 and 15,000. But these assemblies had all disappeared by 1894, except for one or two that struggled on for another year or two. Only four years separated their peak from their end.

Many of the causes of this decline have appeared in earlier chapters. Secrecy and ritual were not to everyone's taste. The insistence of many Knights on arbitration regardless of context often caused problems, either with employers who refused to negotiate or with workers, often members, who preferred to strike whether it be under the Order's banner or not. Sometimes, when Knights led them and they failed, these strikes destroyed assemblies; sometimes assemblies were crippled when their leaders refused to countenance a strike. In some cases, employers were determined enough to keep the assemblies away altogether, as Pilkington's did most successfully and most consequentially for the history of LA3504. Most importantly of all, the assemblies invariably lost ground whenever they threatened the jurisdiction of a trade union with any national stature. In this chapter, we approach the question of the British and Irish assemblies' decline from a wider, international point of view.

Time was always an enemy in the international history of the Knights of Labor. Clifton Yearley writes that 'the order expanded so swiftly between 1885 and 1887 that all of its energies were dedicated to the task of assimilating and consolidating domestic gains, and little attention could be spared to proposals for international action.' After that point, he adds, 'a rapid decline in membership made it increasingly unlikely that it could save itself, let alone the workers of the world.'[1] The Knights emerged in Britain, and then in Ireland, at the high point of the Order's American growth. They grew as the American assemblies began to shrink. They reached their peak membership at a point when their parent body was unmistakeably in decline, and in the 1890s they had to rely on their own initiative and resources. That was easier said than done, however, because the British and Irish Knights had prospered in the 1880s thanks in large part to the organisers and money sent to them from the United States, and to the powerful image that the American Order projected across the intervening ocean. The Order's American decline encouraged similar trends among their assemblies across the Atlantic.

Time was an enemy. But the Order's national origins were not, when it came to organising on an international scale at least. In his study of the Knights in New Zealand, Robert Weir rejects the idea that the Order's American origins – and its 'Americanisms,' as he puts it – impeded its development elsewhere in the world. But if Weir rejects arguments from any kind of national exceptionalism, he concedes that what he calls 'localism,' a general aversion to outside persons, organisations and sometimes ideas, could become an important limit on the Order's international growth.[2] British and Irish Knights were certainly not hamstrung by any kind of exceptionalism. Localism, on the other hand – or regionalism and nationalism if you prefer – did play an important role in the growth and then the decline of the British and Irish assemblies. Some workers refused to join a foreign order; others criticised it on that ground. Knights there, unlike in some other countries, only created a national body comparatively late and when their assemblies were already in serious trouble. They suffered further when their erstwhile officials appeared in police court, charged with embezzling money from the assemblies. Regional splits emerged as the British National Assembly took shape in 1891, and that body ultimately arrived too late to save the assemblies. As we trace the development of the British and Irish assemblies and their attempts to remain inside or escape from their transnational movement, it is often difficult to separate the opportunities they missed to halt their decline from the more or less insoluble contradictions that they faced.

[1] Yearley, *Britons*, p. 65.
[2] Weir, *Knights Down Under*, pp. 206–10.

Those assemblies did not linger on as some American ones did. Most histories of the American Knights of Labor end in 1893 or 1894, when a coalition of western farmers and eastern socialists removed Terence Powderly from his post as General Master Workman and then, less than a year later, split among themselves and soon ensured that the socialists left the Order as a body. Membership fell from 76,300 in 1893 to 54,000 in 1897 and continued to drop further afterwards.[3] We have examined in various ways the events and trends that brought American Knights to this point; but the Order formally continued to exist in the United States until 1917, when its last General Master Workman, former Secretary-Treasurer John W. Hayes, dumped its surviving documents in a leaky shed behind an office in Washington, DC. Its last years mixed tragedy with farce: two rival General Assemblies, each with their own set of general officers, met at Birmingham, Alabama, in November 1900 and ultimately resolved their split through the courts.[4]

The later history of the American Knights of Labor has yet to be properly written, probably because they returned to absolute secrecy in their final years, because their numbers remained so low and because the role they once played in the American labour movement was very firmly assumed, in various ways, by the American Federation of Labor and the Industrial Workers of the World. The secrecy and small size of the British and Irish assemblies makes the task of writing their history difficult enough in the years of their growth. These problems multiply at an exponential rate when it comes to the years of their decline. The leaders and members of most organisations, after all, are keen to promote their successes but not their defeats, and certainly not their dissolution. With these problems in mind, we finally turn to the last years of the Knights of Labor in Britain and Ireland, as best we can uncover them. If the Order arrived there with great expectations it expired, not in some glorious final struggle, but amidst the apathy and disillusionment that more commonly accompanies the death of a social movement.

American Decline and the Fracturing of a Transnational Movement

The growth and development of the British and Irish assemblies was always conditioned by the fate of Knights in the United States. For most of the 1880s Knights in the Old World benefited from the victories and assistance of their colleagues in the New. Powerful assemblies like LA300 were able to organise glassworkers across the Atlantic. The events of the

---

[3] D. Steeples and D. Whitten, *Democracy in Desperation: The Depression of 1893* (Westport: Greenwood, 1998), p. 90.

[4] *New York Times*, 14 November 1900.

Great Upheaval highlighted the inadequacies of British trade unions and encouraged workers in Britain and Ireland to form assemblies themselves. Organisers and financial assistance from the United States encouraged this growth further. From the end or even the middle of the decade, however, all these trends began to reverse themselves. The Order's precipitous American growth soon turned into an equally dramatic decline. The treasury that once allowed cheques and organisers to travel across the oceans ran empty. All the advantages that Knights in Britain and Ireland derived from their connections with the United States now appeared to be disadvantages. The transnational movement the Knights had built began to fracture and, in time, shattered completely.

There were early premonitions of the effect that the Order's American defeats could have on its British and Irish assemblies. When craftsmen from the Black Country built the Midland Counties Trades Federation in 1886, instead of forming assemblies, one newspaper explained that 'recent reverses the Knights have sustained do not seem to have influenced this decision in any way.'[5] English migrants to the United States who opposed the Order also weighed in at this time. In November 1886, one such correspondent to the *Labour Tribune* urged Black Country workers to 'beware of the designing intrigues of the Knights of Labour, who only want your money, and not your disputes.'[6] For several more years it was possible to see these reverses as a temporary blip in the inexorable upward march of the Knights of Labor, and to view these criticisms as the bad-natured rumblings of their rivals.[7]

In 1888, however, the Knights became the target of criticism from publications and workers who had earlier or might otherwise have supported them. The *Labour Tribune* and the *Ironworkers' Journal*, as discussed in the previous chapter, both paid special attention to the Order's American decline as part of their appeals for ironworkers to leave the assemblies for their new union.[8] Knights long remembered this supposed betrayal, as J. Brettell of Stourbridge noted in 1891. 'Many good, union men of the K of L, have withdrawn their support from your paper,' he wrote to the *Labour Tribune*, because 'the Tribune was against the K of L.'[9] The socialist press publicised the Order's decline too. Henry F. Charles, an American socialist, wrote for the *Commonweal* in July 1888 that 'the "Knights of Labour" organisation is

---

[5] *Dundee Courier*, 30 April 1886.

[6] *Labour Tribune*, 20 November 1886.

[7] One Knight claimed that the quoted correspondent was a paid official of the American Federation of Labor: *Labour Tribune*, 5 February 1887.

[8] *Ironworkers Journal*, September 1888; *Labour Tribune*, 25 August 1888.

[9] *Labour Tribune*, 11 July 1891.

practically ruined; all the different district assemblies have been reduced to about one-fifth of their previous strength.' Charles, like many socialists and anarchists on both sides of the Atlantic, hated Powderly for his opposition to his comrades and wrote him off as an 'unscrupulous scoundrel ... on the look-out for new boodle.'[10]

In these papers, and in other socialist or working-class publications, letters and news reports favourable to the Knights began, towards the end of the 1880s, to be outnumbered by those which criticised the Knights and drew attention to the Order's decline. In February 1889, *Justice* correctly pointed out that 'the number of members of the Knights of Labour has now fallen to 175,000, and will, in the course of the winter, dwindle down to 100,000.'[11] In the following year the *Tribune* symbolised the Order's loss of leadership over the American labour movement when it printed a report of the convention of the American Federation of Labor without mentioning that year's General Assembly.[12] Only *Reynolds's Newspaper* continued to present the Knights in a favourable light even after their American assemblies were obviously in dire straits.

The mainstream papers paid equally close attention to the Order's decline. The *Birmingham Daily Gazette*, in a five-part series in February 1889, exposed its secrets and framed the Order's English activities in the context of its American problems.[13] When *The Times* began a campaign in 1889 against the Irish Nationalist leader, Charles Parnell, Powderly was implicated, albeit unfairly, as a support of revolutionary violence in Ireland.[14] The most damaging single report came later in the year, when Henry George, on a tour of the Birmingham area, told the *Gazette* that 'the Order is decaying in America' because 'the chiefs prefer high salaries and a quiet life to active propaganda.'[15]

These reports took their toll. According to the later judgement of another newspaper, the five articles in the *Daily Gazette* 'completely pricked the bladder and produced a fatal collapse' in the assemblies around Birmingham.[16] Frederick Shreeve, the recording secretary of LA395 in Derby, wrote to the *Journal of United Labor* in 1889 about the 'disintegration canard' and added that 'I am sorry to say that it has gotten into some of our papers that the Knights of Labor are going to pieces.' He further hoped that 'some able

---

[10] *Commonweal*, 14 July 1888.
[11] *Justice*, 16 February 1889.
[12] *Labour Tribune*, 13 September 1890.
[13] *Birmingham Daily Gazette*, 18 to 23 February 1889.
[14] See, for instance, *The Times*, 23 November 1889.
[15] *Birmingham Daily Gazette*, 15 May 1889.
[16] *Smethwick Weekly News*, 11 July 1891.

brother will refute it.'[17] James P. Archibald did respond to claims of decline during his time in Britain and Ireland the same year, both in speeches and in print.[18] The *Labour Tribune*, however, rejected Archibald's 'weak defence' of the Order, and demonstrated the enormous extent of its decline in some detail.[19]

The reverses the Knights suffered in the United States did not always or immediately translate into reverses for Knights elsewhere in the world. The Belgian assemblies managed to grow to between 20,000 and 30,000 strong in 1891, at a time when many American Knights contemplated the end of their order.[20] New Zealand Knights peaked even later in the decade, and the Knights only arrived in France in 1893, just as the General Assembly planned to remove Powderly from his post as General Master Workman. British and Irish Knights were not simply the victims of their order's American decline. Instead, this decline exacerbated the problems caused by their defeats in strikes, their failed competition with other trade unions and their commitment to arbitration at a time when newly militant workers sought confrontation more than compromise. As their rivals grew and became more attractive to British and Irish workers, the Knights remained tethered to an order whose time seemed to have passed. Unfavourable news reports were only part of the problem. The gradual withdrawal of direct support helped to fracture this transnational movement too.

The glassworkers of LA3504, with whom the history of the British and Irish Knights began, were hit especially hard by this withdrawal of support. Their assembly owed everything to the organising work and financial resources of LA300 and its Universal Federation of Window-Glass Workers. The leaders of LA300 had justified their assistance to the glassworkers of Europe on the grounds that the assembly could then regulate and restrict their immigration to the United States as necessary. Their lobbying for the Foran Act formed the other side of their strategy, and Marcel van der Linden argues that its passage soon rendered the Universal Federation superfluous.[21] Yet American glassworkers continued to support the Federation over the course of the 1880s because, as one speaker at their 1889 convention put it, 'in the years that the Federation had been in operation it had prevented hundreds of foreign workmen coming to this country.'[22]

[17] *JUL*, 10 October 1889.
[18] *Birmingham Daily Post*, 31 August 1889.
[19] *Labour Tribune*, 6 September 1889.
[20] *1893–4 Royal Commission on Labour: Foreign Reports, Volume IV, Belgium*, pp. 13–14. Found at: HCPP.
[21] Van der Linden, 'Labour Internationalism,' p. 266.
[22] *Smethwick Telephone*, 20 April 1889; 'Fifth National Convention of Window-Glass Workers,' p. 21.

Internationalism based on this kind of self-interest soon ran into problems on both sides of the Atlantic. Through the Universal Federation, LA300 allowed English and Belgian craftsmen to fill vacancies at new American glassworks. Even in April 1889, the *Smethwick Telephone* reported that 'hundreds of people' gathered to see off glassworkers from Spon Lane on their way to take up posts in the United States with the full blessing of LA300.[23] When that assembly imported mainly Belgian members of the Universal Federation to work at a new glassworks in Jeanette, Pennsylvania in the same year, however, they were prosecuted for breaking the very contract labour law that they had lobbied for in Congress.[24] Opposition to the Universal Federation grew among the members of LA300.[25] The European affiliates of the Federation, on the other hand, felt that LA300 used it as a means to 'keep them from going to America to work.'[26] When that assembly raised its initiation fee to $200 in 1889, even for members of the Federation, English and Belgian glassworkers deluged Powderly with their complaints.[27] Representatives of LA300 responded in 1890 that they had the right to set whatever fee they wished.[28] That same year they went even further and formally left the Universal Federation altogether. Albert Delwarte, the head of the Belgian glassworkers, attempted to keep the Federation together but his enthusiasm was no substitute for LA300's enormous financial reserves. LA300 continued to provide LA3504 with some financial assistance in their strikes at Spon Lane and Sunderland, but the days when English glassworkers were part of an international movement based on mutual assistance were over.

The other British and Irish assemblies encountered a similar change in their relationship with headquarters in Philadelphia. Powderly and the General Executive Board never possessed the same determination and financial resources as LA300, or the time needed to properly coordinate a campaign for the international growth of the Knights of Labor, but for much of the 1880s they nevertheless managed to provide the British and Irish assemblies with some measure of assistance. Organisers like A.G. Denny, James P. Archibald and Michael Davitt were hardworking and capable and, in Davitt's case, famous as well. The money that the General Executive

---

[23] *Smethwick Telephone*, 20 April 1889.

[24] *Pittsburgh Dispatch*, 28 November 1889 and 16 May 1890.

[25] See, for instance, a letter by Simon Burns against the leaders of LA300, and an undated letter against the Universal Federation, presumably from the late 1880s, in an unnamed newspaper dealing with the glass trade, in Box 8, JHP.

[26] Quoted in Pelling, 'Knights in Britain,' p. 318.

[27] Albert Delwarte to Powderly, 7 August 1890, Box 61, TVP; James Brown to Powderly, 12 November 1890, Box 64, TVP.

[28] C.H. Oaks to Powderly, 15 September 1890, Box 61, TVP.

Board sent to Knights in the Black Country in the 1880s allowed them to open more assemblies, recruit members and bring Kenrick's, a major manufacturer, to the negotiating table. In the early days of the British and Irish assemblies this assistance had been a powerful asset; as the American Order entered into decline, and its assistance dried up, these connections became a dangerous liability.

In August 1889, as James P. Archibald countered yet more criticism of his order in the pages of the *Birmingham Daily Post*, he added that 'it is not unlikely [that] a permanent organiser for Europe may be appointed by our next general assembly.'[29] British and Irish Knights must have hoped that, just as their appeals in 1887 for a 'paid man among us beyond the reach of capitalistic vindictiveness' had brought them Michael Davitt, they would soon greet Archibald's replacement.[30] But though both DA208 and DA248 asked the General Assemblies in 1889 and 1890 for such a replacement, they received none.[31] The only exceptions were American Knights who arrived in Britain and Ireland on personal business, and John J. Bealin, one of Powderly's enemies, who tried unsuccessfully to claim that the General Master Workman had issued him an organisers' commission in England.[32] Thomas Clarke, the Master Workman of an American assembly, lectured on behalf of Derry's LA1601 while visiting relatives in the area.[33] There are suggestions that Andrew D. Best, an Irish-born Knight, was sent as an organiser to Britain and Ireland sometime in the early 1890s but no further evidence rests behind it.[34] This lack of help from America had serious consequences. William Stewart, the recording secretary of LA1601, told Powderly in 1891 that 'no organizer would do us any good unless one from your side of the water.'[35]

Not all Knights who travelled across the Atlantic proved to be of use to the assemblies there, either. Leonora Barry and Thomas Cavanaugh, both among the Order's leading figures, visited the Paris Exposition in 1889 as part of a workers' delegation organised by the Scripp Newspaper League, and spent time in England *en route*.[36] Barry and Cavanaugh met with the

---

[29] *Birmingham Daily Post*, 31 August 1889.
[30] *Proceedings of the GA* (1887), pp. 1770–72.
[31] *Proceedings of the GA* (1889), p. 44; *Proceedings of the GA* (1890), p. 9.
[32] Powderly to Hayes, 17 September 1889, Box 1, JHP.
[33] William Carroll to Thomas Clarke, 16 September 1891, Box 69, TVP; William Stewart to Thomas Clarke, 19 September 1891, Box 69, TVP; Thomas Clarke to Powderly, 2 October 1891, Box 69, TVP.
[34] *Washington Times*, 11 August 1899.
[35] William Stewart to Powderly, 23 November 1891, Box 69, *TVP*.
[36] For both of them in Paris, after their English leg, see F. Veyssier to Powderly, 20 September 1889, Box 56, TVP.

Birmingham Trades Council and with representatives from assemblies in the city.[37] Barry visited the chainshops of Cradley Heath but, due to poor health or other commitments, she did nothing in the way of organising or lecturing for the Knights while there. Cavanaugh also failed to help any local assemblies.[38] William S. Waudby, a socialist and member of the (American) International Typographical Union, received organisers' credentials from Powderly and Hayes when he went to one of the two International Labour Congresses that convened alongside the Exposition. But Waudby, as he warned Secretary-Treasurer Hayes, 'may not be enabled to do much in the way of actual organization of LAs, owing to my official duties.' In the end he made no impression in Britain or Ireland at all.[39] Paul Bowen of Washington DC's DA66 also visited the Labour Congresses, without the knowledge of Powderly and the General Executive Board. He met with Engels in London, but never met with Knights in the rest of the country except for when he attended the Possibilist Congress in Paris alongside Jesse Chapman, who represented DA208.[40]

But the absence of one Knight in particular provided the most damaging blow to the morale of the British and Irish assemblies, and symbolised the retreat of American Knights from their assistance to foreign branches. Between 1887 and the end of the decade, Terence Powderly made a number of private and public promises to journey across the Atlantic, work on behalf of the Irish nationalists and visit Knights throughout Europe.[41] Michael Davitt predicted that Powderly would receive 'enthusiastic receptions' there and that his visit would 'be productive of wide-reaching results,' both in terms of Irish nationalism and the British labour movement.[42] Powderly himself, according to *Reynolds's Newspaper*, expected 'that his visit to England will have the effect of arousing the industrial masses of that country to the importance of enrolling themselves under the banner of the Knights of Labour.'[43] Given his international fame, the General Master Workman was probably not exaggerating unduly; but in 1887 and 1888 Powderly failed to keep his promise thanks to poor health and his propensity for sea-sickness,

---

[37] *JUL*, 19 September 1889.

[38] *Dudley Herald*, 10 August 1889.

[39] William S Waudby to Hayes, 21 February 1889, Box 53, TVP.

[40] Friedrich Engels to Friedrich Adolph Sorge, 17 July 1889. From MIA. For Jesse Chapman at the Second International see Pelling, 'Knights in Britain,' p. 325; *Report of the International Workmen's Congress... 1889, Published by the Trade Unionist Members of the English Delegation* (London, 1889), p. 1.

[41] Some examples from 1887: *Sheffield and Rotherham Independent*, 9 September 1887; *Newcastle Weekly Courant*, 15 April 1887; *Chicago Daily Tribune*, 3 September 1887.

[42] *Los Angeles Daily Herald*, 15 October 1887.

[43] *Reynolds's Newspaper*, 2 October 1887.

which meant, he told Davitt, that he 'would be poisoning fishes before the ship on which I started would get half way over.'[44] British Knights, who had invited him to visit their assemblies, were naturally disappointed.[45] The decision of the General Assembly in 1888 to appoint Powderly as the Order's representative to the Paris Exposition of 1889, however, which he accepted, suggested that after a number of broken promises the British and Irish Knights would finally get to host their leader and, perhaps, have him lead a resurgence of their assemblies.[46]

Powderly reassured Jesse Chapman that 'I will most assuredly be with you.'[47] Knights waited for their leader with great expectation. Yet Powderly never made the voyage, and justified his decision to the General Assembly in 1889 on the grounds that 'I could not see that any gain would accrue to the Order on either side of the Atlantic.'[48] Privately, he told Chapman that 'I have had a longing to go over for a long time, but somehow I can never see my way clear to make a start, for about the time that I begin to prepare, something turns up to demand my presence and attention.'[49] To Thomas Dean, Master Workman of DA208, he explained that 'while man proposes, Knights of Labor disposes of their GMW pretty much as they please.'[50] These explanations may have satisfied the individuals involved, but Powderly's failure to make good on any of his promises did little for morale at a time when news of the Order's decline was beginning to spread and as hostile newspapers like the *Birmingham Daily Gazette* subjected the assemblies to extended criticism and exposed their secrets to the newspaper-reading public. His visit may not have single-handedly safeguarded the future of the assemblies but it would undoubtedly have boosted their profile and added to their numbers in a way that Denny, Archibald and maybe even Davitt could not. Powderly's broken promises symbolised and coincided with the point at which the affiliation of the British and Irish assemblies became more of a hindrance than a help.

---

[44] Powderly to Michael Davitt, 6 April 1888, Box 99, TVP.
[45] Three examples of these invitations: one from Preston (David Whittle to Powderly, 13 April 1887, Box 32, TVP); one from Smethwick (J. Chapman to Powderly, Jan 1889, Box 50, TVP); one from Sunderland (Joseph French to Powderly, 12 September 1887, Box 36, TVP).
[46] *Proceedings of the GA* (1888), p. 67.
[47] Powderly to Jesse Chapman, 8 February 1889, Box 99, TVP.
[48] *Proceedings of the GA* (1889), pp. 6–7.
[49] Powderly to J. Chapman, 5 March 1890, Box 100, TVP.
[50] Powderly to Thomas Dean, 6 March 1890, Box 100, TVP.

Knights and the Money Power, or the Power of Money

The financial history of the British and Irish assemblies followed a similar trajectory. The Knights of Labor developed in Britain and Ireland as an inexpensive alternative to local trade unions, most of which, at least before the rise of the new unions, combined high dues with a range of insurance benefits for members and often their families as well, and were led by paid officials. Knights proudly claimed that without these benefits and paid officials their order was run on very economical lines.[51] Correspondence to General Secretary-Treasurer Hayes from LA9970 of Winson Green, Birmingham, indicates that Knights paid around 2d per week, with quarterly dues of 1½d and an annual per capita tax of 5 cents (or approximately 2½d).[52] Other sources refer to an entrance fee for new members of 5s.[53] Contributions were higher for the glassworkers of LA3504, who paid 1s 6d a month, presumably along the same lines as members of LA300.[54] Each new assembly paid an initiation fee of £3 6s 7d to headquarters in Philadelphia. That sum paid for the various bureaucratic supplies that it needed, from membership cards to official stationery, as well as for the symbols that graced each assembly hall.[55] The assemblies hired independent auditors where possible to keep their accounts in proper shape.[56]

Even with these low dues some assemblies were able to quickly amass a sizeable reserve fund. In its first year of operation, LA7952 received £127 8s 9½d from members' contributions, paid out £50 8s 11d, and kept £77 4s 10½d in reserve.[57] Charles Chamberlain insisted in 1889 that 'it is an easy matter for any of our lodges to accumulate £100 if they are of a saving disposition,' and other reports in the same year bear this out.[58] According to a report in the *Journal of United Labor* in 1887, this steady accumulation of funds resulted from the fact that English Knights 'pay up their dues a great deal better' than Knights in the

---

[51] The recording secretary of LA443 told one newspaper that 'we have no men with big salaries on the staff of the Liverpool K.O.L. All the officers belonging to L.A. 443 and P. 1, 2, and 3, give their time gratuitously for the benefit of their fellow workmen' (*Liverpool Courier*, 10 February 1890).

[52] Pelling, 'Knights in Britain,' p. 325; Letter from C. Mullineux to Hayes, 22 July 1890, Box 26, JHP.

[53] *Sheffield and Rotherham Independent*, 26 September 1889.

[54] Pelling, 'Knights in Britain,' p. 325.

[55] *Walsall Observer*, 28 December 1889.

[56] *JUL*, 13 August 1887.

[57] *JUL*, 13 August 1887.

[58] *Smethwick Weekly News*, 2 March 1889. Reports that a number of assemblies boasted more than £100 in savings can be found in *Smethwick Weekly News*, 23 February 1889.

United States.⁵⁹ But their finances remained dependent, both in terms of inflow and outflow, on the links between them and headquarters. On the one hand, the British and Irish assemblies sent per capita contributions to Philadelphia, around £350 in total during 1889.⁶⁰ British Knights were also subject to the 'calls' from the district and general assemblies, which ordered a certain amount per member when those bodies urgently needed funds for strikes, administrative costs or other reasons.⁶¹ On the other hand, the assemblies received financial assistance from headquarters. Charles Chamberlain described this financial link as the most important reason to keep the British assemblies affiliated with the United States. If they severed these ties, he told the *Smethwick Weekly News* in 1889, 'in the first instance it would do good, but it would not in the end.' By maintaining them, he added, 'we shall receive treble what we are paying in capita tax, should the occasion arise.'⁶²

In 1889 this assumption began to unravel. DA208 and DA248 both appealed to that year's General Assembly for financial assistance to resist employers who refused to recognise assemblies, and were told there was no money to give them.⁶³ By 1890, the General Executive Board responded to pleas from DA248 with only a public appeal to the generosity of individual Knights.⁶⁴ These decisions further encouraged the critics of the British and Irish assemblies. In 1887, a delegate of the ironworkers at Brierley Hill had rejected affiliation with the Knights because 'he had greater faith in getting some of his money back from the North than from America.'⁶⁵ Samuel Welsh, a trade unionist from Walsall, was even more acerbic in 1889. He described the Order as 'a clever Yankee speculation got up for the purpose of providing good berths for high-paid officials to fatten upon the industry of their dupes,' and added that in return for their assessments to Philadelphia, local Knights 'received goods – including tinselled lances and toy globes – not worth one-third the money.'⁶⁶

So long as the British and Irish assemblies received various kinds of aid from Philadelphia, whether in the form of cheques or organisers, they could justify their contributions to the United States to their critics. But as the money stopped travelling eastwards the 'calls,' which the *Birmingham Daily Gazette* claimed were large and frequent enough to prevent the assemblies

---

⁵⁹ *JUL*, 31 December 1887.
⁶⁰ *Walsall Observer*, 11 January 1890.
⁶¹ *Birmingham Daily Gazette*, 18 February 1889.
⁶² *Smethwick Weekly News*, 2 March 1889.
⁶³ *Proceedings of the GA* (1889), pp. 5, 6.
⁶⁴ *JUL*, 23 October 1890.
⁶⁵ *Birmingham Daily Post*, 1 March 1887.
⁶⁶ *Walsall Observer*, 11 January 1890.

from amassing more sizeable reserve funds, became increasingly unpopular.[67] The workers who joined the assemblies in 1889 'expecting half-crowns for shillings,' as the *Smethwick Weekly News* later put it, were not inclined to stay when all the promises of support from the United States were not fulfilled.[68]

The withdrawal of financial assistance led directly to the end of several assemblies. Even the glassworkers of LA3504 which, as the *Journal of United Labor* put it, received 'large sums of good American money' from LA300 as late as 1891, found themselves that year 'continually asking how it is we receive nothing from the General Assembly.'[69] The sums of good American money, as we saw in Chapter 4, were not large enough to keep the strike at Spon Lane from falling apart and dooming LA3504 as a whole. The Belfast assemblies suffered even more. The ropeworkers of LA7566 went on strike in 1890, and the other local assembly, LA418, subsidised the strikers in the belief that the General Executive Board would reimburse them. The strike failed and LA7566 failed with it. The General Executive Board failed to respond to LA418's appeals for money. Without financial assistance, LA418 followed LA7566 and its leaders disbanded the assembly and distributed its assets among the remaining membership. The history of the Knights in Belfast ended with it.[70]

In nearby Derry, as we saw in the previous chapter, LA1601 actually sanctioned a strike in an attempt to disprove the claims of rival unions that it could no longer rely on financial assistance from the United States. Unfortunately for the Knights in Derry, these claims turned out to be true. William Stewart sent frantic letters to the General Executive Board in 1891 and 1892, one of which explained that 'were it not for the proceeds of letting our hall to other unions we would have been out of existence nine months ago,' and that if they were not bailed out soon 'the Knights of Labour in Ireland will be a thing of the past.'[71] As noted in the previous chapter, the General Executive Board had misplaced the documents relating to LA1601's appeals and had not yet rejected them.[72] Regardless of the cause, however, the lack of financial assistance meant that Stewart's prophesy came true in 1892.

Not all the financial failings of the British and Irish assemblies were so innocently conceived. The most disastrous chapter in their financial history came with the appearance of two of their officials at West Bromwich Police Court in 1889 and 1890 on charges of embezzlement. Charges like these were

---

[67] *Birmingham Daily Gazette*, 18 February 1889.
[68] *Smethwick Weekly News*, 11 July 1891.
[69] *JUL*, 19 November 1891; James Brown to Hayes, 17 September 1891, Box 10, JHP.
[70] Boyle, *Irish Labour Movement*, pp. 104–06.
[71] William Stewart to Powderly, 20 January 1892, Box 71, TVP.
[72] Hayes to Powderly, 11 November 1891, Box 69, TVP.

all too common in the history of the American Order. In some cases simple mismanagement was to blame, as when Charles Lichtman rerouted money from the new Defence Fund to the new *Journal of United Labor* in 1880, only to find that his unrealistic forecasts left the Order deeply in debt.[73] Other cases involved foolish expenditure, as when the General Executive Board moved their headquarters in 1887 to a palatial home that cost $50,000.[74] These apparent symptoms of mismanagement and avarice on the part of the general officers certainly fuelled criticism of the Knights in Britain and Ireland.[75] In other cases, leading Knights siphoned the Order's funds into their own bank accounts or used them as collateral for their own private investments. General Secretary-Treasurer Hayes was the worst offender in this regard, although most of the other general officers also indulged in their own moneymaking schemes, either to restore the Order's financial health or to survive at a time when the Knights could not afford to pay their salaries.[76] In the United States these cases of fraud were generally symptoms of the Order's decline and not its cause.

The two cases of embezzlement in the British assemblies were on a far smaller scale than in the United States, but they were very definitely a cause rather than a symptom of the Order's decline there. In January 1889 the secretary of an assembly in the Birmingham area, Charles Richards, was charged with stealing £7 16s 3d, money intended for Jesse Chapman. In August 1890, Charles Chamberlain, the recording and financial secretary of LA7952, the Order's representative on the West Bromwich School Board, and the Knight most interviewed by the local press, followed Richards into the dock. Knights claimed that he took £2 10s from LA7952 without any justification.[77] In both cases local Knights faced a serious legal problem. To successfully press charges for financial disputes in criminal court, trade unions and friendly societies had to register with the Registrar of Friendly Societies and of Trade Unions under the Trade Union Acts. To register they needed to have their headquarters in Britain or Ireland.[78] The Knights were not registered, nor could they register while they remained affiliated with the General Assembly.

The trials of Richards and Chamberlain illustrated the dangers of operating as an unregistered society. Richards claimed to have lost the money and offered to pay it back; in any case his defence counsel successfully

---

[73] Weir, *Knights Unhorsed*, p. 101.
[74] Ware, *Labor Movement*, pp. 371–73.
[75] See, for instance, *Midland Counties Express*, 12 September 1889.
[76] Weir, *Knights Unhorsed*, pp. 171–73.
[77] *Birmingham Daily Post*, 8 August 1890.
[78] Pelling, 'Knights in Britain,' p. 326.

argued that since the Knights were not registered the court was under no obligation to decide the case.[79] Chamberlain, on the other hand, argued that the assembly owed him the money as back pay for his work on behalf of local assemblies. Local Knights disagreed. Their prosecution, in an attempt to get around the fact that they remained unregistered, turned to novel legal arguments, such as the fanciful idea that the assemblies were, at turns, a profit-sharing enterprise, a joint-stock company and a friendly society. Their case was duly dismissed.[80] In October they tried again, this time accusing Chamberlain of taking £5 10s. Chamberlain's lawyer argued that there was no need to proceed any further as the Knights were not registered. This time, the prosecution introduced legal precedents dating from as far back as 1642 but to no avail. The judge dismissed the case for the second and final time.[81]

The timing of these cases proved extremely unfortunate. In 1889 and 1890 the British and Irish assemblies reached their peak membership and widest geographical extent. The Black Country assemblies seemed to be reviving after the losses suffered at the hands of the Midland Counties Trades Federation, the Associated Ironworkers and the Engineers. The Chamberlain case, especially, exposed schisms within the Knights and suggested that members' contributions to the assemblies were far from safe. 'Investigations at Police Courts,' as one paper aptly put it several months later, 'never did and never will tend to the enhancement of any body of workers.'[82] The assemblies suffered a 'severe' drop in membership soon afterwards.[83] The two cases also came at an unfortunate point in the wider relationship between the British and Irish assemblies and Philadelphia. The assemblies became publicly vulnerable to embezzlement at the same time as they sent contributions to the United States and received increasingly little in return, and as the American Order itself appeared, even across the Atlantic, no longer as vibrant and successful but as divided and in serious decline. At such a crucial turning point in this transatlantic relationship, the financial misadventures of a single secretary became a major factor in the decline of the Knights of Labor in Britain and Ireland.

---

[79] *Birmingham Daily Post*, 30 January and 2 February 1889.
[80] *Birmingham Daily Post*, 9 August 1889.
[81] *Smethwick Weekly News*, 4 October 1890.
[82] *Smethwick Weekly News*, 16 May 1891.
[83] Pelling, 'Knights in Britain,' p. 326.

Nationalism, Regionalism and Internationalism

Of all the objections levelled against the Order, Richard Hill told the *Journal of United Labor* in 1887, 'the chief one is that the Knights of Labor is an American organization, and that our money has to be sent abroad instead of staying with us to do us good.'[84] The argument that the Order was a foreign organisation, and unsuited to British or Irish conditions, remained with Knights there until the very end. In 1891, the *Smethwick Weekly News* concluded, rather prematurely, that 'a foreign society could never root itself kindly on English soil.' What, the paper asked, 'do we know of Master Powderly, and what has he to do with our trade disputes?'[85] Some went even further, and argued that the Knights ran directly counter to the interests of local workers. 'The artisans in this country by sending subsidies to the organisation in America were injuring themselves,' Samuel Welsh claimed in 1889, 'because they were supplying funds which would be used in securing the election of representatives to Congress who would vote for the excluding of British manufactures from the American markets.'[86]

A letter in the *Smethwick Weekly News* made similar allegations against LA300 in 1891. That assembly sent 'a very small levy per man' to keep the strike going at Spon Lane, the writer claimed, and 'that small levy is keeping Chance's glass out of the country. Result: Good trade in America; bad trade here.'[87] This allegation was not completely untrue. LA300 supported the introduction of the McKinley Tariff of 1890, which protected American glass and other industries from foreign competition, at the expense of the very assemblies of glassworkers they organised through the Universal Federation.[88] Welsh's wider accusations also have some merit, at least superficially. 'Touch not the tariff,' Terence Powderly wrote in 1888, and 'raise the duties so high that not a single article of foreign manufacture can come into the country.'[89] This was bluster, however, not an expression of what the Knights seriously hoped to achieve. Nor did Knights expand abroad out of a desire to line their pockets. Instead, as we saw in the first chapter, they organised in Britain, Ireland and elsewhere partly due to their commitment to universal brotherhood and partly in order to stem the tide of immigration. They practised brotherhood from a distance rather than extortion from across the Atlantic.

---

[84] *JUL*, 30 July 1887.
[85] *Smethwick Weekly News*, 11 July 1891.
[86] *Walsall Observer*, 11 January 1890.
[87] *Smethwick Weekly News*, 14 November 1891.
[88] Pelling, 'Knights in Britain,' p. 320.
[89] Newspaper clipping from unknown source, in folder 1888 August 23–26, Box 46, TVP.

If the Knights arrived in Britain and Ireland for practical and principled reasons, and not for devious ones, their local representatives still needed to appear to be something more than a collection of branches that belonged to an American Order. We have already seen that British and Irish Knights benefited from their American connections in the 1880s more than they suffered from the American origins of the Order. They followed the guidelines and strictures – the Americanisms, perhaps – of American Knights, in terms of cultural practices and industrial policy, and yet their assemblies grew in their first half decade. Henry George might agree with the *Birmingham Daily Gazette* that 'the American KL Constitution was quite unsuited for the English Knights,' but then, as one of their supporters insisted, 'the English Order does not endorse all that is done in America.'[90] British and Irish Knights needed, however, to portray their order as a British and Irish as well as an American one; and as decline set in, this need grew only more intense. They spent their last years attempting, unsuccessfully, to build a national movement out of their various local and regional ones.

The Knights of Labor, as previous chapters made clear, consistently proved their willingness to let members outside the United States adapt their assemblies to local conditions, provided they met a certain minimum standard of compliance with the Order's programme.[91] They also proved their willingness to let foreign Knights exercise more control over their own affairs. As early as 1884, delegates to the General Assembly proposed that Knights outside the United States should form their own general assemblies, with full control over revenues and methods of operation, with the American General Assembly left in control of ritual and with each general assembly entitled to send representatives to the others.[92] The General Assembly rejected these proposals, and later ones in 1887, but Knights in Belgium created a State Assembly in that year which effectively operated as an independent national body, sent Albert Delwarte to the 1888 General Assembly in that capacity and severed direct ties with Philadelphia in September 1889 while continuing to work under the name Les Chevaliers du Travail.[93] Knights in New Zealand similarly created their own National Assembly, sanctioned by the General Assembly.

British and Irish Knights were slow to follow their lead. Instead, DA208 asked the 1889 General Assembly 'that the words "of America" be dropped

---

[90] *Birmingham Daily Gazette*, 22 February and 15 May 1889.
[91] Weir, *Knights Down Under*, esp. pp. 233–42.
[92] *Proceedings of the GA* (1884), pp. 741–42.
[93] *Proceedings of the GA*, (1887), pp. 1537, 1689; Watillon, *Knights of Labor in Belgium*, p. 35.

from the name of the Order.' The General Assembly acceded to their request.[94] The district assembly further asked that 'a representative of the Order in America be sent over to that country for a period of twelve months to settle disputes and extend the Order generally throughout the United Kingdom.'[95] The General Assembly refused this request, though it did allow DA208 and DA248 to control their own initiation fees and make some adjustments to the Order's preamble.[96] In each case, British Knights wanted the Order to become more international and less specifically American. Their commitment to remaining part of their transnational movement outweighed their desire to go it alone. The General Assembly appreciated their loyalty and nearly chose Birmingham (in England, not Alabama) as the site of their next annual meeting.[97]

At the same time, the leaders of the British and Irish assemblies slowly began to weld their various local and district assemblies into a national movement. An 'Inter-District Committee' convened a meeting on 4 August 1890 for all the assemblies 'to take into consideration what means can be devised for the further consolidation and strengthening of the Order here.'[98] That meeting was overshadowed by the Chamberlain embezzlement case, which painfully illustrated the urgency of registering the assemblies under the Trade Union Acts. Thus energised, the delegates resolved to create a National Assembly, 'draft an English preamble' and raise membership dues in order to create a common reserve fund and supply funeral benefits.[99] But many Knights initially shied away from any attempt to organise apart from the General Assembly. The leaders of DA208 submitted a copy of their rules to the Registrar at the beginning of 1891 in the hope of registering their district assembly without having to sever direct ties with Philadelphia; the Registrar responded that he would only consider registering the Order as a whole and not any one district of it.[100]

The need to gain registration pushed British and Irish Knights towards independence from Philadelphia. Meetings in April and May 1891 brought together representatives from around 30 assemblies from the Rotherham, Birmingham and Cradley Heath districts as well as some unspecified other

[94] *Proceedings of the GA* (1889), pp. 8, 18, 34.
[95] *Proceedings of the GA* (1889), p. 44.
[96] *Proceedings of the GA* (1889), p. 44.
[97] *Proceedings of the GA* (1889), pp. 78–79. Such a move would have given much-needed publicity to assemblies there even if it remains unclear how an order with enormous financial problems could have paid the travelling costs of nearly 100 delegates voyaging across the Atlantic.
[98] *JUL*, 3 July 1890.
[99] *Birmingham Workmen's Times*, 29 August 1890.
[100] *Smethwick Weekly News*, 11 July 1891.

areas.[101] At this stage the delegates resolved to get 'registered in accordance with the laws of this country … [while] at the same time to keep as close as possible to the American order.'[102] Arthur Nadin described it as '"Home Rule" for Great Britain and also Irish Knights of Labour,' and insisted that 'no separation … will take place between the Knights of Labour of this country and their brethren across the Atlantic.'[103] In August 1891 a meeting of delegates from assemblies across Yorkshire and the Midlands agreed to form the British National Assembly of the Knights of Labour, with its headquarters in Cradley Heath, and the new body was registered on 15 October 1891.[104]

The *Preamble* of the National Assembly described it as 'an off-shoot of the great American Organization, whose principles of action, and methods of work, it has largely endorsed.'[105] In its ritual practices, its strike policy, and the names and functions of its officers, the National Assembly followed existing practice in the American Order except for raising the initiation fees from 5s to 7s 6d, on top of 4d in weekly contributions.[106] At the 1891 General Assembly, the General Executive Board gave the new body its blessing. It described 'a growing feeling among our brothers in Great Britain and Ireland in favour of their being placed in a position to more fully control their own affairs,' and the Board declared itself 'favourably disposed toward anything they may find necessary in this direction.'[107]

The National Assembly, Henry Pelling writes, came 'too late to arrest the decline of membership.'[108] The economic upswing of 1889–90 was already subsiding, and the assemblies were subsiding with it. Conflict and competition with the trade unions had already taken their toll, as had desertions after failed strikes or the failure of Knights to support strikes when workers evidently wanted them. There had already been an exodus of members following the embezzlement cases. Indeed, it took more than a year after the Chamberlain case for the British National Assembly to gain registration. Knights could hardly point to any bureaucratic ineptitude on the part of the Registrar of Trade Unions. Instead, the National Assembly was delayed by deep splits between the assemblies attached to DA208 and those attached to DA248 and DA256. The former, as one newspaper reported, 'wish to establish a National Assembly, with headquarters in England, under a charter to be obtained from Powderly'; the latter, DA248 in particular,

[101] *Smethwick Telephone*, 18 April 1891; *Smethwick Weekly News*, 16 May 1891.
[102] *Smethwick Telephone*, 20 June 1891.
[103] *Rotherham Advertiser*, 29 August 1891.
[104] Pelling, 'Knights in Britain,' p. 326; *Preamble of the British National Assembly*, p. 39.
[105] *Preamble of the British National Assembly*, p. 1.
[106] *Preamble of the British National Assembly*, pp. 27–28.
[107] *Proceedings of the GA* (1891), pp. 1–2.
[108] Pelling, 'Knights in Britain,' p. 326.

'wish to cut the connection with America altogether, and make the Order an English trades union,' doubling dues to create 'a fund which would attract recruits, and enable any serious dispute to be properly fought.'[109]

These disputes resulted in the cleavage of the British and Irish Knights at the very point when they could least afford a split. The assemblies of DA248 and DA256 combined under the banner of the British National Assembly. Those in DA208 remained under their existing constitution.[110] Knights elsewhere in Britain and Ireland were not consulted. LA1601 in Derry, for instance, only found out about the meetings after they had been held.[111] At one meeting in 1891, Arthur Nadin spoke of establishing 'further communications' with the Scottish assemblies, but there is no indication that Scottish Knights were involved in the National Assembly at all.[112] In the northeast, the British United Order and the Independent Order remained aloof from assemblies elsewhere.[113]

These regional splits illustrated one of the dangers facing a transnational movement like the Knights. Their British and Irish assemblies remained as oriented towards Philadelphia as to each other. Individual organisers, to be sure, often moved from one area to another: Thomas Dean of DA208 lectured in Liverpool and Rotherham, for instance, and Haydn Sanders travelled from Walsall to organise around South Yorkshire and the West Midlands.[114] But Knights did not begin to conceive of themselves as more than a collection of local affiliates to an American movement, and as a national, British movement, until 1890 at the earliest. This was partially because the Knights only extended beyond the Black Country in 1888 and 1889, and partially, as we saw in Chapter 2, because as an ecumenical and successful international movement the Knights were able organise Irish and other workers in large numbers. But it was mainly because they had no other choice. Financial scandals required them to conform to the standards of the Registrar of Trade Unions if they wished to stop these scandals happening again. Yet the British National Assembly divided their ranks still further, and came too late to reverse the damage done to the Order's reputation or membership.

These conflicting pressures split the Knights at a moment when only absolute unity could offer them any prospect for survival. They also exposed the ways in which working-class internationalism had changed and were

---

[109] *Smethwick Weekly News*, 11 July 1891.
[110] Pelling, 'Knights in Britain,' p. 326.
[111] Hayes to William Stewart, 7 August 1891, Box 67, TVP.
[112] *Rotherham Advertiser*, 29 August 1891.
[113] Pelling, 'Knights in Britain,' p. 328.
[114] For Dean in Liverpool, see *Liverpool Mercury*, 27 May 1889; for Yorkshire, see *Rotherham Advertiser*, 21 December 1889. For Sanders see earlier chapters in this book.

changing. Marcel van der Linden, as we saw in Chapter 1, divides the history of this internationalism in the nineteenth century into several rough periods. The first, 'sub-national internationalism,' was dominant until the 1870s. It found its highest expression in the First International, with its alliances between workers of different countries at a local or subnational level and with the International itself creating branches in various countries. The second phase, 'national internationalism,' began to dominate from the 1890s and represented instead the coming together of pre-existing national bodies. Its highest expression, the Second International and the trade union bodies that surrounded it, exemplified this trend and the great development of national labour movements in the years between the two Internationals.[115] 'The national framework,' Geert van Goethem writes, became 'the only reality for the labour movement as a whole, when it started to develop in the last quarter of the nineteenth century as a mass movement.'[116] The Knights of Labor emerged in the transition period between these two phases. Its dream of a single supranational organisation, bringing together local bodies of workers in different countries, resembled the First International much more than the Second.

We saw in the previous chapter how the Knights lost out to national trade unions, first the 'old,' then the 'new.' The new unions and new unionists also articulated the logic of 'national internationalism' with particular force. 'When each Trade Union comprises the majority of the workers in its Trade, and when these unions are united in a National Trade Federation,' Annie Besant explained, 'then will come the time for the International Federation, which will mean the triumph of labor and the freedom of the workers everywhere.'[117] John Havelock Wilson used this same logic against Knights in Bootle, as he simultaneously praised the American Knights and attacked their local supporters. 'He believed that it would be more profitable for the working men of this country to organise themselves first,' he told a meeting of seamen and dockers in 1890, 'and then, if possible, to confederate with the Knights of Labour or any organisation which might exist.'[118] The Knights proved acceptable as a national American movement but not as an international one.

The British and Irish Knights were caught in many contradictions between many conflicting pressures over the course of their history. This was one of the greatest. Their assemblies faced powerful and often new national

---

[115] Van der Linden, 'Rise and Fall of the First International,' pp. 325–33.
[116] Van Goethem, *The Amsterdam International*, p. 13.
[117] A. Besant, *The Trades Union Movement* (London: Freethought Publishing Company, 1890), p. 28.
[118] *Liverpool Weekly Post*, 8 February 1890.

organisations in the 1880s and the 1890s, and their assemblies invariably lost. At the same time the whole conception of what internationalism meant in the working-class movements of Europe and the Americas was changing. Internationalism came to mean the alliance of national bodies and not the growth of a single, international one like the Knights of Labor. This is not to imply that Knights outside North America were inevitably doomed to failure. But their success depended in large part on their ability to adapt themselves to the new mood for national movements that would, in time, come together with those from other countries. Knights in Belgium and New Zealand successfully built national movements at a relatively early stage in their history. They survived into the twentieth century; the assemblies in Britain and Ireland did not.

Knights there waited until their assemblies fell into serious decline before trying to build their own National Assembly. They found that in the process of building it, their ranks split along a range of ideological and geographical lines. Regionalism, nationalism and internationalism bred changing and conflicting pressures that ultimately helped to tear the British and Irish assemblies apart. It is hard to see how it could have been otherwise. In the early years of the assemblies the American connection seemed to make the task of building a national movement unnecessary, even undesirable, or at least something that could be put off for several more years. When that task became necessary, after Charles Richards and Charles Chamberlain exposed the assemblies' vulnerability to fraud, it was too late to avoid the divisions that opened between the leaders of the various district assemblies. These trends were not inevitable. Paradoxically, however, the very success of the Knights of Labor as a transnational movement in the 1880s made the task of turning their assemblies into a national movement in the 1890s that much harder, and that much less likely to happen in time to save the assemblies.

Conclusion: The Final Years of the Assemblies

In the waning years of Terence Powderly's tenure as General Master Workman of the Knights of Labor, he and one of his closest associates hit upon a moneymaking scheme to make up for the salary that the bankrupt Order could not pay him. Using the printing presses of the *Journal of the Knights of Labor* they printed a *Labor Day Annual* in 1893, in an effort to cash in on the growth of Labor Day as the main event in the American working-class calendar. The publication yielded little profit for Powderly and his friends. It failed to sell well. It also alienated numerous workers who saw its advertisements and featured articles from some notoriously anti-union employers as a betrayal; its content, especially a chapter on 'Labor in England' by one Carey Taylor, was nothing less than delusional. In Britain, Taylor argued, 'the lines of old-fashioned trades-unionism are too closely followed, and ... British toilers, as a mass, have not yet comprehended the necessity for and the advantages of such an unification and amalgamation of forces as are presented by the Order of the Knights of Labor.' Taylor added that 'a more active and enthusiastic dissemination of its principles by our transatlantic brothers would so consolidate the ranks of English labor as to bring the subjugation of British capital within "measurable distance,"' and claimed it was 'inconceivable that the ablest leaders of the various British labor organizations could not unite in the adoption of the Knights of Labor platform.'[119]

The *Labor Day Annual* symbolises many of the problems that afflicted the American Knights in the last years in which they could claim to speak for an appreciable fraction of American workers. The inability to pay salaries on time, the use of the Order's resources for private gain and the almost predetermined failure of these ventures were all too common in the collapsing scenery of the Knights of Labor in the 1890s. Taylor's arguments were reminiscent of the hopes that *Reynolds's Newspaper* held out for the Knights in 1887, when its writer predicted that they would replace the TUC. In that year, at least, the Order in Britain was a young movement affiliated with the largest labour organisation in the world. By 1893, the British and Irish assemblies had missed any opportunity they might have had to assume a leading role in their labour movements. Now they teetered on the edge of dissolution.

Earlier chapters noted many of the causes of their decline. They lost strikes, or lost many members who wished to strike but were prevented from doing so by leaders wedded to arbitration at all costs. The trade unions defeated them and took their members, and the assemblies could not find a role between the national unions and the Trades Councils. Union opposition was perhaps the most consistently debilitating factor of all, more than opposition from employers, which was powerful in specific instances – notably at Pilkington's – and absent in others. In this chapter we can add to the roll call of causes. British and Irish Knights suffered from their attachment to the American Order as it declined from the end of the 1880s onwards. They suffered in terms of reputation, as the local representatives of an order marching from defeat to defeat; and they suffered as American Knights became unable to give them financial assistance and supply them with organisers to replace Denny, Davitt and Archibald.

In these newly unfavourable circumstances the embezzlement cases encouraged an exodus from the assemblies. These cases pushed Knights to build their own National Assembly, but the process of building it divided

---

[119] Carey Taylor, 'Labor in England,' *Labor Day Annual*, 1893, p. 57, Box 115, TVP.

rather than united the remaining assemblies. It also came too late to spark their revival. At the end, the Knights of Labor remained wedded to a style of working-class internationalism that material conditions no longer supported, and which workers in Britain and Ireland, at least, no longer practised. The initiative lay with resurgent national movements who wished to come together but from a position of independence. The British and Irish Knights could not justify their continued existence in this context, unlike Belgian and New Zealand Knights. Their history as a movement with a future probably ended in 1891, even if their assemblies survived at least until 1894.

We can only guess as to the precise mechanics and timeline of decline for each individual local assembly. Most probably went the way of LA9770 in Winson Green, whose members faithfully paid their per capita tax to Philadelphia right up to the point when they folded, in July 1890.[120] Other assemblies gradually disappeared. The Bootle assembly, LA443, whose members had welcomed the 1890s with such optimism and with plans to open new assemblies in Liverpool, held its last public meeting in October 1890, and seems to have folded soon afterwards.[121] The Walsall assembly, LA454, whose growth had also been rapid and whose future prospects seemed bright in 1890, seems to have collapsed some time in the following year. Not much is known of the Scottish assemblies except that James Shaw Maxwell, by far their leading figure, moved to London in 1891 to restart a radical publication, the *People's Press*.[122] They likely faded away in 1891 without much in the way of publicity. Certainly, when the NUDL arrived to organise dockers at Ardrossan in 1892 the Order's assembly no longer existed.[123]

The assemblies in Belfast and Derry suffered from fierce conflict with powerful rival unions, with financial difficulties and the inability of the American Knights to bail them out. As we saw in Chapter 2, they also suffered from the same religious sectarianism that still plagues Northern Ireland today. Nationalists and Unionists, Catholics and Protestants, all fought for control within the three Irish assemblies and helped tear each of them apart, first the Belfast assemblies in 1890, then the Derry assembly in 1892.[124] In the previous year Derry's LA1601 had also endured its own

---

[120] C. Mullineux to Hayes, 22 July 1890, Box 26, JHP.
[121] *Bootle Times*, 18 October 1890.
[122] Shaw Maxwell to J. Bruce Glasier, 13 March 1891, GP/1/1/ 98, J. Bruce Glasier Archives, Liverpool University. Shaw Maxwell also wrote a letter to the *Journal of United Labor* in February or March 1891 from London, not Glasgow (*JUL*, 5 March 1891). When Secretary-Treasurer Hayes wrote to James Brown in July 1891, he only claimed to have written to DA208, DA248 and DA256, making no mention of Scotland's DA203. See Hayes to James Brown, 16 July 1891, Box 10, JHP.
[123] Levy, *Ardrossan Harbour*, pp. 46–47.
[124] Boyle, *Irish Labour Movement*, pp. 104–06.

version of the Charles Chamberlain scandal: its treasurer, Daniel McGaul, had embezzled £12 13s 1d from the assembly. Knights were unable to recover the stolen money, further worsening their already precarious financial position. With no funds left, the assembly soon collapsed.[125]

As we saw in Chapter 4, the first major assembly anywhere in Britain and Ireland, LA3504, also came to an end in 1893. General Secretary-Treasurer Hayes advised its secretary, James Brown, in August 1892 that even in straitened times, the Order 'ought to be a good organization to boom with, being so far in advance of the average trade union.'[126] But LA3504's few remaining members were by that stage unemployed. There was little chance of a bankrupt assembly of unemployed glassworkers becoming the base for a revival of the Knights of Labor in the Sunderland area, and LA3504 closed its doors some time in 1893, more through apathy than any kind of last-ditch struggle. The fire than ruined Hartley's, at any rate, left the remaining Knights in the glass trade with no one to struggle against.

Many of the British Order's leaders deserted the assemblies too. Shaw Maxwell left DA203 for London. Haydn Sanders left assemblies in Walsall and then Rotherham after he became president of the new National Union of Stove-Grate Workers. Samuel Reeves ended his association with the Knights after LA443 was wound up. Jesse Chapman turned all his attention to Liberal politics in the mid-1890s, and Zebulon Butler returned to his political obsession, the single tax. The departure of leading Knights further encouraged members to leave as well. Only stalwarts like Arthur Nadin in Rotherham, and Thomas Dean and Richard Hill in Birmingham, stayed at their posts to the very end.

DA208 and the British National Assembly both continued into 1894. From 1891 until then, both organisations, now rivals of a kind, tried to keep their assemblies running. They doubtless awaited a miracle from some quarter or other, maybe some sharp upswing of trade, the sudden collapse of their trade union rivals or even the revival of the American assemblies, who might then provide them with assistance once more. No miracle was forthcoming. Arthur Nadin did travel to Derry in an attempt to revive the assembly there, this time under the umbrella of the British National Assembly, and there are some indications that a new assembly emerged in Derry and continued, in a subterranean fashion, until as late as 1896.[127] Knights in Rotherham maintained a presence on their Trades Council and,

---

[125] *Belfast News-Letter*, 26 May 1891.
[126] Hayes to James Brown, 12 August 1892, Box 10, JHP.
[127] *Rotherham Advertiser*, 26 November 1892; Garlock, *Guide to the Local Assemblies*, p. 584. At a meeting of Knights in 1895, the socialist Daniel De Leon referred to assemblies in Ireland (*New York Times*, 22 October 1895).

in a last attempt to garner support in the town, they held 'soup dinners' for poor local children and their parents.[128]

Knights in the Black Country met at Smethwick in April 1892 and planned to hold open-air demonstrations 'at an early date.' Another report, however, suggested that only a dozen people attended the meeting and concluded 'that the order has had its day, and they would do better to let it rest.'[129] The Knights no longer existed outside of these two centres. In 1890, the Order had numbered upwards of 10,000 members. When the British National Assembly submitted its first returns to the Registrar at the end of 1892 it claimed only 434 dues-paying members. According to a later report from the Registrar, it never again exceeded this figure and wound up in 1894.[130] The last two surviving assemblies attached to the Trades Council in Rotherham, the last centre where the National Assembly maintained something like a public profile, dissolved themselves sometime in the same year.[131]

The decline of DA208 mirrored that of the British National Assembly. The despair that accompanied the fall of that assembly is all the more vivid for the correspondence that survives between Powderly and Richard Hill, its recording secretary, and Thomas Dean, its Master Workman. In February 1893, Dean informed Powderly that DA208 now had only four local assemblies in good standing, one less than the minimum necessary to operate as a district assembly, and that Hill was seriously ill.[132] At the same time Hill wrote to Secretary-Treasurer Hayes to seek advice and even suggested that Knights in Birmingham 'simply allow DA208 to be a thing of the past.'[133] Powderly, at least, replied and gave Dean special dispensation to keep DA208 in operation.[134] By June, however, the four local assemblies had been reduced to three, and each, Hill told Powderly, 'have held special meetings, attended by the District officers who have put the whole matter clearly before them, when resolutions have been passed, pledging themselves to stand by the Order, and to do what they can to assert the DA.' Hill still hoped that this pledge would keep what remained of DA208's membership.[135]

---

[128] For the Trades Council see, for example, *Rotherham Advertiser*, 18 March 1893. For the soup dinner see *Sheffield Daily Telegraph*, 28 November 1893.
[129] *Smethwick Telephone*, 16 April 1892; *Smethwick Weekly News*, 16 April 1892.
[130] *Report by the Chief Labour Correspondent of the Board of Trade on Trade Unions*, 1898, pp. 190–91. Found at: HCPP.
[131] *Rotherham Advertiser*, 19 January 1895.
[132] Thomas Dean to Powderly, 8 February 1893, Box 77, TVP.
[133] Richard Hill to Hayes, 9 February 1893, Box 77, TVP.
[134] Powderly to Thomas Dean, 20 February 1893, Box 104, TVP.
[135] Richard Hill to Powderly, 23 June 1893, Box 80, TVP.

Powderly did not reply to this letter. Nor did he receive any more. Jonathan Garlock lists one English assembly, LA584 of Aston, as existing until 1896, and the Independent Order survived in Jarrow with less than 100 members until 1901. The General Assembly in 1895 urged the 'necessity [of] building up the Order in England and other foreign countries as to place the workers in all lands in touch with each other,' but this was as much of a dream as General Master Workman James Sovereign's incredible claim, the following year, that there were 100,000 Knights in France.[136] The end of the correspondence between Dean, Hill and Powderly signified the end of the Knights of Labor as a movement of any importance at all in Britain and Ireland.[137] They ended, as Henry Pelling writes, 'vainly demanding advice from Powderly on how to halt the decline.'[138] But Powderly was not in any state to provide advice. By this time his attention was completely devoted to holding on as General Master Workman. The remaining American Knights evicted him from that post in 1894. And no pledge, no matter how powerful, could save the last assemblies in Birmingham from dissolution. They soon ended up in the well-populated graveyard of other failed movements, broken unions and defunct international organisations that are the subject of much nineteenth-century labour history.

---

[136] *Proceedings of the GA* (1895), p. 41; *New York Times*, 10 November 1896.
[137] Garlock, *Guide to the Local Assemblies*, p. 581.
[138] Pelling, 'Knights in Britain,' p. 328.

Conclusion
The Knights of Labor
in Britain and Ireland

In 1896, M.J. Bishop, the General Worthy Foreman of the Knights of Labor, drew the attention of the General Assembly to 'the attempt to form an international organisation of longshoremen, dockworkers and men employed generally on the waterfront, with the avowed intention of forcing their interests to the fore regardless of all others.' Bishop attacked 'the folly of the whole proceeding' in withering terms. 'We are entering upon an era of competition in the labor market which has never had a duplicate on the earth,' he told the assembled delegates, 'in very skilled occupation inventive genius is putting the craftsman upon a level with the common labourer.' Under these circumstances, he claimed, 'any combination, based upon the lines of trade, craft or occupation, which has for its main purpose an intention to force its views upon employers through a strike, must meet with sudden and disastrous failure.' Bishop concluded that 'the trade union methods which the Knights of Labor were originally formed to obviate and supersede, will no longer serve to protect the toiler from the greed and oppression of unscrupulous employers.'[1]

In the same year the General Worthy Foreman also became a participant in a transatlantic slanging match with James Mawdsley, a veteran of the Parliamentary Committee of the TUC and the general secretary of the Amalgamated Association of Operative Cotton Spinners. Mawdsley was not a typical TUC leader – he resigned from the Parliamentary Committee in 1890 in protest at the rising socialist influence within the Congress and later stood alongside Winston Churchill as a Conservative parliamentary candidate for a two-member constituency – but his words still carried some weight.[2] Mawdsley visited the United States in 1895 and relayed his

[1] *Proceedings of the GA* (1896), pp. 20–21.
[2] C.J. Wrigley, *Winston Churchill: A Biographical Companion* (Santa Barbara: ABC-CLIO, 2002), p. 257.

impressions to *Reynolds's Newspaper*. One report in particular raised the ire of Bishop and other leading Knights, when Mawdsley wrote that 'the "Knights" have, during the past five years, been going down as all systems built on folly must do in the long run.'[3] The *Journal of the Knights of Labor* attacked his 'concentrated pig-headed presumption and asinine assumption of "know-it-all-iveness."'[4] Bishop responded in the pages of *Reynolds's* by referring to the 'large following' that the Order supposedly still had in Britain and Ireland. 'Were it not for such methods' as Mawdsley's, he argued, 'we would now have a much larger one everywhere.'[5] The British trade unionist, however, had the final and decisive word. 'An organisation which cannot publish its number of members and its annual income,' Mawdsley concluded, 'need not be given much thought to by the workers at large.'[6]

There was nothing that Bishop could say to refute Mawdsley's allegation that the Knights of Labor was an order in terminal decline. His broadside against the new international organisation of waterfront workers proved similarly ill-timed. Glass bottle makers from across Europe had created what *Justice* described as 'the first really International Trades' Union' in 1886.[7] The British Sailors' and Firemen's Union had recruited members in various countries along the Atlantic and Mediterranean coasts in the late 1880s. After the London Dock Strike in 1889, in which foreign assistance, particularly but not only from Australia, played a major role in ensuring victory, waterfront workers in Britain began to establish connections with others in western and northern Europe.[8] The organisation that Bishop attacked eventually became the International Transport Workers' Federation, a body that survived into the present day. That federation was not alone. Between 1890 and 1910, workers in a variety of trades and industries created International Trade Secretariats (ITS), bodies designed to promote the international dissemination of information relevant to each craft, to facilitate the international exchange of union cards for migrating workers and to offer support for strikes and prevent foreign scab labour from preventing those strikes.[9] Dubbed 'postbox internationals,' because they acted mainly as centres for correspondence, by 1900 there were ITSs among hatters, glovers,

---

[3] *Reynolds's*, 29 December 1895.
[4] *JUL*, 16 January 1896.
[5] *Reynolds's*, 29 March 1896.
[6] *Reynolds's*, 5 April 1896.
[7] *Commonweal*, 23 October 1886.
[8] International Transport Workers' Federation, *Solidarity: The First 100 Years of the International Transport Workers' Federation* (London: Pluto Press, 1996), pp. 3–11.
[9] Busch, *Political Role of International Trade Unions*, pp. 15–16.

shoemakers, miners, glass workers, tailors, metal workers, textile workers, lithographers, transport workers and other smaller trades.[10]

Bishop, in other words, aimed his attack against the future direction of the international labour movement. In the process he also ignored the contributions the Knights made to that movement. The Universal Federation of Window Glass Workers was created by LA300 five years before any of the ITSs, and two years before the international union of glass bottle makers. 'It was an American idea, this world-wide Union,' John Swinton wrote in July 1885. Swinton's prediction that 'by and by other industries will have like Unions, to take up world-wide questions, and decide them too,' was borne out by events, but only partly, because the Universal Federation went much further than the ITSs ever did.[11] The postbox internationals only sought to keep their affiliates abreast of news in other parts of the world; the Universal Federation aimed to regulate the labour market's trade on a global scale, and for some time the Federation succeeded. The Universal Federation, as with the Order as a whole, represented what Marcel van der Linden describes as subnational internationalism, a tradition that social, economic and political trends were rendering obsolete. But traditions of that kind are never hermetically sealed. The Knights of Labor may have arisen out of older patterns of working-class internationalism, but their global expansion anticipated newer patterns as well. The Knights represented both an end and a beginning, even if Bishop refused to see it.

There were further ironies in his position. In 1888, longshoremen in New York announced their desire to form a National Trade District within the Order and then further declared their intention to send delegates to Britain to lay the groundwork for 'the organization of an international organization.'[12] Knights in Boston hosted Richard McGhee, the president of the NUDL, when he visited the city in 1890. McGhee's goal, the *Journal of the Knights of Labor* reported, was 'to study the situation of the longshoremen and freight handlers, to the end that he may form a grand world-wide alliance of the men following those callings.'[13] The fact that McGhee had once worked as an organiser for Knights in the Black Country, before founding a union that shouldered aside Liverpool's LA443, made that irony only more exquisite. Nor would Bishop appreciate the fact that the Knights of Labor, an order dedicated to eradicating craft and other prejudices, grew in Britain and Ireland thanks to LA300, the most restrictive craft union in the United States.

---

[10] Milner, *Dilemmas of Internationalism*, p. 44.
[11] *John Swinton's Paper*, 19 July 1885.
[12] *New York Evening World*, 29 February 1888.
[13] *JUL*, 31 July 1890.

The Knights also provided an alternative to the development of the international labour movement during the late nineteenth and early twentieth century. Lewis Lorwin divided that movement as it stood in 1914 into three parts. One was the ITSs. Another was 'the association of various national labor federations.' The third was 'international associations of political labor parties and groups.'[14] We have dealt with the first. In terms of the second, the single worldwide order which the Knights hoped to build, an order in which all workers would share the same ritual and answer to the same General Assembly, hardly resembled the loose confederation of national union centres that eventually became known as the Amsterdam International. At the same time, industrial unionists and syndicalists in America and abroad regarded the Knights as one of their own and more illustrious ancestors.

In regard to the third, leading Knights remained firmly outside the Second International of labour and socialist parties that became a powerful political force in the years leading up to the First World War. Powderly assured the 1889 General Assembly that he would never have attended the socialist congresses in Paris that year, one of which, dubbed the 'Marxist' congress, was later regarded as the founding meeting of the Second International.[15] Paul Bowen and Jesse Chapman attended the 'Possibilist' Congress, but that meeting was not the one that led to the new International. In any case, Knights like Powderly preached their own brand of radicalism, one that was distinct from the socialism that drove the Second International and more akin to that which animated the British trade unionists who had helped create the First. A wide gulf separated Bishop from Karl Kautsky and the other leaders of the new International.

In short, the Knights of Labor provided precursors *and* alternatives to future trends in the international labour movement. That serves as the epitaph of the British and Irish assemblies in the labour histories of those countries as well. The Order arrived in Britain in 1883, and more decisively in 1884, with Robert Layton and other leading Knights predicting that assemblies would soon extend throughout all the towns and cities of Britain and Ireland. Those predictions, like all the grand prophecies that attended the rise of the Knights of Labor around the world, never came true.

But from their base among the glassworkers, and among the unskilled workers and craftsmen of Birmingham and the Black Country, the Knights gradually extended their assemblies into new parts of Britain and Ireland. They benefited from the image of their order that was forged during the Great Upheaval, from the material and human assistance that American

---

[14] Lorwin, 'Structures of International Labor Activities,' p. 2.
[15] *Proceedings of the GA* (1889), p. 6.

Knights gave them and from the manifold connections between the Irish diaspora in the United States, Britain and Ireland itself. On the question of Ireland and Irish workers in Britain, the Knights remained far ahead of the British trade unions. Coming from outside the imperial social, economic and political framework that kept Ireland subordinated to Britain, they were able to appeal to Irish immigrants around the latter in a way those unions could not match. They did this without obviously antagonising non-Irish workers in the Midlands, Yorkshire and in northwest and northeast England, although they were less successful in sectarian lowland Scotland and Northern Ireland. In general, where workers – especially unskilled workers – were disorganised, where they were seeking ways to end that disorganisation and where the Order's organisers visited and spoke, the Knights and their assemblies were usually not far behind. By 1889, only five years after A.G. Denny formed LA3504, their movement appeared to have a bright future ahead of it.

In the five years after 1889 their dream came abruptly to an end. The decline of the American Knights prevented them from giving any further assistance to their British and Irish assemblies, and fewer workers wished to attach themselves to an order whose American base was in such obvious decline. The embezzlement cases involving Charles Richards and Charles Chamberlain drove hundreds of workers from the assemblies and made them appear an insecure investment of workers' money. The assemblies found their growth impeded by several craft unions in the 1880s; in the 1890s the new unions shouldered them out of the way. British and Irish Knights never faced the same level of opposition and repression from employers and the state as their American counterparts, but enough employers, carrying sufficient weight in their respective industries, fought against them to stymie their growth. In the all-important case of the window glass industry, opposition from employers led to the destruction of LA3504 and, in turn, to the end of the Knights as a movement with a viable future. The economic downturn in the mid-1890s only created new problems and deepened their old ones.

The British and Irish assemblies faced one central problem throughout their history: how to adapt a foreign organisation to local conditions. American Knights, Powderly in particular, decided to err on the side of flexibility. They let their recruits across the Atlantic make changes to their methods and principles as they saw fit. For their part, British and Irish Knights tried as best they could to make arbitration work and adopted the cultural practices handed down to them from America almost in their entirety. In some cases, the philosophy of the Knights suited local conditions, particularly around Birmingham and the Black Country where workers were sympathetic and accustomed to arbitration. In other cases, most graphically around Liverpool, Knights urged arbitration on newly militant dockers with predictably poor results.

Knights adapted local conditions to their foreign organisation, as it were, rather than the other way around. That does not mean that 'Americanisms,' as Robert Weir terms them, lay at the heart of the Order's failures in Britain and Ireland. Rather, Knights there enacted the principles of the Order in an inflexible way, more so than most American Knights, and that inflexibility became a problem when trade, trade unionism and militancy increased at the end of the 1880s. Further research will show whether that kind of dogmatism is common among workers who join a foreign organisation. British and Irish Knights, at least, seem to have believed that by imitating their American cousins as much as possible they would be more likely to build a similarly powerful movement at home. Unfortunately, that belief was misplaced. Henry Pelling even concluded that 'they provided the workers and their leaders with more lessons of what to avoid than of what to imitate.'[16]

But the history of the Knights of Labor in Britain and Ireland is more than a litany of failures. Their assemblies reached into all the nations that then made up the United Kingdom: England, Wales, Scotland and Ireland. Perhaps as many as 20,000 men – though not, it must be said, many if any women – passed through those assemblies at some point between 1883 and 1894. If we add the organisations that plagiarised the Order's model or name, the Sons of Labour and the British United Order in particular, that number reached upwards of 40,000. The Knights attracted figures of great significance in the social and political life of Britain and Ireland, such as Michael Davitt and Robert Cunningham Graham. They attracted others of more localised fame, such as Haydn Sanders, James Shaw Maxwell, Samuel Reeves and Harold Rylett. Some Knights would go on to become leading trade unionists and parliamentarians, like Ben Turner, James Sexton and Richard McGhee. Their assemblies became part of one of the great international working-class movements of the late nineteenth century, and functioned, for a time, as part of the largest contemporary labour organisation in the world. They collapsed in the renewed depression of the mid-1890s, but in the wreckage of unions and labour bodies in those years they were hardly alone. Their influence, moreover, outlived them.

When Terence Powderly came to write his autobiography in the 1910s, he took great pains to explain that the Knights 'did not live or speak or work in vain.' Examine 'the statutes of the United States and of the various states,' he wrote, 'and stamped there – indelibly it may be – you'll find plank after plank of the platform of the Knights of Labor.'[17] Turning to the Order's foreign

---

[16] Pelling, 'Knights in Britain,' p. 330.
[17] Powderly, *The Path I Trod*, p. 56.

branches, Powderly added that 'though no local assemblies of Knights of Labor exist in any of these countries now, the principles of the Order still live and continue to inspire men and women to strive for the betterment of industrial conditions.'[18] Powderly's autobiography might have been little more than an exercise in self-justification. His suspicion of the historian, who 'weaves the warp of fancy into the woof of fact and gives us the web called history,' reflected his anger at early labour historians who characterised his order as utopian and doomed to fail and put much of the blame for its demise at his feet.[19] Powderly's assessment of the Order's long-term influence, however, whether in the United States or in the other countries where assemblies appeared, was probably more correct than even he knew. The Order became as central to the narrative of Canadian labour history as it did to that of its southern neighbour. Knights helped to lay the foundations of New Zealand's political system, and lobbied for and enacted landmark legislation there. The Order left a lasting impression on the methods and numbers of the trade union movement in Belgium.

The situation in Britain and Ireland was no different. The new unionism followed the Order's example when it came to organising unskilled and female workers, and to building greater unity within the trade union movement. American Knights showed British and Irish workers that both aims were achievable as well as desirable. British and Irish Knights pioneered both objectives themselves in Derry, Liverpool, Glasgow and the Black Country in particular. The Knights were an influence on and a part of the new unionism. They performed a similar if less direct role in the field of labour politics. British and Irish Knights enjoyed some small success in municipal elections, thanks especially to the oratorical abilities of Haydn Sanders in Walsall and Rotherham, but their main impact came at a national level. The political ventures of American workers during the Great Upheaval, Knights prominently among them, had a tremendous effect on many workers in Britain and Ireland. These ventures led directly to Keir Hardie's Sons of Labour programme, modelled on the Knights, on which he ran in the famous Mid-Lanark by-election of 1888. Knights also featured prominently in all the other early landmarks along the road to the British Labour Party, from the birth of the Scottish Labour Party in 1888 to the first congress of the Independent Labour Party in 1893.

In these fields, the principles that the Order espoused took greater root in Britain and Ireland than in the land of its birth. We should remain careful not to claim too much. The new unionism and the Labour Party would almost certainly have come about without the Knights. But they contributed

---

[18] Powderly, *The Path I Trod*, p. 66.
[19] Powderly, *The Path I Trod*, p. 2.

to the context in which both occurred. Far from providing British and Irish workers with things to avoid, as Pelling argued, the Order provided them with many things that they could and did choose to imitate. That record demands that we integrate the Knights of Labor into the mainstream of British and Irish labour history, in the same way that Robert Weir has placed the Knights at the centre of the early social and political history of white New Zealand. The main task that remains for the Order's historians is to provide it with a truly international history, one that leaves students of the Knights in no doubt that its foreign assemblies cannot be reduced to footnotes, and that these assemblies were influential and important in their own right. That history remains to be written. Its contours remain vague and imprecise. But as we continue to uncover evidence of assemblies in different parts of the world, that picture will start to acquire a more distinct shape and carry with it implications for what we know of the history of the Knights in their North American home, not to mention for labour history around the world.

That history certainly has implications for the idea and the reality of American exceptionalism. The achievements of the Knights of Labor undermine any assumption that American workers must inevitably remain less organised and more politically marginal than workers in other industrial societies. The Order also stood at a unique crossroads in the relative histories of the British and American labour movements. Just as American industrial development lagged behind Britain for most of the nineteenth century, American unions followed in the wake of their British counterparts and imitated their development, albeit slightly later and on a smaller scale. In the 1880s, however, American industrial output caught up with Britain and the American labour movement, through the Knights, did likewise. Their American assemblies organised more workers than all the British trade unions combined during the mid-1880s.

It is true that the Knights failed to hold this position for very long. In the twentieth century the American labour movement fell behind its counterparts in Europe and elsewhere in the industrialised world. Kim Voss's contention that American exceptionalism was not inevitable but was made, and that it began when the Order's defeat encouraged American trade unionists to retreat from politics and into the skilled trades, even as labour movements elsewhere went in the opposite direction, fits into this narrative especially well. And the history of the British and Irish Knights allows us to take that argument further still. Even as the Order's American decline led to the *rejection*, at least temporarily, of independent labour politics and of a labour movement designed to represent the entire working class in the United States, its British and Irish assemblies contributed towards the greater *acceptance* of a labour party and a truly mass labour movement across the Atlantic. American exceptionalism is based on a comparison between the United States and Europe, after all, and rests on the strength and progress of European labour movements as well as the weakness and backwardness of American ones. Knights on both sides of the Atlantic had a hand in its construction.

The Order stood at another historical crossroads too. American workers might usually have looked across the Atlantic, or to newly arrived British immigrants, for the latest innovations in trade unionism. What Henry Pelling broadly called the British left, on the other hand, took its political cues for most of the nineteenth century from the United States, where it found the republican institutions and universal male suffrage it still lacked at home. Yet the attraction of the American Republic for British radicals began to wane in the closing decades of that century. The rise of the great American trusts and corporations, the development in the New World of Old World evils like mass unemployment and extreme forms of inequality, and the outbreak of class conflict on a national scale in the United States, convinced a new generation of radicals on the other side of the ocean that more than the franchise and clean republican government would be needed to build a truly democratic society.[20] William Clarke spoke for them when he concluded that 'new institutions were of no use along with the old forms of property … a mere theoretic democracy, unaccompanied by any social changes, was a delusion and a snare.'[21]

The defeat of the Knights of Labor accelerated this seismic shift in British radical thought. Many of the British trade unionists who had looked to the Knights for inspiration in the 1880s looked to America in the following decade with growing apprehension as the unions there retreated and the hegemony of the monopolies seemed assured. They assumed, as John Lovell writes, 'that the current state of affairs in America represented the future state of Britain,' and this assumption encouraged them to strengthen their industrial and political organisations before they suffered the fate of the American unions.[22] It was left to Dodo, whose columns in *Reynolds's* during the 1880s had celebrated American republicanism and the Knights in equal measure, to bring together their mutual demise. Dodo lamented the Order's transformation into 'a merely political party aiding the abominable wire-pulling of machine politicians.' He claimed that it failed when 'the central authority sought tyrannously to impose its will' in every trade dispute. He then posed a question. 'When is the revolution going to break out in that caricature of a Republic, the United States,' Dodo wrote, 'with its cast-iron Constitution,

---

[20] Pelling, *British Left*, chs 4 and 5.
[21] Quoted in Pelling, *British Left*, p. 65.
[22] Lovell, 'Trade Unions and Independent Labour Politics,' pp. 35–36.

designed expressly by the middle class founders of the States to ward off the encroachments of Democracy?'[23] That question was rhetorical, of course. It contained all his disappointment with the Knights and his disillusionment with the American Republic.

The fall of the Knights of Labor presaged the end of several eras and the beginning of several new ones. The Knights represented a continuation of older patterns of working-class internationalism and became both a precedent and an alternative to newer ones. They became instrumental in the changing relationship between working-class movements in Britain and the United States, and in the gap that widened between the movements of those two countries in the following century. They failed at a time when British radicals increasingly viewed the United States as something to avoid rather than imitate. The history of the British and Irish Knights of Labor, in other words, is the history of epochal changes that took place on both sides of the Atlantic Ocean and wrested the transatlantic world from the nineteenth into the twentieth century.

That history should also guard us against anachronism, against reading the present back into the past. The presence of an American working-class movement on British soil remains a powerful corrective against the idea that the special or Anglo-American relationship is a thing only of prime ministers, presidents, corporations and military alliances. The Knights, like other working-class movements before and since, proved that that relationship included radicals and trade unionists too. It is also a potent cure for any easy assumption that this radical and working-class relationship only went one way – westwards from Britain to the United States.

It seemed less clear, until very recently, whether these cures and correctives still had any use in the present. Mass unemployment, economic depression and the evisceration of labour movements on both sides of the Atlantic seemed to rule out a speedy revival of the transatlantic radical tradition. The rise of Bernie Sanders in the United States and Jeremy Corbyn in the United Kingdom in 2015, however, has changed all that. A revival of Anglo-American radicalism now seems close as well as likely. It will probably not be based on the rather archaic model of the Knights of Labor. But their enthusiastic and deep-seated internationalism, and their desire to substitute cooperation for competition, still mark the way for their descendants in the twenty-first century.

---

[23] *Reynolds's*, 9 May 1897.

Appendix
List of Known Assemblies of the Knights of Labor in England, Scotland, Wales and Ireland

District Assemblies

Official Number	Location	Known Existence	Occupations, if Known, and Other Notes
DA208	Handsworth, Birmingham	1887–94	
DA248	Cradley Heath	1887–91	Reconstituted as the British National Assembly 1891–94
DA256	Sheffield and Rotherham	1889–91	Reconstituted as the British National Assembly 1891–94
DA203	Glasgow	1889–90	
British National Assembly of Great Britain and Ireland		1891–94	

Local Assemblies

Name of Assembly	Official Number	Location	Known Existence	Occupations, if Known, and Other Notes
England				
Fruitful Vine	583	Aston	1888–91	
Perseverance	10,792	Birmingham	1888–89	
St George's	10,915	Birmingham	1887–88	
Wilberforce	10,928	Birmingham	1887–88	
Forward	10,101	Birmingham	1887–88	
	923	Birmingham	1891	
	2,125	Birmingham	1891	
Progress	584	Birmingham	1890–96	
Good Intent	1,743	Bloxwich	1889	
	none given	Bootle	1884–85	Dockers
	443	Bootle	1889–91	Dockers
	731	Colley Gate	1888–90	Later reconstituted in Cradley Heath
Talbot	731	Cradley	1890	
Unicorn	755	Cradley	1888	
Lion	9,086	Cradley Heath	1886–89	
	395	Derby	1889	

Name of Assembly	Official Number	Location	Known Existence	Occupations, if Known, and Other Notes
	none given	Doncaster	1890	
	none given	Doncaster	1890	
	468	Dudley	1889–90	
Freedom	10,929	Great Bridge	1887–88	
Excelsior	9,144	Handsworth	1886–88	
Handsworth	9,608	Handsworth	1887–91	
	none given	Hoyland Nether	1890	Coal miners
	none given	Jarrow	1889–1901	Constituted as Independent Order of the Knights of Labor
Excelsior	647	Liverpool	1888–91	
	703	Lye	1888	
Day Dawn	none given	Oldbury	1888–89	
Speed the Plough	none given	Oldbury	1888–89	
	none given	Platts Common	1890	
Live and Let Live	1,266	Rotherham	1888–94	
	none given	Rotherham	1889–90	
	none given	Rotherham	1889–90	
	none given	Rotherham	1889–90	
	none given	Rotherham	1889–90	

Name of Assembly	Official Number	Location	Known Existence	Occupations, if Known, and Other Notes
Fountain of Friendship	1,001	Sedgley	1890–91	
	10,645	Small Heath	1888–89	
Lizzie Lucas	7,952	Smethwick	1886–94	
St George	9,801	Smethwick	1887–88	
Humanity	10,382	Smethwick	1887–88	
Rising Hope	10,227	Smethwick	1887–94	
Onward	712	Smethwick	1887–88	
	none given	Stanningley	1891	
The Faithful	713	Stourbridge	1888–89	
Wonder	982	Stourport	1888–89	
Alpha	3504	Sunderland; preceptories at St Helens, Plank Lane and Spon Lane	1884–93	Glassworkers
	none given	Upper Ettingshall	1890	Black hollowware casters
	454	Walsall	1888–91	
	none given	Walsall	1890	Lathers
Excelsior	10,102	West Bromwich	1888–89	

Name of Assembly	Official Number	Location	Known Existence	Occupations, if Known, and Other Notes
Success	666	West Bromwich	1888–89	
The Ripening Corn	807	West Bromwich	1888–89	
Churchfield	913	West Bromwich	1888	
Prosperity	9,770	Winson Green	1887–90	
Bellfield	none given	Winson Green	1888–89	
Providence	518	Wolverhampton	1888	
	418	Wolverhampton	1888	
Wales				
	2,886	Cardiff	1883–85	Ironworkers and coal miners
Scotland				
	none given	Ardrossan	1890	Dockers
	none given	Ardrossan	1890	
	none given	Glasgow	1889–90	
	none given	Glasgow	1889–90	
	none given	Glasgow	1889–90	
	none given	Glasgow	1889–90	
	none given	Glasgow	1889–90	
	none given	Glasgow	1889–90	

Name of Assembly	Official Number	Location	Known Existence	Occupations, if Known, and Other Notes
	none given	Glasgow	1889–90	
	none given	Glasgow	1889–90	
	none given	Glasgow	1889–90	
	none given	Glasgow	1889–90	
	none given	Glasgow	1889–90	
	none given	Glasgow	1889–90	
Ireland				
	418	Belfast	1889–90	
Erin's First	1,566	Belfast	1889–90	Ropeworkers
Alpha	1,601	Derry	1889–92	
		Derry	1892–96	Reconstituted as part of the British National Assembly

Bibliography

Primary Sources

Online Newspaper Archives
The British Library Newspaper Archive
JSTOR Periodicals Collection
The Library of Congress: Chronicling America
The National Library of Australia: Trove
Proquest Newspaper Archives

Newspapers on Microfilm
Birmingham Workmen's Times
Bootle Times
Commonweal
Dudley Herald
Glasgow Weekly Mail
Halfpenny Weekly
Ironworkers Journal
John Swinton's Paper
Journal of United Labor (renamed *Journal of the Knights of Labor* in 1890)
Justice
Labour Tribune
Liverpool Courier
Liverpool Echo
Liverpool Post
Mexborough and Swinton Times
Midlands Advertiser
Midland Counties Express
Philadelphia Press

Philadelphia Record
Rotherham Advertiser
Smethwick Telephone
Smethwick Weekly News
Stourbridge, Brierley Hill and County Express
The Miner
Walsall Advertiser and Newspaper
Walsall Free Press
Walsall Observer
West Bromwich Free Press
Wolverhampton Chronicle
Wolverhampton Express and Star

Archival Collections

Terence Powderly Papers (TVP), History Research Center and University Archives, Catholic University of America, Washington D.C.

John W. Hayes Papers (JHP), History Research Center and University Archives, Catholic University of America, Washington D.C.

Socialist League Archives, International Institute of Social History, Amsterdam

J. Bruce Glasier Personal Papers, Bruce Glasier Archives, University of Liverpool Library

Trades Union Congress Archives, Modern Records Centre, University of Warwick

Archives of the Liverpool Trades Council, Liverpool Record Office

Minutes of the West Bromwich School Board, Sandwell Local History Research Centre

Walsall Labour Representative Wages Fund, Walsall Local History Research Centre

Terence V. Powderly Personal Papers Microfilm Collection, Library of Congress, Washington D.C.

Online Archival Collections

Proquest. *House of Commons Parliamentary Papers Online* (HCPP), found at: http://parlipapers.chadwyck.co.uk/marketing/index.jsp

TUC History Online. *TUC Reports*, found at: http://www.unionhistory.info/reports

Readex. *U.S. Congressional Serial Set, 1817–1994*, found at: http://www.readex.com/content/us-congressional-serial-set-1817-1994

Internet Archive, found at: www.archive.org

Marxist Internet Archive, found at: www.marxists.org

Printed Primary Sources

British Library
Knights of Labor. *Proceedings of the General Assembly of the Knights of Labor* (Philadelphia, 1878–1900).
Knights of Labour. *Manifesto of the Knights of Labour of South Africa* (London, 1891).

Webb Collection, British Library of Political and Economic Science, London School of Economics
Bernstein, E. *The International Working Men's Congress of 1889: A Reply to Justice* (London, 1889).
Besant, A. *The Trades Union Movement* (London, 1890).
———, and G.W. Foote. *Is Socialism Sound?* (London, 1887).
British Delegation. *Report from Great Britain and Ireland to the Delegates of the Brussels International Congress* (London, 1891).
Dundee Courier. *The Trades' Union Congress: Meetings in Dundee* (Dundee, 1889).
English Delegation. *Report of the International Workmen's Congress … 1889, Published by the Trade Unionist Members of the English Delegation* (London, 1889).
Glasgow Trades Council. *Annual Report of Glasgow United Trades Council, 1889–90* (Glasgow, 1890).
Knights of Labor. *Preamble of the British National Assembly of the Knights of Labour* (London, 1891).
Labour Electoral Congress. *Report of the Labour Electoral Congress* (Southport and Manchester, 1890–91).
Liverpool Trades Council. *1890-1 Report of the Liverpool Trades Council* (Liverpool, 1891).
Mann, T. *What a Compulsory Eight Hours Working Day Means to the Workers* (London, 1886).
Sunday Chronicle. *Chains of Slavery: A Visit to the Strikers at Cradley Heath* (Manchester, 1886).
Sunderland Trades Council. *1890-1 Report of the Sunderland Trades Council* (Sunderland, 1890).

National Archives of Scotland
Rules of the Amalgamated Order of the Sons of Labour, National Archives of Scotland, FS7/75.

Bishopsgate Institute, London
Mahon, J.L. *A Labour Programme* (London, 1888).
Smith, A. *Report of the International Trades Union Congress, Held at Paris from August 23rd to 28th, 1886* (London, 1886).

Working Class Movement Library, Manchester
Baernreither, J. *English Associations of Working Men* (London, 1893).

Marx Memorial Library, London
Engels, F. *The British Labour Movement: Articles from the Labour Standard* (London, 1934).

Other Printed Primary Sources
Bellamy, E. *Looking Backward, 2000–1887* (Cleveland: World, 1945).
Ely, R.T. *The Labor Movement in America* (New York: Thomas Y. Crowell, 1886).
Gronlund, L. *The Cooperative Commonwealth* (Cambridge, MA: Harvard University Press, 1965).
International Workingmen's Association. *The General Council of the First International, 1868–1870: Minutes* (Moscow: Progress, 1964).
Knights of Labor. *Adelphon Kruptos* (Chicago: Ezra Cook, 1886).
MacNeill, G.E. *The Labor Movement: The Problem of Today* (New York: M.W. Hazen Co., 1887).
Mann, T. *Tom Mann's Memoirs* (London: MacGibbon and Kee, 1967).
Powderly, T.V. *The Path I Trod: The Autobiography of Terence V. Powderly* (New York: Columbia University Press, 1940).
———. *Thirty Years of Life and Labour, 1859–1889* (Philadelphia: Excelsior, 1890).
Sexton, James. *Sir James Sexton: Agitator* (London: Faber and Faber, 1936).
Simonds, John Cameron, and John T. McEnnis. *The Story of Manual Labor in All Lands and Ages: Its Past Condition, Present Progress, and Hope for the Future* (Chicago: R.S. Peale & Co., 1887).
Sorge, Friedrich. *Labor Movement in the United States: A History of the American Working Class from Colonial Times to 1890* (Westport: Greenwood, 1977).
Swinton, John. *John Swinton's Travels: Current Views and Notes Forty Days in France and England* (New York: Carleton, 1880).
Sylvis, William. *The Life, Speeches, Labors and Essays of William H. Sylvis* (Philadelphia: Claxton, Remsen & Haffelfinger, 1872).
Turner, Ben. *About Myself, 1863–1930* (London: Humphrey Toulmin, 1930).
United States Immigration Commission. *Report of the United States Immigration Commission 1911–12*, 41 volumes (Washington, D.C.: GPO, 1911).

Secondary Sources

Books
Anderson, B. *Imagined Communities: Reflections on the Origins and Spread of Nationalism* (London: Verso, 1991).
Archer, R. *Why is there no Labor Party in the United States?* (Princeton: Princeton University Press, 2007).

Armstrong, A. *From Davitt to Connolly: 'Internationalism from Below' and the Challenge to the UK State and British Empire from 1879–95* (Edinburgh: Intfrobel Publications, 2010).

Aspinwall, B. *Portable Utopia: Glasgow and the United States, 1820–1920* (Aberdeen: Aberdeen University Press, 1984).

Barker, T.C. *The Glassmakers: Pilkington, The Rise of an International Company, 1826–1976* (London: Wiedenfeld and Nicholson, 1977).

Barnsby, G. *Socialism in Birmingham and the Black Country* (Wolverhampton: Integrated Publishing Services, 1998).

Barrow. L., and I. Bullock, *Democratic Ideas and the British Labour Movement, 1880–1914* (Cambridge: Cambridge University Press, 1996).

Barry, E.E. *Nationalisation in British Politics: The Historical Background* (London: J. Cape, 1965).

Belchem, J. *Popular Radicalism in Nineteenth Century Britain* (New York: St. Martin's Press, 1996).

Benson, J. *The Working Class in Britain, 1850–1939* (London: Longman, 1989).

Bernstein, S. *The First International in America* (New York: Augustus M. Kelley, 1965).

Bevir, M. *The Making of British Socialism* (Princeton: Princeton University Press, 2011).

Boston, S. *Women Workers and the Trade Union Movement* (London: Davis-Poynter, 1980).

Boyle, J.W. *The Irish Labour Movement in the Nineteenth Century* (Washington D.C.: Catholic University of America Press, 1988).

Brake, T. *Men of Good Character: A History of the National Union of Sheet Metal Workers, Coppersmiths, Heating and Domestic Engineers* (London: Lawrence and Wishart, 1985).

Braunthal, J. *The History of the International, 1864–1914* (London: Macmillan, 1966).

Braverman, H. *Labor and Monopoly Capital* (New York: Monthly Review Press, 1975).

Brecher, J. *Strike!* (Boston: South End Press, 1977).

Brown, K.D. *John Burns* (London: Royal Historical Society, 1977).

Brown, T.N. *Irish American Nationalism, 1870–1890* (Philadelphia: Lippincott, 1966).

Brundage, D. *The Making of Western Labor Radicalism: Denver's Organized Workers, 1878–1905* (Urbana: University of Illinois Press, 1994).

Buckley, K.D. *The Amalgamated Engineers in Australia, 1852–1920* (Canberra: National Australian University, 1970).

Burchill, F., and R. Ross, *A History of the Potters' Union* (Hanley: Ceramic and Allied Trades Union, 1977).

Burnham, T.H., and G.O. Hoskins. *Iron and Steel in Britain, 1870–1930* (London: Allen and Unwin, 1943).

Busch, G. *The Political Role of International Trade Unions* (New York: St Martin's Press, 1983).

Campbell, A.B. *The Scottish Miners, 1874–1939, Vol. 2: Trade Unions and Politics* (Aldershot: Ashgate, 2000).

Carnes, M. *Secret Ritual and Manhood in Victorian America* (New Haven: Yale University Press, 1989).

Church, R. *Kenricks in Hardware: A Family Business, 1791–1966* (Newton Abbot: David and Charles, 1968).

Clawson, M.A. *Constructing Brotherhood: Class, Gender, and Fraternalism* (Princeton: Princeton University Press, 1989).

Clegg, H., A. Fox and A.F. Thompson. *A History of British Trade Unions Since 1889, Vol. 1: 1889–1910* (Oxford: Oxford University Press, 1964).

Clinton, A. *The Trade Union Rank and File: Trades Councils in Britain, 1900–40* (Manchester: Manchester University Press, 1977).

Coates, K., and T. Topham, *The Making of the Labour Movement: The Formation of the Transport and General Workers Union, 1870–1922* (Oxford: Blackwell, 1994).

Cole, G.D.H. *The Second International, 1889–1914* (London: Macmillan, 1956).

———. *A Short History of the British Working-Class Movement* (London: Allen and Unwin, 1948).

Commons, J. *History of Labor in the United States: Volume 2, 1860–1896* (New York: Macmillan, 1936).

Corbett, J. *The Birmingham Trades Council: 1866–1966* (London: Lawrence and Wishart, 1966).

Cordery, S. *British Friendly Societies, 1750–1914* (Basingstoke: Palgrave Macmillan, 2003).

Crick, M. *The History of the Social-Democratic Federation* (Keele: Ryburn Press, 1994).

Curran, T.J. *Xenophobia and Immigration, 1820–1930* (Boston: Twayne, 1975).

Currie, C.R.J., M.W Greenslade and D.A. Johnson. *A History of Walsall, Being an Extract from the Victoria County History of Staffordshire, Volume XVII* (Walsall: Staffordshire Libraries, 1976).

Davis, P. *The Development of the American Glass Industry* (Cambridge, MA: Harvard University Press, 1949).

Dean, K.D. *Town and Westminster: A Political History of Walsall* (Walsall: Walsall County Borough, 1972).

Debney, J. *Breaking the Chains: The Story of the Women Chainmakers from Cradley Heath* (Studley: Brewin Books, 2010).

Dommanget, M. *La Chevalerie du Travail Française, 1893–1911* (Lausanne: Recontre, 1967).

Douglas, R. *Land, People and Politics: A History of the Land Question in the United Kingdom, 1878–1952* (London: Allison and Busby, 1976).

Dubofsky, M. *The State and Labor in Modern America* (Chapel Hill: University of North Carolina Press, 1994).

Evans, R.J. *Comrades and Sisters: Feminism, Socialism and Pacifism in Europe, 1870–1945* (Brighton: Wheatsheaf, 1987).

Fink, L. *The Long Gilded Age: American Capitalism and the Lessons of a New World Order* (Philadelphia: University of Pennsylvania Press, 2015).

———. (ed.). *Workers Across the Americas: The Transnational Turn in Labor History* (Oxford: Oxford University Press, 2011).

———. *Workingmen's Democracy: The Knights of Labor and American Politics* (Urbana: University of Illinois Press, 1983).

Fishman, W.J. *East End Jewish Radicals, 1875–1914*, 2nd ed. (Nottingham: Five Leaves, 2004).

Foner, P.S. *History of the Labor Movement in the United States, Vol. I* (New York: International Publishers, 1972).

———. *History of the Labor Movement in the United States, Vol. II* (New York: International Publishers, 1975).

Forbath, W. *Law and the Shaping of the American Labor Movement* (Cambridge, MA: Harvard University Press, 1991).

Fraser, D. *Power and Authority in the Victorian City* (Oxford: Blackwell, 1979).

Friedman, G. *State-Making and Labor Movements: France and the United States, 1876–1914* (Ithaca: Cornell University Press, 1998).

Gale, W.K.V. *The Black Country Iron Industry: A Technical History* (London: Metals Society, 1979).

Garlock, J. *Guide to the Local Assemblies of the Knights of Labor* (Westport: Greenwood, 1982).

Gerteis, J. *Class and the Color Line: Interracial Class Coalition in the Knights of Labor and the Populist Movement* (Durham: Duke University Press, 2007).

Goldman, H. *Emma Paterson: She Led Woman into a Man's World* (London: Lawrence and Wishart, 1974).

Gosden, P.H. *Self-Help: Voluntary Associations in the Nineteenth Century* (London: Batsford, 1973).

Greene, J. *Pure and Simple Politics: The American Federation of Labor and Political Activism, 1881–1917* (Cambridge: Cambridge University Press, 2006).

Grob, G. *Workers and Utopia: A Study of Ideological Conflict in the American Labor Movement, 1865–1900* (Chicago: Quadrangle, 1969).

Groves, R. *Sharpen the Sickle: The History of the Farm Workers' Union* (London: Porcupine, 1949).

Gurney, P. *Co-operative Culture and the Politics of Consumption in England, 1870–1930* (Manchester: Manchester University Press, 1996).

Hammond, J.L. *The Age of the Chartists, 1832–1854: A Study of Discontent* (London: Longmans, 1930).

Hanagan, M.P. *The Logic of Solidarity: Artisans and Industrial Workers in Three French Towns, 1871–1914* (Urbana: University of Illinois Press, 1980).

Hey, V. *Pub Culture and Patriarchy* (London: Tavistock, 1986).
Higham, J. *Strangers in the Land: Patterns of American Nativism, 1860–1925* (New York: Atheneum, 1963).
Hild, M. *Greenbackers, Knights of Labor, and Populists: Farmer-Labor Insurgency in the Late-Nineteenth-Century South* (Athens: University of Georgia Press, 2007).
Hobsbawm, E.J. *The Age of Empire: 1875–1914* (London: Wiedenfeld and Nicholson, 1987).
Holmes, R. *Eleanor Marx: A Life* (London: Bloomsbury, 2014).
Howell, D. *British Workers and the Independent Labour Party, 1888–1906* (Manchester: Manchester University Press, 1983).
Hoxie, R. *Trade Unionism in the United States* (New York: D. Appleton and Co., 1917).
International Transport Workers' Federation. *Solidarity: The First 100 Years of the International Transport Workers' Federation* (London: Pluto Press, 1996).
Jacoby, R.M. *The British and American Women Trade Union Leagues, 1890–1925: A Case Study of Feminism and Class* (New York: Carlson, 1994).
Jeffreys, J.B. *The Story of the Engineers* (London: Lawrence and Wishart, 1945).
Joll, J. *The Second International, 1889–1914* (London: Wiedenfeld and Nicholson, 1968).
Kapp, Y. *Eleanor Marx: The Crowded Years, 1884–1898* (London: Lawrence and Wishart, 1976).
Katz, H. *The Emancipation of Labor: A History of the First International* (New York: Greenwood, 1992).
Katz, P. *From Appomattox to Montmartre: Americans and the Paris Commune* (Cambridge, MA: Harvard University Press, 1998).
Kenefick, W. *'Rebellious and Contrary': The Glasgow Dockers, 1853–1932* (Edinburgh: Edinburgh University Press, 2000).
———. *Red Scotland! The Rise and Fall of the Radical Left, c.1872 to 1932* (Edinburgh: Edinburgh University Press, 2007).
Kent, W. *John Burns: Labour's Lost Leader, a Biography* (London: Williams and Norgate, 1950).
Kirk, N. *Change, Continuity and Class: Labour in British Society, 1850–1920* (Manchester: Manchester University Press, 1998).
———. *Comrades and Cousins: Globalization, Workers, and Labour Movements in Britain, the USA, and Australia from the 1880s to 1914* (London: Merlin, 2003).
———. *Labour and Society in Britain and the USA, Volume 2: Challenge and Accommodation, 1850–1939* (Aldershot: Ashgate, 1994).
Lake, Marilyn, and Henry Reynolds. *Drawing the Global Colour Line: White Men's Countries and the International Challenge of Racial Equality* (Cambridge: Cambridge University Press, 2008).
Lane, A.T. *Solidarity or Survival? American Labor and European Immigrants, 1830–1924* (New York: Greenwood, 1987).

Laslett, J.H.M. *Colliers Across the Sea: A Comparative Study of Class Formation in Scotland and the American Midwest, 1830–1924* (Urbana: University of Illinois Press, 2000).

Laurence, E.P. *Henry George in the British Isles* (East Lansing: Michigan State University Press, 1957).

Laurie, B. *Artisans into Workers: Labor in Nineteenth-Century America* (New York: Noonday, 1997).

Lawrence, J. *Speaking for the People: Party Language and Popular Politics in England 1867–1914* (Cambridge: Cambridge University Press, 1998).

Laybourn, K, and J. Reynolds. *Labour Heartland: The History of the Labour Party in West Yorkshire During the Inter-war Years, 1918–39* (Bradford: Bradford University Press, 1987).

Lee, H. *A Short History of Walsall* (Walsall: T. Kirby and Sons, 1927).

Leikin, S.B. *The Practical Utopians: American Workers and the Cooperative Movement in the Gilded Age* (Detroit: Wayne State University Press, 2005).

Levine, S. *Labor's True Woman: Carpet Weavers, Industrialization and Labor Reform in the Gilded Age* (Philadelphia: Temple University Press, 1984).

Levy, C. *Ardrossan Harbour, 1805–1979* (Glasgow: Workers Educational Association, 1988).

Lewenhak, S. *Women and Trade Unions: An Outline History of Women in the British Trade Union Movement* (London: Benn, 1977).

Logue, J. *Toward a Theory of Trade Union Internationalism* (Gothenburg: Gothenburg University Press, 1980).

Lovell, J. *British Trade Unions, 1875–1933* (London: Macmillan, 1977).

McConnaughy, C.M. *The Woman Suffrage Movement in America: A Reassessment* (New York: Cambridge University Press, 2013).

McCord, N. *North East England: An Economic and Social History* (London: Batsford Academic, 1979).

McFadden, M. *Golden Cables of Sympathy: The Transatlantic Source of Nineteenth-Century Feminism* (Lexington: University of Kentucky Press, 1999).

McLean, I. *Keir Hardie* (London: Allen Lane, 1975).

Marwick, W.H. *A Short History of Labour in Scotland* (Edinburgh: W. and R. Chambers, 1967).

Messer-Kruse, T. *The Yankee International: Marxism and the American Reform Tradition, 1848–1876* (Chapel Hill: University of North Carolina Press, 1998).

Milner, S. *The Dilemmas of Internationalism: French Syndicalism and the International Labour Movement, 1900–1914* (New York: Berg, 1990).

Montgomery, D. *The Fall of the House of Labor: The Workplace, the State, and American Labor Activism, 1865–1925* (Cambridge: Cambridge University Press, 1989).

Newby, A.G. *Ireland, Radicalism and the Scottish Highlands, c.1870 to 1912* (Edinburgh: Edinburgh University Press, 2007).

Nightingale, Carl. *Segregation: A Global History of Divided Cities* (Chicago: Chicago University Press, 2012).
Oestreicher, R.J. *Solidarity and Fragmentation: Working People and Class Consciousness in Detroit, 1875–1900* (Urbana: University of Illinois Press, 1986).
Offen, K. *European Feminisms, 1700–1950: A Political History* (Stanford: Stanford University Press, 2000).
Owen, H. *The Staffordshire Potter* (Bath: Kingsmead, 1970).
Pelling, H. *America and the British Left, From Bright to Bevan* (London: Adam and Charles Black, 1956).
——. *The Origins of the Labour Party* (London: Macmillan, 1954).
Perlman, S. *A Theory of the Labor Movement* (New York: Macmillan, 1928).
Phelan, C. *Grand Master Workman: Terence Powderly and the Knights of Labor* (Westport: Greenwood, 2000).
Phillips, P.T. *A Kingdom on Earth: Anglo-American Social Christianity, 1880–1940* (University Park: Pennsylvania State University Press, 1996).
Pollard, S. *History of Labour in Sheffield* (Liverpool: Liverpool University Press, 1959).
Rachleff, Peter J. *Black Labor in the South: Richmond, Virginia, 1865–1890* (Philadelphia: Temple University Press, 1984).
Reid, A., and E. Biagini (eds). *Currents of Radicalism: Popular Radicalism, Organised Labour and Party Politics in Britain 1850–1914* (Cambridge: Cambridge University Press, 1991).
Rees, D.B. *Local and Parliamentary Politics in Liverpool from 1800 to 1911* (Liverpool: Edwin Mellen, 1999).
Reynolds, D.S. *George Lippard* (Boston: Twayne, 1982).
——. (ed.). *George Lippard, Prophet of Protest: Writings of an American Radical, 1822–1854* (New York: P. Lang, 1986).
Richards, C. *A History of Trades Councils: 1860–1875* (London: Labour Research Department, 1920).
Richardson, H.C. *The Death of Reconstruction: Race, Labor and Politics in the post-Civil War North, 1865–1901* (Cambridge, MA: Harvard University Press, 2001).
Rodgers, D.T. *Atlantic Crossings: Social Politics in a Progressive Age* (Cambridge, MA: Harvard University Press, 1998).
Rupp, L.J. *Worlds of Women: The Making of an International Women's Movement* (Princeton: Princeton University Press, 1997).
Saxton, A. *The Indispensable Enemy: Labor and the Anti-Chinese Movement in California* (Berkeley: University of California Press, 1971).
Simons, J., and R. Simons. *Class and Colour in South Africa, 1850–1950* (London: Harmondsworth, 1969).
Skrabek, Q.R. *Michael Owens and the Glass Industry* (Gretna: Pelican, 2006).
Soldon, N.C. *Women in British Trade Unions, 1874–1976* (Dublin: Macmillan, 1978).

Sombart, W. *Why is There no Socialism in the United States* (London: Macmillan, 1976).

Staples, W., and C. *Power, Profits, and Patriarchy: The Social Organization of Work at a British Metal Trades Firm, 1791–1922* (Lanham: Rowman and Littlefield, 2001).

Steeples, D., and D. Whitten, *Democracy in Desperation: The Depression of 1893* (Westport: Greenwood, 1998).

Stewart, W. *J. Keir Hardie: A Biography* (London: Cassell and Co., 1921).

Sutch, W.B. *The Quest for Security in New Zealand, 1840 to 1966* (Oxford: Oxford University Press, 1942).

Tabili, Laura. *Global Migrants, Local Culture: Natives and Newcomers in Provincial England, 1841–1939* (London: Palgrave MacMillan, 2011).

Taplin, E. *Liverpool Dockers and Seamen, 1870–1890* (Hull: Hull University Press, 1974).

Thompson, E.P. *William Morris: Romantic to Revolutionary* (London: Lawrence and Wishart, 1955).

Thompson, P. *Socialists, Liberals and Labour: The Struggle for London, 1885–1914* (London: Routledge, 1967).

Tomlins, C. *The State and the Unions: Labor Relations, Law and the Organized Labor Movement in America, 1880–1960* (Cambridge: Cambridge University Press, 1985).

Towers, B. *Waterfront Blues: The Rise and Fall of Liverpool's Dockland* (Lancaster: Carnegie, 2011).

Trainor, R.H. *Black Country Elites: The Exercise of Authority in an Industrialized Area, 1830–1900* (Oxford: Oxford University Press, 1993).

Turrell, R.V. *Capital and Labour on the Kimberley Diamond Fields* (Cambridge: Cambridge University Press, 1987).

Tyrell, I. *Woman's World – Woman's Empire: The Woman's Christian Temperance Union in International Perspective, 1880–1930* (Chapel Hill: University of North Carolina Press, 1991).

Van der Linden, M. *Transnational Labour History: Explorations* (Aldershot: Ashgate, 2003).

Van Goethem, G. *The Amsterdam International: The World of the International Federation of Trade Unions (IFTU), 1913–1945* (Aldershot: Ashgate, 2006).

Virdee, Satnam. *Racism, Class and the Racialized Outsider* (London: Palgrave MacMillan, 2014).

Voss, K. *The Making of American Exceptionalism: The Knights of Labor and Class Formation in the Nineteenth Century* (Ithaca: Cornell University Press, 1993).

Warburton, W.H. *The History of Trade Union Organisation in the North Staffordshire Potteries* (London: George Allen and Unwin, 1931).

Ware, N. *The Labor Movement in the United States, 1865–1895: A Study in Democracy* (New York: Vintage, 1964).

Watillon, L. *The Knights of Labor in Belgium* (Los Angeles: University of California Press, 1959).
Watts, C. *R.B. Cunninghame Graham* (Boston: Twayne, 1983).
Weir, R. *Beyond Labor's Veil: The Culture of the Knights of Labor* (University Park: Pennsylvania State University Press, 1996).
——. *Knights Down Under: The Knights of Labour in New Zealand* (Newcastle: Cambridge Scholars Press, 2009).
——. *Knights Unhorsed: Internal Conflict in a Gilded Age Social Movement* (Detroit: Wayne State University Press, 2000).
Wertheimer, B.M. *We Were There: The Story of Working Women in America* (New York: Pantheon, 1977).
White, R. *Railroaded: The Transcontinentals and the Making of Modern America* (London: W.W. Norton, 2011).
Worley, M. (ed.). *The Foundations of the British Labour Party: Identities, Cultures and Perspectives* (Farnham: Ashgate, 2009).
Wrigley, C.J. *Winston Churchill: A Biographical Companion* (Santa Barbara: ABC-CLIO, 2002).
Yearley, C.K. *Britons in American Labor: A History of the Influence of the United Kingdom Immigrants on American Labor, 1820–1914* (Baltimore: Johns Hopkins Press, 1957).

Book Chapters

Anderson, G. 'Some Aspects of the Labour Market in Britain c.1870–1914,' in C.J. Wrigley (ed.), *A History of British Industrial Relations, 1875–1914* (Amherst: Harvester, 1982).
Aspinwall, B. 'The Civic Ideal: Glasgow and the United States, 1880–1920,' in D. Gutzke (ed.), *Britain and Transnational Progressivism* (New York: Palgrave Macmillan, 2008).
Bean, R. 'Aspects of 'New Unionism' in Liverpool, 1889–91,' in H.R. Hikins (ed.), *Building the Union: Studies in the Growth of the Workers' Movement, Merseyside, 1756–1967* (Liverpool: Liverpool Trades Council, 1973).
——. 'Samuel Reeves,' in J.M. Bellamy and J. Saville (eds), *Dictionary of Labour Biography, Vol. I* (London: Macmillan, 1972).
Cronin, J. 'Strikes, 1870–1914,' in C.J. Wrigley (ed.), *A History of British Industrial Relations, 1875–1914* (Amherst: Harvester, 1982).
Fraser, W.H. 'Trades Councils in Nineteenth Century Scotland,' in I. McDougall (ed.), *Essays in Scottish Labour History* (Edinburgh: Edinburgh University Press, 1978).
Gore, V. 'Rank and File Dissent,' in C.J. Wrigley (ed.), *A History of British Industrial Relations, 1875–1914* (Amherst: Harvester, 1982).
Gutzke, D. 'Britain and Transnational Progressivism,' in D. Gutzke (ed.), *Britain and Transnational Progressivism* (New York: Palgrave Macmillan, 2008).

Hinton, J. 'The Rise of a Mass Labour Movement: Growth and Limits,' in C.J. Wrigley (ed.), *A History of British Industrial Relations, 1875–1914* (Amherst: Harvester, 1982).

Hobsbawm, E.J. 'The New Unionism in Perspective,' in Hobsbawm, *Workers: Worlds of Labour* (New York: Pantheon, 1984).

Hutchinson, I.G.C. 'Glasgow Working-Class Politics,' in R.A. Cage (ed.), *The Working Class in Glasgow, 1750–1914* (London: Croom Helm, 1987).

Kenefick, W. 'A Struggle for Recognition and Independence: The Growth and Development of Dock Unionism at the Port of Glasgow, c.1853–1932,' in S. Davies et al. (eds), *Dock Workers: International Explorations in Comparative Labour History, 1790–1970* (Aldershot: Ashgate, 2000).

Kenny, K. 'Labor and Labor Organisations,' in J. Lee and M. Casey (eds), *Making the Irish American: History and Heritage of the Irish in the United States* (New York: New York University Press, 2006).

Laslett, J.H.M. 'State Policy Toward Labor and Labor Organizations, 1830–1939: Anglo-American Union Movements,' in P. Mathias and S. Pollard (eds), *The Cambridge Economic History of Europe, Volume 8: The Development of Economic and Social Policies* (Cambridge: Cambridge University Press, 1989).

Lovell, J. 'Trade Unions and the Development of Independent Labour Politics, 1889–1906,' in B. Pimlott and C. Cook (eds), *Trade Unions in British Politics: The First 250 Years*, 2nd ed. (London: Longman, 1991).

McNeil, L. 'Dissecting Davitt: (Ab)using the Memory of a Great Irishman,' in F. Lane and A.G. Newby (eds), *Michael Davitt: New Perspectives* (Dublin: Irish Academic Press, 2009).

Martin, D.E. 'William James Thorne,' in J.M. Bellamy and J. Saville (eds), *Dictionary of Labour Biography, Vol. I* (London: Macmillan, 1972).

——, and B. Turner, 'Ben Turner,' in D. Howell and K. Gildart (eds), *The Dictionary of Labour Biography, Vol. XIII* (Basingstoke: Palgrave Macmillan, 2010).

Nicoleavsky, B.I. 'Secret Societies and the First International,' from M. Drakhkovitch (ed.), *The Revolutionary Internationals, 1864–1943* (London: Stanford University Press, 1966).

Oestreicher, R. 'Terence Powderly, the Knights of Labor and Artisanal Republicanism,' in M. Dubofsky and W. Van Tine (eds), *Labor Leaders in America* (Urbana: University of Liverpool Press, 1987).

Orwell, G. 'The Lion and the Unicorn,' in G. Orwell, *Essays* (London: Penguin, 2000).

Phillips, G. 'The British Labour Movement Before 1914', in D. Geary (ed.), *Labour and Socialist Movements in Europe Before 1914* (Oxford: Oxford University Press, 1989).

Reid, F. 'Keir Hardie's Conversion to Socialism,' in A. Briggs and J. Saville (eds), *Essays in Labour History, 1886–1923* (London: Macmillan, 1971).

Roth, H. 'Knights of Labour,' in *An Encyclopaedia of New Zealand*, 1966, found at: http://www.teara.govt.nz/en/1966/political-parties/page-7

Shepherd, J. 'Labour and Parliament: The Lib-Labs as the First Working-Class MPs, 1885–1906,' in E. Biagini and A. Reid (eds), *Currents of Radicalism: Popular radicalism, Organized labour, and Party Politics in Britain, 1850–1914* (Cambridge: Cambridge University Press, 1991).

Smyth, J.J. 'The ILP in Glasgow, 1888–1906: The Struggle for Identity,' in A. McKinlay and R. Morris (eds), *The ILP on Clydeside, 1893–1932: From Foundation to Disintegration* (Manchester: Manchester University Press, 1990).

Taplin, E. 'Liverpool Tramwaymen,' in Harold R. Hikins (ed.), *Building the Union: Studies in the Growth of the Workers' Movement, Merseyside, 1756–1967* (Liverpool: Liverpool Trades Council, 1973).

———. 'The History of Dock Labour: Liverpool, c.1850–1914,' in Sam Davies et al. (eds), *Dock Workers: International Explorations in Comparative Labour History, 1790–1970* (Aldershot: Ashgate, 2000).

Taylor, A.J.P. 'Men of 1862,' in C.J. Wrigley (ed.), *AJP Taylor: From Napoleon to the Second International* (London: Faber and Faber, 1993).

Taylor, E. 'Edward Trow,' in J. Bellamy and J. Saville (eds), *Dictionary of Labour Biography, Vol. III* (London: Macmillan, 1976), pp. 187–92.

Van der Linden, M. 'Labor Internationalism,' in van der Linden (ed.), *Workers of the World: Essays Toward a Global Labour History* (Leiden: Brill, 2008).

———. 'The Rise and Fall of the First International: An Interpretation,' in F. van Holthoon and van der Linden (eds), *Internationalism in the Labour Movement, 1830–1940, Vol. I* (Leiden: Brill, 1988).

Weir, R. 'Dress Rehearsal for Pullman: The Knights of Labor and the 1890 New York Central Strike,' in R. Schneirov, S. Stromquist and N. Salvatore (eds), *The Pullman Strike and the Crisis of the 1890s: Essays on Labor and Politics* (Urbana, University of Illinois Press, 1999).

Wood, I. 'Irish Immigrants and Scottish Radicalism, 1880–1906,' in I. McDougall and J. Donald (eds), *Essays in Scottish Labour History* (Edinburgh: Edinburgh University Press, 1976).

Wrigley, C.J. 'Liberals and the Desire for Working-Class Representatives in Battersea 1886–1922,' in K.D. Brown (ed.), *Essays in Anti-Labour History* (London: Macmillan, 1974).

Journal Articles

Archer, R. 'Unions, Courts, and Parties: Judicial Repression and Labor Politics in Late Nineteenth-Century America,' *Politics and Society*, 26:3 (1998), pp. 391–422.

Arnesen, E. 'Following the Color Line of Labor: Black Workers and the Labor Movement before 1930,' *Radical History Review*, 55 (1993), pp. 53–87.

Bean, R. 'A Note on the Knights of Labour in Liverpool,' *Labor History*, 13:1 (1972), pp. 68–78.

Benson, J. 'Black Country History and Labour History,' *Midland History*, 15:1 (1990), pp. 100–110.

Churchward, L.G. 'The American Influence on the Australian Labour Movement,' *Historical Studies: Australia and New Zealand*, 5 (1953), pp. 258–77.

Crowley, D.W. 'The Crofters' Party, 1885–92', *Scottish Historical Review*, 35 (1956), pp. 110–26.

Dudden, F. 'Small Town Knights: The Knights of Labor in Homer, New York,' *Labor History*, 28:3 (1987), pp. 307–27.

Duffy, A.E.P. 'The Eight Hours Day Movement in Britain, 1886–1893,' *The Manchester School*, 36:4 (1968), pp. 203–22.

Fine, Janice, and Daniel Tichenor. 'A Movement Wrestling: American Labor's Enduring Struggle with Immigration, 1866–2007,' *Studies in American Political Development*, 23 (2009), pp. 84–113.

Fink, L. 'The New Labor History and the Powers of Historical Pessimism: Consensus, Hegemony, and the Case of the Knights of Labor,' *Journal of American History*, 75:1 (1988), pp. 115–32.

Fones-Wolf, K. 'Immigrants, Labor and Capital in a Transnational Context: Belgian Glass Workers in America, 1880–1925,' *Journal of American Ethnic History*, 21:2 (2002), pp. 59–80.

Gerteis, J. 'The Possession of Civic Virtue: Movement Narratives of Race and Class in the Knights of Labor,' *American Journal of Sociology*, 108 (2002), pp. 580–615.

Grob, G. 'The Knights of Labor and the Trade Unions, 1878–1886,' *The Journal of Economic History*, 18:2 (1958), pp. 176–92.

Hanagan, M.P. 'An Agenda for Transnational Labor History,' *International Review of Social History*, 49:3 (2004), pp. 455–74.

Hobsbawm, E.J. 'General Labour Unions in Britain, 1889–1914,' *Economic History Review*, 1:2 (1949), pp. 123–42.

Hyslop, J. 'The Imperial Working Class Makes itself "White": White Labourism in Britain, Australia, and South Africa before the First World War,' *Journal of Historical Sociology*, 12:4 (1999), pp. 398–421.

James, B. 'The Knights of Labor and their Context,' found at: http://www.takver.com/history/secsoco2.htm

Kaufman, J. 'Rise and Fall of a Nation of Joiners: The Knights of Labor Revisited,' *Journal of Interdisciplinary History*, 31:4 (2001), pp. 553–79.

Kirk, N., D.M. MacRaild and M. Nolan. 'Introduction: Transnational Ideas, Activities, and Organizations in Labour History 1860s to 1920s,' *Labour History Review*, 74:3 (2009), pp. 221–32.

Laslett, J.H.M. 'Haymarket, Henry George, and the Labor Upsurge in Britain and America during the Late 1880s,' *International Labor and Working-Class History*, 29 (1986), pp. 68–82.

Lorwin, L.L. 'The Structures of International Labor Activities,' *Annals of the American Academy of Political and Social Science*, 310 (1957), pp. 1–11.

McAteer, S. 'The New Unionism in Derry, 1889–1892: A Demonstration of its Inclusive Nature,' *Saothar*, 16 (1991), pp. 11–22.

Marsden, K.G. 'Patriotic Societies and American Labor: The American Protective Association in Wisconsin,' *The Wisconsin Magazine of History*, 41 (1958), pp. 287–94.

Matthews, D. '1889 and All That: New Views on the New Unionism,' *International Review of Social History*, 36:1 (1991), pp. 24–58.

Moloney, D. 'Land League Activism in Transnational Perspective,' *US Catholic Historian*, 22:3 (2004), pp. 61–74.

Moody, T.W. 'Michael Davitt and the British Labour Movement, 1882–1906,' *Transactions of the Royal Historical Society*, Fifth Series, 3 (1953), pp. 53–76.

Parfitt, S. 'Brotherhood from a Distance: Americanization and the Internationalism of the Knights of Labor,' *International Review of Social History*, 58:3 (2013), pp. 463–91.

———. 'The First-and-a-Half International: The Knights of Labor and the History of International Labour Organizations in the Nineteenth Century,' *Labour History Review*, 80:2 (2015), pp. 135–67.

Parlee, L.M. 'The Impact of United States Railroad Unions on Organized Labor and Government Policy in Mexico (1880–1911),' *The Hispanic American Historical Review*, 64:3 (1984), pp. 443–75.

Pelling, H. 'The American Labour Movement: A British View,' *Political Studies*, 2:3 (1954), pp. 227–41.

———. 'The Knights of Labor in Britain, 1880–1901,' *The Economic History Review*, 9 (1956), pp. 313–31.

Peterson, L. 'One Big Union in International Perspective: Revolutionary Industrial Unionism, 1900–1925,' *Labour/Le Travail*, 7 (1981), pp. 41–66.

Rose, S.O. 'Gender and Labour History,' in Marcel van der Linden (ed.), *The End of Labour History? International Review of Social History Supplement 1*, 38 (1993), pp. 145–62.

Roth, H. 'American Influences on the New Zealand Labour Movement,' *Australian Historical Studies*, 9 (1961), pp. 413–20.

———. 'The Distribution of New Zealand Radicalism: 1890–1957,' *New Zealand Geographer*, 15:1 (1959), pp. 76–83.

Sadler, E. 'One Book's Influence: Edward Bellamy's Looking Backward,' *New England Quarterly*, 17:4 (1944), pp. 530–55.

Saville, J. 'Henry George and the British Labour Movement,' *Science and Society*, 24:4 (1960), pp. 321–33.

Scates, B. '"Millennium or Pandemonium?": Radicalism in the Labour Movement, Sydney, 1889–1899,' *Labour History*, 50 (1986), pp. 72–94.

———. '"Wobblers": Single Taxers in the Labour Movement, Melbourne 1889–1899,' *Historical Studies*, 21:83 (1984), pp. 174–96.

Searles, M. 'The Origins of New Unionism on Tyneside,' *North East Labour History*, 25 (1991), pp. 25–50.

Stromquist, S. '"Thinking Globally, Acting Locally": Municipal Labour and Socialist Activism in Comparative Perspective, 1890–1920,' *Labour History Review*, 74:3 (2009), pp. 233–56.

Taylor, E. 'A Craft Society in the Age of General Unions: The Chainmakers and Strikers Association of Saltney, Pontypridd and Staffordshire 1889–1914,' *West Midlands Studies*, 5 (1970), pp. 29–30.

———. 'The Midland Counties Trades Federation, 1886–1914,' *Midland History*, 1:3 (1972), pp. 26–40.

Thistlewaite, F. 'The Atlantic Migration of the Pottery Industry,' *The Economic History Review*, 11:2 (1958), pp. 264–78.

Weir, R. 'A Fragile Alliance: Henry George and the Knights of Labor,' *American Journal of Economics and Sociology*, 56:4 (1997), pp. 421–39.

Wilentz, S. 'Against Exceptionalism: Class Consciousness and the American Labor Movement, 1790–1920,' *International Labor and Working-Class History*, 26 (1984), pp. 1–24.

Young, J.D. 'Changing Images of American Democracy and the Scottish Labour Movement,' *International Review of Social History*, 18:1 (1973), pp. 69–89.

———. 'Evolution of a Working-class Vocabulary,' *Bulletin of the Society for the Study of Labour History*, 21 (1970), p. 15.

PhD Theses

Blackburn, S.C. *Sweated Labour and the Minimum Wage: A Case Study of the Women Chainmakers of Cradley Heath, South Staffordshire, 1850–1950* (University of London, 1984).

Hunt, G. *The Pub, the Village and the People* (University of Kent, 1989).

Medley, G.R.W. *The Geography of Industrial Decline: The Black Country Iron and Steel Industry, 1850–1900* (University of London, 1986).

Rabinovitch, V. *British Marxist Socialism and Trade Unionism: The Attitudes, Experiences and Activities of the Social-Democratic Federation (1884–1901)* (University of Sussex, 1977).

Ross, C. *The Development of the Glass Industry on the Rivers Tyne and Wear, 1700–1900* (Newcastle University, 1982).

Taylor, E. *The Working Class Movement in the Black Country, 1863–1914* (Keele University, 1974).

Wright, M. *Wales and Socialism: Political Culture and National Identity, c.1880–1914* (University of Cardiff, 2011).

Wright, R.A. *Liberal Party Organisation and Politics in Birmingham, Coventry and Wolverhampton, 1886–1914, with Particular Reference to the Development of Independent Labour Representation* (University of Birmingham, 1977).

Index

All-England Royal Order of the Knights of Labour
see also British United Order of the Knights of Labour
Amalgamated Society of Engineers 9, 24, 30, 31, 55, 82n12, 125, 145, 185
　conflict with the Knights of Labor 170–2, 174, 192, 195
American exceptionalism 21–3, 34, 48–9, 167, 194–5, 230–2
American Federation of Labor 3–4, 22, 24, 80, 160–2, 164, 193–4, 198, 200
Arbitration 20, 109–10, 111–15, 118–19, 120–33, 174, 189–90, 218, 227–8
Archibald, James P. 67–9, 72–3, 86, 90, 99–101, 141, 183, 201–5, 218
Associated Iron and Steel Workers of Great Britain 173–4, 192
Association of Cast Iron Hollow Ware Manufacturers 126–7
Aveling, Edward 139–40, 180

Ballance, John 14, 137
Barry, Leonora 98, 100, 203–4
Beaumont, Ralph 135
Bellamy, Edward 33–4, 48
Bernard Shaw, George 33

Bernstein, Eduard 31
Besant, Annie 144–5, 216
Bird, Charles 50–2, 56, 60, 85, 169
Bishop, M.J. 223–5
Bootle 53, 60–1, 86, 89, 101, 115, 129–30, 141, 183, 186, 189, 191, 196, 216, 219
Bowen, Paul 204, 226
boycotting 29, 56, 109–10, 115–17, 122, 130, 133, 181, 190
Brades Steel Works 114, 120
British National Assembly of the Knights of Labour 54, 86, 111, 114, 154, 220–21
　origins 213–17
British United Order of the Knights of Labour 95–7
Broadhurst, Henry 30–1, 137, 168
Brotherhood of the Union 26
Brown, James 55, 99–100, 122–4, 147–8, 187, 220
Burns, John 144, 150, 152, 166, 175
Burrows, Herbert 106–7
Burt, Thomas 43, 168
Burtt, Andrew 10, 46–7, 64
Butler, C.W. 68
Butler, Zebulon 60, 142, 155–6, 220

Callewaert, Jean 11
Cameron, A.C. 39

Campbell, James 65
Catholic Church 72–5, 89–90, 219
Cavanaugh, Thomas 203–4
Chamberlain, Charles 52, 60–1, 84, 117–18, 121, 126–7, 141, 145–6, 206
  and embezzlement case 209–10, 213, 220, 227
Champion, H.H. 150, 181
Chance Brothers 47, 56, 111, 113, 121–4, 193
Chapman, Jesse 60, 67–8, 87–8, 140, 145, 154, 171–2, 204–5, 209, 220, 226
Chartists 29–30, 36, 71, 78, 105
co-operative enterprise 9, 40–1, 117–18
Corcordal, Jules 11
Cline, Isaac 10, 46–7, 64
compagnonnage 36, 40
Cunninghame Graham, Robert 61, 142, 158–9, 228

Davaud, Abel 12
Davitt, Michael 29, 32, 59, 66–8, 71–5, 77, 84, 88, 119, 130, 175, 178–9, 202–5, 228
Dean, Thomas 52, 60, 68, 76–7, 84, 155, 205, 215, 220–2
Be Deers Consolidated Mines 15–16, 136
Delwarte, Albert 10, 12, 202, 212
Denny, A.G. 10, 16, 47–8, 51, 64–5, 69, 81, 168, 202, 227
Dock, Wharf, Riverside and General Labourers' Union 166
Dooling, Thomas 129–30

Eglington, Frederick 149–51
Engels, Friedrich 25, 80, 139–41, 177, 204

Fabian Society 29, 142, 144
Feagan, R.H. 75

First International 4, 30, 37–9, 49, 177, 216
fraternalism 1, 8, 15–16, 26–7, 35, 40, 80–2, 86, 94, 96, 102–8
Freemasonry
  see also fraternalism
French, Joseph 65, 79, 89, 122

George, Henry 9, 31–4, 48, 57, 116, 136, 139, 142–3, 156–7, 200, 212
Gessner, F.N. 46
Glasier, J. Bruce 89
Gompers, Samuel 26, 161–2, 194
Grand National Consolidated Trades Union 24, 26–8, 82, 96, 105–6, 181
Great Upheaval, the 2, 56–8, 62, 77, 105, 109–10, 119, 128, 136, 139, 177, 194, 229
Gronlund, Laurence 33–4, 48
Guest, Thomas 192

Hardie, Keir 89, 93, 137, 156–60, 229
Hartley's 47, 111, 121–4, 132, 193, 220
Hayes, John W. 7, 13, 55, 68, 124, 198, 204, 206, 209, 220
Higgins, John 183, 191
Hill, Richard 60, 62, 65–6, 77, 85, 87, 113, 117, 172, 211, 220–2

immigration 36–9, 41–8
Independent Labour Party 137, 156, 160, 229
Independent Order of the Knights of Labour 97, 215, 222
International Trade Secretariats 224–5
International Trades Union Congresses
  1886, Paris 30–31
  1888, London 31
International Workingmen's Association
  see also First International

Irish Land League 29, 66, 109–10, 115, 142
Irish nationalism 32, 71–2, 66–7, 143, 158–9, 200, 204

Kenrick's 126–9, 203
Knights of Labor
  American history and historiography 1–6
  Britain and Ireland
    By topic
      political views 136–43
      secrecy 80, 82–5, 90, 189–90, 198
      financial history 62–3, 206–10
      political views 136–43
      gender 4, 82, 97–108
    By location
      Ardrossan 182, 186, 219
      Barnsley 53, 72, 90, 121
      Belfast 53–4, 60, 75–6, 196, 208, 219–20
      Cardiff 10, 44, 50
      Cradley Heath 100, 135, 156, 160, 172, 204, 213–14
      Derby 53, 76, 196, 200–1
      Derry 53–54, 60, 72, 75, 88–90, 118, 120, 182–3, 189–90, 196, 203, 215, 219–20
      Dudley 61, 63, 115, 155, 170, 187
      Glasgow 32, 53, 60–1, 68, 72, 129, 142–3, 158–9, 182, 186, 188, 191
      Handsworth 52, 85, 154
      Hull 97
      Platts Common 53–4, 72
      Preston 53, 91, 116, 121, 141
      Rotherham 52–4, 60, 68, 86, 111, 117, 130–3, 142–3, 150–1, 154, 160, 182, 187, 192, 196, 213, 220–1
      Spon Lane 47, 50, 95, 111, 113, 123–24, 202, 208, 211
      St. Helens 46–7, 55, 65, 76, 85, 110–13, 121–3
      Stanningley 53
      Sunderland 47, 55, 76, 79, 95, 108, 111–13, 121, 123–4, 132, 147, 151, 187, 202, 220
      Walsall 60, 61, 68, 73, 85, 114–15, 118, 128, 141, 148–52, 174, 182, 185–8, 219
      West Bromwich 51, 113–17, 120, 125–7, 145–6, 154, 208–9
      Wolverhampton 86, 115, 126–8, 147, 155, 170, 187
      Yeovil 91
  the rest of the world
    Australia 13–14, 17, 81, 92, 136, 165
    Belgium 10–12, 46, 136–7, 212, 217, 229
    France 12–13, 201, 222
    Germany 16–17
    India 17
    Italy 11
    New Zealand 14–15, 81, 88, 92, 98, 137, 165, 201, 212, 217, 229
    Portugal 17
    Scandinavia 17
    South Africa 15–16, 81, 92, 98, 136
  Local Assembly 300, Window-Glass Workers of America 10, 44–8, 63–5, 81, 86, 123, 135, 168, 198, 201–2, 206, 208, 211, 225

Labour Electoral Association 147, 155–6
Labour Party (British) 3, 137–8, 152–3, 163
Layton, Robert 48–50
Lenin, Vladmir 23

Lichtman, Charles 40, 209
Lippard, George 26
Lyght, W.W. 13–14, 92

M'Daid, Michael 75
MacDonald, Alexander 43, 156
McGaul, Daniel 220
McGhee, Richard 67, 143, 180, 191, 225, 228
McHugh, Edward 191
Maddison, Frederick 177–8
Mahon, J.L. 179
Mann, Tom 30, 32, 166, 175
Marx, Eleanor 139–40, 180
Marx, Karl 4, 34, 38
Mawdsley, James 223–4
Midland Counties Trades Federation 50, 56, 126, 154, 169–70, 174, 185, 192, 199
Mitchell, George 91
Morris, William 33

Nadin, Arthur 54, 87–8, 142, 192, 214–15, 220
National Amalgamated Iron Plate Workers Society 174, 192
National Federation of Labour Union 181, 184
National Labour Federation 171, 179–80, 184
National Labor Union 26, 38–9, 101–2, 135
National Order of Potters 20–21, 48, 83, 91
National Union of Dock Labourers 129–30, 180, 183–4, 190–1, 219, 225
National Union of Gas Workers and General Labourers 166, 189–92
National Union of Stove Grate Workers 131, 151, 192, 220
Newcomb, William 140, 183

New Unionism 125, 137, 166–7, 229
  and the Knights of Labor 175–95
Norbury, Joseph 65, 85

Orwell, George 35
Owen, Robert 48

Pilkington's 46, 47, 55, 65, 85, 110–11, 113, 121–5, 132, 196
Powderly, Terence 3, 7, 10, 12, 17, 40, 41, 43, 51, 59, 65, 66, 67, 77, 81, 87–8, 98, 106–7, 133, 136, 138–9, 141, 158, 168, 170–1, 178, 180, 182, 200, 202, 203, 211, 221–2, 226–9
  and Paris Exhibition 12–14, 204–5, 226
  and the Catholic Church 72–3
  fall as General Master Workman 198, 201, 217–18
  on Irish nationalism 71–2, 200
  on internationalism 40, 44, 47
  on immigration 41–2
  on picnics 89
  on ritual 80, 86
  on strikes and arbitration 109–12, 119, 122–5
Price, John A. 66
public houses 85, 104

Reeves, Samuel 61, 101, 115, 141, 142, 155–56, 160, 183, 186, 188, 191, 220, 228
Reynolds Newspaper 30–1
Rhodes, Cecil 15, 136
Richards, Charles 209, 217, 227
ritual
  see also fraternalism
Robertson, Robert 50–51, 56, 60, 85, 87, 124, 169
Rylett, Harold 61, 67, 73, 140, 154, 169, 228

Sailors' and Firemens' Union 183, 186, 190–1, 224
Sanders, Hadyn 61, 85–6, 114–15, 118, 131, 141, 148–51
Sanders, W.H. 149–51
Schilling, George 59, 67
Scottish Labour Party 61, 137, 158–60
Scottish Land Restoration League 32, 143, 157
Second International 4, 9, 216, 226
Sexton, James 50, 55, 61, 71, 83, 120, 191, 228
Shaw Maxwell, James 61, 72, 142–3, 157–60, 186, 219, 220, 228
Sherlock, T.T. 50, 58, 61, 67, 73, 140, 169
Shreeve, Frederick 64, 200
Shipton, George 181
Smethwick 47, 51, 60, 67, 73, 88, 99n121, 115, 118, 124, 140, 145–6, 154, 221
Social-Democratic Federation 29–30, 106–7, 140–2, 146
Socialist League 29, 116, 140–1, 178
Sombart, Werner 21–2
Sons of Labour
   Amalgamated Order of 73, 92–5, 108, 121, 182
   political programme 93, 157–8
Sparling, H. Halliday 58–59, 141
Stephens, Uriah 1, 12, 35, 40, 72, 80, 109, 136
Stewart, William 203, 208
Strasser, Adolphe 26
Swinton, John 58–9, 225
Sylvis, William 38–9

Tanner, J.T. 141, 146, 149
temperance 8, 65, 85, 98, 102–3
Threlfall, T.R. 56, 155
Tillett, Ben 30, 166, 175
trades councils 186–7, 192–3
   Birmingham 141n26, 146, 148, 204
   Derry 90, 189–90
   Glasgow 188
   Liverpool 188–9
   Rotherham 151, 187–8, 220–1
   Sheffield 153
   Sunderland 147, 187
   Walsall 151, 187–8
   Wolverhampton 115, 147, 155
Trades Union Congress 25, 28, 30–1, 49, 62, 125, 137–8, 155, 162, 165–6, 167–8, 175–7, 184, 186, 192, 194, 218
Turner, Ben 61, 178–9
Turner, Frederick 58

Universal Brotherhood 40–1, 44, 48–9, 80
Universal Federation of Window-Glass Workers 10–12, 46–9, 64–5, 121, 168, 200–3, 225

Veyssier, F. 12

Welsh, Samuel 185, 187, 207, 211
Williams, John 180–1
Wilson, John Havelock 191, 216
Women's Protective and Provident League 99, 102